TEACHING ANTICOMMUNISM

TEACHING ANTICOMMUNISM

Fred Schwarz and American Postwar Conservatism

HUBERT VILLENEUVE

McGill-Queen's University Press
Montreal & Kingston • London • Chicago

ISBN 978-0-2280-0186-7 (cloth)
ISBN 978-0-2280-0319-9 (ePDF)
ISBN 978-0-2280-0320-5 (ePUB)

Legal deposit second quarter 2020
Bibliothèque nationale du Québec

Printed in Canada on acid-free paper that is 100% ancient forest free (100% post-consumer recycled), processed chlorine free

This book has been published with the help of a grant from the Canadian Federation for the Humanities and Social Sciences, through the Awards to Scholarly Publications Program, using funds provided by the Social Sciences and Humanities Research Council of Canada.

Funded by the Government of Canada | Financé par le gouvernement du Canada | Canada

Canada Council for the Arts | Conseil des arts du Canada

We acknowledge the support of the Canada Council for the Arts.
Nous remercions le Conseil des arts du Canada de son soutien.

Library and Archives Canada Cataloguing in Publication

Title: Teaching anticommunism : Fred Schwarz and American postwar conservatism / Hubert Villeneuve.
Names: Villeneuve, Hubert, 1979– author.
Description: Includes bibliographical references and index.
Identifiers: Canadiana (print) 20200155431 | Canadiana (ebook) 20200155512 | ISBN 9780228001867 (cloth) | ISBN 9780228003199 (ePDF) | ISBN 9780228003205 (ePUB)
Subjects: LCSH: Schwarz, Fred, 1913–2009. | LCSH: Christian Anti-Communism Crusade. | LCSH: Conservatism—United States—History—20th century. | LCSH: Right-wing extremists—United States—History—20th century. | LCSH: Christians—Political activity—United States—History—20th century. | LCSH: Anti-communist movements—United States—History—20th century.
Classification: LCC JC.2.U6 V55 2020 | DDC 320.52097309/045—dc23

This book was typeset in 10.5/13 Sabon.

Contents

Figures

Acknowledgments

This project, originally a doctoral dissertation, was initiated at a moment when Dr Schwarz was still alive, and his personal records – to the extent they survived the hazards of time – had not yet been given to any library or archival institution. A few pieces of primary source material relevant to this study were being kept by either the Schwarz family in Australia (who still kindly provided some useful information) or other relatives who could be reached. The Christian Anti-Communism Crusade still legally exists as these lines are being written: it has been, since Dr Schwarz's retirement in 1998, de facto integrated into the works of a Colorado-based fundamentalist ministry. However, in order to prevent any confusion concerning this project's independence, I made a deliberate choice not to rely on its archives or to seek the current Crusade's collaboration or assistance. This is not an "authorized" book.

Such circumstances inevitably raised the difficulty posed by this project. It would never have seen the light of day without the help of all those who assisted me in scores of libraries and archival centres across North America, of all those whose advice was key in structuring this work, and of the many who welcomed me along my research trip and gave me any type of support, be it logistical, informational, or moral. I would like to thank in alphabetical order: Douglas Allan and Lynette Adams of Toronto; Anne Bahde (San Diego State University); Gerry Baumgarten (ADL, NY); Chip Berlet (Political Research Affiliates); Andrew Bonnell (Queensland University); Toni Bressler (University of Kansas); Christopher Buckley; Lynn Bycko (Cleveland State University); Lucas R. Clawson (Hagley Museum and Library); Peter Coleman (*Sydney Bulletin*, retired); Roger and

Gwen Congdon, Portland; Don Critchlow (University of St. Louis); Mitali Das (McGill University); Brian Dickey (Flinders University); Darren Dochuk (University of Purdue); Michelle Doré (United Nations); Jennifer Drouin (McGill University); Louis Fagnan (Georgia State University); Alan Ferg (Arizona State Museum); Robert Eric Frykenberg (University of Wisconsin-Madison); Maxime Giroux (Université du Québec à Montréal); Lee Grady (Wisconsin Historical Society); Janet Greene; Debbie Z. Harwell (University of Houston); Kenneth Woodrow Henke (Princeton University); Don Irvine (Accuracy in Media); Vishnu Jani (Hoover Institution Library and Archives); Alan Jutzi (Huntington Library); Bruce Kirby (Library of Congress); Luc Lamothe; Ernie Lazar; Carol A. Leadenham (Hoover Institution Library and Archives); William LeFevre (Wayne State University); Bart and Steven Lidofsky; Vicky Lipsky (Jacob Rader Marcus Center); Sheilah Mann (American Political Science Association); Russell L. Martin III (Southern Methodist University); William Massa (Yale University); Thomas McIntire (University of Toronto); Lisa McGirr (Harvard University); Derek H. Meyers (MD, Australia, retired); Debbie Miller (Minnesota Historical Society); Chris Naylor (National Archives and Records Administration); Mary Nelson (Wichita State University); Marvin Olasky (King's College, NY); Jason Opal (McGill University); Gwendolyn Owens (McGill University); Stuart Patton (Hoover Institution Library and Archives); Stuart Piggin (Centre for the History of Christian Thought and Experience, Sydney); the late Anglican bishop D.W.B. Robinson, Sydney; Greg Robinson (Université du Québec à Montréal); the late Professor Edward Rozek; the late Phyllis Schlafly; John and Rosalie Schwarz and the Schwarz family; Alan M. Schwartz (Anti-Defamation League); Harold Skousen and the Skousen family; Joost Sluis, Chicago; Yorick Small (University of Queensland); Susan Snyder (University of California, Berkeley); Wayne Sparkman (PCA Historical Center, Missouri); James Stack (University of Washington); Rob Swaner (Research Center of the Utah State Archives and Utah State History); Sylvia Stopforth (Trinity Western University); Rachel Taube (*Ecotone* magazine); Helen Taylor (Australia); Brittany Trubody (MacArthur Museum of Brisbane); Robert Walker (Southern Methodist University); Linda A. Whitaker (Arizona Historical Foundation); Pip Wilson, Australia; Ray Wolfinger (UC Berkeley, retired); Melissa Zajicek (Texas

A&M University); and Steve Zeleny (International Church of the Foursquare Gospel).

I would like to express my sincere gratitude to Stephen Holt, who provided me with very useful information from Australia; to Don MacLeod, whose advice and impressive list of contacts were among the most valuable; to Bill Geerhart, who shared with me some of his immense knowledge of Cold War popular culture; to my supervisor at McGill University, Leonard J. Moore, who bore the main burden of discussing this project – and my insecurities related to it – with me for several years; to Deb Pentecost from *Eagle Forum*, whose kindness remains memorable; to Tom Levitt and Anastasia Painesi, whose proofreading skills and comments helped me to come up with a much improved final product; to Michelle Nickerson, whose generosity during my stay in Dallas was overwhelming; and to the entire McGill-Queen's University Press staff, and particularly my editor, Jonathan Crago, whose advice, dynamism, and continuous support proved invaluable during the later stages of this book, and copyeditor K. Joanne Richardson for her outstanding work.

I also wish to thank the following institutions, whose funding made this book possible: the McGill Faculty of Arts; the Foundation for the Advancement of Protestant Education; the Social Sciences and Humanities Research Council of Canada; and the Fonds de Recherche sur la Société et la Culture du Québec.

Finally, this list would not be complete without mentioning the unwavering support I received from my family. This work is dedicated to my mother France and to the loving memory of my father Daniel.

Abbreviations

AAUN	American Association for the United Nations
ACCC	American Council of Christian Churches
ACLU	American Civil Liberties Union
ADL	Anti-Defamation League
AFL	American Federation of Labor
AFP	Armed Forces of the Philippines
AJLAC	American Jewish League against Communism
ALP	Australian Labor Party
AMA	American Medical Association
ANC	African National Congress
ANES	American National Election Studies
ASSs	Anti-Subversive Seminars
BGEA	Billy Graham Evangelistic Association
BMA	British Medical Association
BPP	Black Panther Party
CACC	Christian Anti-Communism Crusade
CIA	Central Intelligence Agency
CIO	Congress of Industrial Organizations
CMF	Cardinal Mindszenty Foundation
CPA	Communist Party of Australia
CPUSA	Communist Party of the United States of America
CRA	California Republican Assembly
ERA	Equal Rights Amendment
FBI	Federal Bureau of Investigation
FCDA	Federal Civil Defense Administration
FCC	Federal Communications Commission
FCC	Federal Council of Churches

FCI	Freedom Center International
FFSGs	Four Freedoms Study Groups
GOP	Grand Old Party
HUAC	House Un-American Activities Committee
ICC	Indian Christian Crusade
ICCC	International Council of Christian Churches
IGM	India Gospel Mission
ILWU	International Longshoremen's and Warehousemen's Union
IOP	Ideological Organizations Project
IPR	Institute of Pacific Relations
IRS	Internal Revenue Service
IVF	Inter-Varsity Fellowship of Evangelical Unions
JBS	John Birch Society
LIC	low intensity conflict
MFU	Minnesota Farmers Union
NAE	National Association of Evangelicals
NBC	National Broadcasting Company
NEP	New Economic Policy
NEP	National Education Program
NFED	National Freedom Education Center
NHS	National Health Service
NPA	New People's Army
NSC	the National Security Council
PLP	Progressive Labor Party
PPP	People's Progressive Party
RMOs	resident medical officers
UAW	United Auto Workers
UF	United Force
UQMS	University of Queensland Medical Society
USSR	Union of Soviet Socialist Republics
WACL	World Anti-Communist League
WASP	White Anglo-Saxon Protestant
WCC	World Council of Churches
YAF	Young Americans for Freedom
YFC	Youth for Christ

TEACHING ANTICOMMUNISM

Introduction

It is 30 August 1961. It is a beautiful late summer evening. The setting is the Los Angeles Memorial Sports Arena, the largest covered auditorium in the United States. For the first time since its opening two years ago, all of the arena's sixteen thousand seats are filled. Thousands of unlucky people who could not get in have gathered outside, hoping to capture some of the inside excitement from the loud speakers that were rushed in.

Coming from all over Southern California, the crowd is composed mostly of well-dressed, middle-class people wearing their Sunday best, many of whom have brought their children. Scores of high school students representing more than thirty Southland cities are also present. These young people are admitted free of charge for this third evening of the week-long Southern California School of Anti-Communism's Youth Dedication Night. Although the Memorial Sports Arena is normally used by the Lakers, the city's new basketball franchise, tonight's crowd has not come for sports but to proclaim its patriotism and its opposition to communism.[1]

A Marine Color Guard enters the arena carrying "Old Glory," generating a spontaneous ninety-second round of applause from the audience and a subsequent rendition of "The Star-Spangled Banner." Next the pledge of allegiance is read by anticommunist star Herbert Philbrick, who is acting as master of ceremonies for the evening, and then the Protestant hymn "God of Our Fathers" is sung by a youth choir. The night's first speaker discreetly walks to the arena's centre stage: Marion Miller, a local celebrity in West Los Angeles, whose story was popularized by a series of *Reader's Digest* articles. Her autobiography *I Was a Spy: The Story of a Brave Housewife* tells of how, on a voluntary basis, she infiltrated a local left-wing group, the activities of which were deemed suspicious by the Federal Bureau of Investigation (FBI). Flanked by her three children, she calls for a national program to educate Americans on the evils of communism. In implicit terms, she attacks the Los Angeles School Board, which had recently decided, amid controversy, to retain in its archives a series of films about Russia and Communist China.[2]

Miller gives up the stage for a much-cheered movie and television star. This is Ronald Reagan. With a commanding air refined by years of having been spokesman for the General Electric Corporation, Reagan proclaims that youth is now a priority for Communists: "You are a target. Communism will appeal to your rebellious nature ... They will make you feel your patriotism is hollow. Then they will full up the vacuum with their philosophy." The speaker decries the trend towards the welfare state and centralized government, which he deems as dangerous for the United States of America as communism: "These advocates of the welfare state fail to realize our loss is just as great if it happens on the instalment plan." After Reagan's short speech, the audience gets on its feet to welcome star singer and Christian activist Pat Boone. He loses no time before singing a few numbers from his pop repertoire and generates the audience's wildest reaction of the night with the following words: "I don't want to live in a Communist United States. I would rather see my four girls shot and die as little girls who have faith in God than leave them to die some years later as godless, faithless, soulless communists."[3]

The outburst of emotion dies down. Master of ceremonies Philbrick then takes the stage and delivers a didactic speech concerning Cold War politics. He berates the Department of Defense for "muzzling" military leaders from speaking against communism and calls for a congressional investigation into the issue. The three-hour rally continues with testimonies offered by stars like John Wayne, Roy Rogers, Dale Evans, and George Murphy. These presentations are interspersed with songs like "This Is My Country" and "Battle Hymn of the Republic." Sporadic references to conservative heroes like General Douglas MacArthur or Senator Barry Goldwater are welcomed by cheers.

And now, Fred Schwarz, forty-eight-year-old president of the Christian Anti-Communism Crusade (CACC) appears. The Australian doctor turned professional anticommunist does not generate the same frenzy as did Reagan or Boone. However, the authority of the man who masterminded this anticommunist Woodstock shines through. Wearing a bow tie, the Australian is a middle-aged man with scant hair. His rigid, long-nosed, and mostly expressionless face contrasts with his eyes, which twinkle behind huge horn-rimmed glasses when he makes a point.

His high-pitched, Australian twang could have been a distraction for this audience. However, it is not. The doctor's eloquence allows him to hold his listeners' attention and to melt away cultural barriers. He sums up the evening's main points and reiterates, as he often does, that "the greatest need that confronts us today is that we have knowledge of the enemy that threatens to destroy us." In a lecture the delivery and efficiency of which has been tested countless times, Schwarz outlines the various means by which communists intend to carry out their blueprint for world conquest: military power, propaganda, demoralization, duplicity, as well as sympathy generated among youth and intellectuals. The anticommunist crusader wraps up his speech with a fiery proclamation of his conviction that the final victory over communism will come through the assertion of the free world's most important assets: respect for authority, God, country, and freedom. The evening concludes with a Statue of Liberty candle-lighting finale and the singing of "God Bless America."[4]

This event was televised throughout Southern California by the *Times-Mirror*-owned KTTV, thanks to the sponsorship of the Richfield Oil Corporation. A few days after this gathering, Times-Mirror Broadcasting Company president Richard Moore indicated in a letter to Republican congressman Walter H. Judd, who gave a speech during the event on that Thursday night, that the public reaction surpassed anything he had seen in the station's twelve-year history, beating even popular shows offered by national corporations (CBS, NBC, ABC). The week-long event was also given prime coverage by the conservative Chandler family's *Los Angeles Times*.[5]

In the following months, anticommunism manifested itself to an unprecedented level in Southern California. Civic clubs organized patriotic rallies in record numbers, businesspeople invited anticommunist speakers to address their chamber of commerce luncheon talks. Suburbanites showed anticommunist films in their churches and joined anticommunist organizations. Housewives formed anticommunist study groups in their homes. Bill Becker, West Coast correspondent for the *New York Times*, wrote that conservatism "is marching in double-time in Southern California to the twin strains of anticommunism and pro-Americanism." For years, this grassroots anticommunist activity had been a common feature across the United States, and especially in the Southwest. However, in late 1961, Southern California saw an anticommunist popular upsurge that expressed a highly conservative, anti-collectivist, and nationalist outlook. Some observers had thought that the demise of Senator Joe McCarthy in the mid-1950s had led to a decline in anticommunism throughout the nation. Clearly, they were wrong.[6]

Many liberal thinkers expressed the fear that this bubbling movement carried the seeds of a threat to American democracy and values. Columbia University sociologist Daniel Bell and several colleagues expanded the book they had published in 1955 on McCarthyism. In the now-titled *The Radical Right*, Bell states that 1950s McCarthyism was not an organized movement but, rather, "an atmosphere of fear." There was no "McCarthy movement" as such, while "the radical right of the 1960s ha[d] been characterized by a multitude of organizations that seemingly ha[d] been able to evoke an intense emotional response from a devoted following." For Bell, the anticommunism schools and seminars, "who adapted old revivalist techniques to a modern idiom" and were held all across the Midwest, Southwest, and California, constituted a clear sign that a right-wing resurgence was taking place throughout the country.[7]

Worried by the situation, President John F. Kennedy travelled to Los Angeles, where he addressed this issue on 18 November 1961 at the Hollywood Palladium, attacking "those fringes of our society who have sought to escape their own responsibility by finding a simple solution, an appealing slogan or a convenient scapegoat." As the president spoke, three thousand people picketed outside the building, carrying signs that read: "Unmuzzle the Military," "Veto Tito," "Disarmament is Suicide," or "CommUNism Is Our Enemy."[8] The scene itself illustrated what Bell had also noted in *The Radical Right*. As long as Republican president Dwight D. Eisenhower had been in power, the anger that conservatives felt at the direction the country was taking had been contained "because 'their' party was in power, and the American political system does not easily invite ideological splits." With Kennedy, "the charge of softness in dealing with Communism could again become a political, as well as an ideological, issue." The stage was set for a clash between an ascendant

American liberalism, captured by Kennedy's vision of a prosperous future, gradually marked by expanded definitions of citizenship, and a growing conservative movement whose very core was its opposition to communism.[9]

THE SUM OF ALL EVILS

This is a story about anticommunism. Its main character, an Aussie doctor turned anticommunist, has already been introduced. Its chronological setting is primarily the era during which the world was mobilized for an impending military conflict of unexampled proportions, though one that ultimately never came to be.

For a long time, the seeming approach of a Third World War resulted in an ongoing state of tension, a "Cold War" that affected American society in many ways. Lodged in the national consciousness by the late 1940s was the conception that the United States was up against a foe like it had never faced before. This enemy was perceived as an outside and an inside threat; it took the shape both of powerful, nuclear-powered foreign countries and affiliated political parties ("Communism" with a capital "C," the international movement involving governments and political organizations) and a philosophy ("communism," with a lowercase "c") that rejected core American principles: individual freedom, belief in God, and private property. The subtle distinction between Communism and communism was easily blurred in public discourses throughout the Cold War, as is shown by the various quotations in this book that use one word or the other, often in a generic manner. Not all communists were Communists, whereas Communists were almost assuredly communists, at least until the mid-1960s. Such nuances, however, were overlooked more often than not during the Cold War, especially in its earliest stages.

"We face a hostile ideology, global in scope, atheistic in character, ruthless in purpose, and insidious in method," President Eisenhower said in his farewell address in 1961. For a long time, opinion polls and studies showed that anticommunism spread so widely across all political, religious, and social boundaries that it became an almost universally shared aspect of the national identity. Of course, the Cold War affected American culture particularly through the 1950s and 1960s, but its various effects were felt far outside the chronological boundaries of these two decades. "For nearly half a century," historian Stephen Whitfield points out, "the geopolitical contest between the two superpowers haunted public life, pervading it so thoroughly that the national identity itself became disfigured."[10]

As opposed to comparable periods of collective fear, such as the aftermaths of the Pearl Harbor attack of 1941 and the terrorist attack of 11 September 2001, the Cold War angst was not linked to any actual physical attack on the United States. Nonetheless, the 1949 to 1954 period, when the Cold War was most intensely experienced in American life, remains the best example in American history of years dominated by a shared feeling of anxiety and vulnerability. Mid-twentieth-century anticommunist mobilization was the end product of a long series of developments that took place in the immediate post-Second World War period, such as the international expansion of Communism and US efforts to contain it, the development of the Soviet atomic bomb, as well as successive outbreaks of several espionage scandals. Communists, the public perceived, were stealthily undermining the United States from both within and without. A wave of anticommunism took American society by storm, dramatically affecting and changing its direction.

McCarthyism grew out of anticommunism. One of the most universally recognized features of the Cold War anticommunist craze was how the climate of suspicion it fostered was exploited to the utmost by an opportunistic politician from Wisconsin who gave the era its name. To this day, Joe McCarthy remains the symbol of how domestic anticommunism unleashed massive encroachments on civil liberties, thus destroying the lives of thousands in all segments of American society. McCarthyism is understood here as including not only McCarthy's personal campaign against alleged Communists in US public institutions but also the climate of intense anticommunist fear and the campaign of political persecution, both of which faded only throughout the second half of the 1950s. Through McCarthyism, anticommunism changed not only individual destinies but also the nation's entire political culture. McCarthyism not only proved disastrous for the left, as it wiped out US Communism and severely weakened the whole network of political groups, labour unions, and cultural institutions constituting the armature of left-wing activism, but it also had a lasting impact on all sectors of society (organized labour, unions, schools, civil rights groups, cultural industries, etc.) as well as deeply affecting the direction of the nation's domestic and foreign policy.[11]

overall movement towards recognition and mobilization after the Second World War. It also constitutes the first scholarly biography of a professional anticommunist, evangelist, and public educator whose influence on several leaders, as well as on countless grassroots activists throughout the United States, made him one of the forerunners of American contemporary conservatism. Until now, with the exception of a period extending roughly from the late 1950s to the mid-1960s (during which social scientists demonstrated a brief interest in the US right wing and the CACC), scholars seem not to have noticed his career.

By the late 1950s, Fred Schwarz was the country's most important anticommunist educator, and the CACC was its largest single-issue anticommunist organization. By giving thousands of speeches, creating scores of recordings and writings, and, most notoriously, holding highly successful week-long anticommunism "schools," Schwarz's teachings reached large numbers of people who, in many cases, experienced as never before the need to become politically involved. Across the nation, and in particular in locations such as Southern California, Texas, and Arizona, Crusade events became key foundational moments that sparked lives of activism in an emerging grassroots subculture composed primarily of small-town or suburban patriotic families, small or average businesspeople, and upper-class professionals. For a time, fighting communism became the prime feature of their activism, before most eventually moved on to other issues. "Darling of the Moral Majority" Phyllis Schlafly summarized this well in a 1998 letter to her friend Fred Schwarz: "You were an indispensable factor in building the grassroots anticommunist movement, which became the conservative movement, which ultimately elected Ronald Reagan."[14]

This mobilizing process was especially true for conservative evangelicals, who constituted an important part of the Crusade audiences during the organization's first decade. By the post-Second-World-War era, the communist issue proved to be the one around which coalesced the political fears of many conservative evangelicals, from the more radical and marginal fundamentalists (Carl McIntire and the American Council of Christian Churches) to the partisans of a softened conservative gospel (Billy Graham and the National Association of Evangelicals). Just as the Cold War and its creation of a climate marked by an impending apocalyptic fear allowed conservative evangelicals to bring their subculture back to the American mainstream, so anticommunism established the groundwork for a renewed evangelical tradition whose Cold War linkage with American nationalism moved it out of the political fringe.[15]

At the earliest stage of this process, figures like Schwarz contributed to the re-emergence of a worldly consciousness among conservative Protestants. Equipped with knowledge of Marxist-Leninist theory, which he acquired over years of self-education, and seasoned by his experience in the academic world in Australia, Schwarz preached his message in countless churches and within the most important institutions of the American evangelical subculture. He did this in a manner that established a clear link between atheism and the abandonment of all morality, thus pushing evangelicals back into worldly matters in order to stand up against perceived manifestations of godlessness in public life.

Hearing Schwarz speak on the campus of Tyndale College in 1954, future fundamentalist leader Norman Geisler was thrilled: "When he spoke of his debates with Communists in universities, my ears perked up. I did not know that Christians could actually debate toe-to-toe with unbelievers in a secular context." Writing of hearing Schwarz for the first time in 1956, Focus on the Family founder James Dobson recalls: "He made quite an impression on me. I still recall [the] things he said, thirty years later, and they continue to influence my life." In a short article about his political awakening at the age of fourteen, free market economist and Christian fundamentalist Gary North summed it all up in the title, "It All Began with Fred Schwarz." In 1987, when he published *Healer of the Nations*, a book promoting Christian Reconstructionism (the idea that Christians should seek to rebuild society according to conservative Christian principles and biblical law), North dedicated it to Schwarz, "whose one-hour lecture got me started on all this over 30 years ago."[16]

Amid this process of mobilization, the Crusade became, despite its limited resources, one of the most active international Christian anticommunist groups. It established and maintained a presence in India, Asia, and Africa using mostly local church networks, thus becoming part of the great upsurge of conservative Protestant missionary activity that took place between the 1950s and the 1980s. The history of the CACC thus highlights the complex and still understudied interactions between global dynamics (evangelicalism and Cold War anticommunism) and US conservatism.[17]

Schwarz had made his way in the Australian evangelical world before coming to the United States with almost no resources. He had an outsider's perspective on North American affluence; he knew how to do a lot with a little. This creative frugality sets the Crusade apart from other American anticommunist groups, who, though sometimes enjoying much greater resources, were far less active at the international level. Finding it absurd, within the context of a planetary struggle for human freedom, to restrict their actions to the United States, Schwarz and his collaborators adopted a global perspective. And they did this in spite of their support for American nationalism, which they accepted as a prerequisite for the success of their activities. "The ideology and program of the CACC," Laura Jane Gifford writes in one of a handful of post-1960s studies on the Crusade, "combines a philosophy of anticommunism deeply steeped in religious motivations with a uniquely international approach to understanding – and combating – the Communist menace."[18]

To the extent that this work focuses primarily on the dynamics of postwar history in which the Crusade participated, its objective is not to provide the reader with a traditional biography of its central character. Schwarz's 1996 autobiography *Beating the Unbeatable Foe: One Man's Victory over Communism, Leviathan, and the Last Enemy* deals in depth with his private personal life, while the current book aims to provide a critical historical perspective on his life story and the role he played in American postwar conservatism. In this endeavour, focusing on Schwarz rather than on the Crusade itself is fitting from both a narrative and a practical viewpoint. The CACC's history is indistinguishable from that of its founder, who, until his retirement, remained its leader, organizer, and primary writer and speaker as well as its most public figure. While it was possible to locate and retrieve an interesting body of correspondence between Schwarz and many others, the number of existing CACC documents that do not bear the crusader's imprint is limited. Also, Schwarz's involvement in evangelical and anticommunist activities, both in Australia and in the United States, was in full swing long before he founded the CACC in 1953. Clearly, it would be impossible to give an account of the organization's history without addressing its origins and, in so doing, the path of its founder.

1

A Crusader's Tale

BIRTH

Frederick Charles Schwarz was born on 15 January 1913 in Brisbane, Australia. His father Friedrich Schwarz (1883–1970) was an Austrian Jew who moved to England at the age of fifteen, converted to evangelical Christianity, changed his name to "Paulus" (like Paul the Apostle), and became an evangelical lay preacher in the Holiness tradition. At the age of twenty, Paulus became a missionary and medical helper. He moved first to Egypt then migrated to Australia, where he worked among lepers in the quarantine station of Peel Island near Brisbane. He met and married a Methodist church deaconess named Phoebe Smith, and the couple settled in Brisbane, in the state of Queensland in the northeastern part of Australia. The Schwarz family had eleven children. Given the same name his father originally possessed, Frederick was the fourth child and the family's first boy.[1]

The family lived in Red Hill, a working-class inner suburb of Brisbane. They were very poor, and eleven children was a huge family size, even by Australian standards at the time. Fred recalled in his late years that his brothers and sisters received an egg as a birthday gift, and he remembered the joy of being offered his first pair of shoes when he was six. Although conditions gradually improved after the First World War, Schwarz once wrote that his father's circumstances remained at best "moderate" throughout his life. By Fred's account, Paulus was a tireless worker who gave everything he had for his family. He would sometimes arrive at home with "some unfortunate who was to be welcomed, warmed, and fed." Across his career, Schwarz would tirelessly attack the idea that communism grew out of poverty, giving himself as an example of someone whose "proletarian" origins never resulted in his being attracted by revolutionary ideas.[2]

Though he had arrived in Australia via the British Isles, as most immigrants did then, Paulus Schwarz belonged to the country's small German-speaking community. This had unfortunate consequences for his growing family. One year after Fred's birth, the outbreak of the First World War created a climate of intolerance for people of German ancestry. About forty-five hundred of the country's twenty-five thousand first-generation German-Australians, most of whom were still subjects of imperial Germany, were interned, and German immigration was not allowed again until 1925. Being an Austrian rather than a German native perhaps helped Paulus to escape legal repression, but it could not prevent him from being discriminated against. Paulus, Fred recalled, "was an object of suspicion and derision. He managed to provide the minimal requirements of life by work as a fishmonger and later as a stevedore." After the war, the family's conditions improved as Paulus made money in the war-surplus goods business. During his youth, Fred developed resentment towards his father's origins. He mentioned in his late years that, as a teenager, he found his father's foreign accent embarrassing: "I was not kind and gracious to him."[3]

Upon his arrival in Australia, twenty-year-old Paulus Schwarz reflected the young median age of a booming country. Australia's population had grown from 3 to 4 million in less than fifteen years, and first-generation immigrants like him constituted a fifth of the whole population. The country itself was also young: the Commonwealth of Australia was born in 1901 as a result of the federation of the six British colonies of Australia. Schwarz's native city of Brisbane was then at the cutting edge of an ascending nation whose identity was not yet definite. The city doubled its population in about twenty years, growing from 145,000 people at the time Fred was born to 300,000 in 1933. Brisbane was the principal shipping centre of Queensland. Since the great strikes of the late 1880s and early 1890s, especially those involving the Queensland Shearers Union, it was also a major centre of labour activism.

Queensland was also more racially and ethnically diverse than other parts of Australia. In several parts of the region, whites were a small minority in thriving multiracial communities like Broome, Darwin, and Thursday Island. The area in which Schwarz grew up in Red Hill was known for the multiple garden plots owned by the area's Chinese, who, like other Asian immigrants, were targeted by legal and extralegal discrimination. Schwarz thus grew up in a frontier-like environment characterized by quick change, social mobility, the spread of people and ideas, and social and ethnic struggles.[4]

FAITH

The crusader's early years coincided with the end of the Golden Age of Australian Protestantism, a time when more than 40 percent of Australians still attended church each Sunday. In the wake of the disestablishment of the Church of England, proclaimed in Queensland in 1860, the whole country had become a competitive religious environment in which evangelical revivalism thrived. Though Australia never underwent the intense kind of religious awakenings that marked American history, some of the world's most prominent evangelical figures (Thomas Spurgeon, Howard Guinness, Reuben Torrey) visited the country during that time, leaving behind them scores of revivalist experiments.

Evangelicalism in Australia spawned an emphasis on urban reform among the Victorian middle class. Concerned by the ills of poverty and the loss of moral fibre associated with urbanization and immigration, middle-class reformers set up organizations in which benevolence and evangelization complemented each other. Schwarz's career was undeniably a product of this voluntarism, which prompted the believer to a personal, individual engagement expressing his or her willingness to reform society. Queensland experienced five notable religious revivals over a period of four decades from 1870 on, though the city of Brisbane itself was hardly an evangelical stronghold. Its population came mostly from the British Isles and included an important number of Catholic Irish. At the outbreak of the First World War, most Brisbaners were nominal Anglicans, with Catholics constituting an important minority.[5]

Raised in an evangelical home influenced by the Holiness tradition, the Schwarz children, who retained apparently very little, if anything, of their father's Jewish origins, belonged to a nonconformist minority that was present mostly in impoverished urban areas and that had come to Australia through the work of Wesleyans, Primitive Methodists, and the Salvation Army. It was an international figure of the latter movement, William E. Booth-Clibborn, grandson of Salvation Army founders William and Kate Booth, who formally allowed Schwarz to experience his "second birth" at the age of eighteen during an evangelistic tour. Holiness movements, which proposed a heart-felt Christianity emphasizing autonomy and free agency, contrasted with the conservative and hierarchical Protestant tradition characterizing the Church of England. Nonetheless, to a greater degree than elsewhere, Australia's sprouting religious scene became characterized by interdenominational influences between High and Low Church Protestantism. An eclectic evangelical tradition blossomed among Australian Anglicans, enabling several of them to work in parachurch institutions that included evangelicals from other traditions. In the years following his conversion, Schwarz was often seen as a Pentecostal, but it was a Brisbane Methodist church that granted him his first lay pastorship in 1931 at the age of eighteen. Around the same time, he befriended D.W.B. Robinson, who later became Anglican archbishop of Sydney and who was an important collaborator in his activities in Australia. In his adult years, the crusader gradually moved towards Baptist churches and a tamer, more middle class-oriented evangelicalism. This capacity to move across denominational boundaries is reflective of Australian religious sensibilities.[6]

But Schwarz's personal religious doctrine remained conservative. Although "he doesn't press it upon you," Schwarz collaborator Arthur G. McDowell once wrote, "Schwarz considers himself a conservative in theology." He was actually a "fundamentalist," in the original early twentieth-century American sense – that is, he was a strict believer in the truthfulness of Protestant theology's "fundamentals." In a 1963 interview, he assented to almost all points on the list of traditional articles of belief characterizing fundamentalism. These included the belief that the Bible "is the revealed Word of God, is without error, and must be understood literally," that "Man is inherently sinful" and can be saved "only by faith in the risen Lord," and that miracles "are historical facts." In a 1981 speech, he made no mystery of his belief that liberal theology "poisons theology and destroys the assurance of the Christian message."[7]

Schwarz always held an almost Calvinistic vision of human nature: "The more society changes, the more human nature remains the same. Allegories and fables written centuries ago to point out the weaknesses and inconsistencies of human nature are as up to date as today's newspapers." He rejected the idea of indefinite progress based on scientific development. "The root of evil in human nature has not been eliminated by education, affluence, sociology, or applied psychology," he wrote. "Every utopian program for a society of happiness has foundered upon the rock of human nature." Communism was thus the quintessence of humanely conceived evil, a Promethean enterprise that was tantamount to intellectual and spiritual fraud. Human nature was immutably rooted in sin and could be freed only through individual salvation. Accordingly, Schwarz never put a great trust in the role of the state in human affairs. He admittedly supported state intervention in dealing with social ills, agreeing, for instance, with the ideas of income tax, gun control, or, in the 1960s, state antipoverty programs aimed at curbing the ills caused by the existence of US racial ghettos. His perspective on those issues always reflected the mainstream Australian centre-right sensibility, which is moderate by the standards of US conservatism and, comparatively, has not been influenced by radical anti-statist traditions.[8]

Schwarz's personality traits were those idealized by much of nineteenth-century literature – that is, "Victorian" values such as self-control, punctuality, orderliness, separate gender spheres, thrift, sobriety, delayed gratification, repressed sexuality, and piety. He remained a tireless worker throughout his life, with his leisure time consisting of activities such as reading the Bible and poetry. He never smoked, and he considered teetotalism a Christian duty, a stance later reflected in many CACC activities from which alcohol was banned. His views of womanhood were in accordance with the traditional gender role ascribed to women: "Motherhood is the birthright and fulfillment of womanhood. Any form of social organization that inhibits the right of a woman to bear and care for her child, is essentially destructive. This function can only be adequately fulfilled in the shelter of the family. Legislative and educational measures that weaken the family do not liberate women; they enslave them."[9]

He did not consider all bodily pleasures to be inappropriate: "Most human activity has been devoted to gratifying the senses of the human body. Consider the arts." But self-indulgence was to be rejected. "Permissiveness promotes the insane cruelties and homicides of certain hippies rather than a climate of love and mutual support," he wrote in 1970 in the wake of a debate over Herbert Marcuse's theories. To borrow sociologist David Riesman's expression, Schwarz was the classic "inner-directed" personality: a self-reliant, self-controlled, self-made man who moved across an ever-fluctuating world empowered by parentally induced principles rather than by the vagaries of other types of social influences.[10]

EDUCATION

Throughout his youth, Schwarz recalled, his father "sacrificed, schemed, and begged in order that each child secure[d] the best education possible." Young Fred enjoyed school and distinguished himself as an excellent student at Brisbane Grammar School. At the age of sixteen, he was accepted at the University of Queensland, unquestionably a privilege in times of economic depression. Having always performed well in mathematics, he registered for a bachelor's degree in science. As early as he could remember, Schwarz wanted to become a medical doctor. However, this was not possible in the early 1930s, as Queensland did not have a medical school. The country's two such institutions were located in Sydney and Melbourne, respectively, and the associated costs to send Fred to either were too great. On the other hand, the University of Queensland's bachelor's program in science was, for him, a good way to acquire a scientific background that could be credited should he get accepted into medical school one day. Also, it opened the door for a teaching career in high schools.[11]

Schwarz's work life was characterized by a slack kind of tension between his passions for evangelism and for science. In this era, in which the clash between science and religion, especially on the evolution issue, had produced rifts in the Protestant world, he had no problem in reconciling these two hemispheres of his psyche. He believed in scientific progress and the way it improved living conditions. In a manner that derived from the old rationalist tradition, he assumed that science was simply the "knowledge of the laws of nature," just as religion concerned the laws of the Almighty. He never joined the battle cry of anti-evolutionism, which split American churches in the 1920s but which had been settled a generation earlier in British churches. He also stayed away from dispensationalist theology (i.e., the idea that history may be seen as a series of successive eras, or "dispensations," through which divine truths are revealed), which was common among US fundamentalists. Besides, he claimed that anticommunism was the outgrowth of his scientific mind: "My fight against Communism was medical activity in the true sense."[12]

Throughout his university years, Schwarz's youthful enthusiasm was committed to the twin goals of earning his degrees and Christian evangelism. "Wherever I went I carried a large Bible and was widely regarded as a religious fanatic," he wrote. He got involved in his university's branch of the Inter-Varsity Fellowship of Evangelical Unions (usually referred to as IVF), an interdenominational umbrella organization of university ministries founded in 1928 in England. The IVF's intent was to maintain a Christian presence on university campuses within a context that, since the late nineteenth century, had been undergoing secularization. The IVF grew internationally as its leaders were eager to establish Evangelical Unions throughout the British Empire.[13]

The IVF suited Schwarz: it rejected the liberalism and ecumenism that characterized the liberal Student Christian Movement. Schwarz became his local branch's leader, adding his sense of energy to the group's Bible study meetings and campus evangelism. Reporting on the University of Queensland branch led by Schwarz, Howard Guinness, an English evangelist who helped set up IVF branches throughout the British world, once wrote: "the leader of the Queensland Evangelical Union was Pentecostalist, and our Union was consequently regarded as extreme and fanatical." It was during his time that Schwarz revealed himself as a powerful speaker. His style combined spiritual fervour, didactic brilliance, and poetic cadence. Usually not using any notes, he could deliver extemporaneous speeches, on any subject of his choosing, that kept audiences captivated. Schwarz's entire political career was an extension of his eloquence.[14]

However, Australian religion changed during the Depression years. The great age of Australian Protestantism had passed. Controversies over liberal theology, which split denominations worldwide, had reached Australia, whose conservative evangelicals were saddled by the pejorative traits (obscurantism and intolerance) of fundamentalism. When Schwarz graduated in 1934, fellow students broke into a sarcastic rendition of the hymn "Onward Christian Soldiers" as he walked up to be hooded. "It was good-natured yet not meant as a compliment," he wrote. "But I accepted it as one." Schwarz's bachelor of science was complemented by a year of study at the Queensland College of Teachers, which licensed him to teach mathematics and science. In 1935, twenty-two-year-old Fred was assigned by Queensland's Education Department to teach science at the high school level in Warwick, a town south of Brisbane. There, his activities as teacher were paralleled by his evangelical involvement. He formed a branch of the Crusader Union, a Christian youth organization devoted to reaching people of high school age. When he was transferred back to Brisbane in 1940, his reputation as a religious leader preceded him. He was seen as an effective leader whose doctrinal conservatism and Pentecostal ties did not impede his ability to address a broad base of evangelicals.[15]

Circumstances then made it possible for him to fulfill his life-long dream. In October 1936, the University of Queensland inaugurated its new Faculty of Medicine, located in Herston, near the Brisbane General Hospital, where new medical graduates completed their residency. Since his evening teaching schedule at the Queensland College of Teachers left him free during the day, Schwarz registered and was accepted in 1940. Under normal circumstances, a medical student was required to go through six years of study to become a doctor. Yet it only took Schwarz four: his bachelor's degree in science allowed him to get the program's first year credited, and the time required to complete the curriculum had been shortened by a year due to emergency measures adopted after the outbreak of the Second World War – measure adopted because a good number of Australia's medical practitioners had been enlisted in the armed forces, thus creating a shortage. Schwarz was not conscripted and spent the war completing his medical training.[16]

Upon returning to Brisbane, Schwarz married Lillian Morton, whom he had met on the train that he took to Warwick four years before. She was a few years younger than he and was still attending high school when they met. The wedding took place in the bride's home parish in the Clifton Anglican Church in December 1939. Shortly after, the new husband and wife relocated to a small apartment in Brisbane near the Teachers' College where Schwarz taught evening classes. Their first child, named John Charles Morton, was born two years later in March 1942 and their second, Rosemary Gay, in October 1944.[17]

FIRST FIGHTS

In medical school, Schwarz resumed his involvement with the University of Queensland's Evangelical Union, which he had left six years before, now embodying a new attitude of self-confidence among young campus evangelicals in many English-speaking countries. He organized prayer meetings and Bible study groups and tried to impress upon his peers the kind of ethic he deemed fit with the medical vocation. In April 1943, he intervened loudly at a meeting of the University of Queensland Medical Society when it was suggested that graduation ceremonies include a ball. A student newspaper reported that "this suggestion drew forth a long spirited and castigating address from Christian Reveler Schwarz, who in no uncertain terms declared his aversion for extra-Christian terpsichorean revels, and demanded rejection of the motion."[18]

Most importantly, for the first time he came into conflict with Communists. Communists were very active on the Queensland campus, where they organized conferences and rallies, as well as being involved in the University Student Union. Australia had a tradition of left-wing radicalism and labour unionism since the great strikes of the 1890s. This ferment led to the founding of the Australian Labor Party (ALP), which rapidly became a moderate, middle-class-oriented mass party that took power in several Australian states (e.g., in Queensland in 1915), prompting disenchanted radical militants to form the Communist Party of Australia (CPA). The CPA recognized the authority of the Communist International (Comintern) and was thus in line with Soviet policies. However, because the Union of Soviet Socialist Republics (USSR) had signed a non-aggression pact with Nazi Germany in August 1939, the CPA found itself in a bad spot when Australia declared war on Germany in September 1939. In accordance with Comintern policy, Communists condemned Australia's war effort, calling the war an "imperialist" conflict in which the Allies were the aggressors. In spring 1940, the CPA was banned under wartime national security regulation. In many Australian cities, its offices were raided, its assets seized, and several of its members detained.[19]

Yet, on the Queensland campus, as in many other places, Communists continued their activities simply by removing the name "Communist" or the party's name. Schwarz was particularly appalled by their anti-war demonstrations, during which they denigrated Australian soldiers by calling them "Six-bob-a-day murderers." Having publicly affirmed that he would challenge any communist in a public discussion, he got a reply through the student newspaper: "I would like to warn F.C. Schwarz that should any worthy exponent of dialectics be sufficiently provoked to accept the rash challenge to Marxian doctrines, Jehovah, and all the heavenly host will avail the said F.C.

Schwarz nothing." Schwarz's opponent was Max Julius, a law student who came from a non-practising Jewish Communist family, a member of the CPA's central committee, and president of the university's Student Union. A debate was organized between the two student leaders in the Men's Common Room in May 1940 on the topic: "Is Communism a Science or a Religion?"[20]

Schwarz's opposition to communism was rooted in its atheism and its conception of God and humanity rather than in its economic and political doctrines. His goal was to explain why communism should be considered a religion: "It possessed a doctrine of God viz., atheism; it had a doctrine of man viz., an evolving animal; it had a doctrine of sin viz., capitalism; it had a doctrine of redemption viz., revolution and it had a doctrine of the end times viz., Communism." Schwarz's rhetoric was part of a global trend during the decades that followed the October 1917 Russian Revolution whereby observers increasingly conceived of communism not only as an economic and political philosophy but also as a full-fledged religious system. "Throughout the 1930s and 1940s," Jonathan Herzog notes, "this idea flourished, which led in turn to a powerful conclusion: if Communism was a dangerous religion, then a powerful weapon in the anti-Communist arsenal was a genuine religious faith."[21]

However, Max Julius swerved away from the debate's proposed topic and, rather, launched an effective attack on the capitalist system, pointing out how it created war, poverty, and social inequities, and robbed workers from reaping the harvest of their labour. Schwarz won the debate basically because most of the hundred people who attended it were Evangelical Union supporters. Yet he was dissatisfied by the experience. He had handed over to Julius control of the stage by allowing him to focus on the ills of capitalism. Fundamental to this blunder was his lack of understanding of communism. He thus decided to become an authority on it: "Each night I read from one of the large volumes that contain the teachings of the Communist founders." Before long he had absorbed enough Marxist-Leninist theory to develop a more solid critical perspective on it. "I'm never alone with Fred. He always has Karl Marx along," his wife Lillian said.[22]

In June 1944, Schwarz and twenty-seven fellow medical students graduated as doctors in medicine during a ceremony at the university's Technical College Hall. Medical graduates needed to serve as resident medical officers (RMOs) for a year in a hospital approved by the Brisbane and South Coast Medical Board to acquire full registration.

Most Queensland graduates, including Schwarz, did their residency at the Brisbane General Hospital. Working conditions were poor. Brisbane Hospital RMOs were paid two hundred pounds per year and worked considerably more than the usual forty-four-hour work week. When residents attempted to gain better working conditions and wages in 1942, the board refused their demand, claiming they were students, not employees. Moreover, wages and working conditions had been frozen for the duration of the war. This setting gave Schwarz his first important political experience.[23]

Since 1941, Schwarz represented the Queensland Medical Students' Association's general committee and became acquainted with associated procedures and politics. In August 1943, during a meeting at which the association was dissolved into the new University of Queensland Medical Society (UQMS), which integrated into a single body both students and RMOs, Schwarz spoke of the need to assist medical graduates. As reported by the student newspaper: "On this point Mr. Schwarz waxed voluble, and in an excellently phrased address, put forward a motion that the society explore and exploit the possibilities of an increased remuneration to graduates employed in the Brisbane Hospital." He suggested that the hospital and the Medical Board be approached directly. If fruitless, this action was to be followed by bringing the case to the Industrial Court of Queensland, the only body that had the authority to increase wartime wages.[24]

Medical resident Ronald Wood recalled: "Schwarz ... began to take a very active role in the affairs of medical students. He was a persuasive speaker who put his case well. His oratory had considerable influence on his audience." In March 1944, Schwarz was elected president of the UQMS and a memorandum on the RMOs' conditions was distributed among students. It recommended a five-hundred-pound annual salary, a forty-four-hour week, and a few health and holiday benefits. After the Brisbane and South Coast Medical Board's refusal to receive their delegation, the RMOs brought their case before the Industrial Court. As the date of the court hearing got closer, the case attracted an increasing amount of attention in medical circles. The Queensland branch of the British Medical Association (BMA) was not pleased and urged the RMOs to stop their action.[25]

On the morning of 8 October 1944, the Industrial Court of Arbitration of Queensland and its justices – T.A. Ferry and W.J. Riordan – heard the case. As president of the UQMS, Schwarz represented the RMOs. His main opponent, Medical Board representative J. McCracken, first complained that, because Schwarz had refused a private hearing, "there might be certain matters discussed and brought out in evidence here which is undesirable should [it] receive the publicity that may eventuate from this discussion." Schwarz responded: "We are doing something that is rather unprecedented in the medical history of Australia ... and our action has been misinterpreted and misjudged by a section of the medical profession and I think now [there is] the opportunity for them to know the full facts of the case as we present it."[26]

Schwarz pointed out that Brisbane Hospital's working conditions and wages were based on the premise that RMOs were single men, which prevented them from marrying and have families. He further observed that the three among them who had families, including himself, had them "by reason of special economic circumstances." He related the RMOs' poor working conditions to the bygone conception of a hospital as a charitable institution funded by philanthropic subscriptions. McCracken counter-argued that residency constituted only a temporary apprenticeship carried out by a graduate whose medical knowledge was theoretical. He added that RMOs had had a wage increase before the war.

As the court was about to adjourn, Schwarz made a passionate plea for social justice in response to an attack from McCracken, who had implied that Schwarz's status as a married man preceded his medical studies and that "consequently his marriage was not a desire created by his studentship at the University." Schwarz responded:

> I desired as early as I can remember to become a doctor but that was rendered absolutely impossible because of the financial position of my parents. I was a member of a large family and my parents were not well-to-do, consequently, I went into the Teaching Service while some of my friends whose parents were well-to-do went to Sydney and Melbourne and qualified as doctors. That indicates to me that the present position is loaded against the sons of poorer parents, and I believe one reason for this claim is that we should eliminate as far as possible any handicaps so that the Medical Profession will be open to worthwhile members of the community irrespective of the financial position of their parents or the size of their families.

A few days later, the court ruled in the RMOs' favour. They were given a £350 per annum salary and their work week was fixed at fifty-four hours. Work shifts could no longer exceed sixteen hours. "Medical History Made," the University of Queensland student newspaper headlined, adding that this success was "a personal triumph for Dr. Fred Schwarz who ha[d] been throughout the driving force behind the movement." A precedent had been set, one that would be emulated in other Australian hospitals where RMOs demanded, and in several cases gained, better working conditions. As Queensland physician Derek H. Meyers wrote sixty years after the case, "Although this industrial action seemed scandalous to older doctors at the time, it is clear that every graduate of an Australian medical school since then owes a debt of gratitude to Fred."[27]

Upon completing his term as RMO at the Brisbane hospital, Schwarz moved with his family 160 kilometres north of Brisbane to the town of Gympie, where he worked for the local hospital, before moving to Wentworth, a town in the Australian southeast. Then, the family made the move to the city. Schwarz bought a house in the Sydney suburb of North Strathfield. Located at 142 Concord Road, this superb sixteen-room home with a large backyard took up the entire southwestern side of a street corner at the intersection of Concord Road and Wellbank Street. Schwarz also established a new office for his private medical practice in the nearby city of Concord. This practice grew in the following years to become one of the busiest in Sydney's western suburbs. Schwarz once estimated that, in US dollars, his practice's gross income in the late 1940s was about $25,000 and that his personal net income was $12,000. Also, the family was again expanding. In July 1948, the Schwarzes had their third and last child, David Frederick. Around this time their eldest child, John, started attending school. He met another boy, also named John (Whitehall), whose father had died during the war and who was informally adopted by the family and became Schwarz's foster son. The "two Johns" followed their father's dual vocation and both became doctors.[28]

Settling down allowed Schwarz to resume his religious activities, notably with the University of Sydney's Evangelical Union. He met John Drakeford, a Baptist preacher who would become one of his life-long friends and who eventually baptized Lillian Schwarz by immersion, bringing her formally to the evangelical faith. Schwarz quickly made a name for himself in the Sydney area's most important churches. Donald W.B. Robinson, at the time an Anglican bishop who had known Schwarz since the late 1930s, introduced him to Howard Mowll, the Anglican archbishop of Sydney.[29]

Sydney Anglicans had, since the nineteenth century, a tradition of cooperating with evangelicals of all persuasions. Schwarz was popular among them during this period, earning the moniker the "Beloved Physician." He lectured at the Moore Theological College and was also invited to address the Annual Conference of Anglican Clergy. His closeness to Anglicans was such that a 1948 newspaper clip even referred to him as "a Strathfield physician and Anglican lecturer." In reality, he had become a member and deacon of Haberfield Baptist Church, located a few kilometres from the Schwarz family home. In 1947, continuing his activities as lay pastor, he was also appointed director of evangelism by the Baptist Union of New South Wales. This, in addition to his entrance into Sydney Anglicanism's upper spheres, shows how far Schwarz had come from the lower-class evangelical nonconformism with which he had been long associated.[30]

DIALECTICS

Schwarz once stated: "[American right wingers] never taught me anything. I learnt all I know about communism in Australia."[31] The fundamentals of his analysis of Marxism-Leninism were established during the Second World War and evolved little thereafter. He read widely from the basic Marxist-Leninist texts, notably using editions made available in the English language by the Communist International's publishing house and, after 1952, by Beijing's Foreign Language Press. Writings included Marx's *Capital*; Marx and Engels's *Manifesto of the Communist Party*; Lenin's *The State and the Revolution; The Proletarian Revolution and the Renegade Kautsky; Left-Wing Communism: An Infantile Disorder*; *Imperialism: The Highest Stage of Capitalism*; Stalin's *Problems of Leninism*; and the writings of those philosophers, such as Hegel and Feuerbach, who had inspired communist theoreticians. After the communist takeover of China in 1949, he read works by Asian thinkers, such as Mao Tse-tung's *On Contradiction* and Liu Shao-Chi's *How to Be a Good Communist.*

From the 1950s on, he also became an intense reader of English-language Communist and left-wing publications throughout the world: the *Daily Worker*, the *Beijing Review*, *Workers Vanguard*, *Soviet Life*, the *Militant*, *World Marxist Review*, and so on. By the late 1950s, he admitted that the only non-communist journal he read with some consistency was the *US News and World Report*. In the United States, each week the Long Beach CACC office received more than thirty periodicals to which it subscribed. These publications became the basic source of information for the CACC newsletter. Schwarz claimed that reading and writing about communism was sometimes difficult since communist propaganda was "often cloaked in Marxist-Leninist jargon which need[ed] to be translated into simple understandable English."[32]

While the *Communist Manifesto* still stands as a model of rhetorical clarity, many Marxist-Leninist writings are arcane and not easy to grasp. Schwarz's professed goal was to "provide information and analysis which is worthy of the greatest universities, but which can be understood by all thoughtful and intelligent readers." Yet it seems that he never availed himself of the vast number of academic works on the subject. His writings have thus sometimes been castigated as overly simplistic, especially by foes from the academic world. Communist theory aside, one of the only books that clearly influenced his take on communism was not an academic work but, rather, the autobiography of Whittaker Chambers, a former Communist whose testimony was the cornerstone of the sensational 1949 Alger Hiss trial in the United States. *Witness* (1952) was for Schwarz "the best book on communism ever written." Schwarz was particularly inspired by Chambers's recollection of how he had initially been drawn in by the promise of world peace through the establishment of a classless society based on rational principles. Schwarz acknowledged that this idea of being the subject of history was a "wonderful vista for the human mind," and he recognized communism as the most attractive vision of hope offered to humankind since the birth of Christ. Chambers's account became the blueprint for all of Schwarz lectures and writings pertaining to the manner in which communists converted young idealists to their cause.[33]

For Schwarz, communism was primarily anchored in the denial of God's existence. He always substantiated this axiom by quoting Lenin's writings on religion, such as the 1905 *Socialism and Religion*, in which the Bolshevik leader claimed his program was rooted in a scientific, materialistic, and therefore atheistic philosophy. Schwarz's emphasis on the atheism-communism connection was almost always drawn from the writings of Lenin, whose atheism was more virulent than that of either Marx or Engels. However, theory aside, Schwarz's emphasis on the atheistic aspect of communism was also strengthened by the concrete experience of Soviet Communism. During the 1920s and 1930s, the Soviet purge of organized religion frightened scores of Christians worldwide. Not only did those waves of anti-religious repressions garner worldwide media attention during the interwar years, but, as Jonathan Herzog notes, anticommunists "held no monopoly on explaining Communist incompatibility with religion. Communists themselves did little to hide their contempt." The awakening of Schwarz's anticommunist praxis in 1940 took place at a time when the Soviet regime was still fully committed to Lenin's virulent antireligious policy – elimination of the clergy, seizure of churches, campaigns against religious belief advocated by the Soviet press – which had been maintained by Stalin. Despite the 1941 Nazi aggression, which compelled the USSR to enlist the Orthodox Church's support (therefore lifting its repression of religion), Schwarz, like many others, never believed communists could be trusted with regard to organized religion.[34]

In 1963, American liberal Protestant churchman Brooks R. Walker criticized Schwarz for placing undue emphasis on atheism: "To suggest, as Schwarz does, that there is an intimate connection between atheism and the repudiation of ethics and morality is to impugn the good names and ethical standards of a multitude of persons who are atheists and, at the same time, ethical and moral." Schwarz later replied that he never claimed godlessness directly caused communism but, rather, that it created conditions favourable to its inception. He also acknowledged that atheists could be anticommunists since communism "conflicts with some of their other convictions such as devotion to individual liberty."[35]

Walker nonetheless concurred with the crusader on one point: "If Schwarz misses the mark in his attack on atheism, he is nonetheless discerning when it comes to identifying one of Communism's main appeals: It has a program to change human nature. It proclaims that the old human nature will die with the passing away of bourgeois society … He perceives the flaw in Soviet utopian idealism because his Christian faith maintains that sinful human nature may be transformed, but only in Christian liberty."[36]

Long before Walkers' objections, it seems that Schwarz had been aware that his animus towards communism, based as it was on the doctrine's atheism, tended to unfairly devalue ideas that had much greater importance in the writings of communist theoreticians – for example, those relating to economic theory, party organization, and historical development. Schwarz thus came to focus his main critical analysis of communism on the concept of dialectical materialism. Dialectical materialism was an outgrowth of Hegel's dialectic, which assumes that history is an evolving phenomenon wherein the resolution of contradictions (thesis-antithesis-synthesis) propels society towards inexorable progress amid apparent chaos. Marx transposed this logic into hard economic reality whereby the whole of human evolution was determined by material forces (i.e., the modes of economic production). Controlling these forces was the key to shaping human character, culture, and society. Marxism thus used the Hegelian concept of contradictions and their resolution to explain the evolution of society. In other words, nature and history themselves are dialectic. This Marxist interpretation of dialectical progress became a theoretical hotchpotch that would dominate the thinking of communist politicians, leaders, and theoreticians throughout the world. Dialectical materialism could in fact be twisted to any purpose, something Schwarz never failed to point out. Lenin used it to explain Russia's modest return to capitalism during the New Economic Policy (NEP) in 1921; Stalin used it to criticize the same program and to promote a collectivization program in 1928.[37]

As Schwarz observed, Marxist dialectics can justify any action deemed necessary to secure and maintain political power: "One obvious conclusion from the Communist adherence to the dialectic is that the Communist goal can never be perceived by observing the direction in which the Communists are moving." Communism was thus first and foremost characterized by total flexibility; economic, political, cultural, and scientific programs were merely expedient tactics. Yet flexibility was not synonymous with dishonesty: "Any lie that advances Communist conquest is, by definition, not a lie but the Marxist-Leninist truth. The maturity of a Communist can be judged by the extent to which he can divorce himself from the evidence of his senses and totally identify himself with the verdict of the Communist Party." Schwarz could thus portray communists as being ideologically induced towards embracing an attitude that enabled them to adopt any stance that happened to fit their immediate interests. And he suggested that their psychology could be understood and their moves predicted through the study of Marxist-Leninist theory. The foundational quality of these writings, Schwarz and many other anticommunists asserted, was validated by the uniform nature of

Communist regimes, which were all single-party states. The communist canon looked like a genetic blueprint. Hence the title of his book *You Can Trust the Communists (to Be Communists)*.[38]

In other words, while Schwarz located the essence of Communism (as a movement) in its classic texts, which he conceived of as statements of purpose to be seriously considered, he also thought that communist doctrines were so intellectually flexible that, as an ideology, communism was almost meaningless. While, since the nineteenth century, anticommunists throughout the world lamented the alleged deceitfulness of Communists, Schwarz went further by suggesting that, apart from its goal of a classless society, communism did not have any genuine program: "Communism has no economics. Economic programs are merely temporary tactics designed to enable the Communist Party to conquer and retain power." This takes Marxist-Leninist theory at face value while, at the same time, seeing it as a tapestry of self-serving slogans. This had a practical advantage as it allowed Schwarz simultaneously to slam Communists for their duplicity and to substantiate his suspicions by citing Marxist-Leninist writings.[39]

Political scientist and *National Review* contributor Edward J. Rozek, who participated in some CACC events in the 1960s, affirmed that Schwarz had a commanding understanding of Marxism-Leninism – an understanding that even impressed some academic specialists. However, he argued that the crusader was wrong to discount the fact that the USSR was a world of its own, to which Marxism was often not applicable. In 1967, questioned by William F. Buckley on the American TV show *Firing Line* on the evolution of the Soviet world since Stalin, the crusader was unwilling to move from his ideology-based analysis. Even though he acknowledged that the USSR had toned down its aggressive rhetoric towards the West during the post-Stalin era, he refused to recognize that this had resulted from the languishing of the Soviet state and its economy.[40]

2

Touching the Multitudes

COLD WAR

By 1948, polarization between the US and the USSR had led to the impending threat of another world war. The chain of events was marked by a series of pivotal dates. In spring 1946, both George Kennan's "long telegram" to the US government and Churchill's "Iron Curtain" speech expressed the Western world's growing apprehension of the Soviet Union. In March 1947, the announcement of the Truman Doctrine affirmed the American resolution to contain Soviet geopolitical expansion. This was followed in June by the Soviet refusal to cooperate with US secretary of state George Marshall's program for European economic recovery. The Berlin crisis in mid-1948 indicated that the world's two superpowers were now deadlocked in a power struggle.

Since the early months of 1948, Australia had been well into the new conflict. Coming out of the Second World War, the British Empire was virtually bankrupt. The integration of Australia into the US strategic orbit increased as the country needed a new protector within the new bipolar world. At the same time, growing American cultural and economic influence substituted for former British ascendency. In Australia, the first decade of the postwar era was largely defined by the country's role as the Pacific stronghold of the West. These were troubled times for the Australian left, and particularly for the Australian Labor Party, which had ruled the country since October 1941. The foreign policy of Premier Ben Chifley, in office since July 1945, was increasingly under attack for its refusal to accept Cold War polarization. By 1948, a reinvigorated centre-right coalition led by Robert Menzies (Liberal Party) and Arthur Fadden (Australian Country Party, the Liberal Party's junior ally) campaigned on "the pattern of coming dictatorship" and assailed each one of the proposals put forward under the Labor Party's social and economic agenda. The ALP was ultimately defeated at the polls in December 1949, thus allowing Menzies to return to power after his first mandate (1939–41). Before the ALP's final defeat in 1949, Premier Chifley's plan to nationalize banks faced an intense and well-organized two-year lobbying campaign, in which public opinion, especially that of the middle class, was mobilized by business sectors and conservatives in opposition to the project. In May 1948, the Labor government's plan to implement price and rent control was defeated by referendum.[1]

Australian medical doctors were overwhelmingly opposed to the ALP's health policy. One clash took place over the National Health Service (NHS), adopted in December 1948. This plan covered some medical services at government expense. Menzies's Liberal Party, Fadden's Australian Country Party (then in opposition), and the British Medical Association organized a very effective one-year boycott of the NHS and other "socialized medicine" schemes. In spite of its non-political stance, the BMA put its case forward in newspapers and in letters to its members. Australian doctors closed ranks in opposition to the dual prospect of competition between private practice and state-financed clinics and the imposition of state control over the payment of medical services. In October 1949, the BMA appealed to the Australian High Court, which invalidated governmental measures aimed at forcing doctors to apply an ALP program – the Pharmaceuticals Benefits Act – designed to provide a limited number of free medicines to patients.[2]

Schwarz did not publicly join his fellow physicians in the outcry over Labor Party policies; rather, he was preoccupied by the Communists themselves, whom he saw as the more dire threat. Despite its small size – about thirty thousand members at its peak just after the Second World War – the CPA was run by dedicated Stalinists and had established a solid foothold in some powerful and militant trade unions. Between 1948 and 1949, Schwarz became more active as an anticommunist. During a 1948 series of lectures he delivered at the St Andrew's Cathedral (Anglican), he challenged L.H. Gould, member of the CPA's Central Committee, to a debate. In 1949, in Adelaide, Schwarz and Drakeford debated with Alf Watt, the secretary of the Communist Party of South Australia. In 1950, Schwarz had lectured on or debated in the most important universities of his country: Queensland, Sydney, Melbourne, and Adelaide.[3]

His name became one with which Australian Communists had to reckon. Schwarz took pleasure in telling the anecdote about a time he once lectured on dialectical materialism to a CPA chairman who had no real idea about the concept. In September and October 1955, two years after he had founded the CACC, Schwarz returned to Australia for a rest with his family. A debate was arranged with J.J. Brown, head of the Australian Railway Union. But twenty-four hours after accepting the challenge, Brown cancelled it. Several other Communists were contacted, with similar results. "It seems," Schwarz quipped, "a central directive was issued that they should not debate with me."[4]

By May 1948, the Cominform, which had replaced the Comintern as the main coordinator of international revolutionary efforts, had adopted a position that prompted Soviet-affiliated parties throughout the world to denounce the United States and its allies as agents of imperialism. This included Australia's Labor government, which, according to the CPA, was composed of reformist betrayers. The policy was now to forcefully substitute the CPA for the ALP as the workers' party. On 27 June 1949, during a harsh Australian winter, the Communist-led Australian Miners' Federation went on general strike in New South Wales and was later joined by most workers in the coal industry. Since the country has no oil or natural gas, Australians experienced dreadful living conditions during that winter. Economic activity halted and shortages were felt everywhere.[5]

Schwarz was outraged by this strike, which had been called before any ruling from the arbitration authorities came out. A year later, he explained the consequences for Australia in a speech:

> In the middle of winter one bulb, and one bulb alone, was allowed on the night. No heating appliances of any make whatsoever were allowed, except on a Doctor's prescription. Cooking was allowed for one hour in the morning and one hour in the evening, and the gas was turned off at other times. Hospitals everywhere had to close down their operating theatres, to cease accepting patients. They could not carry on. A considerable number of elderly people died, were gassed, in effect were murdered, because they would ignore the restrictions and go to bed with their gas fire in their room.

Moreover, the fact that most of the strikers were non-Communists showed that: "the vast bulk of the Union membership is helpless, where all the decisions, at the critical moment when they are important, are made by the executive membership." For Schwarz, the 1949 strike had shown the danger of Lenin's prescription for seizing power through implementing strategies of social and political unrest initiated by a few dedicated advocates.[6]

The strike was exceedingly unpopular among Australians. Under pressure, the ALP government adopted emergency measures. Bank accounts of members of the CPA and striking unions were frozen, and their leaders imprisoned. On 2 August the army reopened the coal mines; nine days later the strike was over. The whole episode weakened the Australian left considerably. The ruling ALP struggled with parts of its own constituency while at the same time being criticized by conservatives for its lack of action. Australian Communism never recovered. Diminished and isolated, having wasted its reserve of public sympathy, it was eventually eradicated from nearly all trade unions. Calling Communists "opponents of religion, of civilized government, of law and order, or national security," Liberal Party leader Robert Menzies declared that, if elected, he would introduce legislation to outlaw the CPA. After Menzies's December 1949 win at the polls, he soon introduced the Communist Party Dissolution Act.[7]

It was in this context that Schwarz had his last important debate with a Communist in Australia. The crowd, wrote one journalist, was composed of "prominent Communists and prominent churchmen," with support "of the two contestants evenly divided." The burning question of the day – concerning the legal banning of the Communist Party – made this contest a rather fiery one. L. Aarons, Newcastle district secretary of the Communist Party, commented: "such previous efforts to ban a movement which represents the progress of humanity have failed." This prompted Schwarz to slam the communist concept of progress, which he asserted meant violent revolution. Schwarz also called Communists hypocrites for their call to "keep the trade unions free" in light of the fact that Communist countries did not allow trade unions. Schwarz later deplored the fact that, in spite of Menzies's electoral victory thanks to his "promise to drive the Communists underground," in the months following the election the bill to prohibit the Communist Party had been "weakened by Labor amendments and at present is stymied."[8]

That Schwarz supported the ban is hardly surprising. He never showed any leaning towards civil libertarianism. Many times in the United States he would scorn "pseudo-liberals" who defended the presumption of innocence and used the US Constitution's Fifth Amendment with regard to Communists. "I believe that nobody is entitled to go into a private home without a warrant," he once said. "But, if the house is on fire, I'd be prepared to forgive the fire brigade when they did it." He also opposed allowing Communists to teach in schools and universities. In 1962, Schwarz debated this issue at the University of California, Berkeley, with William Mandel, a liberal journalist known for having been dismissed from Stanford University during the McCarthy era. Mandel made a plea for academic freedom and hailed Communists for having "fought for the equality of Negroes when nobody else would touch the subject." Schwarz tried to ridicule Mandel's logic, which "would have allowed Nazis to teach at U.C. while Jews were being fed to the gas chambers." A Communist in a university, he said, was "a soldier dedicated to destroy this institution … and in favor of the enslavement of all mankind."[9]

The considerable dwindling of Australian Communism in the post-strike aftermath did not mitigate Schwarz's conviction that it remained a genuine threat to his country. Years later, he wrote that Communists in Australia were "active, advancing, and aggressive." "Australians," he added, "are, generally speaking, complacent and confused. This serves the communist purpose exceedingly well."[10]

THE PROPOSAL

In early 1950, two important figures of North American Protestant fundamentalism visited Australia. Their encounter with Schwarz would change his life and that of his family. The first visitor, Thomas Todhunter ("T.T.") Shields had been pastor of Jarvis Street Baptist Church in Toronto, Ontario, since 1910. A hard-shelled fundamentalist and separatist who railed against liquor consumption, dancing, movie-going, and, more intensely, against Roman Catholicism, Shields had been for two decades president of the Union of Regular Baptist Churches, which he tried to purge from its modernist personalities before he was himself voted out in 1949. At the age of seventy-seven, when he met Schwarz, his influence on the fundamentalist movement was receding, though he remained a figure of authority among conservative Baptist churches.

The second visitor, Carl McIntire, then forty-four, was pastor of the Bible Presbyterian Church of Collingswood, New Jersey. Just like Shields, McIntire waged war against a changing culture. He attacked not only all signs of moral decay as he understood them (drinking, dancing, jazz music, movie theatres) but also the civil rights movement, the revised version of the Bible, Roman Catholics, the United Nations, the US Post Office, Gandhi and the Indian Congress, sex education, water fluoridation, socialized medicine, and labour unions. Formerly a student at the Princeton Theological Seminary, McIntire had followed his mentor, J. Gresham Machen, who left the institution in 1929 and founded the Westminster Seminary in Pennsylvania, from which McIntire graduated in 1931.

In 1933, the Presbyterian Church of America appointed McIntire, then aged twenty-seven, pastor of the one-thousand-member Collingswood Presbyterian Church in New Jersey. In 1938, he left his denomination along with his whole congregation and founded his own church, where he preached for the next sixty-six years. In 1941, in reaction to the US Federal Council of Churches (FCC) – officially the Federal Council of Churches of Christ – which, since 1908, had regrouped most of the larger, mainline Protestant churches, McIntire founded his own parachurch organization, the American Council of Christian Churches (ACCC).[11]

In the 1940s, while a new generation of evangelicals – Billy Graham, Carl F. Henry, and Harold J. Ockenga, often labelled the "neo-evangelicals" – rejected extreme separatism and turned towards a more moderate outlook that was institutionalized in the National Association of Evangelicals (NAE), Shields and McIntire were among those who clung to an uncompromising fundamentalist faith, which they incorporated into an ultraconservative political ideology. In his 1945 book *The Rise of the Tyrant: Controlled Economy vs. Private Enterprise*, McIntire located the origins of capitalism in the Bible itself and stated that the United States would soon be struggling for its survival in the context of a spiritual clash between a free and a controlled economy. Using religious terms to emphasize the superiority of capitalism, McIntire fused his hatred of atheistic, materialistic communism with economic libertarianism.[12]

In August 1948, McIntire, Shields, and other hard-shelled fundamentalists in several countries (the United States, Canada, Switzerland, Sweden) founded the International Council of Christian Churches (ICCC) in response to the creation of the World

Council of Churches (WCC), which had regrouped 147 more mainline Protestant churches worldwide. Looking forward to expanding the ICCC, which at this point simply amalgamated ACCC churches in the United States and some small ones abroad, McIntire announced an ICCC conference in Geneva in August 1950 that would be aimed at increasing the organization's visibility and inviting other churches to join. In January 1950, McIntire asked Shields to accompany him to Australia to hold talks about a possible ICCC affiliation with Australian denominations, notably the Australian Free Presbyterian Church. McIntire convinced Shields that his presence was essential to the ICCC's fortunes.[13]

Recalling his encounter with both men, Schwarz noted that those arranging the visitors' itineraries experienced difficulties: "I was asked to help as I had friends in all evangelical circles. I cooperated willingly and well remember my visit to the Anglican Primate of Australia, Archbishop Mowll, on their behalf." The two visitors learned of Schwarz's reputation as both medical practitioner and conspicuous Christian leader. They were greatly impressed with the extent of his self-education on communism and his success in debating Australian Communists. McIntire invited him to speak in ACCC-affiliated churches in the United States as well as to attend the ICCC Geneva conference in August 1950. In April 1950, after McIntire and Shields had returned home, Schwarz wrote McIntire that an Australian church had voted to disaffiliate from the WCC and had applied for ICCC membership under a new name (the Bible Union of Australia), making it possible for Schwarz to attend the Geneva congress as a representative of the new body. Schwarz suggested inviting a well-known Australian soprano church singer named Clarice Inglis, who travelled with her husband Bob, an evangelical businessman, and McIntire agreed to this. Schwarz's wife Lillian would also accompany her husband during the tour. A family friend was ready to take care of the children during the parents' absence, and a doctor was hired to run the medical practice. Due to the high cost of the plane ticket – intercontinental air transportation was still in its earliest stages – Schwarz was forced to sell his car to make the trip.[14]

Schwarz was to be paid for his speeches in the United States not by the ACCC but by the churches themselves. McIntire guaranteed that he would advertise the tour and pressure ACCC-affiliated churches to book the Australian visitors. McIntire's religious newspaper the

Christian Beacon promoted the event on its front page during the months leading up to May. The lecturing honorariums in each location were to be fixed between the visitor and his hosts, who were to pay what seemed reasonable. "I am sure the only expense that you would need to care for," McIntire confidently wrote, "would be the plane because so far as accommodations and entertainment, that would be all cared for along the line at various places where you would be speaking."[15]

On 28 May 1950, Schwarz, his wife, and the Inglises left Australia aboard a propeller-driven DC6B plane. The next day, the Australians arrived in Honolulu, where addresses were scheduled in local fundamentalist congregations, the Kaimuki Community Church, and Honolulu's First Baptist Church. Schwarz lost no time in picking on the WCC. During this stay in Hawaii, a WCC-affiliated minister, John C. Bennett, had stated that no particular element of the communist creed was, "by itself[,] a 'great evil.'" Schwarz replied in a letter sent to Hawaiian newspapers that he found it strange that a minister could assert that atheism and violent revolution could not be considered as "evil." Pleased, McIntire republished the letter in his *Christian Beacon.*[16]

THE SEA OF FAITH

On 1 June 1950, Schwarz arrived at the San Francisco International Airport and began the first of two speaking tours (1950 and 1952) whose success led him to change his life and career path. This early North American success was due not only to his competence as a speaker but also to an auspicious combination of other factors. Schwarz and his new peers shared a common global subculture that often rendered national differences irrelevant. Schwarz's career highlights the transnational dynamics of Protestant evangelicalism, which has always been permeated by a global, frontierless sensibility. It provided Schwarz and North American evangelicals with a common structure of thought, sensibilities, and tastes, which was more influential than their respective national traits.[17]

Moreover, these first tours took place at a moment when the popular demand in the United States for faith had reached levels unprecedented in the twentieth century. In September 1949, two days after President Truman announced the first Soviet atomic test, evangelist Billy Graham opened the tent revival in Los Angeles that turned him into a national celebrity. Boosted by the support of W.R. Hearst's media empire, Graham's sermons tapped into popular fears over the new atomic age. In late January 1950, Truman authorized research on the hydrogen bomb. Times were appropriate not only for a faith that would provide immediate salvation but also for one that would appease the collective need for patriotic assertion. Throughout these years, church attendance became a way to profess one's commitment to the United States of America as well as a marker of freedom from subversive influence.[18]

Meanwhile, the nation saw the rapid expansion of its suburban population as the country's economy reshaped itself around the increasing number of white-collar, salaried professionals. Churches adapted well to the suburbs, where they provided communal stability. The year Schwarz arrived in the United States, church affiliation had risen to 55 percent of the total population, up from 49 percent in 1940. Even if the postwar revival affected all American religious groups, conservative Protestants constituted the cutting edge of the phenomenon. Between 1941 and 1961, conservative Presbyterian, Methodist, Lutheran, Baptist, and Reformed churches increased their membership by ranges that went from 60 to 100 percent. Congregations were expanding and so were financial resources. With the founding of Bible institutes, colleges, parachurch institutions, and journals, the renaissance of an evangelical theology and social ethic was under way.[19]

Last but not least, Schwarz arrived at a time when the issue of Communism in the collective psyche was about to reach its apex. From 1948 on, a series of spy cases underlined the idea of Red infiltration: the Alger Hiss, Harry Dexter White, and Judith Coplon cases as well as the arrest of twelve leaders of the Communist Party of the United States of America (CPUSA), followed by a nine-month trial for sedition. In January 1949, Beijing fell to Mao's armies; in September, the first Soviet atomic bomb exploded. In early 1950, Alger Hiss was declared guilty of perjury. In the summer of 1950, Julius and Ethel Rosenberg were arrested for spying for the Soviet Union and passing on US atomic secrets. Meanwhile, in Wheeling, West Virginia, Joseph McCarthy delivered the speech that made him a dominant voice in American national politics for four years. On 25 June, Kim-Il Sung's troops invaded the Republic of South Korea. In August 1950, a Gallup poll reported that 57 percent of respondents affirmed that their country was actually involved in the Third World War.[20]

On 4 June 1950, Schwarz spoke in Oakland at the First Independent Baptist Church, initiating a tour across the United States "by plane and by car in a zigzag path from west to east" and lecturing in "small Bible-believing churches." On 12 August1950, Schwarz ended his tour at the Bible Presbyterian Church of Collingswood by addressing McIntire's own congregation two days before the departure for Geneva. By this time, he had delivered forty-five paid church sermons in thirteen different states, plus an unknown number of unpaid lectures in churches, as well as in civic clubs and schools where meetings had been arranged on the spot. The Australian travellers often spent entire days on the road (interstate highways were built only a few years later). All visited churches were affiliates of McIntire's ACCC, which, in 1950, comprised several tens of thousands of uncompromising fundamentalists, including twelve thousand members in McIntire's own denomination. "Dr. Schwarz," the promotional "visit card" sent by the ACCC's head office to its affiliates indicated, "has been actively linked with the evangelical movement among students and has resisted modernism with brilliance of scholarship and saintliness of character." Congregations were taken by this preacher whose sermons and lectures on Marxist-Leninist dialectics gave spiritual meaning to daily headlines.[21]

With the start of the Korean War in late June, the secular press also began to show some interest. In Grand Rapids, Michigan, a local paper covered Schwarz's visit with the headline: "He 'Foresaw' the Korean War." In fact, Schwarz was no psychic. But he was already developing his skill at taking past declarations by Communist leaders and relating them to current events in a way that impressed audiences. "Korea is no accident," he said. "Trouble there was planned by Stalin 25 years ago when, in a lecture at Sverdlov university [in 1924], he stated that revolution in Korea and China would join hands with Russia for an inevitable clash with 'imperialist' powers of the West." While, in the same interview, he warned that communism and socialism should not be lumped into one single group, a few days later, another article saw him expressing more typical ACCC attitudes. "The churches of America need a great housecleaning to rid them of communists," he said, observing that the infiltration of Australian churches was already well established. McIntire rejoiced over this "splendid news coverage."[22]

On the day the Korean War started in late June, Schwarz arrived in the American Midwest. For three days the "Schwarz Party," as it was now called, was welcomed in Iowa by Dr William E. Pietsch, pastor of the Walnut Street Baptist Church in Waterloo and the ACCC's main representative in the Midwest. Pietsch invited Schwarz to his "Rev. Pietsch's Hour," broadcast each day on radio KXEL, for Schwarz's first radio appearance in the United States. Schwarz made an impression on Pietsch. This encounter was significant: in May 1953, Pietsch was co-founder of the CACC.[23]

Schwarz visited two other Midwestern evangelical hotbeds. On 5 July 1950, near Chicago, in "the evangelical capital of the U.S.A.," he delivered a sermon at the College Church of Wheaton College, Billy Graham's alma mater. Three days later, moving to Michigan, he brought his message to a Youth for Christ (YFC) rally in Grand Rapids as well as to local churches. The Schwarz Party then proceeded to T.T. Shield's congregation in Toronto for what Schwarz later described as "the great thrill of our tour." An overflowing crowd of about fifteen hundred gathered in the largest Baptist church in Toronto to listen to Schwarz deliver, extemporaneously, one of his most effective sermons. "What Shall the End Be? According to Joseph Stalin" covered his usual themes. But the training provided by weeks of speaking, as well as the critical situation in Korea, where UN troops were being pushed back to the extreme southeast corner of the peninsula, gave the lecture both gravity and suspense. Schwarz drew on his usual tricks. He explained the perilousness of the global political situation and related it to quotes from Communist leaders, in this case taken from Stalin's aforementioned 1924 speech.[24]

Schwarz then transitioned into a description of nuclear warfare, whereupon, drawing on his scientific background, he explained the principle of fusion reaction and how it accounted for the existence of stars as well as describing its role in creating lethal radioactivity. Then he raised the prospect of the creation of hydrogen bombs, "one million times as powerful as the atomic bomb," which would, in fact, be developed only two years after: "The scientists of the world, not the preachers, are saying that the world faces its own annihilation; the very possibility of universal suicide is facing the world today." He ended his presentation with a parabolic story about a man and his son drowned by the Deluge and affirming that Christian faith was the only glimpse of hope in an age of darkness. Schwarz used a two-hundred-year-old formula dating back to George Whitfield: the sermon starts with current events, describes Hell in a terrifying manner, and concludes with a message of salvation and hope. The twist was to introduce the Cold War and to present the mushroom cloud in eschatological terms.[25]

Shields rejoiced in the headline of his publication *The Gospel Witness*: "We are not easily swayed, and we confess that we are not easily satisfied with the content or manner of much modern public speaking, but Dr. Schwarz surpassed all our expectations." He pressed on: "But fine as was the character of his speaking, the content of his messages was still more extraordinary. We regard him as the most brilliantly intellectual man we have had the privilege of meeting in many a day." Shields urged Schwarz to give up his medical practice and to embrace a new career. Physicians were plenty; evangelical authorities on communism were not. "Dr. Schwarz ought to be free as a lecturer and preacher on these tremendous matters so that he might touch through the multitudes the intelligence and the conscience of mankind."[26]

Having publicly issued a challenge to debate any Communist during his first US trip, Schwarz found at least one man up to the challenge: Philip Frankfeld, chairman of the Communist Party of Maryland. In the boiling context of 1950, Frankfeld was among the few CPUSA leaders who had not been convicted amid the wave of arrests that had started in 1948. The ACCC obtained permission from the University of Maryland to use its Coliseum. The debate was booked for the evening of 8 August 1950. But in an unexpected twist, the event was cancelled on the eve of the scheduled date. The reason: Democratic Maryland governor William P. Lane's intervention urging the university president to withdraw permission to use the institution's facilities. The politician stated: "With Americans being shot down on the battlefields of Korea in defense of our way of life against insidious forces of communism, I cannot and I will not permit the representatives of this malevolent conspiracy the freedom of the University of Maryland campus." Frankfeld called the governor a bigot. Schwarz was equally upset, having been denied the opportunity to display of his hard-earned debating skills: "I could have answered Mr. Frankfeld's arguments easily. I could have wiped up the floor with him."[27]

In mid-August 1950, when Schwarz ended his two-month tour, he had earned $3,060 for an average of sixty-seven dollars per lecture. Admittedly, the costs associated with multistate travelling were such that most of the money grossed was spent during the trip. Yet Schwarz, an absolutely unknown name in the United States, netted in two months of lectures more than an American family physician averaged for the same period of time. He must have realized at this point that, should he tour alone in the US with a greater amount of publicity, a sustainable full-time career as lecturer was a possibility.[28]

On 14 August 1950, Schwarz, McIntire, and other ICCC officials took a plane to Geneva to participate in the ICCC's week-long congress. Several hundred fundamentalists were present, most from the United States or Western Europe, meaning that the proceedings had to be translated into several languages. The armature of the ICCC consisted of religious leaders who composed the Congress's committees and commissions. Schwarz was part of the International Affairs Commission and, as such, was in charge of the ICCC's platform pertaining to communism. But, no matter how burning the communist issue was in this summer of 1950, his lecture before ICCC delegates was an ill-attended bust. Schwarz was an unknown figure to non-American delegates, and the Geneva proceedings were dominated more by talks about organization than about doctrine. Additionally, historian Markku Ruotsila, in his work on McIntire and the ICCC, notes that, by the time of the Geneva Congress, there was among ICCC bodies "full agreement" with McIntire's hardline anticommunist stance, which made lengthy discussions on this issue seemingly unnecessary. Schwarz's only influence on the Congress ended up being to help the ICCC to draft its platform on communism. He returned to the United States in late August 1950.[29]

Lillian took the plane back to San Francisco and then returned to Australia, but her husband did not. Schwarz had decided to prolong his US stay. He was again invited to Jarvis Street Church in Toronto, where this time he spent an entire week. Before returning to Australia, he headed back west and delivered several other speeches. He was learning how to sustain an independent lecturing career wherein each lecture led to another as members of the audiences invited him to speak to yet other groups.[30]

Schwarz returned to Australia in late November 1950. In a letter to McIntire, he described his visit to the United States as a life-changing experience. He was doubly thrilled since the last part of the tour, which he made alone with few travelling expenses, allowed him to earn $2,350, which he donated to the ICCC. However, appeals for Schwarz to embrace a full-time ministry began coming in. "I think Dr. Shields has a real point, Dr. Schwarz," McIntire wrote, "and I think that you should consider it seriously before the Lord. Is the

Lord calling you into full-time Christian service? You have a ministry, a gift, a message, and all this has now been gloriously confirmed by the blessing of God."[31]

Returning to daily life was anti-climactic for the Australian, and world events in 1951 only increased this sentiment. The UN forces found themselves confronted by a Chinese intervention in North Korea, which forced them to retreat in the winter of 1951. In Australia, the Menzies government moved forward in the fall of 1950 with legislation that prohibited the Australian CPA. But in early March 1951, Australia's High Court ruled the legislation invalid. Menzies replied by calling a federal election, held in late April, which allowed conservatives to retain power in a context within which polls showed that more than 80 percent of Australians supported banning the CPA. However, on 22 September 1951, after several months of a bitter campaign that saw one of the largest opinion swings in Australian politics, in a referendum the electorate narrowly rejected (by a 50.5 percent margin) the Menzies government's proposal to ban the CPA.[32]

By the time the March election was called, McIntire informed Schwarz that the National Broadcasting Company (NBC) had just allowed the ACCC thirty minutes of free time to discuss the question of "socialism in the Church," and he expressed his wish to reach out to a greater number: "Would you be at all interested ... in giving yourself in to full time service in the ministry of the International Council of Christian Churches? It would mean ... giving up your medical practice, but giving the rest of your life to the promotion of the work of the Lord on a world-wide basis." The replies Schwarz sent to McIntire throughout 1951 reveal that he was torn between his personal and professional duties and his desire to embrace a lecturing career. This pleased McIntire: "I think you have a real responsibility to Christ and the whole Christian church when He has given you such gifts and such information concerning the issues confronting the church." He also invited Schwarz to participate in the ICCC Conference scheduled in Manila, Philippines, in November 1951. By the fall of 1951, Schwarz announced to McIntire that he had decided to give up his medical practice.

During the few days he spent in the Philippines for the ICCC Conference, Schwarz delivered talks to four different radio stations and before local delegates. The ICCC delegates were received by Philippine president Elpidio Quirino, a US ally who was himself battling a Communist insurgency in the archipelago. Schwarz delivered a keynote address during the meeting. He and McIntire agreed that the Australian would return to Sydney for Christmas and then leave for a new US tour in early 1952. "Dr. Schwarz and his wife," McIntire announced in December 1951, "have been invited to the U.S.A. in March for another speaking tour under the auspices of the ICCC. He plans to visit the British Isles and attend the Edinburgh Regional Conference in July, 1952. He is on his way now to Japan for ten days to speak on communism. He is keen and quick, accurate and unanswerable. The illustrations from the medical world slay the World Council's Goliath."[33]

DRIFT FROM MCINTIRE

Throughout 1952, daily headlines in US newspapers were still dominated by Communism and the Cold War. McCarthyism was still in full swing. The United States detonated the world's first hydrogen bomb and launched its first supersonic-guided missile. The Korean War came to a frustrating stalemate. Harry Truman announced in March that he would not seek re-election, paving the way for the presidential contest between former Illinois governor Adlai E. Stevenson and General Dwight D. Eisenhower.

Schwarz's second US tour began in March 1952 and marked the genuine beginning of his life as a full-time crusader. Shortly after his arrival in the United States, he informed McIntire of his plans. He would fulfill the two commitments he had made to McIntire: (1) to participate in the thirty-minute block of radio airtime given to the ICCC by the NBC and (2) to attend the ICCC's regional conference in Edinburgh in July 1952. He would also agree to speak before ACCC churches. However, he now rejected the idea of a pre-planned itinerary and no longer wished to be lecturing exclusively before ACCC audiences. Thus McIntire quoted Schwarz in a letter to two collaborators: "I will be happy to spend a month on the West Coast where I know the opportunities to be vast … The idea is not to concentrate in American Council Churches, but to get the American Council message across to as wide a circle as possible." Whether or not this new modus operandi was decided upon before the tour began, Schwarz had little reason to regret it: from day one, he rode a wave of success. In April 1952, he was in the studio of the San Francisco NBC affiliate and, during the free airtime the ICCC had been granted, spoke on the Sunday show *Faith in Action*. The NBC received so many requests for copies of the tape of this show that it thought it more convenient to send the original to McIntire so that the ICCC could make its own duplicates. The show generated such a response that Schwarz's schedule was filled with proposals for speaking engagements. As he realized, each single lecture opened the door to several others, initiating an endless chain reaction.[34]

For two months, he toured Southern California without any clear schedule, speaking an average of three or four times a day. This was a rehearsal for what his life became after the CACC's founding in 1953. His policy was to accept any invitation to speak, even if no honorarium was offered. McIntire's office lost track of Schwarz's whereabouts and could not offer clear answers when people interested in hiring him asked for his contact information. After weeks of radio silence, McIntire finally received a message from Schwarz, who told him that he was postponing his visit to the East because his lecturing schedule in the west kept filling up in a stunning manner.[35]

During this 1952 tour, the Australian quickly established contacts with some of Los Angeles's most important conservative evangelicals. One was Reverend James W. Fifield, pastor of Los Angeles's First Congregational Church (then the world's biggest congregational church) and founder of Spiritual Mobilization – a movement that was dedicated to arousing the clergy against "the trend towards pagan stateism" and that attracted contributions from leading businessmen such as J. Howard Pew (Sun Oil) and J. Frank Drake (Gulf Oil). Another contact was Robert "Fighting Bob" P. Shuler, pastor of Los Angeles's Trinity Methodist Church (one of the city's largest congregations) and arguably the most notorious fundamentalist from the fast-growing community of expatriated white Southerners who flocked to Southern California amid the wartime and postwar boom. Schwarz, said Shuler in a letter of recommendation, "delivered one of the most illuminating, practical and convincing messages on the plan and purpose of communism that it has ever been my privilege to hear." Schwarz also addressed several thousand people at the Church of the Open Door. Since 1949, this immense church had been led by Texas-born fundamentalist J. Vernon McGee, who invited Schwarz to preach a few times in the following years and joined the Crusade's "advisory committee" in 1956.[36]

Churches and religious institutions apart, the greatest demand for lectures came from civic organizations: service clubs such as the Lions, Kiwanis, and Rotary, and veterans organizations such as the American Legion. Schools were also interested, as were private businesses and chambers of commerce. By word of mouth, one lecture could lead to another, maximizing the potential offered in each area. For instance, after leaving California in spring 1952, Schwarz addressed a Rotary Club in Portales, New Mexico, where he met Floyd D. Golden, district governor of the local Rotarians and president of the Eastern New Mexico University. Impressed by the Australian, Golden arranged speaking engagements for him for an entire week in Albuquerque. This week was later described in a letter of introduction Golden wrote for Schwarz: "Dr. Schwarz spoke twenty some-odd times to service clubs, civic organizations, our University Assembly, special groups at the University, churches, and a few times in the neighbouring communities."[37]

In effect, Schwarz somehow updated an old American religious tradition, that of the travelling preacher. Preaching wherever he could, admitting new members to the fellowship, and often relying on the hospitality of the faithful for food and shelter, the travelling preacher was well adapted to the huge distances of North America. Unscheduled touring was cheap, efficient, allowed for giving several lectures a day, and created a large pool of contacts in different locations. However, this approach dealt a blow to Schwarz's collaboration with McIntire, who showed disappointment: "With a plan such as you are thinking of you would only have about 10 cities in which to operate." But he respected the decision. "Every man knows his own way of operating and we want you to have all the liberty you possibly can, and the Lord certainly has ways of going ahead of you as He has so definitely indicated."[38]

As historian Erling Jorstad wrote, Schwarz separated "himself from the separationists." As his US career began for good, he gradually severed his association with the ACCC and the ICCC. Schwarz nonetheless remained a member of the ICCC's Commission on International Relations for some time. His last recorded appearance as such was in 1954, when he participated in the ICCC's Third Plenary Congress in Philadelphia. In 1982, McIntire tried to re-establish contact with the Australian and invited him to address the delegates of the ICCC's next congress, but Schwarz kept his distance and politely declined the invitation.[39]

A legacy of Schwarz's collaboration with the ICCC is titled *A Christian Manifesto on World Communism and the Christian Church*. It was a document that he and Reverend Samuel Doyle, a Reformed Presbyterian who had worked as a missionary in China, co-wrote and whose final draft was adopted as a policy statement by a regional branch of the ICCC (the Far Eastern Council of Christian Churches) in Manilla in November 1951. The imprint of Schwarz, whose knowledge of communism easily surpassed that of his ICCC peers, can be seen in the *Christian Manifesto*'s passages rejecting Communism's "dialectical materialism which is militantly atheistic" and its "theory of the economic determinism of human character, a theory which is anti-Christian and debasing to human dignity." It denounced the USSR for its atheism, its "denial of moral and spiritual virtues," its "repudiation of the value of the individual and his heritage of freedom," and its "persistent vision of world conquest." The manifesto deemed socialism and theological liberalism to be "pathways" to Communism and called Christians to recognize "and admonish all pro-Communists who are in the churches." The Australian's prose added some substance to the ICCC's statement. "It was," Markku Ruotsila notes in his biography of McIntire, "the most thorough summary thus far of McIntire's own, most American fundamentalists', and the broader ICCC community's passionate faith-based anticommunist convictions, to be repeated time and again in the following four decades."[40]

Still, the drift away from McIntire highlights several differences between Schwarz and the most conservative wing of US fundamentalism. Schwarz was willing to engage the secular culture and society in a way that McIntire and his followers could not. While McIntire remained primarily obsessed by battles over doctrinal and theological purity, Schwarz's perspective was broader and did not share the sheer anti-intellectualism of the ACCC. Moreover, coming from Australia, where levels of interdenominational cooperation were higher, Schwarz was unaccustomed to the separatist bitterness found among McIntire and his associates. As Ruotsila points out, McIntire "would sorely need a man such as Schwarz" to grow his interdenominational appeal, especially in light of the crusader's later collaboration with Catholics and secular anticommunists. Schwarz's natural sensibility was much closer to the larger, more inclusive (albeit still fundamentalist) National Association of Evangelicals. Also, NAE leaders were more promising in terms of helping Schwarz open doors to a wide variety of religious and secular institutions. In 1956, Schwarz formed for his Crusade an "advisory committee" composed of known evangelical leaders. Significantly, none of them was associated with the ACCC, and several – Paul James, H.H. Savage, J.V. McGee, and World Vision founder Frank C. Phillips – had known NAE ties.[41]

THE CHINA LOBBY MAN

On 31 May 1952, Schwarz addressed a Youth for Christ rally at the Church of the Open Door Auditorium. Before the meeting took place, he notified McIntire's office that he would remain in California until 8 June and then proceed eastwards, adding that the number of requests he had received had led him to seriously consider hiring a manager. On 2 June 1952, back in the Los Angeles region, Schwarz spoke at a stadium rally for YFC in Inglewood, marking the end of a two-month presence in Southern California, where he had planted the seeds of what was to become decades of his presence in the region.[42]

After stays in Texas and Oklahoma, Schwarz arrived in the East, where he was to depart for the ICCC meeting in Edinburgh. However, new opportunities had been opened by a letter he had received in California from Alfred Kohlberg, an importer from New York City who ran Alfred Kohlberg Inc. – Chinese Textiles. Kohlberg wished to organize for Schwarz, upon his return from Europe, a reception before selected guests in New York. In early September 1952, the event took place at New York's Metropolitan Club on Sixtieth Street before a small crowd.[43]

A short, bald, mild-mannered sixty-five-year old Jew, Kohlberg was unknown by the broader public but was one of the most important behind-the-scenes men in the world of American anticommunism. Kohlberg had never finished college, nor had he ever held elected office. Still, he was the driving force of the "China Lobby," a coterie that supported Chiang Kai-shek's Republic of China, which had been established in Taiwan in 1949. The China Lobby included politicians, businesspeople, scholars, religious people, institutions (especially those with links with pre-Revolutionary China), military leaders, anticommunist Chinese Americans, and Chinese agents of Taiwan's Kuomintang government. For years, it successfully spread the idea that people active in the US government, especially in the State Department, had "lost" China to Mao Tse-tung. More importantly, during the 1950s and 1960s, it effectively lobbied against the United States formally recognizing Communist China.[44]

For almost twenty-five years, starting in 1915, Alfred Kohlberg Inc. bought Irish linen and shipped it to cottages in China, where workers transformed it into handkerchiefs that were sold on the US market. Kohlberg became close to the Kuomintang elite, including Chiang Kai-shek. His business ended after the Communist takeover of China in 1949. During and after the Second World War, having grown furious over American liberals' criticism of the Kuomintang, he completed his conversion to militant anticommunism. Kohlberg eventually located his chief target: the Institute of Pacific Relations (IPR), a private body of national councils interested in Asian affairs. The IPR, he claimed, had been infiltrated by Communists and their sympathizers who were trying to influence US foreign policy. In early 1950, as agitation over the "who-lost-China?" question reached its height, the IPR, and especially Owen Lattimore, editor of its magazine *Pacific Affairs*, became targets of Joe McCarthy. When McCarthy's charges against Lattimore appeared to be unsubstantiated, Kohlberg came to the senator's rescue, feeding him information he had amassed on Lattimore, notably concerning his condemnations of US policy towards Chinese Communists.[45]

Kohlberg's (and the whole China Lobby's) infatuation with China embodied several elements of American nationalism, the most important of which was the westward gaze. Since the early days of the republic, US nationalism and westward expansion fed each other to the point of becoming an integrated scheme. Upon the end of continental expansion, Asia and the Pacific became the new focus, supported by the conviction of many that overseas expansion, be it economic or territorial, was vital to the nation's prosperity and freedom. In the context of the Philippine-American War, that fixation on China and Asia became a tradition within the Republican right, which formed an ideological faction that was distinct from the party's "moderate" eastern wing (whose foreign policy was more centred on Europe). Hence, it comes as no surprise that, in the early 1950s, the China Lobby constituted a largely Republican line-up: Senators Kenneth Wherry, Joe McCarthy, William Jenner, and William Knowland; General Claire Chennault; Representative Walter H. Judd (the "Asian Firsters"); and, to a lesser extent, *Time Magazine* publisher Henry Luce.[46]

The reception Kohlberg organized in New York in September 1952 enabled Schwarz to meet several figures active in both anticommunist networks and the China Lobby. Among attendees were two journalists: Ralph de Toledano, conservative intellectual and writer for *Newsweek*; and columnist Irene Kuhn, former press relations head for Thomas Dewey's 1944 campaign. Also present was Louis Budenz, a professional anticommunist who had helped Kohlberg to feed information to McCarthy.[47]

Kohlberg proved an invaluable ally from this time on. He introduced Schwarz to powerful people, one of whom was Texas oil tycoon H.L. Hunt from Dallas, to whom Kohlberg sent a copy of Schwarz's Metropolitan Club speech. Hunt had just set up Facts Forum, a million-dollar initiative to warn the United States about communism. In 1955 and 1956, whenever Schwarz was in the Dallas-Fort Worth area, Facts Forum extolled him in its publication *Facts Forum News* and on its radio broadcast hosted by Southern conservative stalwart Dan Smoot. Another powerful person was Chiang Kai-shek's wife, whom Kohlberg introduced to Schwarz in a 1953 letter. When, a few years later, Schwarz travelled to Taiwan, he met the presidential couple and established contacts with the Kuomintang elite. Through Kohlberg, in April 1958, Schwarz also met William F. Buckley, whose *National Review* was becoming the country's most important conservative magazine. Buckley introduced the crusader to the small, lofty community of New York conservative intellectuals. Some of Buckley's collaborators, such as Anthony Bouscaren, Eugene Lyons, Edward Rozek, Stephan Possony, and Frank Meyer, offered their intellectual credibility to various CACC events until the 1970s.[48]

COMING TO LONG BEACH

As the end of 1952 drew near, Schwarz crossed the United States westward with plans to spend Christmas in Australia. By this time, he had reached the conclusion that he needed a better strategy going forward, not only with respect to booking his lectures but also with respect to allowing him to raise money and/or print literature. In other words, he needed more than an agent – he needed an organization. He already had a collaborator: Dr Pietsch, who again invited him to stop in Iowa to give a series of lectures at KXEL radio. These lectures became the core of Schwarz's first booklet, published by Pietsch: *The Heart, Mind, and Soul of Communism*. During this visit, the two men agreed they would form an organization when Schwarz returned from Australia in January 1953.[49]

Pietsch, a Los Angeles native of sixty-one at the time, began his religious career in the 1920s as associate pastor for the Church of the Open Door in Los Angeles. In the 1930s, he was known for his radio lectures, in which his theological creed supported a conservative interpretation of world politics (he once claimed that the increase in chain stores was perhaps "Preparing the Way for the Mark of the Beast"). During the Second World War, Pietsch settled in Iowa and became pastor of Waterloo's Walnut Baptist Church, where he associated with McIntire and became the ACCC's main Midwestern representative. Admittedly, like McIntire, Pietsch was limited by an inability to appreciate secular reality; however, he shared Schwarz's active interest in anticommunism. His Walnut Street Baptist Church in Waterloo would provide the headquarters for the new organization.[50]

Schwarz met his second original collaborator when he returned to the United States in early 1953. After a lecture at the LIFE Bible College of Los Angeles (training ground for preachers and missionaries of the International Church of the Foursquare Gospel) he was contacted by Reverend James D. Colbert, director of the Long Beach YFC, who had already seen Schwarz on television and was looking for him. Colbert invited Schwarz to address a Long Beach YFC rally. In Colbert, Schwarz had found a formidable organizer who, along with Pietsch, formed the Crusade's original triumvirate. A California native, Colbert was in his mid-thirties and looked like John Wayne – tall and with a sportsman's physical attributes. He had been a truck driver for years before embracing the Baptist ministry. Trained at Biola University (a private Christian university) and the Los Angeles Baptist Theological Seminary, he was recruited by the YFC movement, itself the fundamentalist response to the emergence of 1950s youth culture. The YFC proved immensely popular in the postwar years, and, under Colbert's leadership, Long Beach's YFC grew into one of the most active units on the West Coast. YFC meetings catered to teenage audiences and featured many stars of the day, including Billy Graham, singing cowboy Stuart Hamblen, and humorist Bob Ringer.[51]

On 12 May 1953, Schwarz reconvened with Pietsch in Iowa, and they incorporated the Christian Anti-Communism Crusade. Schwarz was the CACC's only full-time employee, having the official function of being main lecturer and executive director. Pietsch became president, handling administrative duties and promotional work, plus delivering radio lectures on behalf of the CACC. Colbert became organizational manager.[52]

Schwarz thought up the organization's name, which he claimed was in harmony with his beliefs and goals. The name came to be a source of a few problems. The CACC was often confused with the Christian Crusade, run by Oklahoma fundamentalist Billy James Hargis, a mistake deepened by the fact that Hargis also started his career with the help of Carl McIntire. By the late 1950s, as the CACC began to move into the mainstream, some claimed its name pigeonholed the organization as fundamentalist. Others thought it excluded non-Christians. Schwarz's collaborators often suggested changing the name, but the crusader remained stubbornly opposed to any such idea. "My personal motivation", he once wrote, "is a Christian motivation. I am a narrow-minded, Bible believing Baptist ... What we need is multiplicity, not unity. It is foolish to cancel out the Protestant motivation, the Catholic motivation, and the Jewish motivation in a helpless unity. Let each come to this struggle against Communism with his own personal motivation."[53]

While the CACC was officially headquartered and incorporated in Iowa, its founder had already developed closer ties with Southern California, especially with Long Beach, where he had met Colbert in early 1953. In the early 1950s, this community of about a quarter of a million souls enjoyed the mild Mediterranean-type climate that characterizes Southern California but with the addition of a pleasant southwest breeze that gave Long Beach better air quality than most of the region's cities. Downtown Long Beach was also only some thirty-two kilometres from the Los Angeles International Airport, a convenient factor for Schwarz, who already knew he would frequently have to travel by plane.[54]

Southern California was the region that most welcomed his message. Midwesterners and Southerners were flocking to the area by the millions, bringing with them their evangelical faith and creating new congregations and megachurches. The local culture was also deeply permeated by a growing military presence. Long Beach itself exemplified the "military facility" town, being the location of the US Naval Drydocks, the largest such facility on the West Coast, along with the Douglas Aircraft, Lockheed Martin, and Boeing plants. Despite being essentially government-funded, Southern California's prosperity intensified its hawkish, defence-oriented, and anticommunist tendencies, which were already present before the war. According to historian Lisa McGirr, many who embraced the region's strong anti-statist and anti-collectivist outlooks did not conceive of themselves as benefitting directly from state spending "since they made their fortunes in private businesses, in construction, and as professionals serving the new communities."[55]

The Los Angeles region – which was then not only the US's fastest-growing area but also a laboratory for the suburban lifestyle based on the single-family house – also seemed a perfect place to raise a family. Schwarz and Lillian agreed that the family would settle in this area. After the CACC's founding in May 1953, Schwarz rented a cottage in Long Beach, where the family came to live. However, seasonal differences resulted in John Schwarz (then aged eleven) being enrolled in a class that was a year and a half below his level. His father was constantly absent from home, as he had been over the last three years. Dissatisfied, Lillian and the children moved back to Australia after only one year in the United States.[56]

For the next four decades, Schwarz's life would take place in the United States, broken up by trips back to Australia. There is no doubt that being away from his family for extended periods of time was the most painful component of his new career. It would not have been possible without Lillian's acceptance of raising the family almost alone. This detail was not lost on Schwarz, who praised his wife in his memoirs, calling her the "center of all the family activity." He and Lillian managed to remain close throughout the years of their long-distance relationship. "Nobody's closer than we are... we write every day," he told a journalist in 1976. By this time, all his kids had grown into married adults, three of them, including his foster son John Whitehall, becoming medical doctors. In the early 1980s, the crusader and his wife had seventeen grandchildren, whom he saw during his stays in Australia. Over the years, he affirmed that he and Lillian would again make the same decisions if faced with the same choices. However, the children felt their father's absence. "There has never been any doubt in my mind that what my father was doing was important and that it was right," Schwarz's elder son John once said, adding, "I must say that, in truth, it was quite difficult. It was difficult for all the family, but possibly more so for my younger brother and sister."[57]

The return of the Schwarz clan to Australia deepened the financial dilemma posed by Schwarz's career change. During the Crusade's first years, neither Pietsch nor Schwarz had a salary. The CACC covered only Schwarz's travelling, eating, and lodging expenses. Lillian and the three kids needed support. This problem was momentarily solved through the establishment of a CACC "Australian office," of which Lillian became secretary. By the late 1950s, she earned an annual salary of $5,400 – more than the CACC paid Schwarz himself. In the early 1960s, however, the Crusade ran into trouble with the IRS, who suspected that this branch of the CACC was only a decoy to channel money to Australia.

Not long after the Schwarz clan returned home, the Crusade itself moved to Long Beach. In 1955, Pietsch suffered a stroke that left him incapacitated for two months. This episode made it even more urgent for the CACC to secure a more suitable location for its headquarters than the Walnut Street Baptist Church in Waterloo. Schwarz and his growing team needed to bring the CACC closer to the West Coast (and Australia) and to find new facilities where the organization could be managed in a more efficient, business-like way. Pietsch dedicated his last years to the Crusade. He left Waterloo and moved to Long Beach, though crippled by diminishing health. He died in 1959 at the age of sixty-eight.[58]

In May 1956, the CACC settled in its new central office, located at 124 East 1st Street in the heart of downtown Long Beach. This office remained the CACC's main headquarters until Schwarz retired in 1998. In the early 1960s, when the CACC was at its height, Southern California was where a little less than half of its supporters (nationwide) lived and also where much of its financial support originated. The Crusade's cocktail of evangelicalism and anticommunism provided a language that contributed to the assertion of the region's conservative culture.

3

The CACC: Functioning, Clienteles, Status, and Global View

TURNING PRO

The Christian Anti-Communism Crusade remained in Long Beach for four decades. However, it was only in 1971 that Schwarz bought himself an apartment there as, due to his incessant touring, he never stayed in Long Beach for long. When he did, a typical office day saw him rise early and pass the day reading and replying to his mail, plus studying communist literature while also writing and planning future tours and events. Janet Greene, part of the CACC staff for three years in the 1960s, described him as an "early bird" and a "workaholic." The Crusade had a small, stable staff, with the fixtures being Schwarz, Colbert, Pietsch (until his death in 1959), and, from the mid-1950s on, Ella Doorn, a former schoolteacher from Wisconsin who would remain Schwarz's secretary over the next four decades. In the 1960–62 period, the staff briefly expanded to twenty before contracting. This does not account for workers in other CACC offices.[1]

Early 1954 saw the creation of the *Christian Anti-Communism Crusade Newsletter* (CACCN). Schwarz always remained its main contributor. Until the 1960s it came out about every second month. Later, the publication appeared on a regular, bi-weekly basis, and the format improved. Most of its space was initially devoted to accounts of Schwarz's tours. The irregular rhythm of the 1950 issues attests to the difficulty of producing such a publication with a small staff and a main writer who is constantly on the road. Nonetheless, it was an indispensable means of reaching pools of supporters scattered across multiple states. Any subscriber was a potential financial supporter to whom appeals for funds could be made.[2]

One of the rare accounts of Schwarz's relationships with his office staff is provided by the Anti-Defamation League's full-fledged attack on the crusader in the 1964 book *Danger on the Right.* Relying on the anonymous testimony of one of the CACC staffers, the book portrays an ill-tempered, irascible Schwarz, incapable of admitting mistakes, rarely talking with his employees, and habitually rude, particularly when annoyed by a trifling incident. The staffer described Schwarz as a "fussy autocrat" who could "throw a childlike temper tantrum over a typist's error. Once, when his staff failed to have enough collection envelopes for the whole audience at a rally, he raged for hours about the stupidity of his help." Whether this account is accurate or not, the fact was that the Long Beach staff often did not have to personally interact with their boss for long periods of time since he was touring the country with his advance man Jim Colbert.[3]

And Schwarz did lecture. His lecturing continued almost on a daily basis until 1960, when the success of CACC schools caused him to decrease speaking engagements. During this seven-year period, he basically lived out of a suitcase. By 1956, he had settled on the habit of a summer and a Christmas visit to Australia. In the United States, his life consisted of lectures plus debates, radio addresses, fundraising pitches, and selling promotional material. He estimated that he travelled about 170,000 kilometres yearly. "My home here is a hotel room in whatever city I happen to be," he affirmed. He liked this existence. "I don't consider myself a martyr," he said, "I'm enjoying it up to the hilt."[4]

Unscheduled touring did not mean working without a prepared itinerary. Schwarz actually preferred travelling to a given area with a plan. However, a single engagement could be enough reason for him to travel to a region. He would then ask his supporters in the area to fill up the schedule. Also, a great deal of the booking work was done by Colbert before Schwarz visited an area. Then, lectures would usually generate invitations to speak elsewhere, sometimes on the same day.[5]

Thus, a workday could well include three or four lectures. On 9 February 1955, he spoke in the morning at Hamline University in St Paul, Minnesota. At noon he spoke before a few hundred people at the St Paul Masonic Lodge. Later, he returned to Hamline University for a public discussion, and he ended his evening by addressing a rally sponsored by the Northwest Nurses Association and Allied Health

Groups. "It is amazing," he wrote, "that my voice has been standing up to a schedule of meetings most people would consider impossible." Three months later, on 3 May 1955, he addressed the State Assembly of California in the morning, the assembly of the Sacramento Junior College at noon, the Senate of California in the afternoon, before finishing the day addressing a rally in a high school auditorium. Once, in Hawaii, he delivered twenty-four lectures in six days.[6]

While the CACC was conceived primarily as a vehicle for Schwarz's lectures, its founders also thought about the possibility of creating a mass movement when they incorporated it in 1953. A formal membership was created (a ten-dollar annual fee was later established as well as a one-hundred-dollar life membership). Members were encouraged to organize whatever activity they wished, providing it was in accordance with the CACC's principles and followed written notification to the organization. But from the mid-1960s on, CACC literature and promotional material ceased to solicit membership affiliations and simply asked for regular donations or a willingness to volunteer for specific events. In 1962, in a memo, Marvin Liebman, direct-mail fundraising pioneer and Schwarz's brief adviser, suggested that the crusader build a serious mass organization. Liebman described the CACC as a "barnstorming" operation. "I would suggest," Liebman wrote, "that this is not quite sufficient and that a continuing organization – no matter how informal – should be in existence to continue educational work which would stimulate broader action." Schwarz, however, was not interested in this idea if it meant losing control over his organization.[7]

As opposed to medicine, professional anticommunism did not require degrees and registration: anybody could claim to be an expert on communism. Full-time anticommunists never formed a professional order, and most remained unknown to the public, even if some achieved some degree of public fame. However, in the two decades following the Second World War, anticommunism enabled many individuals to make a living. In the internal memos related to the activities of CACC and similar groups, FBI staffers used the expression "professional anticommunists," albeit in a derogatory manner, thus marking the difference between law-enforcement professionals and privately paid anticommunists. For a long time, Schwarz disliked the expression "professional anticommunist." However, he eventually made peace with it. During a television appearance in 1967, he said: "I didn't know that there was anything particularly wrong with the word 'professional.' If you go to a surgeon for a delicate operation, you prefer to go to a professional rather than an amateur, I presume."[8]

During the decade following the Second World War, professional anticommunism was dominated by informers, a subcategory featuring mostly ex-Communists. Richard Gid Powers points out that, during the height of their popularity in the 1930s, the Communist Party of the United States of America and its fronts "became schools for anticommunists" in that many officials who left them – either through expulsion or voluntarily – ended up becoming champions of McCarthyism. In the late 1940s, as the machinery of political repression got under way, they offered their knowledge in the context of congressional hearings, trials, and deportation proceedings. Such individuals, Ellen Schrecker writes, "became disproportionately influential in shaping the political repression of the McCarthy period." Louis Budenz was a good example. A former *Daily Worker* editor, he broke with Communism in 1945. He published an autobiography titled *This Is My Life* and became one of the FBI's and the House Un-American Activities Committee's (HUAC) most cherished witnesses, spending about three thousand hours detailing the CPUSA's internal functioning as well as becoming the most in-demand expert witness for trials involving Communists. In 1953, he said he had earned about $70,000 over a period of a few years for his expertise. Benjamin Mandel's career followed a similar trajectory: former managing editor of the *Daily Worker*, he was expelled from the CPUSA for "deviationism" in 1930. In the late 1930s, he started a career as a researcher for such clients as HUAC and the Senate Internal Security Subcommittee. His Communist-hunting career spanned three decades.[9]

Among professional anticommunists, Herbert Philbrick was the top celebrity, and his path became closely linked with Schwarz's. In 1940, Philbrick, then a twenty-five-year-old advertising executive from Boston, attended the meetings of a pacifist group that he realized was controlled by Communists. He told FBI staffers about the situation, and they suggested that he become an informant. Over the next eight years, he ascended in the CPUSA and fed authorities internal information about the party. The FBI decided to use him in April 1949 to testify at a trial at which twelve CPUSA leaders were accused of seditious conspiracy. That trial, which took place from January to October 1949, was a highlight for professional anticommunism. In a context within which evidence to support the charge of seditious conspiracy was scarce, the task assigned to Budenz, Philbrick, and other pro anticommunists by the prosecution team was to demonstrate that Marxist-Leninist writings on revolutionary violence should be taken at face value, while calls by Communists for peace should be seen only as attempts to conceal the revolutionary objective. The strategy worked: the whole CPUSA leadership was declared guilty. Philbrick published an autobiography, *I Led Three Lives*, which was adapted for television and became one of the decade's most popular shows, running 117 episodes between 1953 and 1956.[10]

However, on his first and second tours in the United States, Schwarz made a niche for himself not as an informer but as an educator. He was one of the first of such "teachers," whose numbers grew considerably in the following years. The growth of public anticommunist education corresponded with a slackening of Cold War tensions. Prior to this point, professional anticommunism usually involved being employed in an intelligence division or as an expert witness. But a change took place as McCarthyism subsided. The spring of 1954 marked the collapse of McCarthy's influence on national politics. Meanwhile, the conflict in Korea stalled. On 5 March 1953, Stalin died, initiating a phase of reassessing Soviet foreign policy. In July 1953, the Korean Armistice Agreement put an end to hostilities in Korea. By the mid-1950s, the expression "peaceful coexistence" had appeared. This very concept was rejected by most anticommunist activists. While Schwarz always prioritized the need to defend free peoples and to aggressively liberate the unfree behind the Iron Curtain, he also affirmed that any idea "that we can 'negotiate' or 'coexist' or 'compromise' with this cancer is plainly symptomatic of the mental illness on which [the Communists] depend for their ultimate success." But coexistence became a reality. This new state of affairs was confirmed in August 1954, when the Taiwan Strait Crisis over the islands of Quemoy and Matsu quickly ended, showing that both sides were unwilling to take military action.[11]

As coexistence set in, a growing demand for information pertaining to communism appeared as the menace was now perceived as a permanent reality that would not be eradicated in the foreseeable future. Billy Graham urged Christians to "study Communism from stern to stern that we may have some understanding as to the nature of this great world-wide force." Moreover, the US and the USSR presented themselves as leaders of competing visions, which necessitated new methods for instilling and disseminating their values. Education became an important Cold War battlefield. In 1950, the Truman administration created the Federal Civil Defense Administration (FCDA), whose purpose was to teach the public basic emergency preparedness in the advent of Soviet attack. By 1952, FCDA programs had been implemented, in one way or the other, in more than 88 percent of American schools. In 1955, Schwarz was invited, like other pro anticommunists before and after him, to address FCDA staffers.[12]

By the mid-1950s, professional blacklisters were increasingly unemployed, with HUAC, the FBI, and other government institutions beginning to run low on targets, and with the CPUSA no longer existing as a viable political entity. Moreover, the US Supreme Court took a turn towards civil liberties after the 1954 appointment of Chief Justice Earl Warren and progressively dismantled the legal framework that had been used to prosecute Communists since the 1930s. Some blacklisters were able to keep their jobs for a few more years. HUAC continued its work until 1975. As McCarthyism was fading nationally, it developed in the South amid the turmoil produced by the breakdown of the racial status quo after 1954. People such as J.B. Matthews found opportunities there as Southern authorities were eager to discredit civil rights organizations by tying them to Communists. However, by the second half of the 1950s, most professional anticommunists had taken the educational turn. They became lecturers, advisors for educational departments, school book writers, contractual columnists, or advisors for any institution willing to hire them. Philbrick exemplifies this shift. Transformed into a national celebrity by the 1949 trial and the popularity of *I Led Three Lives*, Philbrick embraced a lucrative lecturing career. He spent the following two decades delivering speeches at civic clubs, patriotic rallies, schools, churches, and seminars. While Schwarz usually accepted all opportunities to speak, sometimes without a salary, Philbrick charged an average of $600 per contract and had to turn down most of the requests during the second half of the 1950s.[13]

In 1956, Pennsylvania became the first state to initiate a two-week course on communism for high school students. Within a few years, the movement to implement programs to teach communism in schools had spread. By 1962, legislation mandating special classes on communism had been voted in in six states, and thirty-four education departments had, in some form, included such teaching in state curriculums. This movement varied according to different regional subcultures: whereas in Northern states promoters of teaching communism often advocated for an "objective" approach, in Southern states students were often exposed to right-wing rhetoric connecting communism to the welfare state or desegregation.[14]

Education on communism thus became a multi-million-dollar industry. By the late 1950s, any citizen willing to acquire such knowledge had access to an embarrassment of riches: affordable accounts of any dimension of communism were readily available everywhere. This literature was to be found in bookstores and was distributed at civic clubs, corporation meetings, churches, and patriotic rallies. Lectures by professional anticommunists were regularly accompanied by the sale of educational material. "There's a difference," Schwarz said, "between the educational and the police function. We're not an investigative organization – people ask, 'How many Communists have you uncovered?' None – none at all – that's not what we try to do."[15]

CLIENTELES

Schwarz's busiest period as lecturer extended until 1960, when his schedule mostly switched to the holding of CACC schools. His most intense centre of activity was the Pacific area, followed by the Midwest, with occasional trips to the Northeast and the South.[16] Iowa, location of the CACC's first central office, virtually disappeared from its projects after the relocation to Long Beach. In 1962, a survey conducted by researchers at Iowa State University showed that only one in eight respondents could recognize Schwarz. This contrasted sharply to other polling data, which showed that the crusader's visibility was much higher in the Pacific, the South, and the West than it was in the Midwest.[17]

Across the country, most of Schwarz's talks were given in faith-based institutions or settings (churches, Bible institutes, seminars or colleges, and evangelical gatherings), civic institutions (veterans organizations and service clubs), and secular schools. Combined, these three groups were the locations of the overwhelming majority of his talks. Half of them, however, took place in faith-based institutions alone. In spite of Schwarz's efforts to diversify his pool of secular supporters, churches and other religious institutions, especially conservative ones, formed the core of his clientele. In 1964, a survey confirmed that the Crusade was significantly better known among respondents who belonged to evangelical, fundamentalist, or Pentecostal denominations.[18]

During the Cold War, American evangelicals were beginning to establish a new relationship with the larger culture. While the thesis whereby, between the Scopes Trial and the Cold War, evangelicals underwent a period of seclusion from the broader world has been exaggerated, it remains true that anticommunism was, to borrow sociologist Robert Horwitz's words, "the ideological hub around which conservative Christians mobilized in the public arena" from the late 1940s on. Figures like Schwarz helped them embrace American nationalism and renew the terms of their worldly involvement in a proactive way. This was especially true for small independent churches that had broken with mainstream culture and apprehended divine wrath in the form of communism. In a few instances, Schwarz's lectures were delivered in major churches with large congregations, such as the Church of the Open Door in Los Angeles, the Moody Church in Chicago, the Foothill Baptist Church in Oakland, and the First Baptist Church of Dallas. Schwarz also participated in mass rallies, such as the Winona Lake Bible Conferences and YFC rallies, with crowds numbering in the thousands. Yet small congregations constituted the bulk of his church audiences.[19]

The crusader brought his message to many of those who had not yet been reached by the neo-evangelical call to re-engage the culture. In late 1954, he visited the Detroit Bible Institute (later renamed William Tyndale College), whose president, Roy L. Alldrich, affirmed that the Australian offered the "most stimulating picture that I have ever known to be presented." This talk by Schwarz impressed future fundamentalist leader Norman Geisler, co-founder of North Carolina's Southern Evangelical Seminary. In December 1956, in Pasadena, twenty-year-old James C. Dobson heard Schwarz speak. "I was," the future founder of Focus on the Family later wrote, "deeply impressed and influenced by his words that day. I still remember that compelling speech, which nudged me towards a conservative point of view."[20]

Schwarz's emphasis on the atheistic root of communism was particularly effective with these audiences. As he put it: "When [communists] deny God, they simultaneously deny every virtue and every value that originates with God. They deny moral law. They deny absolute truth and righteousness." It might come as a surprise that this emphasis was not common in the evangelical world before the 1950s. As sociologist Robert Wuthnow writes, communism was initially rejected not so much because of its atheism but, rather, because of its totalitarian nature, which was conceived as bringing economic solutions to spiritual needs. "It represented a collapse of the essential biblical distinction between ultimacy and the mundane, between creator and created; it identified ultimate authority with the state, a concrete social institution." Schwarz's twist was, obsessively, to identify the Godless nature of this materialism. Communism, he said, had three laws that Christians needed to reject: atheism, materialism, and economic determinism, the latter being the idea that everything merely reflects the economic environment.[21]

Moreover, he relentlessly outlined the link between atheism and the repudiation of ethics and morality. This identification opened the door for an extension of the struggle between different spheres of society. During the early 1960s, the United States saw the earliest manifestations of the rise of a fundamentalist right wing that was evolving more or less alongside the more secular conservative movement. One of the first observers of this dynamic, reporter David Danzig, noted the role played by anticommunism in this mobilization. The conflict "is not one of blocs, but of faiths, part of the unending struggle between God and the devil. The danger of communism, therefore, is from within – from the corrosion of faith by insidious doctrines." Danzig also observed the appreciation several new fundamentalist leaders had for Schwarz's work. In 1962, Gerri Von Frellick, a lay Southern Baptist leader, founded Christian Citizen, an early Christian Right political group that sought to help "evangelical Christians to control the local, state and Federal Governments." He praised the CACC as a "terrific" organization, "doing a fabulous job." As Darren Dochuk notes, anticommunism had definitely picked up steam among conservative evangelicals throughout the 1950s, thus contributing to the politicization of their various cultural and religious identities: "Hungary's failed anti-Soviet revolution in 1956, China's ascendancy, clashes between communist and nationalist interests in Africa and Latin America, and Fidel Castro's peasant revolution of 1959 made evangelicals more receptive to the hard-line solutions that Hargis, McIntire, Bundy, and Schwarz could deliver." Evangelical anticommunists of that era had more visible leaders than did those of previous decades and were noticeably more active at the grassroots level. No longer content to pray for the nation's victory over communism, according to Jonathan Herzog, they "also traveled to attend lectures, subscribed to a variety of shoe-string-budget newsletters, discussed their beliefs with their neighbours, and campaigned for the removal of anti-Christian, anti-American literature from library shelves."[22]

While anticommunism emerged as a feature of the evangelical worldview, denominational strife among evangelicals waned, paving the way for Schwarz and other conservative preachers to carry their gospel across American Protestantism and, sometimes, beyond it. Taken as a whole, Baptist institutions were Schwarz's most consistent faith-based clientele (receiving roughly a third of all his known lectures until 1960), but the remainder of his presentations were given in a wide array of denominations: Methodist, Pentecostal, United Brethren, Disciples of Christ, Lutheran, Churches of the Nazarine, Presbyterian, Salvation Army, and various smaller denominations.[23]

This illustrates that, from the Cold War on, American religion underwent a "restructuring" process, whereby ideological differences, rather than denominational differences, gradually became the main polarizing force within churches. Divides over communism were the first visible signs of this new dynamic: evangelical churches became increasingly characterized by their strong anticommunist stance, while mainstream churches went in the opposite direction.[24]

In the spring of 1955, several Christian leaders wrote to the dean of Sacramento Junior College to protest his inviting Schwarz to lecture before students. In times when "calm judgements" were needed, "I can not feel that bringing in a paid professional rabble rouser is in that interest," Wesleyan Methodist minister Correll M. Julian wrote. The talk was held, but Schwarz editorialized that the fuss over it was "indicative of the extent to which sympathy towards godlessness has penetrated the official Christian churches." A similar episode took place in 1958 when Schwarz was about to address students of a state college within the context of the Religious Emphasis Week program. The visit was cancelled on short notice by the church body overseeing the program. The cancellation letter informed Schwarz: "your message is not sufficiently grounded in the spiritual strength of liberal Christianity to justify its presentation at a Religious Emphasis Week program." "I cannot say I am surprised," the crusader replied, "as I have had previous experience of the illiberality of the so-called liberals in religious as well as other realms."[25]

A lesser, though important, part of Schwarz's clientele consisted of civic institutions, which provided a sense of community and belonging in times of suburbanization and social change. In 1955, a survey showed that more than 36 percent of American adults were members of a voluntary association, excluding churches and unions. The great majority of civic institutions that constituted the professional anticommunists' bread and butter belonged to two categories: veterans associations and service clubs. Both began showing interest in Schwarz's lectures early on. In May 1952, during the crusader's second US tour, he addressed the American Legion for the first time at Hollywood Post 43. His correspondence during the same tour also contains numerous accounts of addresses before Rotary or Lions Clubs. As the Crusade was about to relocate to Long Beach in May 1956, its popularity among veterans associations and service clubs had reached a plateau that remained unchanged until 1960. This success opened the doors to huge, nationally entrenched associations that proved one of the CACC's most consistent sources of support.[26]

The American Legion was anticommunist from the very outset, having been founded in March 1919 by a group of high-ranking officers from the First World War American Expeditionary Force, with the financial help of Wall Street institutions such as J.P. Morgan and Company. One of its objectives was to shelter US soldiers from the revolutionary ideas that spread in Europe during the postwar period. It became the country's most important veterans organization. The Legion took active part in the first "Red Scare" (1919–20) as its members helped police authorities to repress Communists, members of the Industrial Workers of the World (IWW) labour union – the "Wobblies" – and other "radicals." Throughout the 1920s and 1930s, it remained at the forefront of conservative patriotic organizations, notably through its campaigns to Americanize immigrants and eradicate subversive activity.[27]

In the early 1950s veterans associations grew substantially as soldiers returned from the Second World War and the Korean War. In 1950, the Legion had about 2.5 million members, and the Veterans of Foreign Wars had 1 million. These organizations were an essential ingredient of Cold War anticommunist activism at the grassroots level. They gathered information on left-wing activists and collaborated with the local police, FBI, and congressional investigators against real or alleged subversion. They also coordinated and organized anticommunist cultural life in communities, furnishing public and college libraries with literature and holding events. In May 1950, the Legion, aided by professional anticommunist Ben Gitlow, staged a mock Communist takeover in the town of Mosinee, Wisconsin.

The local police chief was "shot" and the mayor dragged from his bed into the snowy streets, where he was denounced as an "enemy of the people." Restaurants offered "communist meals" (potato soup and black bread) and stores inflated their prices to reflect living costs in Communist countries. The experiment was brought to an unfortunate end when the mayor died from a heart attack a few hours after it began.[28]

Schwarz's routine thus included stopovers in American Legion posts. In each community, the Legion was one of the most prestigious local forums, where a presentation often guaranteed several bookings elsewhere. In January 1955, after the Legion sponsored a rally organized for Schwarz at Minneapolis's Lyceum Theater, its members asked him to speak at another event in Texas the following day and chartered a plane to fly him directly to there overnight. In May of the same year, the Legion chartered another plane to bring him from Sacramento to Indianapolis, where he was the evening guest speaker for the National Commander's Banquet for the Legion's executives. Schwarz then received a police escort, thanks to Legion contacts among local law-enforcement authorities, so that he could return to the West Coast in time for another series of lectures. By the end of the same year, he was invited to address the Legion at its National Convention in Miami.[29]

Service clubs constituted the other important type of civic institution. Throughout the 1950s, most of these clubs were local branches of one of the organizations that had formed in the early twentieth century, with 90 percent belonging to the "big three": Kiwanis International, Rotary International, and the International Association of Lions. Once a week, in most American communities, prominent citizens – local doctors, bankers, lawyers – met for lunch, socialized, conducted business, and set up community service initiatives. Reflecting the middle-class mindset, service clubs drew their numbers primarily from white-collar workers who wished to protect community life from the effects of big business, bureaucratization, and state expansion, notably by trying to infuse moralism and order into local business activity.[30]

Service clubs were useful for any publicity-seeking lecturer, even though Schwarz noted that they generally did not offer high honorariums. Invariably, word of him travelled the various organizations' grapevines. Demand for his services among service clubs reached its height in the late 1950s. In March 1959, the New Hampshire Lions

Clubs and the state's five major veterans organizations organized a rally featuring Schwarz. In the audience of fifteen hundred people was state governor Wesley Powell. The public was admitted free of charge "because the sponsors [felt] everybody should hear Doctor Schwarz and his vital message." Earlier that day, the crusader had addressed the state's legislature.[31]

Secular educational institutions composed the third main clientele for Schwarz's lectures. This category includes talks delivered to school board officials and professional educators' associations, though the demand for his services came primarily from high schools. Drawing effortlessly on his own teaching experience, Schwarz knew how to capture the attention of young audiences, making use of self-deprecating humor, joking notably about his accent. "Invariably, the students were interested and responsive ... Questions from junior high school students were direct and straightforward, but those from high school students were somewhat more sophisticated." He also delivered a few lectures in higher education institutions such as the University of Minnesota, Hamline University, Baylor University, the University of Southern California, and Michigan State University. In 1959, he made his only known appearances at the country's eastern elite institutions when he addressed students from the Massachusetts Institute of Technology and later appeared at Harvard University to debate the chairman of the Communist Party of the Commonwealth of Massachusetts, Otis Archer Hood.[32]

Lecturing in high schools required the approval of local or state educational administrations, and the crusader knew how to establish peer-like relationships with educational professionals. A superintendent wrote Schwarz after he delivered a lecture to an audience composed of the teachers, supervisors, and principals of Berkeley's public schools: "We want all our teachers to have a sufficient background on this subject so that they will be in a position to help children to learn something of the lives of people living under Communism as compared to the wonderfully privileged lives we live in the United States." In May 1955, Schwarz's tour of Sacramento schools was officially sponsored by Sacramento Junior College and the local superintendent. In October of the same year, the governor of Hawaii, Samuel Wilder King, proclaimed an Education for Freedom Week, and the CACC got a contract to be the official sponsoring agent for the information drive in public high schools. The crusader saw this school work as one of the most important of his deeds: "Many people have been deluded that the foundation of Communism rests in the labor unions. This is untrue. The vast majority of Communist leaders throughout the world became Communists as students, atheistic in outlook."[33]

By the end of the decade, Schwarz's booklets and recordings were being used in some high schools in Southern California and Texas, and he was a regular speaker at schoolteacher conventions. When the Crusade began its schools of anticommunism in the late 1950s, the support and collaboration of local school boards proved an important factor in their success.

HELEN BIRNIE, THE IRS, AND POLITICS

The Crusade's finances were initially scarce and remained so for years. CACC staff only began earning salaries from 1955 on. Pietsch's annual wage was $1,375 and Schwarz's was $2,800. Considering the cumulative rate of inflation of the US dollar (855.8 percent) between 1955 and 2019, in the latter year this would have left Schwarz with a yearly purchasing power of about $26,700. Colbert joined Schwarz as the other full-time employee. He earned $6,600 per year, making him the highest paid CACC staffer. By the time the organization moved to Long Beach in 1956, revenues had risen to $57,806, up from $18,862 when it filed its first tax report to the US Internal Revenue Service (IRS). But expenses had risen too, resulting in a deficit. This fragile financial outlook made it crucial for the CACC to obtain tax-exempt status as non-profit organization operating for educational and religious purposes, thus allowing contributions to it to be tax-deductible. However, specific IRS rules had to be respected if one was to be eligible for tax exemption. Pietsch's request, submitted in July 1954, was denied on the grounds "that the organization was engaged to a substantial extent in promoting the circulation of books of an individual setting forth his view on a particular subject." A year later, another application was refused for the same reason, even though other speakers had sporadically been hired.[34]

The drive to convince the IRS that the CACC was more than Schwarz's one-trick pony took, in part, the form of a woman named Helen Wood Birnie. Schwarz met Birnie, then a frail forty-year-old woman, in the fall of 1953. Raised on a Minnesota farm, Birnie initially wanted to become a novelist. In 1932, in Montana, her talent for public speaking attracted the attention of local Communists.

She worked for the CPUSA's legal arm, known as the International Labor Defense. She broke with Communists in 1934 but waited until 1952 to publicly denounce her former comrades. However, the disclosure of her past resulted in her losing her job at the Nebraska Historical Society. Thereupon, she resettled in Long Beach, where she met Schwarz and Colbert.[35]

Birnie was included in the CACC as a part-time staff worker and given equal billing with Schwarz when they shared the same stage in dual appearances. Her duties were similar to Schwarz's: lecturing in civic clubs, American Legion posts, churches, and schools. "Of all the ex-Communist speakers I have heard in the US," Schwarz once said, "she is far and away the best speaker." In July 1954, in addition to sponsoring her lectures, the CACC financed the publication of Birnie's story in an eighty-page booklet. A 1960 editorial in the Communist newspaper *People's Voice* stated: "The effectiveness of this woman should not be underestimated according to many who have heard her. She has a dramatic and commanding manner." Nonetheless, one opponent observed: "In general, she is clever as to her manner of hitting the emotions, but she is inconsistent with her facts, and upon being challenged by the audience, or questioned, she has different answers for different times." She once claimed that there were "900 million Asiatics being scientifically educated and prepared to be the executioners of the boys and girls of America." In another speech, she declared that the Boy Scouts of America were infiltrated by Communists.[36]

During the winter of 1955, both she and Schwarz blitzed her native state of Minnesota. While Schwarz focused on the Twin Cities area, Birnie toured in the state's rural northeast, but she faced a controversy. The Minnesota Farmers Union (MFU) officials did not appreciate her allegation that their organization was Communist-infiltrated. This deepened the bitterness between the MFU and the Minnesota Farm Bureau, a competing, more conservative union that had sponsored some of Birnie's appearances. The Bureau was accused by an MFU representative of having brought Birnie "to the rural areas in an attempt to further discredit the Farmers Union program." Angry MFU supporters disrupted one of her meetings in Bernadotte, forcing its cancellation. Schwarz editorialized on how heartening it was to see that "whenever she has been under attack, the Christian friends of the Crusade have rallied most warmly to her support."[37]

When tax exempt status was denied to the Crusade in 1954 and again in July 1955, Pietsch wrote the IRS in protest, "We want to make it crystal clear that this work is not centered around one man, but he is a splendid worker in this as well as Mrs. Birnie." Pietsch turned for help to Kohlberg, who recommended that the Crusade approach his New York law firm to deal with the issue. This advice, plus Birnie's contribution, probably helped as the CACC received its tax-exempt status in September 1956. From this point on, the Crusade, now categorized as a "religious and educational institution," was allowed to accept contributions that were tax deductible for the donors.[38]

In April 1956, Birnie made her last appearance alongside Schwarz during a rally in Iowa. The granting of tax-exempt status to the CACC more or less coincides with the removal of Birnie's name from the organization's documents. She pursued a lecturing career of her own but remained associated with other minor controversies, like when she claimed in 1960 that the University of Iowa was heavily infiltrated by Communists. She was later recruited by Billy James Hargis's Christian Crusade but later disappeared from the public eye.[39]

Tax-exempt status came at a price. The IRS letter bringing the good news in September 1956 warned: "Your exemption will be revoked if any substantial part of your activities consists of carrying on propaganda, or otherwise attempting to influence legislation, or if you participate in, or intervene in (including the publishing or distributing of statements), any political campaign on behalf of any candidate for public office."[40]

In plain English, the IRS banned the CACC from partisan political activity and put limitations on its production and distribution of "propaganda." However, the IRS did not elaborate on what constituted propaganda, nor did it explain how it was to be limited. Schwarz took no risks. While he had always been careful to present himself as a man who stayed above the fray of mundane debates, from 1956 on this tendency became systematized. Communism, he often said, was not a liberal or a conservative issue but, rather, one that concerned the whole free world. Still, the problem was that it *also* remained a political issue, and one that liberals and conservative often did not address in the same way. Often solicited by friends and foes alike to take stands on partisan issues, Schwarz found a convenient way of not answering by evoking his non-American status: by 1965, he was entitled to apply for US citizenship, but he never did, probably because Australian citizenship laws did then not allow dual citizenship. While Schwarz's fence-sitting on politics posed no problem during the CACC's first years, it became harder to maintain once the organization became widely known by the late 1950s.[41]

Whereas IRS regulations forbade participation in political campaigns, the prohibition of "propaganda" did not mean that tax-exempt organizations could not take stands on policy matters. The CACC had the freedom to address issues related to its mission. For decades, Schwarz dealt at length in speeches and writings with the geopolitics of the Cold War, which was unquestionably in the realm of the CACC's vocation, but he tended to be much more selective regarding US domestic politics. Also, while the Crusade could not endorse politicians, politicians could endorse the Crusade. Several elected officials appeared at CACC events, and, until the early 1960s, Schwarz was many times invited to speak before congressional luncheons, state congresses, and political meetings. In 1964, the closeness between the CACC and the Goldwater movement was such that the CACC's professed neutrality was almost facetious. During George Murphy's 1964 Senate campaign and Ronald Reagan's gubernatorial bid of 1966, both men refused to sever their ties with Schwarz, despite Democratic attacks on both candidates for their association with the "Radical Right."

Schwarz would have perhaps invested himself more in politics had it not been for IRS regulations, as is shown by the more politically charged public interventions he made while he still had the freedom to speak his mind. In the US context, one speech stands out in particular, and it was delivered in September 1952, at the end of his second US tour. Before Reverend James Fifield's Freedom Club of Los Angeles (an all-Republican audience), Schwarz argued that, in 1933, Roosevelt had been "seduced" by Soviet diplomat Maxim Litvinov "into granting the recognition of Russia by the American nation." At the same time, he sang the praises of General MacArthur. He also implied that Communists had infiltrated US governments and institutions, and he blatantly appealed to the West Coast's anti-Asian sentiments, asserting that China had fifth columns in every country in which "Chinese colonists" were present. Chinese propaganda was a "body of hatred directed against this country that will one day be loosed in an avalanche of destruction and death that will deluge you and your family and children into the nightmare of catastrophe and darkness."[42]

The crusader's comments on Joe McCarthy are very few, a remarkable fact for a Cold War anticommunist personality. In June 1954,

Schwarz privately wrote Kohlberg sarcastically expressing how sad he felt for the intellectuals persecuted by McCarthyism. In late 1954, with McCarthy now offstage, in his newsletter Schwarz lamented, without further comment, that McCarthy's investigative work had been halted. Still, by the late 1950s, the crusader could not ignore the extent to which McCarthy, who had since died, was controversial among the general public, despite his continued popularity among his own supporters. Asked about his take on McCarthy in 1962 during an interview in Australia, Schwarz replied: "Oh, he was an anarchist. Here, have a soft drink."[43]

TURNING GLOBAL

In early 1955, Schwarz received a twelve-page letter in minute handwriting from Ch Devananda Rao, a twenty-two-year old evangelical Baptist from Krishna District in Andhra State in South India. Rao worked as a teacher in a small school established by a Baptist mission and led by his father Ch Pushpanadham. Rao wrote Schwarz about how Communists were attempting to deceive Christians in Andhra, notably by promising them freedom of religion, and explained how he had endeavoured to persuade his fellow citizens not to vote for them. Despite the CACC's dim financial situation at the time, Schwarz pledged he would try to find a way to help his correspondent.[44]

Andhra was one of the Indian states with a particularly large Communist membership. During the 1951 state elections, Communists picked up forty-one out of 140 seats in the legislature and formed the main opposition to the ruling Congress Party. They had been present in Andhra since the Depression but expanded their following in the postwar years. By the time Rao wrote Schwarz, Andhra Communists had been defeated at the February 1955 election and had lost almost all their representatives in the state legislature. However, their votes in absolute numbers had more than doubled to reach the 2.5 million mark (31 percent of the total vote). By the end of 1955, Schwarz was particularly alarmed at the tour Khrushchev undertook in Burma and India. Khrushchev embarked on his Southeast Asia tour to assert his new position as world leader and to take diplomatic advantage of the decolonization process. Schwarz related the huge crowds that gathered to see Khrushchev (2 million people in Delhi and Bombay; about 4 million in Calcutta) to the great amount of Communist propaganda disseminated in India.[45]

In 1956, as the CACC's financial resources improved after the granting of its tax-exempt status, supporting Rao became a possibility. However, sending missionaries to India was not an option: "The missionaries are members of an alien race, speaking the native language with difficulty," and Communists would easily brand them as "agents of foreign imperialism." The alternative was to provide financial and logistical help to Rao, who would oversee a homegrown project. Rao envisioned the founding of an Indian Christian Crusade: "Ten evangelical, paid, full-time workers are immediately needed to work in key places." He also claimed he needed bicycles, phonographs, cameras, and money to secure an estate where his group would be headquartered. Schwarz decided that he would visit India to assess the situation.[46]

On 30 November 1956, Schwarz arrived at the Hyderabad airport where he was welcomed by Rao, who took him on a five-day trip to Vijayawada in central Andhra. "Brother Rao," Schwarz reported, "was everything he had presented himself to be. An intelligent, educated Christian Indian, small in stature, wearing English style dress." For a few days, he visited Rao's Baptist mission, met Rao's wife Suvarna Devananda Rao and their five children ("They all live in this pathetic hut," he editorialized, shocked by their living conditions), and visited nearby villages. The CACC subsidization of the Indian Christian Crusade (ICC) was agreed upon. Schwarz opened an account at the State Bank of India, where he deposited $5,000, mostly to buy a building for the ICC's office in Vijayawada. Judging Indian newspapers to be very biased against the United States, he also authorized the purchase of equipment to put out a newsletter in Telugu (a Dravidian language spoken in Andhra). Rao's team of mobile evangelists each received fifteen dollars per month, enough to support a family.[47]

Between 1957 and 1961, as CACC finances soared, the amounts sent to Andhra increased and reached a plateau of about $2,100 yearly. Raising expenditures resulted from two factors. The first was the increase in the number of evangelists supported by the ICC (a few hundreds by the time Schwarz retired in the late 1990s); the second was the inception, in 1960, of a Christian orphanage managed by Rao. This project allowed Schwarz to counter criticism that he did not have a positive program, but the crusader was genuinely shaken by the extreme poverty of India. Returning from his 1956 Indian trip, Schwarz described what he had seen in his newsletter:

people living in huts, crowds assailing railway trains, roads being used "day and night as a toilet by old and young ... How to give you an idea of the scenes, I don't know." In 1967, the ICC Orphanage moved into a new building. By then, it provided care for 125 boys; in the mid-1990s, the number had reached three hundred.[48]

Appraising the political impact of the Andhra projects is rather difficult. Shortly before retiring, Schwarz claimed that, through its work, thousands had been converted and educated on the evils of communism. Nonetheless, Christians always remained a tiny minority in Andhra, and Telugu Baptist churches like the one to which Rao belonged were a minority among the minority of Protestant churches in the Indian south. For its part, the impact of the ICC's newsletter, which was distributed to government officials, students, and high-caste Hindus, was undoubtedly quite limited at best. In any case, the fortunes of the Andhra Communist Party declined sharply after 1955. By the end of the decade, Communist influence in Andhra had subsided.[49]

The orphanage aside, the Andhra project's biggest impact was on the CACC itself. Almost from birth, the Crusade adopted a globally framed perspective in which skin colours and national borders were irrelevant to two larger colliding transnational forces: religion and communism. While acknowledging that patriotism could be a bulwark against communism, Schwarz saw in it a double-edged sword, as evidenced by the many "national liberation wars" Communists supported throughout the twentieth century. An observer who attended one of his lectures in 1965 noted: "He continually used the expression, 'nationalism and Racism' as though these words were synonyms, interesting in view of the flag-draped stage, the anthem-singing and the pledge of allegiance, etc." While paying lip service to US patriotism, the crusader wished to operate on a global scale and, as such, conceived of the United States of America less as the primary Cold War battlefield than as the free world's stronghold. Accordingly, the CACC newsletter would often devote as much space to international developments as to the domestic front.[50]

The CACC thus adhered to a form of internationalism, albeit a conservative brand, one that showed distrustfulness towards liberal internationalism and institutions such as the United Nations. Though the Crusade did not have an official anti-UN policy, it featured collaborators who displayed an anti-UN stance, such as Robert Morris, who wrote an article in 1964 in the CACC newsletter decrying the UN's disarmament programs. Schwarz himself never showed much confidence in the organization either in public or in private exchanges. Distrust of the UN's liberal internationalism was also in keeping with Schwarz's tendency towards realpolitik as far as communism was concerned. As he wrote in the wake of the 1964 coup in Brazil that established an anticommunist military dictatorship, "A military coup is like a cut in the abdomen, undesirable in itself, but necessary sometimes to preserve life." Among conservative Protestants this rejection of liberal internationalism ran as deep as it did in the years following the First World War, when many disapproved of the United States's projected adherence to the League of Nations and to such concepts as supranational authority, the equality of creeds, and/or multilateralism.[51]

Schwarz's embrace of a global perspective was epitomized by the keynote address he delivered in April 1956 at the Freedom Forum on the campus of Harding College in Searcy, Arkansas. Later published as a tract, this speech helped establish his reputation among US conservatives. The Freedom Forum was the magnum opus of George S. Benson, who had heard of Schwarz through Kohlberg. Benson and Kohlberg shared an experience with pre-revolutionary China and strongly supported Taiwan's Kuomintang regime. Raised among the Disciples of Christ, a church for which he acted as missionary in China during the 1920s and 1930s, Benson returned to the United States in 1936 to assume presidency of Harding College, an institution affiliated with his church. Within a few years, through the support of prominent citizens in the business community, Benson had transformed this small college in Arkansas into a centre of conservative propagation. In the early 1940s, Benson launched the National Education Program (NEP), designed to "promote Americanism, patriotism, and the free enterprise system." The NEP's printed material, films, and Freedom Forum agendas quickly morphed into aggressive anticommunism, often of a conspiratorial mindset.[52]

The NEP's most effective organ was the Freedom Forum, which was held for the first time in February 1949. Held three or four times a year, the event welcomed a cross-section of conservative types (business executives, politicians, clergy, activists). Attending employers were urged to educate their employees on the benefits of free market capitalism as well as on the threat posed to freedom by socialism and the overextension of the state. Before long, professional anticommunists were invited to attend. Louis Budenz made appearances at the tenth and eleventh forums in October 1951. Herbert Philbrick was invited for the first time in 1954, soon to be followed by J.B. Matthews. "Between the mid-1950s and mid-1960s, anyone who had any clout in Goldwater's Right spoke in Searcy, Arkansas; Leonard Read, Clarence Manion, Albert Wedemeyer, and Fred Schwarz were just a few of the popular conservative pundits invited to share their expertise with attendees," Darren Dochuk observes. Schwarz appeared for the first time at the sixteenth Freedom Forum in May 1955.[53]

The speech Schwarz delivered in April 1956 for his second Freedom Forum appearance epitomized his embrace of a new global perspective and contained several elements he would emphasize for the rest of his career. Schwarz reconceived the communist threat as a gradual geostrategic encirclement of the United States in the context of a series of coups and undeclared wars (such as that in Korea) coupled with general apathy on the part of the American public. This paradigm put the communists in position to win the Cold War not through espionage or stirring up a domestic revolution in the United States but, rather, by eroding the nation's fighting spirit. This thought was eventually synthesized into a simple equation that became Schwarz's mantra: "External encirclement, plus internal demoralization, plus thermonuclear blackmail, equals progressive surrender." Communists no longer proceeded by taking out countries; rather, they struck incrementally, by patiently weakening their target's social, cultural, and political system while isolating liberal democracies.[54]

These schemes could be countered, Schwarz asserted, by blocking them at the outset. Successful containment implied reaching out to the youth in every country. For the rest of his career, Schwarz supported hard military measures against Communism but made it clear that such intervention alone could not counter the enemy. "On the world-scene, the Communists are reaching the *people* of many lands, while our contacts are reserved for the *government* … Suddenly the surge from the grass roots sweeps the government out of power, and in its place we are confronted with a pro-Communist government," he once pointed out. A spiritual and ideological war could not be won through military means.[55]

Both the Andhra project and the 1956 Freedom Forum speech announced what the CACC's international strategy would be from then on. Working largely outside government apparatuses, it focused on channelling resources from the United States – its only genuine financial base – to local anticommunist forces by way of private, faith-based networks. Taking the form of seminars and literature especially targeting students, ministers, and professionals, these international programs were often executed by people from local Protestant churches. From 1958 on, these projects accounted for roughly a quarter to a third of CACC yearly expenses. But with relatively modest amounts of money, the CACC operated continuously on several continents for decades.

Benson was delighted by Schwarz's performance. He sent a copy of the speech to Kohlberg, who distributed it to the most important names on his mailing list. Kohlberg hailed Schwarz's work and informed him that his speech would probably be widely circulated and make an impact. While not all Schwarz's confreres chose to utilize his ideas about the importance of youth or to employ his particular internationalist vision, they were in harmony with his sense that the battlefield had, to a degree, moved inward.[56]

4

"Operation Testimony"

THE SCHLAFLYS

In February 1957, Schwarz received an offer to give a series of four lectures at the St Louis Medical Society in Missouri. The invitation came from Phyllis Schlafly, then a thirty-two-year-old Catholic housewife and mother of two who had already made a reputation for herself among Midwestern conservatives by running in 1952 as a Republican candidate in the heavily Democratic 21st Congressional District of Missouri. Representing the Taft wing of her party, Schlafly had won an upset primary victory against an opponent supported by the GOP establishment, making her an instant sensation, despite her predictable loss in the fall election against a fifth-time Democratic incumbent. Campaigning as the underdog who stood for ordinary people, and as a woman in the male-dominated world of politics, her story was quickly picked up by the press. Her husband Fred Schlafly, a lawyer in a firm in Alton, Illinois, was a member of the American Bar Association's Committee on Communist Tactics, Strategy and Objectives, the report of which, submitted to the American Bar Association in 1957, drew attention and controversy due to its criticism of the Warren Supreme Court's decisions on anti-subversion laws.

The Schlaflys were well-known conservative activists in the Alton-St Louis area. Notably, Phyllis organized regular visits for speakers to address local activists. In 1956, she had set up a series of lectures featuring professional anticommunist Louis Budenz, who, like other former blacklisters, had shifted his career towards the goal of educating the public, resulting in a three-day seminar in June of that year, covering such topics as "The Nature of Communism," or "Subversive Influences on Education."[1]

Schlafly planned a follow-up to the experience for the next year, but in February 1957, the ageing Budenz suffered a heart attack and was hospitalized. In her search for a stand-in, Schlafly recalled an article she and her husband had read that same month in the *American Mercury*, then common reading among conservatives, as its pool of contributors included a who's-who of the country's staunchest anticommunist fighters (such as J. Edgar Hoover, James Burnham, and Ralph de Toledano).[2]

Schwarz, who had already met Budenz, accepted Schlafly's proposal to hold a four-day class in St Louis. The seminar was planned to take place at the St Louis Medical Society, which could only be used once a week. Hence, the four sessions were set up on a weekly basis on Tuesday evenings, from 30 April to 21 May. Schwarz managed to fill the rest of his April–May schedule, allowing him to spend a month in St Louis, where he had never been. He was a hit for local activists. Fred Schlafly compared him to other "great American anti-Communists" like Martin Dies, Louis Budenz, Francis E. Walter, and Senators Pat McCarran and Joe McCarthy. "Able and informed as these men have been on the subject of Communism, I believe that your knowledge ... is greater and your ability to impart it to your audience is even more effective." St Louis would become one of the Crusade's strongholds in the Midwest. Schwarz's collaboration with the Schlaflys was his first important contact with Catholics, who then formed more than a third of St Louis County's population. By substituting for Budenz, a protégé of the high Catholic clergy, Schwarz had managed to once again cut across denominational barriers.[3]

In 1958, when Schwarz was back in the St Louis area, a meeting took place involving him, the Schlaflys, Fred's sister Eleanor, and Father C. Stephen Dunker, a Catholic priest and former missionary who had been detained and tortured by Chinese Communists. The Schlaflys proposed to the crusader the creation of a united Protestant-Catholic anticommunist group. Schwarz refused: "If we do that we will paralyze each other. I am a fervent, evangelistic Protestant Christian. When I speak to a Protestant church group, I want to be able to speak without reservation. If I go in with you Catholics around my neck, I am suspect before I start ... When you Catholics go to speak to the Knights of Columbus or the Newman

Society, or one of the many Catholic societies, you are speaking to a group whose basic objective is to get me converted to the Catholic religion."[4]

Schwarz's rejection of a Catholic-Protestant group was grounded in his life-long praxis: any political or religious group should follow the core motivation of its founder. "There is," he said, "a great power in conserving our multiplicity of motivations. That is the genius of our Free Enterprise system." And Schwarz's motivation was a conservative evangelical one. Over the years, Schwarz would regularly collaborate with anticommunist Catholics; yet accepting them in leading Crusade positions was never a possibility. When once asked his opinion on William F. Buckley, Schwarz answered, "I don't accept his Catholicism, but he's a good man." Moreover, he was undoubtedly not disposed to share his leadership at a moment when his organization was becoming increasingly popular.[5]

Schwarz suggested that his hosts create their own group. This advice led to the founding of the Cardinal Mindszenty Foundation (CMF), named after the Catholic Primate of Hungary who, successively, had been imprisoned by the Nazis and by the Hungarian Communist government. Phyllis Schlafly's sister Eleanor directed the CMF, and, in the coming decades, it was to become one of the world's most militant Catholic anticommunist organizations, spreading information on the ills of communism in a manner similar to that of the CACC. However, until the pontificate of John Paul II, which began in the late 1970s, the CMF's stance was at odds with the Vatican's more moderate anticommunism.[6]

Although it never saw the light, Schlaflys' idea of a joint Catholic-Protestant effort reveals the changing dynamics of the Cold War American religious landscape. The Roman Catholic Church, and especially its conservative wing, had been one of the most notable sources of opposition to communism since the nineteenth century, both in the United States and internationally. By the 1950s, due to their traditional anticommunism, American Catholics, spurred on by the Cold War climate, often tended to identify their faith with the United States itself. Joe McCarthy's anticommunist crusade had its roots in his own Catholicism, even though, according to Robert Horwitz, "he tended not to tie the two together in any public way." However, among lay conservative Catholics in the 1950s, anticommunism was often framed in eschatological terms: it was seen as a struggle to preserve Christian Western civilization, and it was often coupled with calls to halt the march towards secularization and atheism in a manner that was similar to that of evangelicals.[7]

To an unusual degree, this context brought anticommunist evangelicals closer to their foes from the Catholic Church. McCarthy was highly esteemed by several of the most radical fundamentalist Protestant leaders, despite their outright contempt for his church affiliation and their diatribes against the Vatican's perceived or real influence on domestic and international issues. Some evangelicals began to see in a positive light the common front against communism that the Cold War had created among Protestants, Catholics, and people of other faiths. Schwarz's collaboration with the Schlaflys demonstrates well how anticommunism was fostering unity among religious conservatives of all stripes. Nonetheless, denominational identities remained strong enough in the 1940s and 1950s to prevent the systematic collaboration between Catholics and evangelicals that, by the late 1970s, had became a feature of the Christian Right. The Schlaflys' idea of an ecumenical anticommunist group was only one among several such failed attempts during the Cold War. Later in her life, Phyllis Schlafly acknowledged that the respective messages and constituencies of the CACC and the CMF were probably too different for this uneasy alliance to have worked out.[8]

In spite of Schwarz's unwillingness to turn ecumenical, the Schlaflys remained life-long CACC backers. They played a central role in organizing the first school of anticommunism in St Louis in the spring of 1958, and Fred Schlafly would be on the "faculty" of several CACC schools, lecturing on court cases involving communism. Phyllis Schlafly later left her imprint on US politics by founding the conservative interest group STOP ERA in 1972 as well as by successfully waging a decade-long battle against the ratification of the Equal Rights Amendment (ERA). In a letter to Schwarz in 1998, she recalled the crusader once said, commenting on the success of her husband's report on Communism for the American Bar Association: "You'll have other projects just as big."[9]

THE BILLY GRAHAM CONNECTION

Schwarz's 1957 springtime stay in St Louis was followed by a visit to Washington, where he had already been scheduled to make his first appearance before a congressional committee during a hearing regarding the Hawaii statehood bill. He had been summoned by Texas representative Walter Rogers, who, like most Southern Democrats, opposed including Hawaii as a state as doing so would mean two more pro-civil rights senators in Washington. However, Rogers's arguments were framed in terms of the cost for taxpayers and national security, which provided an opportunity to invite Schwarz. Before the committee, Schwarz recommended that the US government exercise a good deal of caution. Communists, he pointed out, could influence civil life and have "potential power over the entire Hawaiian economy" since they controlled several key labour unions in the archipelago, in particular the International Longshoremen's and Warehousemen's Union (ILWU) led by Australian native Harry Bridges (a professed Communist who was naturalized in 1945). The ratio of Communists to the total population was probably lower in Hawaii that it was in New York or California, Schwarz said; however, in the latter states Communists did not control anything of importance, while in Hawaii their stranglehold on the ILWU made them "a real danger."[10]

Schwarz's network of government contacts can be traced back to his first trip to Washington and his meeting with Billy Graham. In February 1953, the crusader had made a short trip to Arizona before proceeding to Detroit, where he met his old friend Max Bushby, a lay Methodist pastor from Tasmania who introduced him to Graham. Graham was then at the peak of his popularity. National press coverage of him was more extensive than that of anyone else in the country, including the president himself. Having supported Eisenhower during the 1952 election, Graham hoped that Ike's tenure would mark the return of evangelicals to prominence in national life. Shortly after Eisenhower took office in January 1953, the nation learned that the new president had been baptized and confirmed in a Presbyterian church that Graham had recommended to him.[11]

Schwarz was not unknown to Graham, who had already heard the Aussie talking on a Christian radio program. "Billy had friends in Congress," Schwarz wrote, "and he wanted me to take my message to Washington." Soon after the 1952 election, the Billy Graham Evangelistic Association (BGEA) had opened a new permanent office in the capital city for the purpose of bringing spiritual guidance to Washington. Though his network of political contacts was not limited to Southerners, Graham had more friends among politicians of his native South than among any other groups. These friends included Senator John C. Stennis from Mississippi, Representative L. Mendel

Rivers from South Carolina, and Governor James C. Byrnes from South Carolina. Like him, many of his contacts were traditional Southern Democrats who had supported Eisenhower in 1952.[12]

Graham got in touch with the man who was perhaps his closest contact in Congress – Frank Boykin, the Democratic Alabama congressman who, since 1936, had represented the 1st Alabama District based in and around Mobile. With an undistinguished political record, Boykin was widely seen as a House backbencher who had more interest in his prospering business in the lumber and chemical industries than in his congressional duties. Nonetheless, the convivial Boykin was also known for his loyalty to his friends. He promptly arranged for Schwarz to give a bipartisan address during a luncheon meeting for members of Congress, senators, and their senior political staff in the Congressional Dining Room in Washington, DC, in February 1953. When contacted by Boykin, Schwarz had already returned to the Southwest from Detroit and was in El Paso. Graham covered the costs of the Australian's direct flight to the capital city.[13]

Schwarz's first Washington lecture was delivered before a lunching crowd, in the kind of informal context characteristic of scores of his other meetings. Most leaders from both parties were present. Schwarz exclusively stressed secular issues. His main target was the pacifist rhetoric often found in Communist literature. "Peace," he explained in a manner that showcased his savvy use of Marxist buzzwords, "is the dialectic synthesis which emerges when the progressive thesis of the proletariat utterly overwhelms the reactionary thesis of the bourgeoisie and ... there is established Socialism, under the dictatorship of the proletariat, which is peace." Boykin thanked Graham for "bringing us another great message through your friend, Dr. Fred Schwarz. It was terrific. He knocked them cold." Graham wished Schwarz good luck: "I am certain the Lord has opened a wonderful door there, and that much good will come of it." Schwarz left Washington with several letters of recommendation, notably from Boykin but also from Republican senator Homer S. Ferguson and from Democratic representative James C. Davis, from Michigan and Georgia, respectively. Schwarz ended up speaking in front of the legislatures of both states.[14]

In 1957, four years later, Schwarz's trip to Washington to address the issue of Hawaii was his sixth visit to the "hub of the world," as he called the capital city. Visits to Washington had become a routine each spring, with Schwarz arriving during the weeks when both chambers of Congress were about to recess for the summer. In 1955, he had the opportunity to address another bipartisan congressional meeting of senators and representatives. In the spring of 1956, he made two short trips to Washington, where he had the "thrilling experience" of addressing leading institutions of the military-security establishment, starting with the Pentagon, where "70 to 80 of the leaders" of the US Department of Defense gathered to hear him. Shortly afterwards, he was invited to present the last official lecture of the academic year at the National War College and, later, he addressed a group of Central Intelligence Agency (CIA) executives. The crusader's contacts among Washington's political establishment and the national security apparatus provided opportunities not only in Washington but also in federal institutions around the country. Examples of this are his speech to the staffers of the Federal Civil Defense Administration in Battle Creek, Michigan, in 1955 and his first address on a military base in Colorado Springs in July 1956.[15]

Early on, the Crusade's most solid political contact was Minnesota Republican representative Walter H. Judd. Schwarz and this tall Midwesterner were both evangelists and physicians. Upon completing his medical degree in 1923, Judd worked as a medical missionary in China until the late 1930s, where he became a supporter of Chiang Kai-shek. Moderately conservative in economics, liberal on race issues, and anti-isolationist in foreign policy, Judd was elected as representative in 1942 and became a star in the anticommunist world. He corresponded with all the important anticommunist figures: J. Edgar Hoover and George S. Benson; business backers of the China Lobby like Alfred Kohlberg and Henry Luce; foreign leaders such as South Korean president Syngman Rhee and Chinese nationalist leader Chiang Kai-shek. He also contributed to forming groups such as Aid Refugee Chinese Intellectuals in 1951 and, in 1953, the Committee for One Million, which became one of the most important fronts of the China Lobby.[16]

In 1956, Judd refused to be part of the Crusade's advisory committee when Schwarz's new right-hand man Bill Strube invited him to join. Judd wrote, "I have felt that as long as I am in this present public position, I ought not to join officially in the many, many good causes and organizations from which invitations come every month." However, he added, "I can help you and Dr. Schwarz quite as much without being officially a member of your advisory board." In April 1959, he assisted in organizing a luncheon in Schwarz's honour at

4.1 | Dr Walter H. Judd, Minneapolis Newspaper Photograph Collection.

the Chevy Chase Club. Until the late 1970s, Judd appeared at CACC events, refusing to accept any fees and even contributing financially.[17]

While in 1957 Schwarz's first official testimony before the US Congress regarding the Hawaiian issue went almost unnoticed by the press, it drew the attention of Representative John R. Pillion of Buffalo, one of the few Republicans who opposed Hawaiian statehood. Pillion invited Schwarz to address a private meeting of GOP members of Congress and immediately took steps to refer him to the House Un-American Activities Committee. Shortly upon returning to his hotel room after the meeting, Schwarz received a phone call from Richard Arens, HUAC's director, who invited him to give a full report on Communist strategy. Schwarz asked "when?" and the answer was "now." He replied, "Certainly."[18]

THE HUAC

Ten minutes later, the crusader was at the Capitol. He found himself in a bare room with two staffers and HUAC's Richard Arens, one of Capitol Hill's leading congressional officers, who had worked with some of Washington's prime Cold War fighters, including Joe McCarthy and Pat McCarran.[19]

Schwarz appeared as an expert witness on communist theory. Many other pro anticommunists had come before the same committee, testifying that Marxism-Leninism meant revolutionary violence and that its proponents should be considered public enemies. Schwarz did the same thing, but he did it better. On the Communist interpretation of peace, he said, "If they take a gun, they take a peaceful gun, containing a peaceful bullet, and kill you peacefully and put you in a peaceful grave." On the fallacy of equating strength with numbers: "One hole can sink the ship. Communism is the theory of the disciplined few controlling and directing the rest." On whether Communists were trustworthy: "As long as keeping their promise would advance their program, they could be trusted to keep it." And on whether they were hypocrites: "They have merged the techniques of hypocrisy with the virtues of sincerity, creating a powerful instrument."

The hard-nosed Arens, who would become a Crusade collaborator, was won over. Schwarz not only had a superior command of the Marxist-Leninist stance but also framed the clash as a global struggle to control hearts and minds – a struggle that the enemy was winning.

As an example – one in which he uncritically adopted the US view – Schwarz cited the Rosenberg case. The Rosenbergs had been given what he considered "a fair trial" and had been sentenced to death for high treason. Yet the case had been exploited by Communists and framed as an anti-Semitic conspiracy. They demonstrated their command of propaganda by joining the international outcry to have the Rosenberg sentenced commuted. However, they were at the same time persecuting Jews themselves: during the Slansky trial in the fall of 1952, eleven high-ranking Jewish Communist bureaucrats in Czechoslovakia were executed after having been accused of participating in a "Trotskyte-Titoite-Zionist conspiracy." "In Czechoslovakia," Schwarz said, "these Jews were practically murdered after the most summary of judicial farces. What hypocrisy!"

Unbounded by frontiers, Schwarz also mentioned a case in India, which he had visited the year before. "To the Indian his religious faith, whether it be Hindu, Moslem, or Christianity, is important. His family relationship is important. His moral code is important. Communism is against all these things." Given this, he explained that those Christians in India who voted for the Communists did so because Communists operated by targeting subgroups and exploiting narrow issues to their advantage. Also, they knew how to present a friendly image: people in India voted Communist "because the Communists sent a very fine young student to their village with glorious magazines showing them how much their life will be improved under communism."

Much of the exchange dealt with the issue of the role of students in the Communist plan for world "conquest without war." Here, Schwarz offered a detailed exposé of the type of student intellectual targeted by Communist propaganda:

> He accepts that materialist foundation on which Communist ideology and morality is built. He is recruited in terms of his ideological pride. He is more intelligent than the average man, and he sees the opportunity to mold man and create history, whereas the dull, brutal, driven herd sweeps on unaware of the forces that create it and that drive it forward. He is one of the elite, the chosen, and the intellectual aristocracy. In combination with this intellectual pride, the religious nature of a man demands a purpose in life; they find in this vision of human regeneration, a religious refuge for their Godless hearts.

According to Schwarz, education and counter-propaganda were the only solutions to this state of affairs: "The first thing is to educate young people who believe in their God, their country, their family, their Constitution, their liberty under law and who are proud of their heritage." That each year the United States devoted $40 billion to the military, $3 to $4 million to foreign aid, and only a minute percentage to educating the world's populations amounted to relying on short-term measures that could only temporarily hold back the menace.

The whole presentation was a masterful demonstration of casual erudition. While skirting anything controversial, Schwarz offered a synopsis of his main ideas in a two-and-a-half-hour rant disguised as a scholarly lecture. However, in the last two minutes of the hearing, he took a major risk. Asked by Arens how long would it take for Communists to control the world if their expansion continued, he stated: "I think the Communists have more or less tentatively set the deadline for about the year 1973. Mao-Tse-tung and Stalin in their last conference thought it would take four more 5-year plans, approximately 10 years for the conquest and consolidation of Asia, with the immediate threat of Africa and Europe, while the weakening, softening, and degeneration of America, continues, and avoiding an atomic-hydrogen war, their conquest is contemplated about that time."[20]

Schwarz had no evidence to substantiate this claim. He later acknowledged that the 1973 deadline had not been taken from any official Communist source: "The actual date was suggested by Free Chinese intelligence agents as the date agreed upon by Stalin and Mao Tse-tung at the last conference." What he meant by "last conference" is unclear. Stalin and Mao had only two face-to-face meetings, one on 16 December 1949 and one on 22 January 1950. These were held in private, and their transcripts were kept secret until after the fall of the USSR. If Schwarz had been fed the content of the Stalin-Mao conversation, as he claimed, by some Nationalist Chinese source, the information was incorrect. The disclosed transcripts from the Stalin-Mao meetings mostly consisted of casual exchanges about the mutual interests of China and the USSR, especially regarding issues such as Soviet interests in northeast China and the question of Korea.[21]

Nonetheless, the prophecy of a communist takeover planned for 1973 was given considerable weight. A man who appeared to know the enemy inside out was putting forth the prospect that the United States of America would be sovietized in less than two decades. This contributed to making Schwarz's HUAC testimony one of the most widely read documents in the conservative subculture of the late 1950s and early 1960s. Two years after this testimony, an anonymous apocalyptic novel titled *The John Franklin Letters* became an underground sensation among the American grassroots right wing. It portrayed a United States that, in the early 1970s, had been taken over by Communists. The result was economic collapse, suburbs being invaded by city mobs, and the death of 20 million US citizens. All of this was brought to a halt by a group of American vigilantes who, under the leadership of a patriot named John Franklin, mounted a counter-revolution that kicked the Communists out of the country. Though it remains hard to tell whether this scenario had or had not been influenced by Schwarz, it demonstrates to what extent the crusader had captured widespread fears among conservatives in the late 1950s.[22]

Schwarz later admitted that the concluding paragraph of his HUAC testimony "stimulated criticism and controversy." Aware that relying solely on vague estimates taken from an intelligence report "would be highly speculative were it not supported by a great body of indirect evidence," he tried for years to find such evidence. He jumped on Khrushchev's confident claim in January 1959 that the USSR would become the world's leading economic power "fifteen years hence." In 1959, he used a statement from CIA director Allen Dulles affirming that, by 1970, the USSR would "advance to first place in the world both in absolute volume of production and in per capita production." As late as 1996, Schwarz returned to the issue, this time using an excerpt from *The Private Life of Chairman Mao*, written by Mao's former physician Li Zhisui, in which the author describes a speech made by the Chinese premier in 1957 predicting that, within "fifteen years," Communist economies would surpass those of the West.[23]

The few newspaper articles that covered Schwarz's HUAC appearance focused almost exclusively on the 1973 prediction. While a HUAC appearance was an established status symbol for a pro-anticommunist, by 1957 the media buzz around the committee's hearings had substantially diminished. Schwarz did not initially make much of it and continued his Washington tour, resulting in private meetings with Republican senator William F.

Knowland (senate minority leader), Senator Lyndon Johnson (senate majority leader), and Bryce Harlow (assistant to the president). The Australian also had a meeting with people from the United States Information Agency.[24]

HARRY BRADLEY WEIGHS IN

The transcript of the May 1957 hearing was published as a booklet and distributed two months later to the HUAC mailing list. One recipient was Alfred Kohlberg, who was making his way back to taking up his activities two years after a prolonged rest caused by heart attacks in 1955. He and Schwarz had not corresponded for a year, but he was glad to see that his friend Fred had been heard on Capitol Hill and considered the HUAC document worthy of wide distribution. In August 1957, while the crusader was back in Australia, Kohlberg wrote in a letter that, through the American China Policy Association (his pro-Taiwan organization), he had sent the HUAC testimony to a "list of something over 2,000, not including members of Congress. About 1,500 of these were editors, writers, columnists and so forth, connected with newspapers." Upon his return from Australia in mid-September 1957, Schwarz was stunned at the extent of his friend's all-out effort, but Kohlberg tried to keep expectations low.[25]

One name on Kohlberg's mailing list was that of Norman Beasley, a journalist who had been hired by businessman Harry L. Bradley to write a book about the history of the Allen-Bradley Corporation, leader in the field of factory automation equipment. Beasley showed a copy of the HUAC testimony to Harry Bradley. Reading the document, the Allen-Bradley owner experienced the classic mix of joy and terror countless audiences had felt listening to Schwarz. Starting in December 1957 and continuing a few months into the new year, Allen-Bradley saw that the entire transcript of Schwarz's HUAC testimony appeared as a paid ad in most of the nation's major newspapers. The ad appeared under two different titles: "How Much Freedom Do We Have Left – Not Much" and "Will You Be Free to Celebrate Christmas in the Future?" The cost of the operation was once estimated at about $50,000.[26]

This new Crusade benefactor, Harry L. Bradley, was, since the death of his elder brother Lynde in 1942, the last remaining founder of Allen-Bradley. Founded in 1903, Allan-Bradley was prospering with the establishment of a permanent military-industrial complex.

The Allen-Bradley plant in South Milwaukee was one of the biggest of its kind in the Midwest, with four thousand employees by the mid-1950s. The pious and industrious Bradley brothers embodied the values (God, country, and belief in free market) they had acquired in their youth in the heartland of Wisconsin. By the late 1950s, Harry Bradley began sponsoring right-wing activity, notably by subsidizing the radio broadcasts of commentator Bob Siegrist and William Buckley's *National Review*.[27]

Schwarz's Houston collaborator Bill Strube was the first CACC official to learn about Bradley's sponsorship. He contacted Schwarz who, once again, happened to be in Australia for Christmas. Upon his return to the United States, the Crusade had received hundreds of letters of support from every social stratum across the country, and Allen-Bradley had set up a special department to handle the thousands of requests for copies.[28]

On 24 February 1958, a meeting was finally arranged between Schwarz and Harry Bradley in Milwaukee. Kohlberg gave his friend a few tips before the meeting with his new sponsors: "I think the only guidance they really need is to keep them from going off at less useful angles and wasting their money on side issues, which always seem to be the fate of businessmen who get excited." A moved Schwarz, "hoping to be forgiven a slight moistness in my eyes," detailed to Bradley the Crusade's most important needs and spent the rest of the day at Bob Siegrist's studio, where he was featured during the evening broadcast.[29]

Between March and May 1958, Allen-Bradley spent an additional $100,000 to print the HUAC testimony in more than thirty newspapers. By late spring, the number of requests for copies had reached a quarter of a million. In April 1958, a $10,000 cheque was received at the CACC's office in Long Beach, the largest single amount ever donated to the organization at that time. Allen-Bradley's support of the CACC lasted, Schwarz wrote, "as long as Harry Bradley and [Bradley's right-hand man] Fred Loock lived." By 1963, about 4.5 million reprints of the testimony had been sent out. The company also sponsored Schwarz's tour in Milwaukee in the fall of 1958 as well as the CACC school in Milwaukee in 1960. However, Allen-Bradley's peak aid to the CACC was between 1958 and 1960. Afterwards, as Kohlberg had predicted, it extended help to other groups and dispersed resources that otherwise might have been channelled to the Crusade.[30]

By mid-1958, various groups and institutions followed Allen-Bradley's lead. The CACC thus established Operation Testimony, which consisted in encouraging its supporters to buy copies of the HUAC transcript and sponsor its printing in newspapers. The Crusade's Houston branch organized its own distribution service, charging sixty dollars per thousand copies. The National American Legion sent a copy of the HUAC transcript to all Legion posts and local Legion posts paid for its publication in newspapers. In Montana, the transcript appeared in six newspapers, thanks to the sponsorship of the First National Bank and the Security Bank and Trust Company from Gallatin County. In Texas, the Texas Power and Light Company distributed seven thousand copies to its employees, while the Southwestern Savings and Loan Association mailed ten thousand copies to its accounts. Schwarz wrote Kohlberg in June 1958 that the HUAC transcript also circulated easily within the educational system due to its being a congressional document. Thus, for years, the HUAC testimony was disseminated by independent sponsors nationwide, and only amid the controversies of the 1962–64 era did this fad die out.[31]

Moreover, the document began circulating in other countries. Texas oilman Jack Danciger paid thousands of dollars to get the testimony translated into Spanish and distributed south of the Rio Grande. In Taiwan, Taipei's state information agency translated the document into Mandarin and distributed it to Taiwanese civic leaders and government officials before the Taiwan Air Force dropped thousands of copies over Mainland China in 1959. Kuomintang general Andrew K.T. Ming read a copy of the document and decided to contact Schwarz.

This led to a further expansion of the Crusade's international activities. In November 1959, Schwarz embarked on a twenty-eight-day trip. After a stop in England, he flew to the East. His DC 6B plane landed for refuelling in Hong Kong, which the Australian described as "the living proof that the claim of the Chinese Communists to be the legitimate representatives of the Chinese people is a lie" since about a million refugees from Mainland China had flocked to the British colony. He then proceeded to Taiwan, where he was met by a small crowd holding a "Welcome Dr. Fred Schwarz" banner while a musical band played. Andrew K.T. Ming, "president of the Chinese Christian Anti-Communism Crusade," was Schwarz's host for the week. Himself a reverend, Ming belonged to Taiwan's influential evangelical Christian minority, a group whose anticommunism had been reinforced by the Chinese Communists' wiping out nearly all of the churches in Mainland China. Not unlike what had happened in India four years earlier, a local group of evangelicals exposed to Schwarz's writings had formed and had invited him to pay a visit. In the meantime, this Chinese CACC organized an evangelical anticommunist conference attended by two hundred Taiwanese church leaders, and it translated CACC writings into Mandarin.[32]

Schwarz's visit came after the second Taiwan Strait Crisis of 1958, which had seen Chinese Communists on the mainland and Nationalists in Taiwan trading shells and military threats over control of Quemoy and Matsu Islands. The crisis furthered Taiwan's integration into the US strategic apparatus in Asia. Since 1949, when Taiwan saw the arrival of 1.5 million Kuomintang sympathizers (military, bureaucrats, businesspeople) who ruled as conquerors, the island underwent transformations favouring the emergence of groups such as this Chinese CACC. The Kuomintang, aided by a large infusion of US money, reorganized the country's economy and opened it to the West. In a few years, Taiwan welcomed Christian missionaries, many fleeing from Mainland China, while other came directly from the United States, especially from conservative denominations (e.g., Southern Baptists and Assemblies of God).

Schwarz's new friends were themselves members of a conservative Baptist group tied to the Baptist Evangelization Society, which had kept contacts with Christian mainlanders whose religious faith had been driven underground. This relationship between Taiwan's ruling regime and Christian missionaries was strengthened by the fact that Chiang Kai-shek, his wife Soong Mei-ling, and an influential minority among the Kuomintang establishment adhered to the Christian faith. Missionaries were welcomed in Taiwan and, in return, their churches became lobbyists for its regime. Missionaries helped Taiwan's development as they supplemented the state's social programs by opening relief agencies, hospitals, colleges, and even universities. During his guided tour, Schwarz marvelled at Taiwan's healthcare infrastructure and its education system, which fostered some of Asia's highest rates of school and university attendance.[33]

The crusader's visit culminated in a series of meetings with the Kuomintang elite, including one with Chiang Kai-shek and his wife, who perhaps recalled the visitor from some of his writings, which Kohlberg had forwarded to her in 1953. "The President," Schwarz wrote in his newsletter, "appeared serene in his position of great responsibility and his concern for the Chinese people is tempered by a vibrant faith in their future." Ironically, Schwarz, who claimed that it was a waste of time to visit the USSR since Communists could constrain the visitor's tour to carefully selected areas, thus presenting a false tableau, was probably himself deceived, at least to a degree, by Kuomintang officials: only two years before, an Indigenous uprising against the Kuomintang's corruption-ridden management and its exclusion of local elites had been crushed, resulting in thousands of civilian deaths.[34]

Despite the eventual cessation of the Chinese CACC's activities for reasons unknown (there is no mention of this group in Crusade literature and correspondence after 1961), Schwarz's visit shows the extent to which the success of the HUAC testimony had resulted in a bonanza of free advertising. Schwarz's collaborator Bill Strube told a journalist in 1961 that the testimony "had wider circulation in this country than any document except possibly the Bill of Rights, the Declaration of Independence and the Constitution."[35] While this statement was hyperbolic, there is no doubt that, at this point, the HUAC testimony constituted the most important factor in making Schwarz and his organization known to the larger public, both in the United States and internationally.

BIG MONEY

Widespread dissemination of the HUAC testimony increased the crusader's visibility and reputation. From early 1958 on, in articles covering his activities Schwarz was referred to with superlatives. He was presented as a "top authority on the Communist technique"; a "world renowned speaker"; an "internationally recognized authority"; "one of the Free World's best informed analysts of communist ideology"; an "outstanding foe of communism for 20 years"; and even "the 20th Century Paul Revere." With fame came the ability to make new friends. During the year 1957, the number of new lifetime CACC members – who paid the a $100 life membership fee, and whose names were displayed in CACC newsletters until 1961 – was twenty-nine. During 1958, this number jumped to more than 132, including prominent figures such as actor Roy Rogers and his wife Dale Evans, and Rear Admiral A.C. Burroughs.[36]

A significant addition to the 1958 list of life members was that of Southern California businessman Walter Knott, of Knott's

Berry Farm fame, "a warm-hearted and generous lover of liberty," as Schwarz put it, who sent the CACC an unsolicited $500 check, the first of many across a twenty-three-year period. Knott was the American Dream incarnate, an industrious and religious farmer who lifted himself from poverty to fortune during the Depression by introducing the boysenberry to the market and later opening a successful roadside chicken dinner restaurant in Buena Park, near Anaheim. In the 1940s, a Ghost Town was built near his business, originally to please waiting crowds but which evolved into an amusement park and remained popular even after the opening of nearby Disneyland in 1955. In the mid-1950s, Knott became engaged in conservative politics and established himself as a major financier of various right-wing causes. Knott remained one of the Crusade's regular major contributors until his death in 1981.[37]

Later in 1958, Schwarz met oil magnate J. Howard Pew, former president and owner of Sun Oil (later Sunoco), after an address he delivered at a meeting for Dr Howard Kershner's Christian Freedom Foundation, which Pew sponsored. By the time Schwarz met him, J. Howard Pew was at the centre of a huge web of conservative groups, business and religious associations, and various media outlets. Supporter of Robert Welch, Pew was a staunch defender of classical liberalism in the face of government interference. He was also a devout evangelical for whom defending economic freedom in the United States was indistinguishable from protecting old-fashioned religion from liberal Protestantism.[38]

Pew invited Schwarz to Philadelphia, where he met other members of the city's richest family. These people included Pew's brother Joseph Newton Jr and his sister Mabel Pew Myrin. Shortly after their meeting, Schwarz wrote Pew, thanked him for his "gracious counsel and generous donation of time," and summarized four "immediate projects ... which may commend themselves to you for your prayerful support": the establishment of an East Coast Crusade office, with estimated costs of $10,000 for the first year of operation; the distribution of the HUAC testimony "in the Spanish language to the students of the Universities and Colleges of Central and South America," at the same cost; the organizing of an anticommunism school in Indianapolis or in Pew's own turf of Philadelphia (at a cost of $5,000 each); and the establishment of an anticommunist newspaper in Kerala, India, at the projected cost of $50,000. Though the real costs incurred by these projects were higher than this, all came to fruition in one form or another.[39]

Schwarz's encounters with Knott and Pew, both of which came shortly after Harry Bradley's efforts, marked Schwarz's first genuine inroads into the world of big business. The CACC had already received a few big business contributions before 1958, the earliest instance being that of Charles Stewart Mott, founding member of General Motors, who offered a $1,000 cheque after Schwarz addressed a dinner meeting of engineers in Flint, Michigan, in June 1955. At that time, however, this was a single case in an otherwise grassroots financial base that consisted mainly of contributions of one hundred dollars or less. A few years later, the CACC was financed by a few more big business sponsors.

In one respect, Mott's initial contribution paved the way for the many that would come after: it did not take the form of a personal cheque. The money was channelled through the Mott Foundation, the private philanthropic organization Mott had founded in 1926. In a similar way, Harry Bradley's $10,000 cheque in 1958 came from the Lynde and Harry Bradley Foundation, Harry Bradley's philanthropic organization established in 1942, which, by the 1980s, became an important subsidizer of right-wing causes in the United States. As time passed, most of the Crusade's large contributions came from private foundations, making the CACC, way before the age of the "New Right," an early recipient of the private and charitable philanthropic organizations that, by the late twentieth century, would constitute one of the American right wing's most consistent sources of power and support.

To conservative businesspeople, channelling money through private foundations was not only fiscally preferable: it also maintained a distance that prevented the possible pitfalls of a closer association while, at the same time, establishing a managerial setting through which sums could be properly allocated and administered. The largest and most important sources of big money for the CACC were piped through the several foundations established by the Pew family, including the Memorial Trust, the Freedom Trust, the Joseph N. Pew Jr, Charitable Trust, and the Mabel Pew Myrin Trust. These were closely managed by the Glenmede Trust Company, allowing the Pews to avoid direct involvement in politics and to remain out of the spotlight. Nonetheless, playing behind the scenes never prevented them from supporting almost exclusively causes and people with whom they had established close-knit, personal contacts – and Schwarz was one of these.[40]

Apart from Pew, the CACC's most important supporter until the early 1970s was Patrick J. Frawley. One day in 1960, Frawley, then president of Eversharp and its subsidiary the Schick Safety Razor Company sent the CACC an unsolicited $10,500 cheque and invited Schwarz to visit him in Bel Air, an affluent suburb near Beverly Hills. In contrast to Mott, Bradley, Knott, and Pew, all men over seventy when Schwarz met them, Frawley was only thirty-six. Equally noteworthy was the fact that Frawley was a devout Catholic. Frawley and his wife Geraldine, Schwarz wrote, "were the personification of Irish hospitality. With nine children, their home was a hive of constant activity." According to author Russell Adam, headstrong and mercurial, Frawley was "a temperamental individualist whose erratic traits were magnified by a drinking problem."[41]

Frawley's path to fortune took the form of a ballpoint pen. In 1948, he secured the rights to a new type of ink that allowed the creation of the Paper-Mate pen, the ink of which "stayed put, neither blotted nor smeared." After Frawley sold Paper-Mate in 1956, he bought Eversharp in 1958, which he transformed with the introduction of the new stainless-steel razor blade. He also acquired enough shares of the colour film corporation Technicolor to become its chairman. Until the late 1950s, Frawley was widely seen as a young marketing genius, but his name was not associated with politics. That changed in 1959, when a Schick plant he had opened in Cuba was nationalized by Fidel Castro's new regime. "That woke me up. … They were stealing property and I'm a large stockholder. How did I know they might not begin stealing our plants in the United States?" Frawley's first two anticommunist initiatives consisted of (1) his becoming a wholehearted backer of the CACC and (2) his vigorously supporting the GOP during the presidential campaign of 1960, convinced that a Nixon presidency would have overthrown the Castro regime. Until 1970, Frawley was a major money provider for conservative causes in the United Sates.[42]

Big business benefactors provided important support for logistics and networking. Knott's 1961 chairmanship of the CACC's Orange County anticommunist school was crucial to its success. Knott also helped the Crusade to hold fundraising or patriotic events, to the point at which Schwarz recalled in his later years Knott's Chicken Dinner Restaurant as being "the favourite location for Crusade rallies." In 1959, Pew used his contacts to fill Schwarz's schedule in the Philadelphia area. The following year, his backing was vital to the success of the CACC school in Philadelphia, whose chairman,

Allyn Bell, was president of the Glenmede Trust Company. Frawley organized a meeting between Schwarz and some of his corporate executives right after their first encounter. These included his Jewish right-hand man Edward Ettinger, a skilled public relations man who contributed to the advertising of several CACC events.[43]

First and foremost, big business backing meant big donations. In a matter of weeks after he initially met Pew, Schwarz received a $10,000 cheque from the Pew Memorial Trust. This gift was not only renewed each subsequent year until the mid-1970s, but it increased over time to compensate for rising inflation. Other trusts administered by the Glenmede Company donated as well, such as the Pew Freedom Trust, which was established, as its statement of purpose reads, to "acquaint the American people with the evils of bureaucracy and the vital need to maintain and preserve a limited form of government." Tax returns from the 1966 fiscal year indicate that, when all trusts administered by the Glenmede Trust Company are totalled, the CACC received $40,000 from the Glenmede Trust Company that year. By the late 1960s, support from all the Pew Trusts combined amounted to almost one-tenth of the Crusade's income.[44]

Frawley was unique among the many Crusade supporters, big or small, since his assistance was often channelled, as long as he was able to do so, through the corporations he managed or with which he was associated. Support sometimes took the form of "public service" advertising. Frawley was also the Crusade's biggest financial supporter in the early 1960s. "Dr. Schwarz will not lack for money while I'm around," Frawley said in 1961. He donated a cumulated amount of about $50,000 in 1962 alone, comprised of his personal donations and those from Technicolor and Schick. Though this support was reduced in subsequent years, as Frawley spread his generosity to many other organizations, it nonetheless remained high throughout the 1960s.[45]

However, those CACC benefactors belonged to a minority among the nation's business elite. Their level of political involvement and eagerness to promote conservative views were far superior than average. Since the implementation of the New Deal, attempts by conservative businesspeople to set up movements outside the realm of partisan politics (such as the du Pont family's Liberty League in the 1930s) had failed.[46] The big business community had reluctantly come to accept the new role the state played in the economy during the Second World War and the ensuing prosperity. Some factors that made Schwarz's benefactors more susceptible to supporting right-wing causes can be suggested. No one among Mott, Bradley, Pew, Knott, Frawley, and Harry Casey (the co-builder of UPS, who became a Crusade supporter in the 1980s) belonged to the country's old dynasties. As members of the country's wealthiest class of citizens, they were all "first-generation" cases who had built their respective empires from scratch and who connected their success to a deep faith in the meritocratic, entrepreneurial philosophy with which they were familiar. Frawley excepted, all had lived through the prosperous 1920s, an era of unimpeded business in which entrepreneurs were often considered the nation's most valuable citizens. This nostalgia combined with a deep resentment towards the new power that state technocrats and big labour imposed over US businesses. Mott's philanthropic initiatives aimed at providing an alternate model of welfare from that offered by unionism, which, as head of General Motors, he had fought for years. Bradley's first clashes with the Congress of Industrial Organizations (CIO), which successfully organized his company's unionization in 1939, turned him and his brother Lynde into bona-fide union-busters. Bradley decried what he considered Washington's interference in favour of the unions, and, for the next two decades, Allen-Bradley fought an exhausting legal war with the American Federation of Labor (AFL) and the CIO over several issues.[47]

By and large, these were also highly pious men who stressed morality and faith in a nation besieged by atheism and moral decay. Walter Knott, himself the son of an evangelical preacher and rancher, was said to have taught Sunday school on his theme park's train. J. Howard Pew's prime motivation to get politically involved was his deep conviction that American churches needed to be shielded from the dangerous influence of liberal thought. Despite their personal successes and postwar prosperity, Schwarz's backers shared a pessimistic view of the nation's future. As opposed to other business leaders, they considered the domestic growth of big government and big labour to be part of the same dynamic as Soviet expansion abroad. They saw, like Schwarz, the social order being threatened by the breakdown of faith and morality, which opened the door for the spread of atheistic communism. And for two of the crusader's most ardent supporters, Alfred Kohlberg and Patrick Frawley, the danger was more than a mere abstraction: it was personal. Both had embraced militant anticommunism overnight after having themselves experienced seeing their businesses wrecked by Communists, making their activism a personal, bitter affair.[48]

5

"We Could Reach Everyone in the World"

CACC SCHOOLS: BEGINNINGS

A crowd of more than thirteen hundred people had jammed into the largest hall of Phoenix's dashing Westward Hotel on this morning of March 1961. A forty-eight-year-old Fred Schwarz was delivering his routine on communism, provoking laughter, applause, and thoughtful silence as he spoke with his usual ease. Freelance journalist Donald McNeil, sitting in a front row seat, described the scene in his personal notes: "[Schwarz] points, jabs, and waves his fingers, reminiscent of John Kennedy." McNeil had not remembered seeing an attentive audience for a long time. Almost everyone, he observed, was taking notes. The audience was mostly white, Protestant, from a middle- or upper-class background. Numerous teenagers were present, having been excused from class by the local school board. Yet the bulk of the audience ranged from thirty to forty-five years of age.[1]

Seven months earlier, the great majority of them had voted for Nixon over Kennedy, though their natural preference would have been for their revered federal senator, Barry Goldwater, had his name been on the ballot. In fact, at the end of this Phoenix School of Anti-Communism, several attendees contacted the office of "Mr. Conservative" to say that the week-long event had been a life-changing experience. A husband and wife declared that they feared for their children upon learning that Communists set 1973 as the year of world domination. A woman demanded that similar initiatives be set across the nation. A Mesa pediatrician wrote that he now reluctantly agreed with Goldwater's hardline foreign policy outlook. In his syndicated column, Goldwater hailed the event as responsible popular anticommunism. "The men and women who attended this school were community leaders ... there were in fact sober, industrious, thoughtful citizens who have helped to shape the culture and the prosperity of the Southwest."[2]

Between 1958 and 1964, the Crusade held thirty schools of anti-communism, in addition to those organized by its branch in Houston, where the formula somewhat differed. These events gradually became the organization's main activity, its potential seemingly limitless (at least for a time). It was based on a formula that brought together grassroots activists, professionals, businesspeople, and some of the most important private institutions of any given community: service clubs, churches, and professional organizations. Their success increasingly hinged on the participation of public bodies such as school boards, local police forces, the military, city councils, and mayoral offices. By the end of 1960, they had evolved into huge patriotic happenings that inflamed the nation's most conservative strongholds, each one providing the CACC with effective new fundraising opportunities. For a time, all this made the Crusade the nation's fastest-growing and highest-grossing anticommunist organization.

This was remarkable considering how low-key these schools were when they began. The first school opened on 24 March 1958, at the Tower Grove Baptist Church of St Louis, Missouri. It consisted of a week-long seminar of twenty one-and-a-half-hour sessions, stretching from 8:00 a.m. to 4:30 p.m. Attendees were taught about communism by a "faculty" of seven people, which included, apart from Schwarz and Strube, two Washington insiders – Representative John R. Pillion and HUAC staffer Richard Arens. "Tuition" fees were twenty dollars for the full seminar or five dollars for a single day. Morning sessions began with Schwarz's presentations on communist philosophy. Other topics included "Psychology of Communism" (by Arens), "Communism and Business" (by Strube), and "Communism and the Law" (by Pillion).[3]

The St Louis gathering was the CACC's largest initiative in the United States up to this time. A request for financial support that Schwarz sent to Pew in the fall of 1958 mentioned that such a school required a minimum expenditure of $5,000; however, the cost seems to have been double this figure since, around the same time, he mentioned to Kohlberg that he had to refuse Arens's proposal for a school in Washington because he needed about $10,000 to make it possible. The school was an ambitious follow-up to

Schwarz's spring 1957 seminar in St Louis under the auspices of Fred and Phyllis Schlafly. However, this time, the St Louis Medical Society refused to authorize the use of its building, prompting organizers to hold the event at the Tower Grove Baptist Church. An agent was hired to promote the school, but he found the task to be difficult and urged Schwarz to cancel the project. "But I knew," Schwarz noted, "that if we cancelled this one, we would meet up with the same problems the next time and cancel it. So I said let's go ahead with this one, and if no one comes, so be it." The project came into being with the help of local supporters, many of whom came from the Schlaflys' network. Financial backing came from Missouri industrialist F. Gano Chance and the Pepsi-Cola Bottling Company of St Louis, the latter initiating a practice that became common among corporate sponsors: some of their employees were paid to be present as a "patriotic duty." There was little advertising, and only a few newsletters published by small anticommunist groups seem to have taken notice of the event.[4]

The idea of week-long seminars had been on Schwarz's mind for some time. The formula offered a way of educating individuals who came to him rather than having him tour endlessly to reach the corners of any given state. This model would also allow for the recruiting and educating of new activists in a manner similar to that of George Benson's Freedom Forum. Moreover, by the late 1950s, popular demand for Schwarz's lectures had risen to the point at which he had to turn down an ever-growing number of requests. "I find it impossible," Schwarz observed upon launching the first school, "to fulfil all the possible engagements that are open in this great land." Forming leaders was a better strategy: "On the other hand, if I spoke to one person a week and convinced that person, and together we each spoke to another person the following week and convinced that person, and this process continued, we could reach everyone in the world in less than twelve months."[5]

The week-long seminar format was also in line with the evangelical culture and its tradition of collective happenings, such as the old-fashioned camp-meeting, in which attendees could, without interruption, be immersed in a transformative experience. Schwarz had appeared at many YFC rallies, and the CACC had itself organized a five-day seminar at the Winona Lake Bible Conferences in 1956. However, the biggest influence on CACC schools was, by Schwarz's admission, Billy Graham's revivals. "Look," he once told a journalist, "if you're trying to find out about my religious beliefs, I'll tell you, I very much admire Billy Graham and I try to pattern my rallies after his approach."[6]

Given the circumstances, the St Louis school was a success. The CACC's resources were so scarce then that anything more than a hundred attendees would have been deemed a success. In the end, 130 people showed up. Schwarz particularly liked the opportunity of seeing, under the same roof, audiences that, up until that time, he had encountered separately. "There were preachers from many denominations including Catholic priests. Businessmen mingled with men of manual labor. Attorneys jostled with housewives." A representative sent by the Associated Industries of Missouri wrote to Schwarz: "Without exception, this was one of the great experiences of my life. Others have told me the same thing. A good number of us were utterly exhausted from the emotion stirred by a number of the speakers, the excitement of working together as an organization, and watching you perform daily with such vigor and enthusiasm."[7]

It took four CACC schools before Schwarz came up with a definitive formula that would be successfully applied over the years. The Crusade's second school got under way in December 1958 at the First Brethren Church of Long Beach. Walter Judd appeared for the first time at a CACC school, initiating two decades of regular appearances. All of the school sessions were recorded, allowing for the subsequent selling and distribution of tapes. Another novelty was that the Crusade wooed public authorities for some level of endorsement, thus providing the event with local respectability. Schwarz stated afterwards that the "attendance at the Long Beach School included Security Officers of the Los Angeles Police Dept. and the Los Angeles Sheriffs Dpt." The Long Beach school produced two future directors of Crusade branches.[8]

The third CACC school was held in Indianapolis in late September and early October 1959. Expanding financial resources permitted for a distinctly secular location: the Washington Hotel in downtown Indianapolis. The daily sessions were extended by a few hours with the addition of an evening session, making each school day an eleven-hour event ending at 9:30 p.m., and bringing the week's exhausting schedule to fifty-five hours (at least for those who did not miss a session). Schwarz elaborated an "academic freedom" policy, according to which ideas expressed by his collaborators were deemed not to represent the opinion of the Crusade.

The Indianapolis school initiated the logistical blueprint that characterized all later schools. This is perhaps where Schwarz's admission of Billy Graham's influence is most apparent. Though many people attributed the success of his revivals to the miraculous work of the Holy Spirit, Graham's urban mass gatherings were in fact carefully prepared. The Billy Graham Evangelistic Association did not undertake a citywide crusade before securing a critical mass of local support. Once a location had been chosen, the BGEA's team sent a staff member to oversee preparations (this was often James Colbert's job in the CACC). A local office was set up, from which the groundwork was undertaken: linking the national organization to the local community, recruiting volunteers, setting up local committees, raising funds, appealing for the support of local citizens and institutions.

The Crusade would choose a city in which it was deemed that a core of activists would be able to support a week-long event. The most dedicated local supporters formed a central committee in charge of providing logistics, advertising, and financial support. This group had to be composed of prominent citizens whose names conferred respectability. In Indianapolis, it included as chairman Reverend Russell Blowers, minister of the East 49th Street Christian Church; local radio commentator Don Bruce, who, in 1960, would be elected GOP representative of Indianapolis; and John Lynn, an executive for the Eli Lilly and Company pharmaceutical group who, in 1961, would join the Lilly Endowment as general manager.[9]

Supporters formed subcommittees to meet the school's specific needs. Local preparatory rallies designed to stimulate interest in the school, raise funds, and enlist more supporters or attendees were later set up. The Indianapolis school also initiated the ritual of ending each event with a banquet. With time, this event took on huge proportions with, in some cases, thousands of people attending. An important part of the money grossed by each school came from banquet contributions and sales.[10]

The Indianapolis school was also the first school in which the CACC managed to enlist a local politician to proclaim an "Anticommunism Week" – that is, effective, free advertising. Organizers approached GOP governor Harold W. Handley, who encouraged the electorate to learn of "the insidious workings of an international conspiracy that [was] dedicated to the destruction of our fundamental constitutional rights as free men." Handley also paid an unexpected visit to the school during one class. Such endorsements facilitated attempts to garner support from other public institutions. In Indianapolis, for the first time, the CACC had the formal backing of the local school board, which sent off teachers to attend the school's hour-and-a-half sessions. Four hundred people registered for the Indianapolis school, more than twice the number that did so in St Louis and Long Beach the year before.[11]

Most importantly, the 1959 Indianapolis school saw the addition of two new "faculty" members: W. Cleon Skousen and Herbert Philbrick. By and large, Schwarz, Skousen, and Philbrick ran the show. They even came to be called "The Big 3" on some records containing lectures sold across the nation.

Skousen was a Mormon lay pastor who had worked for the FBI until 1951. In 1956, he was appointed chief of police of Salt Lake City, but, in 1960, he was fired by the city's mayor, J. Bracken Lee, after raiding an illegal card game attended by the mayor himself. Meanwhile, Skousen devoted much time to writing and lecturing, where he revealed himself as an unabashed right-winger whose views were often expressed in conspiratorial fashion. His 1958 book *The Naked Communist*, an exposé of Communism that became a bestseller due to its breezy style, wove within its rather conventional text threads of bombastic sensationalism. Skousen claimed the USSR designed *Sputnik* with plans stolen in the United States and that FDR's secretary of commerce, Harry Hopkins, attempted to provide the Soviets with the secrets of the A-bomb in 1943 (when it had not yet been developed). Internal FBI correspondence indicates that, from 1960 on, Skousen angered his former employers, who felt he inflated his counter-subversive record given that his former FBI job was largely secretarial in nature. Of all of the CACC schools' "faculty" members, he became the only one who genuinely tested the Crusade's rather extensive "academic freedom" policy – to the point at which Schwarz had to cut him loose. Nonetheless, the Mormon trail-blazer added such rhetorical firepower to the schools that he proved a great asset during the three-year period he and Schwarz collaborated.[12]

Herbert Philbrick accepted the invitation to Indianapolis on short notice despite his busy schedule. He was then the United States's most in-demand anticommunist lecturer as it appeared he could spend the rest of his life getting mileage out of his undercover agent fame. The continuing success of *I Led Three Lives*, both as a book

5.1 | Herbert Philbrick signing autographs at the Los Angeles School of Anti-Communism, 1961. *Los Angeles Times* Photographic Archives.

and as a TV series that was rerun several times, kept his name in circulation in popular culture. Philbrick did not have the oratorical flair of either Schwarz or Skousen, but his personal story added such a sense of drama to the proceedings that he was the most popular speaker at CACC schools. Most of his speeches were in fact variations on one theme: his experience as an infiltrator of Communists.

While frequently scorning liberals, Philbrick remained careful not to lump them and Communists in the same category. A journalist who attended one of his lectures noted that "he always left the feeling that there was a conspiracy going on and that you had better look hard at your neighbors," but "he was careful not to say anything without crediting it to the HUAC or the Senate Internal Security Subcommittee or the Congressional Record."[13]

Philbrick was so satisfied with his experience in Indianapolis that he continued to make appearances at CACC schools for little compensation. He had an exclusive contract with his lecturing agency, but a special clause permitted him to address "educational" institutions. The CACC thus paid him a mere one hundred dollars, plus covering travel and accommodation expenses. As Philbrick explained to one of his contacts, he did this because he felt indebted to Schwarz for his work of awakening the American public. Before long, Schwarz's influence on Philbrick was apparent. A few days after the closing of the Indianapolis school, he began feeding his supporters CACC material and affirming that the communist domination of the world could come as early as 1973.[14]

In February 1960, Milwaukee, Allen-Bradley's turf, was the site of the fourth CACC school and the one in which the formula took its classic form. It was in Milwaukee that the CACC commenced the policy whereby, if possible, each school would feature at least one lecture given by a military officer and another given by a recognized conservative academic. In Milwaukee, the military was represented by Rear Admiral A.C. Burrows, former commanding officer of the Great Lakes Naval Training Center. Academia was represented by political scientist Anthony Bouscaren, a *National Review* collaborator. In spite of a snowstorm that had blanketed Milwaukee area, the school attracted more than eight hundred "note-jotting students." "Nothing in my experience," Schwarz concluded in his newsletter, "can have such a dramatic influence in any area as one of these schools. They awaken the slumbering, encourage the despairing, inspire the patriotic, set hearts on fire and Christians to work in the service of Christian liberty." Each event had been followed by its share of exuberant testimonies. An article published in June 1961 on the anticommunist movement in Milwaukee indicated that numerous conservative militants "got their start after attending" the CACC school of February 1960.[15]

ROOTS TO BRANCHES

With Schwarz's growing notoriety, his new friends in the big business community, and the success of the CACC schools, the Crusade's financial resources flourished. From about $63,000 in 1957, the amount netted by the CACC rose to $110,000 in 1958, $197,000 in 1959, and $369,000 in 1960 – a sixfold increase in four years. Nonetheless, the CACC never amassed any substantial surplus during these years as its expenses also increased. During the 1958–1960 period, these expenses amounted to more than $600,000, of which more than 38 percent were devoted to administration. This was largely caused by a new development for the CACC: the opening of subsidiary branches.[16]

Between 1958 and 1961, the Crusade grew from having one to having eight different US branches, with new locations established in Houston, San Francisco, San Diego, Seattle, Philadelphia, Ypsilanti, and Indianapolis. The main office in Long Beach was renamed "international headquarters and executive office." Upon W.E. Pietsch's death, the Crusade's main managerial position was taken over by Colbert, who took the title of vice-president and became responsible for the Long Beach office. Colbert was confirmed in his role as Schwarz's right-hand man.[17]

Schwarz only allowed branches to be led by persons whom he knew personally and who held respectable positions in their communities. Only one branch director, Bill Strube in Houston, worked on a full-time basis, and, as such, he was the only one to receive a salary from the Crusade. The Houston branch was also the only subsidiary that developed a notable team of staffers. Two branches, in Houston and San Diego, respectively, published their own newsletters. The CACC provided each branch with a great deal of material to sell, rent, and distribute. Branches solicited contributions, advertised local events pertaining to the good fight, and helped organize the visits of Schwarz and his friends. In 1960, the CACC's administrative costs reached the threshold of $100,000, and the organization bought more than $40,978 worth of books, tapes, and films.[18]

Some subsidiary branches were short-lived. A good example is the Seattle branch, founded by Charles Sarvis, a restaurant-owning businessman known for his involvement in the YFC movement and in Baptist churches in the Seattle area. This branch's activity did not extend past 1961. The Philadelphia office, located in the National Bank Building and led by a former missionary named Richard W. Hightower, who had worked in refugees' camps in Kenya, lasted for two years, from 1960 to 1962. An office was opened in San Diego in May 1961 but closed after its director, E. Richard Barnes, a retired military captain who first collaborated with the CACC in the 1960 school in Milwaukee, was elected as Republican state representative in 1962.[19]

The four Crusade branches in Indianapolis, Ypsilanti, San Francisco, and Houston lasted longer than those mentioned above. The Indianapolis branch existed until the late 1960s. Its local director, Floyd E. Burroughs, and his wife Ruth remained on the board of the CACC until the late 1980s. A Second World War navy veteran, Burroughs founded in the 1950s Floyd E. Burroughs and Associates, Inc., a civil engineering firm. The CACC branch in Indianapolis was maintained through the devotion of a small group of volunteers. One such volunteer was Jan Conner, a housewife whom the Burroughs met through their common involvement in the Goldwater movement in 1964. Over three decades, Conner could regularly be seen in public places in Indianapolis wearing her red-white-and-blue outfit and selling the flag pins, greeting cards, and sweat shirts that allowed her to amass a total of $40,000 for the Crusade.[20]

In Ypsilanti, Michigan, the branch lasted until the late 1960s. Its director was Dr George Westcott, another personal friend of Schwarz, and one of his earliest US supporters. This graduate of the University of Michigan Medical School and former missionary in Africa who had a medical practice in Ypsilanti met Schwarz in 1953. Westcott brought with him his expertise in radio technology and became the CACC's recording technician. Each time a Crusade event of some significance took place, he would leave his practice under the care of a colleague and come down to do a recording. In the early 1960s, Westcott spent a lot of time as medical missionary in the Caribbean, especially in Haiti, where he spread the anticommunist message using his knowledge of the French language, which he had acquired in Africa.[21]

The two most important Crusade subsidiary offices were those in San Francisco and in Houston. In San Francisco, the local director was Joost Sluis, another medical doctor-turned-evangelist. Sluis was a Netherlands native whose family immigrated to the United States in 1935, when he was twelve. Raised in the Dutch Reformed tradition,

5.2 | William Strube in 1961. *Los Angeles Times* Photographic Archives.

he attended Calvin College, accepting Jesus as his personal saviour during this time. He graduated as an MD from Harvard University in 1951. He settled in the San Francisco area, established a practice as an orthopaedic surgeon, and became part of the University of California's medical faculty. As with many others, his life changed when he heard Schwarz speak, in this case before a meeting of the Christian Medical Society in July 1958. Sluis tried to return to his normal life but often spent wakeful nights wondering "whether patient care and possible personal contributions to improved orthopaedic surgery were the highest services I could render to humanity." He later attended the CACC school in Long Beach, which convinced him to open, in 1959, the San Francisco Crusade branch office. For a few years, the buttery baritone voice of the tall, eternally baby-faced Sluis belonged to the Crusade in Northern California.[22]

The Houston chapter, led by William P. Strube, was the Crusade's most important subsidiary branch. It kicked off in March 1958. Strube, then a Missouri native in his mid-thirties, was the living incarnation of Southern culture's blend of folksy traditionalism, energetic anticommunism, commitment to the spirit of free market capitalism, and conservative evangelicalism ("I am a Bible-reading, Christ-honoring Christian who believes the Bible and Jesus are exactly what they say they are"). Navy man during the Second World War and founder of the Mid-American Life Insurance Company, Strube had first heard Schwarz in Redondo Beach, Southern California, in 1952. He told a reporter, "I shivered and shook for ten minutes, took a towel of apathy and went about my way." Two years later, he wrote: "Here in Houston, the message began to penetrate into the frontal lobe of my brain. Many of the predictions of the first message had already become a reality." When Schwarz toured in Houston in the spring of 1955, Strube ran into the Australian again and considered this to be a sign. Within months he found himself "executive secretary" of the Crusade. In the organization, Strube was the fieldworker who, apart from Schwarz, went the furthest along his own path.[23]

The Houston chapter was housed in a large pink stucco mansion on Montrose Boulevard in Houston, home to Strube's business. Strube's anticommunist activities were initially a non-salaried sideline to his insurance business, but they soon evolved into a full-time involvement. By his own count, Strube spoke 150 times during the Houston office's first year, but the figure jumped to three hundred times in 1959 and about four hundred times in 1960. Journalist Philip Horton from the *Reporter* magazine gave more precise figures, noting that in 1960 the Houston branch "offered 314 lectures to sixteen thousand students and forty-six thousand adults." By the spring of 1960, Strube was conducting seminars in Miami, Colorado, Louisiana, Missouri, and New Mexico. Strube's audiences were the same as Schwarz's: churches, service clubs, veterans associations, schools, chambers of commerce, conservative meetings, and occasionally elected representatives (e.g., Strube addressed the Louisiana state legislature in May 1960). Strube, a handsome blue-eyed man in his mid-thirties at the time, was, as *Harper's* journalist Willie Morris noted, a "fearsome platform orator, often hypnotic in effect," employing the rapid-fire delivery characteristic of the Southern Baptist tradition. Strube's 1962 book *The Star over the Kremlin*, is a readable rehash of Schwarz's ideas.[24]

In 1961, at its peak, the Houston branch office had more than fifteen staff members and had evolved into what a journalist called "a nerve center of a new, modern evangelism." While Schwarz preferred live audiences to electric media, Strube was a fervent proponent of technology and was instrumental in persuading Schwarz to remain abreast of the times. "By using tape-recordings," Strube said, "the experts can be taken into homes, schools, Sunday schools, classes." The Crusade had its own recording studio in the Houston office and Strube busied himself with making tape recordings. One journalist who visited the office noted that it was filled with "nine portable tape recorders, worth about $4,000, tended by earphoned technicians making tapes of the talks of Strube," an "automatic typewriter, worth $3,000," along with "three giant tape-reproducing machines putting out taped lectures, suggestions and instructions for conducting study groups, clinics and seminars."[25]

In 1961 and 1962, Strube designed two comic strips for children, *Two Faces of Communism* and *Double Talk*, both available for a time in various supermarkets and stores across the South and Southwest. Both cartoons expand on the same concept. Two white, middle-class kids who have just heard about communism begin to ask questions of an adult. The adult is a "father-knows-best" suburban character who is the spitting image of Bill Strube – and is in fact called "Bill." In one strip, he talks to his nephews, while in the other he addresses his own children. The main narrative is interspersed with evocative images in which communism is personified by Khrushchev himself. In *Two Faces of Communism*, arguably the better-written of the cartoons, Bill admits that he had once been under the influence of a foreign-born college professor who organized secret meetings at which Bill and two of his peers were indoctrinated with communist propaganda. Torn between his loyalties to the proletariat on the one hand, and to God and his country on the other, Bill found strength in the Bible and informed the police about his teacher, who was quietly removed from his position and deported as an undesirable alien. Freed from the influence of their teacher, Bill and his classmates "found other outlets for their energies. Today they are both successful businessmen!" Bill also tells his kids of the potential effects of a Soviet agent let "loose in our slum area": such a person would incite the homeless to invade private homes. *Two Faces of Communism* is a caricatured encapsulation of McCarthyism. It contains a polemic against left-wing intellectuals; a celebration of the fatherly figure as a source of guidance; a belief in God, country, and capitalism; a touch of xenophobia; as well as a glorification of the informant.[26]

As the Crusade's schools of anticommunism were taking off, Strube began organizing his own seminar-type events. In 1958, in the wake of the first CACC school in St Louis, the Houston branch assembled its first seminar, a project in which Schwarz was not involved (apart from delivering an address at the event's closing session). The 1958 edition was successful enough to produce annual sequels in the following years. In March 1960, Strube managed to gather one thousand people at Rice University's S.P. Martel Auditorium of Houston. Another seminar, held at the Shamrock Hilton, drew more than twenty-five hundred people in 1961.

THE SOUTHERN STRATEGY AND RACE

The Houston branch allowed the Crusade's visibility to soar in the western part of the old South. In March 1959, three years after he spoke before the General Assembly of the State of Georgia, Schwarz was invited to address the Texas state legislature in Austin, delivering his routine from the speaker's rostrum in an atmosphere of solemnity and gravity. As opposed to what happened in Georgia, where there was a tradition of not printing speeches made by outside speakers in the official record, Texas legislators overrode this rule and voted to include his speech in the House journal.[27]

Schwarz's first Texas tour in 1955 occurred just after the Supreme Court's *Brown* decision on school segregation, at a moment when Dixie saw the upsurge of the White Citizens' Council movement in defense of racial orthodoxy. Almost immediately, the South, where anticommunism had until then less traction than it had in the rest of the nation, underwent its own "black-red scare," which kicked off after the *Brown* decision. This black-red connection (i.e., the idea that the civil rights movement was infiltrated, or even controlled by, communists) was to be found in the segregationist imagination – and thus in a significant proportion of the white population – in the following years.[28]

In Houston, the CACC's only genuine Southern base, white resistance to integration was not higher than in other areas of the region.

Still, African American Houstonians only began to have equal access to public transportation and accommodation from the mid-1950s on, and the public school system did not integrate before the mid-1960s. Considering that most public facilities remained segregated as long as the CACC Houston branch existed (from 1958 to 1962), it is likely that the great majority of the organization's public activities in the area took place in non-integrated settings. Besides, anticommunist meetings were not likely to attract more than a small minority of African Americans, even if the venue allowed them to attend.[29]

Interestingly, Schwarz did not openly exploit the black-red theories his Southern audiences were craving during that era. None of the available speeches he delivered in the South during that period contain references to the race question. When interviewed in Dallas by conservative radio host Dan Smoot, a man who believed that the "evil bondage to the white man ... was, physically, an actual improvement upon the life which [blacks] had made for themselves in Africa," and who saw the civil rights movement as part of the "communist program of racial agitation in the United States," the issue was skirted, and the exchange was devoid of any references to desegregation, states' rights, or "outside" agitation. Bill Strube, the CACC's Southern ambassador, was equally silent on the race question. In interviews, pamphlets, speeches, and his 1962 book *The Star over the Kremlin*, he did not address the race issue, even in a coded way. Race was almost absent from all topics addressed in the Crusade's published material and during the events it organized across the nation, except for occasionally criticizing communist propaganda for its attacks on the United States over its record of ethnic and racial discrimination. Throughout the postwar years, both Soviet and Chinese propaganda efforts in the developing world continuously and effectively emphasized the irony inherent in the sheer contradiction between US rhetoric on democracy and liberal values and US repression of racial minorities at home. US officials were well aware of the negative international impact of civil rights struggles on the country's image, especially within a global context of decolonization.[30]

The crusader's quietism on the race issue derived from both personal and strategic factors. On a personal level, he never showed any inclination towards racial prejudice. During his youth, Queensland was an ethnic and racial patchwork within which diversity coexisted with a high degree of discrimination against immigrant communities. Being an immigrant's son whose family had itself experienced stigmatization and intolerance, and having grown up in a nonconformist tradition that was much less affected by the imperialistic and nationalistic overtones that characterized early twentieth-century evangelicalism in Australia, Schwarz never internalized this feature of his native region's culture. Also, his scientific background probably exposed him to the artificiality of racial differences. Another probable factor was his concern to protect the CACC's tax-exempt status by avoiding addressing issues deemed to be too linked to domestic politics.[31]

But his outlook on this issue was mostly faith-based. "Christianity," he once wrote, "is anti-racist. Christianity teaches that all men are sinners and are equal before God." In due course, he would always, both in public writings and private correspondence, refer to friends and sympathizers from any country as "brothers" regardless of their ethnicity, origin, or skin colour. However, Schwarz's individualized theology, common among conservative Protestants, tainted his approach to racism. Racism was a human flaw like any other, the unfortunate consequence of ethnic groups living together. Because "race consciousness has its roots deep in human nature and not merely in the external economic environment," the only solutions to it are grounded in the individual. To that extent, Schwarz's approach was in harmony with that of his core white evangelical supporters, whose "long-standing antistatism" reinforced a general "reluctance to act on racial issues or to support the nascent civil rights movement," which, by the mid-1950s, had evolved into a general blaming of the judicial branch and the courts for undermining American freedoms, as historian Matthew Sutton points out.[32]

When, in the mid-1960s, he began addressing the issue of urban race riots, he made sure that his tirades on the allegedly Communist-inspired racial strife in the United States were accompanied by condemnations of racism: "Racism should be eliminated entirely from human consciousness and conduct. Unfortunately, that situation has not been reached anywhere in the world, not even in the U.S.A." However, such denunciations of racism did not come until the mid-1960s and were always framed in general, vague terms. Before that, the only exception was an extract from a 1963 interview in which he compared the ideological blindness of liberals who rejected the HUAC's work to that of "Southerners who reject the Supreme Court's ruling on segregation."[33]

CACC's approach was also basic common sense for Schwarz and his collaborators. They considered the race issue rather unimportant amid the grand power struggle between freedom and tyranny, and even though they were not disposed to encourage black-red gibberish to grow in the South, it would have been surprising if they had passed up on the opportunity the area presented from the mid-1950s on. Schwarz thus applied the same strategic ambivalence to segregation as he did to any other topic deemed overtly controversial: he let audiences read their own meanings into his words. He could not ignore the fact that any headway made in the South through openly embracing black-red theories – for which he never showed any interest before the mid-1960s urban race riots – might have cost him credibility elsewhere, especially among his upper-class, educated supporters in other areas of the country. This fence-sitting perhaps lessened the CACC's appeal among some white supremacists, but it still left the organization attractive enough to many across the country who embraced anticommunism as a back-door way to slam desegregation. Also, polling data on the CACC shows that, even though its non-Southern supporters rejected segregation in proportions comparable to Northern whites, many of them shared traits with conservative Southerners in their political outlook: they were hostile towards bureaucratization and federal intrusions in the realms of education and business, and they deeply loathed the Warren Supreme Court.[34]

In October 1961, the CACC held two successive anticommunism schools in Louisiana, the only ones ever to have taken place in the Deep South, and both were held in all-white, fully segregated settings. In Shreveport, one of the strongholds of the White Citizens' Council movement and one of the last cities in the state to fully desegregate its public spaces and transportation, sessions took place at the Hirsch Youth Center and the Municipal Auditorium. Two weeks later, in New Orleans, the Crusade held a similar event at the Jung Hotel, a facility that was racially integrated only two years later, in 1963. Yet, in both cases, discussions on race were avoided largely by way of not including local personalities among the school's "faculty." Surprisingly, none of the crusader's liberal detractors ever seems to have used the holding of these schools against him (assuming they had knowledge of them).[35]

Successful as they were, something about these schools seems to have made Schwarz uncomfortable. The Crusade never held any subsequent major event in the Deep South. In 1966, the CACC organized a two-hour rally in Virginia Beach designed to assess the local interest for a week-long anticommunism school. It was attended by a non-segregated, though overwhelmingly white, audience of two thousand and was supported by the local mayor Frank A. Dusch. However, not only was the financial response disappointing but Schwarz told a reporter that the CACC did not wish to be associated with people or groups promoting racism. With regard to this, he mentioned having "encountered some people [at the Virginia Beach rally] who ha[d]n't grasped that point." The project of a Virginia school was dropped.[36]

Schwarz exercised the same calculated, yet uneasy ambivalence in the Crusade's relationships with religious groups from South Africa, the country in which the CACC organized most of its (rather few) African initiatives during the 1950s, and in which Afrikaner elites often justified their racial outlook by framing it within Cold War politics. The policy of apartheid was implemented after the 1948 election, which saw the rise of the main Afrikaner nationalist political force, the Herenigde Nasionale Party. The Communist Party of South Africa was declared illegal in 1950, but anticommunist laws became a convenient tool for white elites to use to oppress anti-apartheid militants.[37]

During the Eisenhower years, the US government remained noncommittal on the apartheid issue. Washington was not only ill-suited to criticize South Africa, in light of its own domestic race problem, but it also wished to maintain good relationships with that country. This was because South Africa was both an important player in the Western alliance (due to its key geographical location) and an important supplier of uranium and ore. Things only began to change in 1960 with the widely condemned Sharpeville massacre, in which the South African police killed dozens of black protesters. The shooting coincided with the rise of the US civil rights movement and the Kennedy presidency, which took a harsher stance towards apartheid than had previous administrations. The World Council of Churches, which had been silent on apartheid for fear of alienating the Dutch Reformed churches, also now began condemning it. Upon his first African tour in early 1960, Billy Graham declined to preach in South Africa due to his inability to conduct integrated meetings.[38]

Schwarz did not face the same choice as Graham, as his relationship with South Africa was limited to providing anticommunist material and some funding. In 1956, he began requesting financial contributions from his supporters to send material to small South African evangelical institutions. By late 1957, Schwarz gave his copyright for *The Heart, Mind and Soul of Communism*, his best booklet for church audiences, to South Africa's Evangelical Alliance Mission. In 1957 in Houston, Strube met Don and Faye Smith, missionaries of the South Africa General Mission, established in the late twentieth century, and the work of which extended to numerous African countries. They told Strube about their idea for a Christian anticommunist magazine in South Africa, a project that was given consideration when the CACC's resources widened. In late 1958, the first copies of *Our Africa*, printed, with the help of four reporters, in the garage of a missionary in Johannesburg, were sent to Schwarz, who had invested $1,000 in this project. "To say that we are astonished by the superb quality is an understatement. The magazine is the size of 'Life.' It has 36 pages." For a few years, *Our Africa* was published and distributed on a monthly basis, allowing its circulation (about thirty thousand copies) to spread in the African south and west (South Africa, Kenya, Uganda, and Southern Rhodesia, now Zimbabwe).[39]

Reflecting the South Africa General Mission's official policy, *Our Africa*, which featured the work of black Christian leader S.E.M. Pheko, opposed apartheid, while the great majority of white South African churches upheld the racial status quo. Still, the magazine and its publishers seemed in line with the Crusade's realpolitik stance: no cause was worthy enough to justify the support of Communists. In 1958, commenting on a famous trial that saw 156 anti apartheid leaders (including Nelson Mandela) prosecuted for alleged treason, one of the Mission's members wrote a letter to Strube that was partly reproduced in the CACC newsletter. "By subtly and persistently stressing the wrongs of the white government," it lamented, "[communism] is twisting a legitimate cause to its own ends. Communism becomes the champion – whites and their Christianity become the oppressor."[40]

The amount of money the Crusade sent to South Africa dropped after 1961. While it remains impossible to determine whether this drop resulted from the backlash following the Sharpeville massacre and the growing hostility towards apartheid, this does not appear to be the case. In 1960, Schwarz consented for his *You Can Trust the Communists (to Be Communists)* to be translated into Afrikaans by a Johannesburg publishing house. Until the early 1990s, when the apartheid regime collapsed, his message was unchanged: apartheid was admittedly bad, but the Communists' exploitation of the issue was even worse. He condemned Nelson Mandela's left-wing party, the African National Congress (ANC), because, he thought, it was "controlled" by Communists. When, in 1973, Billy Graham made his first trip to South Africa, where he condemned apartheid before integrated crowds, Schwarz made no comments. When the Crusade's finances soared again in the 1980s, allowing it to once more ship literature in huge quantities worldwide, South Africa was again on the mailing lists.[41]

The Crusade's racial policy (or lack thereof) reflected several elements: Schwarz's own view of bigotry as an individual, not a collective, sin; his strategy to stay above the fray of controversies while capitalizing on the colour-blind potential of anticommunism to quietly reach various audiences, some of which he knew adhered to black-red theories; and his life-long conviction that communism dwarfed all other problems afflicting the world, thus commanding a policy that, provided it stopped the expansion of communism, gave little attention to civil liberties.

However, considering his core strategy – that is, winning the anticommunist struggle primarily through arguments rather than might – this approach was somewhat inconsistent. Schwarz, ardent promoter of an aggressive propaganda-based strategy, seemed oblivious to the fact that the race issue constituted one of the biggest problems to the credibility of the United States (and the Western world) in the Cold War, thereby providing Communist individuals, parties, and regimes with endless stories to feed their anti-American or anti-imperialist tirades. And the crusader's criticism of Communists for taking advantage of racial strife to undermine the free world, both in the United States and abroad, was deceptive in light of his own strategy on racial matters. But, as with many subjects, his approach to race was incidental to his central commitment.

6

The Changing Face of Anticommunism

THE GRASSROOTS

In an address delivered in April 1954, President Eisenhower reaffirmed Washington's commitment to fighting the Kremlin's ideology and "plans to enslave the world." But Eisenhower also implicitly cautioned the public against any anticommunist craze, stressing that not only had the domestic fear "been greatly exaggerated as to numbers" but also that "our great defense against those people is the FBI." It was no coincidence that this address was delivered during the televised hearings of the Senate's Subcommittee on Investigations into alleged communist infiltration in the army, which had turned public opinion against Joe McCarthy. Eisenhower's message, targeting McCarthy's base and, more generally, the Republican right, was clear: fighting Communism was a job for professionals.[1]

At this point many could only agree with the president that the communist threat was essentially external. By the mid-1950s, especially among liberals, the prevailing perception was that Communism should be resisted through progressive social and political reforms at home, coupled with an international containment strategy framed in political (rather than military) terms, embracing, for instance, collaboration with the UN and the negotiation of arms control agreements. This was, in a nutshell, the essence of the "Cold War liberalism" (also called the "liberal consensus" or "Vital Center") theorized by Arthur M. Schlesinger Jr and other intellectuals. This line of thought saw little, if any, use for popular anticommunist activism since the state was the sole entity with the proper resources and conscientiousness to take on the challenge. Schwarz once deplored: "While many liberals may not be pro-communist, they tend to be suspicious of anti-communists. They examine critically any statement by an anti-communist and seek to find some minor flaw which will justify them in rejecting it." For him, this was an absurdity: "Marxism and liberalism are incompatible. Marxism is based on class and liberalism on the individual. The Marxists have long recognized this incompatibility and have always regarded the liberals with withering contempt."[2]

At the peak of McCarthyism, many liberals had committed themselves to the domestic anticommunist drive. Communists were driven out of most of organized labour and the Democratic coalition. But as McCarthyism subsided, anticommunist militancy became an almost exclusively conservative trait. By the late 1950s, this shift was clearly perceptible in the way the left rejected popular anticommunism, disdaining the zealous intensity that characterized grassroots conservatives. Schwarz's two liberal collaborators – Democratic senator from Connecticut Thomas Dodd and labour leader from the Upholsterers' International Union of North America Arthur G. McDowell – were regularly castigated among their peers for their association with the Crusade.[3]

Like other anticommunist figures, Schwarz began to be criticized for suggesting that public authorities were not capable of adequately informing the public about communism. "The very notion that a vigilante committee is necessary in our country is, of course, a manifestation of an outrageous disregard for American legal tradition," wrote one of Schwarz's foes, liberal pastor Brooks Walker, in his 1963 book *The Christian Fright Peddlers*. For their part, conservatives believed that communism remained the most important problem facing the United States and that government initiatives alone were far from sufficient. In 1962, during a luncheon talk before hundreds of entrepreneurs in San Francisco, Schwarz tapped into conservatives' most heartfelt anxieties by pointing out that exclusive state control over the anticommunist fight amounted to handing over to the state a monopoly that could ultimately "result in complete governmental control of education, foreign trade, information, management and labor."[4]

By the mid-1950s, the mounting evidence regarding the Soviets' appalling human rights record reinforced the right wing's determination to keep the fight alive. In February 1956, Soviet leader Nikita Khrushchev delivered his "secret speech" at the USSR's 20th

Congress, detailing the crimes of Stalin. Three months later, the *New York Times* headlined the story. The "secret speech" confirmed the worst fears about the Soviet Union. This document became one of Schwarz's favourite talking points. In it, Khrushchev explained that ninety-eight of the 139 members of the committee that had elected Stalin had been executed, a fact Schwarz once compared to the pope suddenly declaring that "70 per cent of the Cardinals had been disguised Presbyterians all their lives and would need to be excommunicated." Additionally, because Khrushchev criticized these purges from a Marxist-Leninist viewpoint, since 60 percent of the victims were in fact of working-class origin and thus unlikely to be enemies of the people, Schwarz concluded that, had Stalin "merely arrested and executed 40 per cent of the central committee, Khrushchev could not have spoken a word against his act."[5]

In 1956, President Eisenhower ran for a second term. To right-wingers, his record against the Communist Bloc was disappointing. Promises to "liberate enslaved countries" were long gone. Eisenhower had settled for a peace in Korea that came without a victory, and no assistance was sent to support Hungary's 1956 anti-Soviet uprising. Many resented that in 1954 Eisenhower had stood up against the Bricker Amendment, a piece of legislation that would have invalidated any part of an international treaty that conflicted with the US Constitution. Domestically, right-wingers found the president's record equally condemnable. The return of the GOP to the White House did not alter the fact that "the pattern of American fiscal policy," as General MacArthur put it, "[was] being brought into consonance with the Karl Marx communist theory that through a division of the existing wealth mankind [would] be brought to a universal standard of life." Furthermore, the Supreme Court's "pro-red" decisions kept piling up.[6]

In sum, on the one hand, there was mounting evidence of the Communist Bloc's calamitous human rights record; on the other, the anticommunist struggle seemed to be on a losing path. The combination of these two factors fuelled the vehemence that characterized the right wing during the second half of the 1950s. Complicating the matter was the fact that the face of the enemy had evolved. During the McCarthy years, the paradigmatic figure of internal subversion in the conservative subculture was the spy or the traitor, a deceitful Communist working under a cloak of respectability (like Alger Hiss and Harry Dexter White or, in popular culture, murderers in Mickey

Spillane's novels). However, by the end of the decade, many were inclined to see the whole structure of postwar liberalism as a communist enterprise. While this viewpoint was already present in the rhetoric of some opponents of the New Deal in the 1930s and 1940s, by the late 1950s, this view had undeniably gained momentum. Numerous books published by this time captured these fears. With its self-explanatory title, Frank Chodorov's 1954 *The Income Tax: The Root of All Evil* traced back the conspiracy to the days of Woodrow Wilson. In the same year, right-wing journalist Chesly Manly framed things in similarly terms in *The Twenty-Year Revolution: From Roosevelt to Eisenhower.* "The Communists," Manly wrote, "and their Marxist cousins, the Socialists, have worked for revolution since the advent of the New Deal twenty-one years ago by infiltrating government offices, labor unions, schools and colleges, churches, radio and television, the movies, the publishing business."[7]

Robert Welch and his John Birch Society came to embody this sensibility. A North Carolina native established in Boston, Welch was a retired businessman – he won the Candy Industry Man of the Year award in 1947 – who had begun writing on political issues in the early 1950s. One of his books, *The Life of John Birch: In the Story of One American Boy, the Ordeal of His Age*, popularized the story of John Birch, a Baptist missionary murdered by Chinese Communists at the close of the Second World War. Birch, Welch wrote, had uncovered a communist plot to take over China, and his death had been hidden by the State Department. Welch found in Birch the hero for his epic narrative of the clash between freedom and collectivism. By the late 1950s, Welch had become convinced that communists would not take over the United States by military means or by electoral politics but, rather, would incrementally seize institutions from within – an interpretation of history that made sense of the continuous expansion of state power. Even if Welch never clearly distinguished between large "C" Communism and small "c" communism, such a distinction would have been immaterial since the global collectivist juggernaut against which Welch fought had a life of its own, regardless of party affiliations. Welch founded the *American Opinion*, a magazine that published a yearly scoreboard estimating the level of communist influence over the world's important countries: 100 percent for the USSR; 40 to 60 percent for countries such as France, Norway, and Chile; and 20 to 40 percent for the United States, Britain, and Argentina.[8]

On 9 December 1958, Welch undertook a two-day speaking marathon in Indianapolis before a group of wealthy supporters. The lecture's transcript later became *The Blue Book of the John Birch Society*, a summary of Welch's thought. According to him, the extension of state control "has constituted the greatest tragedy of the twentieth century." The surrender of US sovereignty to the UN, the race riots destabilizing the country, plus the continuous rise of inflation, taxes, and the national debt could only be explained by communist influence. The government could not be depended upon to educate Americans about the conspiracy that had led to this state of affairs; therefore, what was needed was an underground educational program that would be carried out by an organization named after John Birch.[9]

From his office in Belmont, Massachusetts, Welch oversaw the development of the John Birch Society (JBS), which, by its first anniversary in December 1959, had chapters in more than fifteen states and a few thousand members. The JBS was designed to operate outside the public eye: members were encouraged to keep their identity secret, and rules specified that, in order to make infiltration difficult, chapters were to split once a certain membership threshold had been passed. As Rick Perlstein notes, "being a Bircher was *fun*," especially in those very early stages before 1961 when the organization was not yet known to the public and had not yet become a highly polarizing institution. The JBS made it possible for members to think of the secret meetings in their kitchens and living rooms as part of an all-out effort to safeguard freedom. Meanwhile, Welch also developed an interest in the writings of Nesta Webster, which led him to conceive of communism as the latest manifestation of a plot whose origins could be traced back to the Bavarian Illuminati of 1776. By the early 1960s, in the wake of the media's discovery of the JBS's existence, Welch's contentions that communists were "in almost complete control of our Federal government" became, in the eyes of liberals, the classic example of right-wing lunacy. Nonetheless, as Jonathan Schoenwald points out, by expressing a belief shared by millions, Welch filled the void between the end of the McCarthy era and the late 1950s: "Just as McCarthy understood what Americans feared and played a role that took advantage of those fears, Robert Welch realized that he was not alone in his thoughts and that there were plenty of Americans who felt similarly and wanted to do something before it was too late."[10]

While these beliefs reinforced the stigma of insanity that came to be associated with conservative activists, they also undeniably galvanized these people to stand up and fight. In effect, their mobilization, fuelled by a sense of "dispossession," as Daniel Bell puts it, led to their various activities displaying a high level of efficiency and spirit. Within this polarized context, conservative citizens reacted against liberalism nationwide – in education, culture, politics, and economics – by forming or joining local or national groups. Anticommunist, anti-statist, traditionalist, religious, and libertarian free enterprise groups proliferated, with many other groups focusing on specific issues, such as segregationism and anti-Semitism as well as anti-fluoridation, educational, and foreign issues.[11]

The spread of right-wing groups struck many observers of the political and social scene. *Newsweek* conservative columnist Ralph de Toledano wrote: "The fact remains that the American people, for the first time in their history, see defeat looming. Since they get no leadership from their elected officials ... they are seeking it in voluntary associations." Reporting in 1960 on the multiplication of anticommunist groups in Milwaukee, a journalist observed that local anticommunists were more organized and active than ever before: "For concerned action they eclipse even the grassroots effort made in the era of the late Senator Joseph R. McCarthy ... Most groups have formed within the last year." By the end of 1961, columnist John Corlett noted the anticommunist activity in small-town Idaho: "Not since the heyday of Joe McCarthy has there been such interest in anti-communism." A few months later, *Partisan Review* contributor Norman Birnbaum gave a similar assessment from a liberal perspective, remarking that "the decline of anti-Communism among the intellectuals has been accompanied by a recrudescence of a popular anti-Communism which has assumed forms far more malignant than McCarthyism." Astute observers agreed that, somewhere between the early and late 1950s, anticommunism had taken the form of a popular movement, with hundreds of organizations engaged in it throughout the nation.[12]

By the late 1950s, older groups such as the CACC, Carl McIntire's Twentieth-Century Reformation Hour, and Billy James Hargis's Christian Crusade coexisted with a broad constellation of new organizations: the JBS, the Cardinal Mindszenty Foundation, Phoebe Courtney's Conservative Society of America, Constructive Action, the Congress of Freedom, Myers G. Lowman's Circuit Riders Inc., the Foundation for Economic Education, the National Indignation Foundation, We, the People !, the Christian Freedom Foundation, Moral Re-Armament, Inc., and others. Segregationist groups also proliferated during the same period. They appeared overwhelmingly in the South in the wake of the Supreme Court's 1954 *Brown* decision. Besides White Citizens' Councils, which were organized by both Southern elites and grassroots militants, and vigilante groups such as the Ku Klux Klan, about fifty such notable grassroots groups emerged, including the Defenders of State Sovereignty and Individual Liberties, the Patriots, the North Carolina Defenders of States' Rights, and the Federation for Constitutional Government. These groups gradually identified with several conservative traits, such as opposition to statism, bureaucracy, and the New Deal, as well as a virulent form of anticommunism that was unseen during the days of the Dixiecrat Revolt in the late 1940s. Southern resistance to challenges to its racial culture laid the groundwork for its incorporation into the conservative camp.[13]

On a national level, this conservative subculture was highly fragmented. Grassroots conservatism in the mid-1950s was a movement inasmuch as its activists read the same books and newsletters, listened to the same radio broadcasts, and were moved by the same popular anticommunist films (such as *The Iron Curtain* [1948], *My Son John* [1952], and Herbert Philbrick's *I Led Three Lives* TV series). But despite their relative isolation from each other, more prominent groups, including the JBS and, to a lesser extent, the CACC, were able to develop national networks. Newsletters and promotional material from one group often circulated to activists from other areas. Towards the end of the 1950s, the pools of local activists often found themselves supporting larger organizations. For instance, the CACC's anticommunism schools involved members of the JBS and other local groups. In many instances, Schwarz's visit to a given location sparked local activists to form a group that affiliated itself with either the CACC or some other organization. In spring 1960, his tour in St Louis led to the forming of the Four Freedoms Study Groups (FFSGs), which oversaw the forming of smaller anticommunist cells in Missouri and southern Illinois. At the popular level, groups such as the FFSGs acted as multipliers for larger organizations, often using and distributing material from Benson's National Education Program, the JBS, or the Crusade. The FFSGs relied so much on Crusade literature that, in a 1965 audit, IRS officials considered that both groups "should be treated alike for tax purposes."[14]

Estimating how many organizations comprised this macrocosm would be pointless. Groups formed and vanished quickly, with very few attaining national recognition. Many consisted only of a flag-waving citizen, his wife or a few relatives, a stencil duplicator, and a mailing list. Others were new fronts created by activists already involved in other operations. In 1960, the *National Directory of "Rightist" Groups* came up with the figure of a thousand groups by lumping together all conservative, religious, libertarian, segregationist, anti-Semitic, and other far right groups – a number that rose to eighteen hundred in 1961. But even in 1961–62, when this bubbling popular conservatism reached the peak of its influence and activity, it only involved a minority of Republican voters or Democratic voters in the South. Of course, many groups did not issue membership cards, or, like the CACC, did not differentiate between members and other supporters. In 1962, political scientist Alan Westin, building upon rare survey data, estimated that, among the 56 million Americans who had heard about the JBS, only a "hard core" of about 4.5 million (8 percent) held favourable views of the organization and were thus susceptible to actively supporting it.[15]

Moreover, grassroots conservatism was not ideologically homogenous, with activists often experiencing disunity on many issues. Not all groups, let alone individuals, placed the same emphasis on the idea that communism was an imminent threat, and not all ascribed to, or promoted, conspiratorial views. In the realm of foreign policy, a long isolationist tradition, especially popular among libertarians (who connected foreign interventions with domestic governmental expansion), coexisted with a growing call for involvement in world affairs to defeat the Communist Bloc. This aggressive stance, promoted notably by Buckley's *National Review*, aimed at containing, and if possible rolling back, international Communism wherever it existed, and it became increasingly popular among the right wing throughout the 1950s.[16]

Another example is the issue of water fluoridation, which many saw as illegitimate state intervention in an aspect of daily life. In 1962, the National Committee against Fluoridation listed more than fourteen hundred communities that had rejected fluoridation nationwide. Fluoridation was perceived as socialized medicine because the government, not a doctor, "prescribed" the medication and because tax revenues were used to fund it. Some even claimed that it was a communist plot to physically weaken the American public. But others, like Schwarz, had no interest in the issue. The Australian considered it to be pure distraction, if not tripe. A member of a liberal group who once sneaked into a CACC event reported about Schwarz's response to a question on how fluoridation and communism related to one another: "Schwarz seemed to ridicule the idea implying the premise was immature."[17]

Whereas the majority of Southerners supported racial segregation, conservatives in the rest of the country had no coherent position on this issue. Outside the South, in fact, it seems that many conservatives did not wish to concern themselves with race issues as the anticommunist fight remained their prime obsession until at least the mid-1960s. In fact, one of the most consistent observations made by social scientists about the postwar right was how, outside the South, it was free from overt racism when compared to some former manifestations of popular conservatism in the United States. Of course, many conservatives nationwide, even those who disagreed with the Southern position on race, eventually found themselves at odds with the civil rights movement and its calls for federal intervention in state and private matters (e.g., education, business). And this was independent of the deep antipathy they shared with Southerners for the Warren Supreme Court, which dismantled anti-subversion laws, liberalized obscenity standards, and ended school prayer. In 1958, a campaign to "impeach Earl Warren" began, most notably among the Birchers, and came into full swing by the end of the decade, with "Impeach Earl Warren" bumper stickers and billboards springing up across the country. As opposed to the CACC, in order to gain an audience, especially in the South, the JBS capitalized considerably on black-red theories and opposition to federal civil rights legislation on the grounds that such legislation usurped state powers. While this strategy reflected the JBS's liberty to address political and partisan issues freely (a privilege tax-exempt groups did not have), it also reflected Welch's personality and origins, which were a far cry from Schwarz's. Welch was, Schoenwald writes, a native-born Southerner whose "vision was that of the white patrician who knew what was best for blacks."[18]

Nonetheless, some traits were universal among grassroots conservatives nationwide, the most important being their militant anticommunism, around which all cultural, economic, political, and moral issues seemed to be converging. The fact that, by the late 1950s, the Communist Party of the United States of America had been reduced to an insignificant political force had no bearing whatsoever on its perceived dangerousness: it was believed to be a criminal conspiracy masterminded by a foreign government, and the threat it posed to the nation was real. Grassroots conservatives also overwhelmingly saw themselves as upholding the principles of classical liberal individualism enshrined in the Republic's foundational texts. These values were seen as standing in contrast to a newer collectivism that, since the New Deal, had steadily come to dominate American politics and policy.[19]

Last, the great majority of conservatives expressed concern over declining moral standards. "A list of only a few of the elements in the picture includes the growing traffic in narcotics and liquor, illegitimate births, an almost unbelievable divorce rate which continues to grow, homosexuality and juvenile wanton violence," wrote Schwarz's disciple Bill Strube in 1962. These issues took centre stage throughout the 1960s.[20]

"THE SLUMBERING PEOPLE OF AMERICA"

By the late 1950s, another shift was perceptible among the general public, as a majority of Americans grew worried over the possibility of a nuclear clash. In 1959, 77 percent of respondents to a Gallup poll supported a nuclear test moratorium between the United States and the Soviet Union. A series of books and films depicting a fictional nuclear doom, such as Nevil Shute's *On the Beach* (published in 1957 and adapted for the big screen in 1959) and Peter Bryan Geroge's *Two Hours to Doom* (1958), illustrated how pervasive fears over the mushroom cloud were becoming. Right-wingers saw such works as creating a climate aimed at inducing Americans to support self-disarmament. Others did not go so far but still saw these books and films as expressions of a gullible mindset. During the midterm elections of November 1958, which took place during a recession, Communism was largely overshadowed by economic issues.[21]

While conservative militants felt alienated from the broader public over the issue that was closest to the core of their political and ideological identity, the United States seemed to be losing the Cold War. From 1950 to 1965, the Soviet economy grew at a 4.9 percent annual rate, higher than that of most Western democracies. In 1957, the Soviets tested their first intercontinental missile and launched the space satellite *Sputnik*. Though the United States's edge in atomic warheads was never threatened, a series of overestimations of the Soviet military capacity popularized the idea that the exact opposite was true. This "missile gap" became a political tool for Democrats, who saw it as evidence of Republican bungling. John F. Kennedy successfully emphasized the issue during his re-election campaign of 1958 and his presidential run of 1960.[22]

Angst among right-wingers flew through the ceiling when a Communist regime was established in Cuba, 145 kilometres from American shores. Fidel Castro's real intentions were initially unclear: in April 1959, he stated, as he had before, that he opposed all forms of dictatorships, including Communist ones. But, once he was in power, evidence that the new Cuban regime was evolving towards authoritarianism mounted. In contrast to the "Who-Lost-China?" outcry of the McCarthy years, Democrats now had an opportunity to criticize Republicans for losing Cuba, while conservatives tried to dodge these attacks by placing the blame on those who duped the public into considering Castro as a mere reformer rather than as a Communist. However, the "Who-Lost-Cuba" outcry never reached a level comparable to that of the China post-mortem, a clear sign that the nation's mood had changed in a decade. Based on the West Coast, Schwarz initially had little interaction with the Caribbean. He only commented on the Cuban issue when it became clear a year later that the Castro regime was aligning itself with the Soviets. After the Bay of Pigs fiasco of April 1961, the CACC established contact with Cuban exiles. Two months after the failed invasion, the CACC organized a well-attended school of anticommunism in the growing anti-Castrist hotbed of Miami.[23]

In contrast, Schwarz reacted immediately to the American visits of Soviet statesmen Anastas Mikoyan and Nikita Khrushchev in 1959 – visits deemed by conservatives to be a terrifying demonstration that the United States was losing its mind. At the time the Kremlin's number two man, Mikoyan, was the highest-ranking Soviet official to have ever visited the United States. His trip in January 1959 was part of Khrushchev's strategy to initiate direct talks with Eisenhower on the arms race question. When news of Mikoyan's visit leaked out, scores of organizations across the United States invited him to address their members, including prestigious bodies such as the Council on Foreign Relations and the Economic Club of New York.

Mikoyan, dashing and well-spoken, looked like anything but a dangerous Soviet apparatchik, and his trip rapidly evolved into "a presidential campaign," as the *New York Times*'s Harrison Salisbury put it. The visitor was being followed by a crowd of reporters everywhere he went, meeting Jerry Lewis and Sophia Loren, and delivering speeches to halls crowded with factory workers or businesspeople.[24]

Conservatives were outraged. In a telegram, Walter Judd and his wife rejected an invitation to attend a dinner meeting with Mikoyan "for the same reasons would not attend social function honoring Hitler, Himmler, Nero, or Genghis Khan." *US News and World Report* columnist David Lawrence wrote that never in US history "has any high official visiting this country displayed such effrontery and defiance of the American government and its policies." Schwarz wrote in his newsletter that Mikoyan embodied Communist duplicity at its best. He was one of the few Old Bolsheviks who survived the purges of the 1930s, which he managed by closely associating himself with Stalin, which implicated him in the death of millions. However, these crimes were ignored by the businesspeople and clergy who welcomed him "because he ha[d] an urbane manner, a ready wit and a quick tongue." Schwarz also gave his support to those who picketed several appearances by "this man of evil," despite Eisenhower's appeal that the visitor be treated courteously. In a private exchange Schwarz had with one of Judd's assistants, he suggested that a congressional investigation was in order to shed light on what had led to the US government's acceptance of this tour.[25]

In May 1959, John Foster Dulles, who had advocated a staunch anticommunist foreign policy as secretary of state since 1953, died. This opened the door for an agreement between Khrushchev and Eisenhower that they would trade visits to each other's countries and conduct face-to-face talks on arms control, beginning with the Soviet leader's tour of the United States in the fall of 1959. While Eisenhower's attempts at improving relations with the USSR had for years met stiff opposition from the Republican right, news of Khrushchev's visit caught conservatives off-guard. "The change," Schwarz wrote in his newsletter, "is so sudden, the revelation of national perfidy so complete that the mind cannot comprehend the truth. Three months ago it would have been unthinkable. John Foster Dulles has only recently laid to rest in his grave and this overwhelming reversal occurs." In spite of the generally courteous reception Khrushchev received throughout the country, he was also welcomed by protesting crowds. With other members of Congress opposed to the visit, Judd founded the Committee for Freedom of All Peoples, which grew to include members in all the cities on Khrushchev's itinerary. William Buckley, whose *National Review* launched a series of tirades against the Eisenhower administration, led a showcase protest at Carnegie Hall before twenty-five hundred people who wore black armbands symbolizing the victims of Communism. "Protest, protest, protest," wrote Schwarz, who urged his followers to wear the armband as well. "A groundswell of moral indignation may thwart this cruel tragedy."[26]

Nonetheless, conservatives were once again minorities. Among respondents to a Gallup poll in the summer of 1959, only 36 percent opposed the visit, while 50 percent agreed the Soviet leader ought to be invited. In Washington, GOP politicians were not ready to break with their party leader in the White House. Thus, few prominent members of the political class went as far as Judd in completely opposing the visit. Similarly, caught between a rock and a hard place, the conservative press could not take a firm stand against Khrushchev's visit. Even the *Chicago Tribune* editorialized: "we can expect to gain from the visit if it teaches our visitor some fundamental facts about this country that he doesn't know." Schwarz tried to ridicule this argument: "Khrushchev has an espionage system that can secure for him the intimate secrets of America's classified scientific knowledge, yet it is assumed that he does not know what types of houses are occupied by the American people, and that it will come as a bright burst of revelation when he discovers that the great majority of American workers drive automobiles." Khrushchev, the crusader wrote two months after the Soviet leader's visit, had fooled Americans. The country that "holds the hopes of the oppressed of the earth" was losing its spine, its will to fight. Still, it was a battle that had been lost, he wrote, not the war. "We must redouble our efforts to awaken with the truth the slumbering people of America and free lands."[27]

This gradual change in the national mood was paralleled by the waning of fear over domestic Communism. The *Daily Worker* closed in January 1958 and the CPUSA's membership had shrunk to Lilliputian numbers. With the fears of domestic subversion easing, a growing number of voices were heard calling for the dismantling of the institutional inheritances of McCarthyism. Mounting criticism targeted HUAC, whose hearings, which were continuing throughout the country, were deemed by many to be obsolete. In 1957, a Californian branch of the American Civil Liberties Union (ACLU) launched a petition campaign urging Congress to eliminate the committee. Operation Abolition, as the anti-HUAC campaign was named, rapidly picked up supporters from several student and civil rights groups. In May 1960, the HUAC road-show came to San Francisco to investigate subversive activities among local schoolteachers and unions, and was welcomed by protesting crowds composed mainly of students from University of California, Berkeley and San Francisco State College. Protesters were denied access to the hearing room, while inside hostile witnesses staged demonstrations against the committee. The situation degenerated into a rehearsal for the coming decade, with city police turning high-pressure hoses on white, preppy students, dragging them down the marble stairs of San Francisco City Hall. The riot sparked protests across the country.[28]

Schwarz, who owed a great deal of his fame to HUAC, promptly defended the committee's work. A few shrewd and dedicated Communist agitators, "utilizing volatile students," provoked violence so as to undermine the constitutional authority of the US Congress. For the most part, evidence that the riot was Communist-induced was flimsy (e.g., the presence among protesters of figures such as union leaders Archie Brown and Harry Bridges). Still, Schwarz's reading of the event reflected how conservatives saw and framed it. "These university students, perhaps as many as 400, were not all Communists, but the leadership was Communistic," conservative columnist George Sokolsky wrote.[29]

The post-riot outcry prompted HUAC to produce a documentary film defending its work. Made with news footage subpoenaed from two TV stations, *Operation Abolition* gave credence to the Communist-induced riot theory. The film opened with a speech by the HUAC chairman, Representative Francis E. Walter of Pennsylvania, who explained that Operation Abolition was "what the Communists call their current drive to destroy the House Committee on Un-American Activities … and to render sterile the security laws of our government." This introduction, wrongly attributing the anti-HUAC movement to Communists, set the tone for the rest of the film. The narration used the word "Communists" generically to describe anti-HUAC opponents, and the film's depiction of the riot contained edited distortions suggesting that arrested students violently confronted the police, when in fact the great majority were hosed as they were sitting down civil rights-style. The film could have gone unnoticed, but it was released during a summer in which student riots took place in several countries (Japan, Uruguay, Turkey), suggesting that the phenomenon was part of a worldwide campaign.[30]

In July 1960, Schwarz was one of the first anticommunist activists to be aware of and comment on *Operation Abolition.* "My first reaction," he wrote, "was to order the purchase of several copies for the use of our Crusade." For a few months the buzz over *Operation Abolition* remained limited to right-wing circles, but by the fall of 1960 politicians and the conservative press began praising it. Within a year, millions saw the film. A *Time* magazine journalist observed that prints of the film were "booked months in advance by Army camps, student groups, American Legion posts, political meetings, churches and corporations." When the CACC shifted the bulk of its activities towards anticommunism schools by the fall of 1960, their programs included screenings of *Operation Abolition.* In March 1961, a journalist attending the CACC school in Phoenix noted that the film was received with delight by the crowd, who "laughed uproariously at the scene where the students were bounced down the stairs." But as *Operation Abolition*'s success mounted, so did the controversy surrounding it. Many denounced the film's inaccuracies. When the film's narrator, Fulton Lewis III, a HUAC staffer, began a tour to show the film on colleges and universities in late 1960, viewings were systematically picketed.[31]

Another popular and controversial film, *Communism on the Map*, was released in May 1960. Produced by the National Education Program and narrated by Herbert Philbrick, it offered an account of the progress of worldwide Communism since the early twentieth century. Since the film did not clearly distinguish communism from socialism, it presented the United States as being almost completely surrounded by the enemy, which included most Western countries. According to the National Education Program, *Communism on the Map* was seen by millions within a year. But it was also widely criticized for its inaccuracies. In January 1961, ninety-two professors at the University of Washington in Seattle wrote a joint protest against the film's "gross distortion of historical events." In April 1961, six-time socialist presidential candidate Norman Thomas held a press conference in New York, where he slammed the film as "paranoid" and "false and misleading." In early 1961, the *Los Angeles Times* reported that both *Operation*

Abolition and *Communism on the Map* "are blowing up a lively controversy across the nation from Syracuse to Seattle."[32]

When Ike left office in February 1961, *National Review* voiced the viewpoint of many conservatives when it bade him good riddance: eight years in power had been even more frustrating than twenty years in opposition. After the election of Kennedy in November 1960, conservatives were again free to mobilize, discharged from the burden of defending an administration in which they had invested their hopes and then lost them. As the world was about to enter the 1960s, Communism was gradually pushed from daily headlines by civil rights struggles and the cultural transformations that were sweeping the country. The nation retained its universal opposition to communism, but the rift among Americans regarding how to express this core principle of their culture was about to widen considerably.[33]

7

"The Triumphal Spirit of These Days": 1960–61 Success

"YOU CAN TRUST THE COMMUNISTS"

On 7 August 1960, Schwarz's first book, titled *You Can Trust the Communists (to Do Exactly as They Say)*, was released. The book seems to have been noticed at first exclusively among conservatives and right-wing bookstores, the number of which mushroomed from a handful to a few hundred across the nation between 1955 and 1964. Within a year, the book was a moderate bestseller among the general public, but among conservatives, it gradually became a true success.[1]

That this book summarizing the crusader's thoughts wasn't published until he was forty-seven was not only the result of schedule constraints. The written word did not fit his personality as well as did the oral word. Schwarz's many previous booklets were all written versions of his extemporaneous speeches. His book was produced in a similar manner: he rented a hall in San Francisco and had a few of his lectures delivered therein transcribed and edited. Schwarz also toned down the religious dimension of his rhetoric and signed a publishing contract with Prentice-Hall, which had long been a leader in producing educational material. Prentice-Hall's president John Powers showed such an interest in the manuscript that he later agreed to appear among the "faculty" of a few Crusade schools. In 1961, free copies of the book were distributed nationwide, including to high school students in Florida and Louisiana. The book's original title, *You Can Trust the Communists (to Do Exactly as They Say)*, was changed in the second and all subsequent editions to *You Can Trust the Communists (to Be Communists)*.[2]

The book was aimed at a readership unfamiliar with communism. It contains several passages in which the author introduces his readers to the history of communism and its most important figures, and assesses the latter's respective contributions to the theory and practice of Marxism-Leninism. These passages are supplemented by the author's comments, in which the main tenets of Marxism-Leninism are criticized. A sense of crisis suffuses the text. Schwarz suggests that the communist onslaught of world conquest has reached a point beyond which the tide cannot be turned. He backs this claim by citing evidence of Communist superiority in the realms of military science, economics, education, and propaganda. The book concludes with a "Program for Survival," where the author affirms that, while free governments could act to contain the menace, constitutional and legal factors would severely limit these actions when it came to the battle for hearts and minds. Therefore, private citizens had to act on their own: "The urgent need is to discover individuals and groups in all countries with motives that will lead them to effective service against Communism and to provide them with the knowledge and the tools of communication to make their work effective."

The book's writing style is elegant without being overtly literary or academic. *You Can Trust* is at its best when Schwarz the propagandist bows to Schwarz the teacher. The opus contains accessible accounts of the origins of communism, particularly in the third chapter, "The Molding of a Communist – Communist Party: Origin and Organization," which is a reliable introduction to the topic. The tenth chapter, "The Difficult, Devious, and Dangerous Dialectic," despite its formidable title, is an example of Schwarz's ability to make difficult philosophical material accessible. "In his book," *Time* magazine noted in 1962, "his treatment of such a difficult subject as dialectical materialism is a model of instructive popularization."[3]

Schwarz slams Communism's use of organizational façades, or "fronts." In his 1919 book *Left-Wing Communism: An Infantile Disorder*, Lenin urged Communists to work within the boundaries imposed by bourgeois society and to rally to whatever cause was held dear by the public to gain political capital. Schwarz relates this prescription to the various fronts founded by US Communists, notably those whereby they attempted to pick up support among African Americans, which he saw as hypocritical attempts to exploit civil rights issues. He gives the example of Robert Welsey Wells, an African American sentenced to death in 1954, for whom the Communist

Party of the United States of America launched a campaign to have the sentence commuted: "After some months of agitation, [the Communists] prepared a book of some eighty or ninety pages showing what they had allegedly done on Well's behalf. The book did not help Wells very much but it presented the Communist Party in a very benign and humane light."[4]

In this book the crusader develops for the first time a critical analysis of Marxist economics. Marx and Engels, he posits, could not have predicted elements in the evolution of capitalism that invalidated their theories. The dynamic nature of money, as evidenced by the development of credit consumption, is an example. Goods "are purchased not with money presently owned, but by a promise to pay in the future. This has become such a large factor in the economy that any analysis which does not consider this is obviously fallacious." Another example is the role of government and legislation in regulating the economy. These reflections are interspersed with more polemical statements. Schwarz affirms without evidence that "a majority of the students in the world today are attracted to Communism." He defends fellow pro-anticommunist J.B. Matthews's estimate that "the largest single group supporting the communist apparatus in the United States today is composed of Protestant clergymen," a controversial declaration that had forced Matthews to resign as executive director of the McCarthy investigating committee in 1953.[5]

Schwarz chastises liberals for their defence of the Communists' civil rights. Most of these "pseudo-liberals," as he calls them, "are to be found in the ivory cloisters of colleges and universities, frequently occupying professorial chairs, and usually characterized by a pseudo-intellectual outlook." The same people erred in defending the rights of Communists to take the Fifth Amendment as this amendment "refers merely to imprisonment and legal penalty. Any attempt to project it beyond that realm is not intellectualism or liberalism but stupidity."[6]

You Can Trust's weakest section consists of a chapter on the concept of "Communist brainwashing," which reproduces passages from a booklet Schwarz had published in 1956 that depicts what is involved in the process of coercive indoctrination: exhaustion, confusion, physical pain, and emotional fear, followed by a Pavlovian-based injection of ideas. These stories, which shocked 1950s sensibilities, were mostly based on reports, popularized by one of Schwarz's acquaintance, reporter Ed Hunter, on the alleged brainwashing of US prisoners of war in Korea. Such contentions were false. The agitation concerning Communist brainwashing was based on far-fetched evidence, and the work of Pavlov, who had actually been critical of the Soviet regime's ideology and its attempts at curbing the autonomy of science, had been aimed at understanding the human mind rather than controlling it. The brainwashing discussions in *You Can Trust* are among the crusader's weakest work.[7]

You Can Trust demonstrates above all the unchanging nature of Schwarz's anticommunism. As always, his nemesis is an all-empowering force with the ability to turn the brightest human minds into witless zombies, while, through the dialectic, offering its supporters a way to adjust to any circumstance and thus further its ultimate goal. The book's opening statement illustrates this well:

> The thesis of this book is very simple. It is that Communists are Communists. I intend to show that they are exactly what they say they are; they believe what they say they believe; their objective is the objective they have repeatedly proclaimed to all over the world; their organization is the organization they have described in minute detail; and their moral code is the one they have announced without shame. Once we accept the fact that Communists are Communists, and understand the laws of their thought and conduct, all the mystery disappears, and we are confronted with a movement which is frightening in its superb organization, strategic mobility and universal program, but which is perfectly understandable and almost mathematically predictable.[8]

You Can Trust's rigid view of the communist mind reflects an obsessive cast of thought that has stood up poorly to the test of time. However, in 1960, with the memory of Stalin and the fall of China still fresh, it was one of the book's most appealing aspects. It explained the origins of communism, described how it functioned, gave answers to most important questions about it, all the while empowering the reader with the belief that communist behaviour could be predicted through simple knowledge. After the book's first edition sold out, a second edition was released in February 1962, and a third one two months later. In 1964, when Prentice-Hall gave the copyright to the CACC, the book had been through thirteen hardcover printings and had sold about a million copies. By the end of the 1970s, about 2 million copies of *You Can Trust* had been either sold or distributed for free worldwide and it had been printed in about twenty languages.[9]

Reviews of the book were polarized along the left-right divide. Ernest S. Pisko from the *Christian Science Monitor* wrote that Schwarz made several arguments that did "not stand closer examination." Liberal churchman Herman F. Reissig panned the book in the *United Church Herald*, criticizing several of its contentions, such as the insistence that most students worldwide are attracted to communism. This contrasted with appraisals from the conservative press. An impassioned assessment came from the *Free China Review*, published by Taiwan's nationalist regime, in which D.J. Lee praised Schwarz as a man who is "too much a scientist as to permit any prejudice to color his observations and to mislead him to jump to conclusions." William Henry Chamberlain from the *Wall Street Journal* hailed Schwarz's hard-hitting style, which, he stated, "may attract attention that would have been denied to a more scholarly work." Louis LaCoss, from the *St. Louis Globe-Democrat*, called the book an "invaluable" work that was "suited for classroom study and would make a fine textbook for high school and college."[10]

Along with the thousands of lectures Schwarz delivered, the CACC schools, and the various groups spurred or inspired by the Crusade, *You Can Trust* is another of the main ways that Schwarz left his imprint on the American Right. Conservative writer Lee Edwards notes that, in the mid-1960s, it was "widely acknowledged as one of the best primers on communism." Fundamentalist author Tim LaHaye called it a "masterpiece"; John Stormer, author of the best-seller *None Dare Call It Treason*, claimed that it influenced his anticommunist awakening. Reagan-era organizer Richard Viguerie claims it inspired many who would later form the "New Right." The book had an international career because the CACC and evangelical churches saw that it was distributed worldwide. It still circulates in conservative circles.[11]

You Can Trust became a classic of the post-McCarthy anticommunist subculture. It presents Schwarz's work in intricate miniature, laying out virulent conservative assaults on communism in the form of well-crafted, scholarly explanations. It represents "my fullest statement," its author said.[12]

CACC SCHOOLS: GOLDEN AGE

In July 1960, as *You Can Trust* was about to be released, Schwarz informed his supporters through the CACC newsletter that the upcoming fall was "to be the season of Anti-Communism Schools," with more than five already planned: San Diego (23–27 August), Chicago (29 August – 2 September), Dallas (20–24 September), Los Angeles (18–22 October), and Philadelphia (15–19 November). While the Crusade had been struggling only a year before to set up one school per year, in eleven months (between August 1960 and June 1961) it organized ten successful ones. This brief period was the Golden Age of CACC schools as they were not yet seen as controversial and opposition to them was minor and uncoordinated. "Words are inadequate to express the triumphal spirit of these days," Schwarz wrote in late 1960.[13]

These schools adopted an effective, business-like management style. The CACC now requested that its supporters take care of logistics and raise a guarantee of $5,000. A team was designated with the task of assuring maximum attendance. An internal CACC document instructs: "Obtain the names and addresses of all of the known organizations in a particular group. For example – Professional Organizations – Legal, Medical, Dental, etc. – Civic and Service Organizations." The goal was to acquire "their membership list so that personal invitations [could] be mailed to members." Supporters were even to send "a speaker to one of their meetings if they want[ed] the story about the school explained orally." With the establishment of a CACC recording studio in early 1961, the sale of recorded material (for about five dollars per recording) became systematic. In 1962, a report from the California attorney general concerning one of the schools noted: "Those who attended the 'crusade' received a Schwarz price list. If an individual bought one of each available tape and one of each booklet, it would cost him $689.10." In Phoenix, outside the lecture hall an attendee noticed a stand displaying reprints of Schwarz's speeches, copies of *You Can Trust*, pamphlets (a hundred for two dollars), and books such as Skousen's *The Naked Communist*. "By just after lunch they were sold out and the attendants were taking orders."[14]

Of all the schools held between August 1960 and June 1961, more than seven (San Diego, Dallas, Los Angeles, Phoenix, Anaheim, Tyler, and Miami) were set up in what, by the late 1960s, came to be called the "Sunbelt": the stretch across the South and Southwest comprising the country's southern rim, which underwent continuous demographic and economic growth after the Second World War. Five events were particularly successful, all of them taking place in air-conditioned, barbecue-all-year-long cities that had grown into sprawling military-industrial communities: San Diego, Los Angeles, Orange County, Phoenix, and Dallas.[15]

In San Diego, the local Marine Corps Recruit Depot San Diego and the Naval Training Center had greatly expanded their activities during the Second World War, and the school benefited from the participation and implicit endorsement of the local military. Los Angeles harboured in its ports the headquarters of the US Pacific Fleet, while Orange County was the location of the Santa Ana Army Air Base, Seal Beach's Naval Ammunition Depot, and El Toro's Marine station. Phoenix was home to the nation's biggest defence contractors – Motorola, General Electric, and Reynolds Aluminum. In Dallas, "[the] Southwest's capital of aviation, insurance, finance and manufacturing," the school was organized under the auspices of the City-County Civil Defense and Disaster Commission, whose mandate was to prepare the population to take emergency measures in the eventuality of war or disaster.[16]

Following a trend established in 1958, the number of attendees increased from one school to the next. Whereas the Milwaukee school of the previous winter had attracted about eight hundred people, the number in San Diego, in August 1960, reached two thousand people when all sessions were included. A month later, attendance rose again as more than twenty-five hundred people attended the Crusade school in Dallas at the Adolphus Hotel. Weeks later, the Crusade once again broke its record, with thirty-five hundred people gathered at the Biltmore Hotel in Los Angeles. These records were then dwarfed in Phoenix and Orange County, where attendance surpassed ten thousand.[17]

Schools garnered significant support from business elites. In San Diego, free advertising was provided by two newspapers, the *San Diego Union* and the *San Diego Tribune*, both property of conservative publisher James S. Copley, whose right-hand man, retired commander Paul Terry, a collaborator of George Benson and the NEP, acted as the school chairman. Before the event began, the *San Diego Union* ran a Sunday supplement detailing the gravity of the communist threat and later gave the school front-page headlines. In

November 1960, the school in Los Angeles was backed by Walter Knott and Patrick Frawley, whose right-hand man Ed Ettinger was chairman of the finance committee. Knott was also chairman of the Orange County school in March 1961. In Anaheim, the *Orange County Register*, owned by libertarian businessman Raymond Hoiles's Freedom Press Group, provided extensive coverage.[18]

In Dallas, a local reporter noted that the Civil Defense, which mobilized its resources for the school, was "so conspicuously important in community affairs that it ha[d] attracted the support and active participation of the cream of the business community." Numerous members of the Dallas business elite sponsored the event: W.W. Lynch, chairman of the school, president of the Texas Power and Light Company; J.M. Fulliwinder, vice-president of V-F Petroleum, of Midland; James A. Collins, president of Fidelity Union Life and future GOP representative. The organization was handled by Dallas Civil Defense's chairman John W. Mayo, a mortgage businessman whose name had popped up in national newspapers in 1956 when he tried to stop the Dallas Museum of Fine Arts from exhibiting paintings by alleged Communist artists.[19]

In Phoenix, the city's two most important papers (the *Arizona Republic* and the *Phoenix Gazette*), owned by publisher Eugene Pulliam, called the citizenry to arms and advertised the school as a unique opportunity to do something real against Communism. A few names from the list of prominent sponsors of the school included Robert W. Goldwater, brother of Barry Goldwater and president of Goldwater's, the family's locally famous specialty store; Walter Lucking, president of the Arizona Public Service Co.; and C. Lester Hogan, head of Motorola's Arizona activities.[20]

Another important feature of CACC schools during this period was the support they drew from educational authorities. In San Diego, the school board, led by Dr Ralph Dailard, included the event in the ongoing professional development program offered to its members, who attended and participated. In Dallas, the school prompted the local school board to initiate a "hard-hitting course of study concerning Communism." This initiative was organized on such short notice that the new material was worked into existing classes. Schwarz was later re-invited by the Dallas Independent School District to deliver lectures in high schools.[21]

In October 1960, the Greater Los Angeles School of Anti-Communism saw the collaboration of school authorities increase further with the establishment of a youth-centred activity (a "youth day" or "youth night"), to which high school and college students were admitted free of charge. Three speakers were selected for their specific appeal to the fifteen hundred teenagers who showed up. The first was the ever autograph-signing Herbert Philbrick, while the other two were Rafer Johnson, Olympic decathlon champion, and actor Ty Hardin, famous for his TV impersonation of a former Confederate officer in the ABC series *Bronco* and future founder (in the 1980s) of the Arizona Patriots – a paramilitary right-wing group eventually dismantled by the FBI.[22]

The Youth Day event reached immense proportions in Arizona, where it was not only endorsed by the school boards of Phoenix and Mesa but also drew the support of the teachers' union associated with Phoenix's high schools and colleges, which urged its members and students to attend "any morning, afternoon or evening session of the school period." One mid-week afternoon, seven thousand high school students flocked to Phoenix's Montgomery Stadium to listen to Philbrick, and another crowd of ten thousand took over the stadium in the evening. Present was Canadian journalist Elmore Philpott, who expressed amazement in his *Vancouver Sun* column: "At first glance, it might seem incredible that the followers of Barry Goldwater could really be so genuinely scared of a handful of local Reds that 10,000 citizens would pay to hear about them." A week later, in Orange County, the Phoenix figures were surpassed: a crowd of twelve thousand students overflowed Anaheim's La Palma Stadium, where the limited seating capacity compelled thousands to sit on the ground to hear the "Big 3": Schwarz, Philbrick, and Skousen. Students interviewed by a reporter after the event expressed consternation. "I am shocked that communism is in our schools"; "Communism is getting into America slowly but surely and we got to watch out"; "Kids nowadays need more religion in their lives and more guidance and we need to be more patriotic."[23]

Of all schools that took place during that period, the two in Phoenix and Orange County, held one week apart in the winter of 1961, stand out as hallmarks. Both locations shared characteristics that made them some of the country's most intense hotbeds of grassroots conservative activity: thriving economies based on military-aerospace dollars, important proportions of expatriated white Southerners, and probably the most libertarian and anti-statist business elites of the nation.

Phoenix was not a location where the CACC had been established before the schools. The organization, however, benefited from a truly favourable climate. By the end of 1960, a series of highly emotional political fights had erupted on the local scene. One took place when an ACLU-member high school teacher protested the extensive showing of *Operation Abolition* in the city's clubs and churches, prompting angry responses from parents and conservative organizations. Another involved local Birchers who successfully blocked a municipal plan for urban renewal, deemed communist-inspired. Journalist Donald McNeil, who investigated the city's bubbling right-wing activity, noted with amazement that "this type of conservatism ... battles anything governmental" (the UN, income tax, even local authorities' plans for slum removal) as un-American and communist. A word-of-mouth campaign was in full swing almost two months prior to the opening session of the school, with businesses, school boards, politicians, and churches buying and selling advance tickets.[24]

McNeil's personal notes provide an account of the event at the Westward Hotel. Hundreds of properly dressed students, some wearing patriotic badges ("I am an American," or "Stay American"), packed the hall. Crowds "stamped their feet, yelled, clapped, and chanted their approval as Philbrick quoted Skousen and Skousen quoted Schwarz and Schwarz quoted Morris quoting Skousen." At the end of each afternoon, short sessions featuring audience participation were organized. Attendees were divided into several groups, and workshops were held in which people were given the opportunity to express themselves and describe their commitment to the good fight. McNeil's notes describe a high school girl, in her Sunday dress, shyly talking about having troubles with a Tucson teacher who is "pink," and another boy affirming that several teachers at Arizona State University were communists, especially those in the social sciences. Local reporters estimated that the school earned a total of $40,000 when registration, sales, and donations were included.[25]

Most records set in Phoenix were surpassed a week later during the school at Orange County. Planned at Knott's Berry Farm and held at Anaheim's Disneyland Hotel in early March 1961, this event symbolically unified the United States's two great western theme parks. Publicity for the school had begun months earlier in Orange County newspapers. Tickets were sold out even before the event began. Schwarz's 9:00 a.m. Monday presentation drew more than fifteen hundred people, jammed together to hear the crusader kick off the school, followed by Fred Schlafly's castigation of the Supreme Court for the decisions "which virtually ha[d] given Communists a stamp of approval in their operations." Right from day one, to handle the large number of attendees, the organizers had to hold double sessions and send crowds to the Anaheim High School auditorium.[26]

As opposed to Phoenix, Anaheim was pure Crusade country, located just next door to the CACC's Long Beach central office. Orange County, pejoratively nicknamed "nut country" by the magazine *Fortune*, represented in a nutshell the post-Second World War Southern Californian boom, which quickly transformed the whole region from a rural backwater into a collection of suburbs. This dynamic was nowhere more fully captured than at the Disneyland Hotel itself, which, along with its surroundings, stood on land where only ranches had existed a few years before. The county was a haven of vanilla homogeneity, a large portion of its quick growth during the second half of the 1950s being due to its absorption of much of Los Angeles's white flight and the migration of thousands of expatriate Southern whites. With 75 percent of its inhabitants being Protestants, Orange County also had some of the nation's fastest-growing megachurches, such as the one founded in 1955 in a former drive-in movie theatre in Garden Grove by Robert H. Schuller, who served as chairman of the religious committee of the school.[27]

The Orange County event was notable for the virulence of its rhetoric. On the first day, Dr Margaret Wold, a local Lutheran doctor of ministry, delivered a speech titled "The Role of Women under Communism and Freedom." She delivered a frightening account of women's condition in the USSR. Soviet women, she said, were forced to work in steel or saw mills, with the state taking care of the kids. "Well, its [sic] not exactly babysitting service," the *Orange County Register* reported: "They'll take care of your children between the ages of one month and 17 years in a state nursery and perhaps you'll be able to see them on weekends if you're lucky. And listen. Don't worry about the husband situation. If you're tired of your old man, they'll help you get rid of him and the Russians will provide you with one from the state's pool."[28]

On the second day, Paul Terry announced in a McCarthyesque manner that he had in his possession "a Communist plan drawn in Moscow which calls for the downfall of the Philippine Islands by 1963." Skousen detailed his theory that FDR's advisor Harry

Hopkins had transmitted atomic bomb secrets and uranium to the Soviets during the Second World War. Former Joe McCarthy aide Robert Morris, who had joined the "faculty" members in Dallas, voiced common right-wing theories about the State Department's perfidy ("25 Americans are responsible for the downfall of China"), before speaking out against the *New York Times*'s Herbert Matthews for his reports on Castro before the fall of the Battista regime: "Castro was created here in the United States." One journalist reported that Philbrick levelled "a verbal barrage at Hollywood," notably lambasting Frank Sinatra for his movie project – scripted by one of the blacklisted Hollywood Ten writers, Albert Maltz – on the life of Eddie Slovik, the only US soldier shot for desertion during the Second World War. The next evening, Knott's right-hand man William E. Fort, "educational director" of the libertarian California Free Enterprise Association, instructed the audience on the merits of the free enterprise system.[29]

More than $18,100 was donated during the closing beef and lobster banquet alone, and this was above the $20,000 already earned in registrations and sales. The *Orange County Register* mentioned that sixteen thousand persons attended the school. The Long Beach *Independent* gave a higher figure of 17,500. The *Register* described the event as "the most successful, one punch anti-communism movement in the history of the nation."[30]

Despite its keyed-up rhetoric, the Orange County event drew little controversy,[31] in part due to the marked absence of opposition watchdogs. For instance, the ACLU, which was keeping an eye on civic displays of anticommunism, was relatively weak in Orange County and did not send any observers. One exception to this absence of watchdogs was the weekly left-wing newspaper *National Guardian*, based in New York, which published a text from its correspondent Clancy Franks. "Schwarz organized a 'school' at the Disneyland Hotel, where professional anti-communists and right-wing fanatics preached a dogma reminiscent of the late Sen. Joe McCarthy." Franks objected to the local school boards allowing teenagers to be exposed to the school's rhetoric. "Right-wing organizations flourish," Franks warned. "They are riding the crest of a wave of unrest and fear set off by the greatest population growth in the nation and the changeover from a feudal-type agricultural economy to an industrial economy."[32]

By the spring of 1961, the Crusade's annual projected revenues had nearly tripled from 1960 and were set to reach the million-dollar mark before the end of the year. Its audiences and supporters were multiplying, its visibility soaring. CACC schools were now highly profitable ventures that not only mobilized activists but also received the endorsements of important political, business, and civic institutions, putting at the CACC's service the most efficient tools available for mass mobilization. Yet this public support constituted a fragile web and underlined the consensual nature of the school formula. Hence, the mobilization necessary to conduct such mass meetings remained liable to fizzle away.

8

"Schwarz Stirs Them Up, Welch Signs Them Up": First Controversies

THE GLENVIEW SEMINAR

While the Crusade experienced a series of successes in the country's southern rim, a demand for its schools had also appeared elsewhere. In August 1960, immediately after the closing of the school in San Diego, Fred Schwarz, Herbert Philbrick, and Richard Arens flew to Chicago, from where they proceeded to Glenview, a suburb located about thirty-two kilometres north of the Windy City. Their destination was the Naval Air Station of Glenview, a US base that served as an important terminal for naval warfare drills throughout the Cold War. On the base, everything had been prepared for another week-long school, one that this time would use military facilities, including the base's auditorium with its capacity for a crowd of twelve hundred. The event was not officially a CACC school – it was a five-day Education for American Security seminar.

Schwarz was not an unknown quantity to the US military. He had lectured in 1956 at the National War College and later that year at the EntAir Force Base in Colorado Springs. In San Diego, the CACC school had featured the extensive participation of the US military. As Philbrick wrote to one of his correspondents, even if the event did not take place on the base itself, its navy personnel participated, wearing their full gear and apparel. The CACC's "military" credentials were further enhanced by the involvement of the local Crusade branch director, Captain E. Richard Barnes.[1]

This apparent violation of the political neutrality of the armed forces went unnoticed in San Diego. In fact, while this school was the first one at which some notable opposition was levelled, objections did not address the role of the military. Publisher Simon Casady, editor of the El Cajo *Valley News*, complained in an editorial titled "The Hysteria Peddlers are Back!" that the local city council had some public officials attend the week-long event at taxpayers' expense. Casady compared Schwarz, Philbrick, Skousen, Arens, Sluis, and Barnes to "quacks who sell cancer cures."[2]

The political neutrality of the armed forces was a potentially explosive issue in this era of unprecedented military buildup. Only a decade before, a congressional committee had severely condemned the War Department for its use of public funds to publicize policies of the Truman administration. What had made the military participation in CACC activities in San Diego and Glenview possible was a directive issued by the National Security Council (NSC) in 1958 making it a policy of the US government to "make use of military personnel and facilities to arouse the public to the menace of the cold war." A document titled "American Strategy for the Nuclear Age" was prepared to implement the directive. Secretary of Defense Robert McNamara was still unaware of the 1958 NSC directive by the summer of 1961, several months after taking office.[3]

While the directive gave clearance for the holding of seminars on military facilities, the Glenview event was a result of the initiative of a Chicago businessman, Frank Vignola, who had attended a CACC school in California. A reserve lieutenant, he organized a school with the agreement of the Glenview Station commanding officers. The event "was arranged quite independently of myself and the Crusade," Schwarz wrote in a letter. Nonetheless, the Glenview event was a photocopy of the by now classic school formula. A "faculty" of noted anticommunists offered a "re-examination of the principles of our American Heritage" as well as an "exposure of International Communism." The week-long event also ended with a banquet.[4]

Even before the school began, registrations for daytime sessions numbered in the hundreds, with many "students" having their attendance paid for by major sponsors. General Electric and Sears, Roebuck & Co. sponsored five and fifteen people, respectively, while the local chamber of commerce and the Rotary Club paid the "tuition" of one hundred college students from the Glenview area. A large portion of the "student" body was composed of navy personnel. Among thirteen speakers, five were associated with the CACC (Schwarz, Philbrick, and Arens as well as Fred Schlafly and Anthony Bouscaren), but they accounted for half of the thirty lectures given during the week. "Vignola," wrote one journalist prior to the school's opening, "said the 'faculty' had been picked with care to avoid a charge of playing politics." In that regard, Vignola failed.[5]

The controversy began after one of the *Chicago Tribune*'s front-page headlines featured Philbrick, who, during a presentation, warned of Communist activity in Chicago. The ACLU protested to the navy, claiming that the hosting of such events on military facilities was inappropriate, to which a navy spokesman replied that the naval station had not sponsored the school but was "merely the host in a community project." Jack Mabley, columnist for the *Chicago Daily News* and president of the Glenview Village Board, hailed the school in his column and sponsored a resolution commending the event. The resolution passed with only one negative vote, that of Mrs Norma Morrison, who received anonymous nighttime telephone calls in the following days. In April 1961, Morrison was re-elected to the board over conservative opposition. "We won the election," she said, "but there has been a great deal of bitterness left over from it. Our town is divided in a way I've never seen it before."[6]

Tyler Thompson, professor of religion at Northwestern University and Democratic candidate for the House's Illinois 13th District in 1960, assailed the seminar as an "alarming example of McCarthyism." In the following weeks, an anonymous leaflet circulated in local mailboxes attacking Thompson for his alleged Communist links. The FBI eventually arrested Miles M. Vondra, an insurance broker involved in the local John Birch Society, for violation of the Corrupt Practices Act. Vondra, a veteran of the Second World War and Korea, was later declared not guilty after convincing a jury that he was unaware of the prohibition over the distribution of unsigned electoral material. He admitted during the trial that he had been infuriated by Thompson's comments and that he considered him "as much an enemy of mine as the Chinamen who shot me in Korea." Meanwhile, Thompson had been handily defeated at the polls during the 1960 election.[7]

Two weeks after the Glenview school ended, the Chicago-based liberal Protestant magazine *Christian Century* ran an editorial claiming that organizations "which incite hate and suspicion against American citizens should not be permitted to use any arm of the government as their instrument." The editorial absolved the military and blamed Schwarz, under whose "complete control" the seminar allegedly had been. The crusader replied that his role in the Glenview school had been limited to giving lectures and acting as moderator. He invited any individual named by the *Christian Century* to debate him publicly, a challenge that remained unanswered.[8]

The military eventually admitted to participating in the school's organization. In a letter he personally sent to Democratic candidate Tyler Thompson, Secretary of the Navy W.B. Franke, while recognizing that the Glenview Base officials might have gone too far in leaving the impression of "navy sponsorship" of the project, nonetheless affirmed that the practice of using military facilities for activities providing "patriotic indoctrination for naval personnel" was "in the best interests of the navy, the nation, and freedom itself." Philbrick wrote to one of his supporters that the navy fully cooperated with the school but simply did not sponsor it openly. All things considered, the school was so like CACC schools that there is no doubt the CACC was involved in organizing the event to some extent. Moreover, the CACC had provided educational material and advertised the event in its newsletter under the upcoming "anti-communism schools" column. In his 1996 memoirs, no longer needing to dodge the controversy, Schwarz wrote: "The truth is that my lectures were the core and essence of the school. I delivered two major lectures each day, and I also served as 'master of ceremonies.'"[9]

THE BIRCHER STIGMA

During the two years that followed its founding in December 1958, the John Birch Society remained unknown to the overwhelming majority of the American population. While *The Blue Book of the John Birch Society* did not specifically prescribe that the JBS remain a secret organization, a certain level of obscurity was obviously what Welch had had in mind when he designed his group's arcane method of functioning: backdoor meetings, secret membership rolls, and instructions to split local chapters once they passed a certain number of members. Discretion, however, was not compatible with growth in membership. Welch wrote: "We are ought to get a million members truly dedicated to the things in which we believe." This target was never reached, but, after two years, the JBS had so-called "working" chapters (operational chapters with a local leader) in thirty-four states and "home" chapter members (where local chapters did not yet exist) in all fifty states. By the winter of 1961, *Los Angeles Times* journalist Gene Blake reported, based on inside information, that the membership was expected to soon reach 100,000.[10]

Welch insisted that JBS members totally accept his leadership. Through the organization's bulletin, he sent instructions that were to be followed: organizations were required to expand the circulation of conservative periodicals, especially Welch's *American Opinion*; to set up fronts; to stop communistic activity in their local community; and to organize coordinated letter-writing campaigns. By Welch's own admission, the society's cell-like, underground structure emulated Leninist organizational principles, which posed no problem as the JBS was ready to draw on all successful models. While the prospect of attending covert meetings where freedom-loving Americans could schmooze about how to save the nation was exciting to some, others found this secrecy unsettling. In January 1959, an FBI informant who had attended a meeting in Milwaukee sent a memo to J. Edgar Hoover. Participants, the document reported, were "exceedingly prominent and influential individuals in the Milwaukee area," and "the meeting was conducted by Welch in a very secretive manner. Those in attendance were instructed not to divulge what had transpired to their office personnel or even to their wives at this juncture."[11]

In May 1959, Herbert Philbrick, who had maintained ties with the FBI, attended a private seminar hosted by Welch himself. He later reported to his FBI contact about the "cloak-and-dagger" atmosphere and Welch's insistence on the treachery of the nation's leaders. Should Birchers reach their objective of enlisting a million members, Philbrick warned the FBI, they could become an "explosive" force. In the following months, Philbrick refused Welch's offer to join the JBS, invoking his busy schedule, but he exchanged friendly letters with him, of which he made carbon copies and sent them to the FBI. By early 1961, once the JBS had become public, Philbrick ceased feeding the FBI. He remained a supporter of the society, but his initial reaction to it reveals just how spooky the JBS looked to many conservatives.[12]

Welch intensely believed that communists had infiltrated all segments of American society, which meant that JBS literature was saturated with conspiracy theories of all sorts. Senator Robert Taft might have died from a cancer "induced by a radium tube planted in the upholstery of his Senate seat"; Joe McCarthy might actually have been assassinated; New York governor Nelson Rockefeller was "definitely committed to trying to make the United States a part of a one-world Socialist government." Welch's most infamous fantasy can be found in his book *The Politician*, which he wrote in 1958 before he founded the JBS. *The Politician* can best be summarized by quoting from its final passage: "The Communists can now use all the power and prestige of the presidency of the United States to implement their plans, just as fully and even openly as they dare. They have arrived at this point in three stages ... In the third stage, in my own firm opinion, the Communists have one of their own actually in the presidency. For this third man, Eisenhower, there is only one possible word to describe his purposes and his actions. That word is treason."[13]

The Politician was not designed for publication; Welch wished it to remain an in-house document. Until late summer 1960, *The Politician* circulated exclusively among a limited number of conservative leaders across the nation, not all of whom approved of Welch's conclusions. Barry Goldwater was one of the first to read the manuscript. He returned it to Welch with the comment that if he could not back his statements with clear evidence, he would be well advised to destroy all copies and issue a retraction. Should *The Politician* be revealed to the general public, the Arizona senator thought, it would bring heat upon all those connected to Welch.[14]

No record, public or private, indicates that Schwarz and Welch met in person. Naturally, each knew about the other. Concerning Welch, Schwarz wrote, "It does seem strange that we have not come face to face as we have so many actual friends, such a common interest and concern." For instance, Schwarz's friend Alfred Kohlberg had known Welch at least since the early 1950s. He later joined the JBS's council prior to his death in April 1960. Both Welch and Schwarz had greatly benefitted from the backing of Harry Bradley, and Welch himself wrote: "I once heard Harry Bradley tell others that, so far as he was concerned, there were only three really effective anti-Communists in America; they were Fred Schwarz, Bob Welch, and Doctor Nyaradi" (the latter was an economist and proponent of the free enterprise system). Welch had read several of Schwarz's writings and had a high opinion of them. He especially appreciated the 1959 address to the Texas legislature, reprinted in a booklet titled *The Disease of Communism*, and *You Can Trust*, though he strongly disagreed "with the three last pages" (i.e., in which Schwarz warns his readers against "the temptation to try to form a totalitarian organization modeled on Communism").[15]

Schwarz did not hold Welch in the same esteem that Welch held Schwarz. The crusader never showed any interest in Welch's theories.

He reported having once seen a copy of *The Politician*, when Fred Loock – Allen-Bradley's general manager – read excerpts from it. "While I did not agree with the conclusions," Schwarz noted, "I did not express my opinion." But between 1959 and 1960, Schwarz began to receive an increasing number of inquiries about the JBS. Aware that any harsh criticism of the JBS on his part would alienate a good percentage of his supporters, he said that it was "a fine organization of fine people doing a splendid work." Yet many questions were also asked about the desirability of organizations with rigid, clandestine structures such as that of the JBS. Here, Schwarz got off the boat: "I do not believe in collectivism in the battle against collectivism." More than once when addressing this peculiar issue both in private and public exchanges, Schwarz used the word "fascist" to describe the JBS's organizational structure, and before long Welch knew this. Though he considered it an unprovoked attack, he chose not to reply.[16]

The Australian privately admitted that his work and Welch's "complement each other very much": the CACC was "instrumental in stimulating the concern of people who have been recruited by the John Birch Society," and the CACC had "received the honest and wholehearted support of the John Birch Society." Many Birchers had joined the organization committees of the CACC schools of Milwaukee and San Diego after Robert Welch himself had encouraged their involvement. Phoenix probably saw the peak in the support given to a school by high-profile Birchers: the school's steering committee was composed of seven prominent citizens, five of whom later admitted to a reporter to being JBS members. As Barry Goldwater once told William Buckley, every prominent citizen of the Phoenix area was at that time a Bircher: "I'm not talking about Commie-haunted apple-pickers of cactus drunks, I'm talking about the highest cast of men of affairs."[17]

Welch also encouraged his supporters to attend the seminar the Crusade organized on the Glenview Naval Air Station in late August 1960. But prior to the Glenview school an incident occurred involving Frank Vignola, the Chicago businessman who initiated the event. At a meeting in Glenview, after a few attempts, Vignola was able to obtain from local Birchers a copy of *The Politician*. After having assured them as to his discretion, Vignola unexpectedly read passages from it to those gathered, which included *Chicago Daily News* columnist Jack Mabley. After obtaining a copy himself, Mabley broke out the story in *Chicago Daily News* headlines on 25 and 26 July 1960. The JBS, wrote Mabley, "is not a secret society in the normal sense of the word, but it tries to avoid publicity. Until this moment, it has been successful." In a second report, he warned readers that the JBS was a potential threat to democracy. To this end, he used quotes from Welch's *Blue Book*, notably the one in which the JBS leader wrote that democracy "is merely a deceptive phase, a weapon of demagoguery, and a perennial fraud."[18]

Mabley's scoop was far bigger than its impact. The *Chicago Daily News* was only the third most read newspaper in Chicago, and the story broke on virtually the same day that the Republican Party opened the convention in Chicago that nominated Richard Nixon as presidential candidate. The story generated discussion and perhaps some havoc among GOP leaders and delegates but was quickly drowned in the coverage of Nixon's hard bargaining over his platform with the party's moderate and conservative wings, represented, respectively, by Nelson Rockefeller and Barry Goldwater. Shortly after the convention ended, Mabley sent a copy of the story to the *Milwaukee Journal*. After a short investigation of the JBS, on 31 July 1960 the *Journal* ran the headline "Group Branding Ike as Red Has 10 Chapters in Wisconsin." Other articles appeared in the following days in other Midwestern papers (such as the *Chicago Sun-Times*) as well as in the *Boston Herald*, the *Miami Herald*, and the *Louisville Courier-Journal*. The story had spread, but it melted away amid the 1960 presidential campaign.[19]

Welch blamed Schwarz for the leaking of *The Politician*. In a nine-page letter to Schwarz, Welch pointed out that his organization had always collaborated with other groups. "You have done," he told Schwarz "a superb job of waking up a great many Americans to the dangers which we face. We have been trying to take those who were awakened and alarmed, give them an action program which coordinated their individual efforts and made those efforts cumulative." Welch also claimed he once thought that some CACC-JBS collaboration could be possible "without making any slightest change in the nature of our respective programs." Welch then accused Schwarz, writing:

> We know that you personally have repeatedly been making extremely derogatory remarks about myself and The John Birch Society, to various groups and audiences; and that you have been

> reading from my private manuscript, called *The Politician*, to support your disparaging comments. We know that you have privately said things about me and the Society, to important conservative leaders, which – in some cases anyway – has caused these leaders to discontinue strong support ... But most important of all it was one of your men in Chicago, a close associate of yours and a life member of your organization, who deliberately set off the publicity about the *Politician*, which has caused such a furore in several Midwestern papers and at some of other points in the country.[20]

Welch speculated as to why Schwarz might have wanted to harm the JBS. He theorized about one former (unnamed) CACC member in Texas who had broken with Schwarz and joined the JBS, and conjectured that Schwarz's unwarranted aggressive behaviour could have been provoked by his disagreement with *The Politician*'s conclusion. Still, none of these reasons, Welch thought, justified Schwarz's hostility.

In his reply, Schwarz denied any involvement in the leaking of *The Politician*, claiming that he had learned about this indiscretion after it had occurred. "Frank Vignola", Schwarz wrote, "is not active with the Christian Anti-Communism Crusade and is in no sense under my direction." The crusader considered that the JBS included "some of the finest, most patriotic and most dedicated people in America," that it had a "highly commendable" program and was led by a man whose "leadership and literary eloquence speak for themselves." Schwarz acknowledged having used the word "fascist" in his criticism of the JBS's functioning: "I have meant this in the technical sense ... referring to unified discipline and control, but since Communism has made fascist a smear word, I am sorry that I have used it."

Schwarz concluded the letter noting that he had at one time personally commented on the JBS to the American Security Council, a group promoting a hawkish foreign policy that regrouped businesspeople and retired military leaders who had helped implement anticommunist educational programs using military facilities in accordance with the NCS 1958 directive. Members of the American Security Council had received copies of *The Politician* and had asked Schwarz questions regarding the book's controversial conclusions. Schwarz admitted to Welch that these circumstances forced him to keep his distance from the JBS: "I appreciate fully the right to express your personal opinion, but unfortunately the material had become public and could be very damaging indeed particularly to military personnel if they could be linked to this accusation against their Commander-in-Chief. I therefore relayed the information to a few military personnel believing that I would be failing in my duty if I did otherwise."

This exchange, probably the first and last between the two men, remained secret until 1964, when some of its extracts were made public, prompting Schwarz to release the full correspondence to the press. In 1960, the exchange had no immediate impact on the respective activities of either man. Welch told his interlocutor that however angry he was at Schwarz, he would not instruct Birchers to stop aiding the Crusade since "our job is to fight the Communists, and not to be sidetracked by personal animosities." When the press began intensely scrutinizing the JBS in early 1961, Welch exonerated Schwarz by claiming that the attacks on the JBS had a communist origin. Later, Welch blamed all the attacks on the Soviets.[21]

The next round of troubles also came from the conservative camp. By February 1961, JBS membership had grown to the point at which, when Welch gave instructions to write letters demanding the impeachment of Earl Warren, a flood of mail poured into newspaper offices. After the editorial section of the *Los Angeles Times*, owned by the conservative Chandler family, had received what it called "a shower of letters," the *Times*'s editorial board asked one of its seasoned reporters, Gene Blake, to investigate. Blake published a series of five articles about the JBS's beliefs, organization, and objectives. While this series was descriptive and nonjudgmental, one *Times* editorial, signed by Otis Chandler himself, condemned the organization. Otis Chandler restated the *Times*'s conservative stance but affirmed that the "argument for conservatism" cannot be won "by smearing as enemies and traitors those with whom we sometimes disagree." The *Los Angeles Times* had just strikingly alienated a sizable share of its readership: in the following weeks, the newspaper received more than fifteen thousand subscription cancellations.[22]

The controversy spread rapidly eastward and became the talk of the day. In Washington, some members of Congress voiced concern, including conservative Republicans such as Senator Milton Young of North Dakota, who called Welch's beliefs "beyond anything … Sen. McCarthy ever thought of." California Democratic governor Pat Brown proposed that HUAC scrutinize the Society and met with state general attorney Stanley Mosk to discuss an investigation of the JBS. On 1 April 1961, the story reached the front page of the *New York Times*. Journalists exposed the extent of the Society's presence in many states and its support among retired military officers and many prominent businesspeople.[23]

For some time, everybody, so it seemed, was taking a stand on the JBS. The Justice Department released a statement in which new attorney general Robert Kennedy called the JBS "a matter of concern." Cardinal Cushing of Boston affirmed that he was a Welch supporter, while Catholic periodicals such as *Ave Maria* and, two months later, the monthly *Extension* denounced the JBS. Richard Nixon criticized the Society, while other GOP members of Congress from Southern California admitted their JBS membership. Ohio Democratic senator Stephen Young called Welch a "little Hitler" leading a team of "right-wing crackpots." The controversy increased further when, on 14 April, the *New York Times* headlined a JBS-related story. General Edwin A. Walker, commanding officer of an army division in Germany, had been "urging the views of the ultra-conservative John Birch Society on his troops for the last six months," prompting the army to relieve Walker from office three days later.[24]

The CACC, which had schools planned in St Louis in April and Miami in June 1961, was not initially affected by the story. In the short term, the public unearthing of the JBS even helped Schwarz as, at first glance, he and his collaborators benefited from the contrast. To appease its readership, the *Los Angeles Times* published a series on "the blessings of Americanism" and widely covered the activities of the Crusade, seen as a respectable alternative to the JBS, until the end of 1961. The television station KTTV-Channel 11, also owned by the Chandler family, later provided extensive visibility to the CACC. This treatment was emulated by other newspapers in the Southwest, including the *Los Angeles Examiner*, the *San Francisco Chronicle*, and the *Albuquerque Tribune*. In a private letter, Barry Goldwater criticized Welch but praised those who had organized the CACC school in Phoenix, which he deemed a responsible form of anticommunism.[25]

Three weeks after the Orange County school ended, and when the debate over the JBS was at its peak, Schwarz was in Albuquerque talking to fifteen hundred people in the crowded hall at the University of New Mexico. Here, he politely voiced his disagreement with Bircher beliefs while condemning "the size and the intensity" of the attack on the JBS. "He was staggered," one reporter noted, "because people apparently unafraid of a billion Reds 'were scared out their wits by the John Birch Society.'" A few weeks later, Schwarz's series of lectures in Southern California was given prime coverage by the *Los Angeles Times.* The Australian stood on the middle ground, stating that concern "without knowledge leads to fanaticism" but warning against trial and condemnation by newspapers.[26]

On 12 April 1961, the JBS vanished from the headlines. Khrushchev announced that the Soviets had launched the first astronaut into space. After an hour and a half in orbit in the Vostok 1 shuttle, Yuri Gagarin returned alive to Earth. On 18 April, four days before the CACC was scheduled to open its school in St Louis, the nation learned that an invasion of Cuba was under way. Two days later, the Bay of Pigs invasion was over, with the complete obliteration of a CIA-trained landing force of Cuban exiles. The American public's attention refocused on Communism, and, for a time, the right-wing threat appeared pretty mild by contrast.[27]

But the Bircher controversy would not go away. On 7 February 1961, a legislative assistant of Democratic senator Edward V. Long of Missouri contacted the ACLU's headquarters in Washington and asked for any information it might have on the Crusade as Senator Long had been invited to be part of the advisory committee of the CACC school in St Louis scheduled for 24–28 April 1961. The only information the ACLU had at this point was a biographical sketch of Schwarz and a short description of how CACC schools functioned. In its communication with Long, the ACLU added that, even though the CACC promoted an "extreme" brand of anticommunism, it was not associated with religious or racial bigotry. Senator Long accepted the invitation, as did several other Missouri politicians, including Democratic governor of Missouri John M. Dalton.[28]

"Our hearts are filled with expectation as we revisit the city where the anti-Communism school movement was born," Schwarz wrote of St Louis in his newsletter. This second St Louis school, held three years after the first school in 1958, was indeed another success. A surplus of more than $34,000 was earned, including $20,000 during the closing banquet alone, making it the most financially profitable of all schools to this point. The Orange County school having demonstrated that audiences could overflow hotel conference rooms, organizers rented the Keil Auditorium in downtown St Louis for the biggest evening sessions, where two thousand earnest people heard Schwarz and Philbrick.[29]

Yet this time the crusaders had unsolicited guests. Realizing they lacked information on the CACC, the ACLU suggested that the St Louis Civil Liberties Committee send observers to the event. The content of the speeches alarmed them. In one lecture, Schwarz attacked the ACLU for its campaign to have the Bible withdrawn from public schools. Paul Terry affirmed that communists had infiltrated Hollywood, giving them power "to sell the Communist idea to a guaranteed weekly audience of 100 million Americans, including 11 million children." Fred Schlafly delivered his routine against the Warren Supreme Court. ACLU's director Alan Reitman requested that ACLU branches nationwide monitor CACC activities.[30]

The CACC had also captured the attention of the *New York Times*. Its veteran reporter Cabell Phillips attended one of the school's evening sessions at the Keil Auditorium. The full-page article was published in the Sunday issue of the *Times* under the title "Physician Leads Anti-Red Drive with 'Poor Man's Birch Society.'" The piece was infused with the feeling that something was disturbingly wrong about the CACC. Phillips wrote that the resemblance with the JBS was "comparative rather than specific … The Christian Anti-Communism Crusade … stops a good deal short of the vehement summons to retaliation advocated by Robert W. H. Welch." Phillips commented that the charges "that certain individuals or institutions have been duped into 'serving the communist cause' were implied rather than directly stated." A St Louis reporter anonymously stated that, whereas earlier such events "created little more than a ripple of public interest," this one "ha[d] not only drawn quite substantial crowds, but they seem[ed] to be a cut or so above the social and intellectual average of such turnouts." More importantly, Phillips was able to get hold of Schwarz as he was "relaxing shirt-sleeved in his hotel suite" and quoted the crusader as saying: "Certainly these people – these dedicated anti-Communists want a leader. They want to be led; they want me to lead them. But I won't do it. If Bob Welch wants to do it he can; he's got a program of action and a lot of ready resolutions. But it's not my business. You know … I sometimes get the notion he follows me around the country, signing up the people after I've worked them up."[31]

When the article came out, Schwarz sent a letter to the *Times* claiming it was filled with mistaken information, in particular in its closing lines where he spoke of Welch. He dismissed these "alleged quotations" as not being "direct quotations but an attempted synthesis by the reporter of an extensive conversation and should be so designated." Three and a half months later, he received a reply from the *Times*, which apologized for its late response but denied that readers had been misled. Accurate or not, the closing passage of Phillips's piece posed a clear problem: it was an admission that the CACC indirectly acted as a JBS recruiting agent, echoing Welch's statement seven months earlier that his group was targeting for recruitment those whom the crusader had "awakened and alarmed." Schwarz always denied the veracity of this quote. In 1962, before journalist Lawrence Spivak on the TV program *Meet the Press*, he referred to it as "a false statement." Unhappy to see his professionalism challenged on national television, Cabell Phillips wrote to his colleague Spivak that the quote was in fact a verbatim transcription.[32]

The *New York Times* article was a major factor in Schwarz's being profiled among liberals as toxic. By the end of 1961, it was now commonly remarked that "Schwarz stirs them up, Welch signs them up." However, this had no negative effect in terms of his popularity among Birchers. Between 12 and 16 June 1961, the CACC held a school in Miami at the Everglades Hotel. The spectre of the Bay of Pigs fiasco created an atmosphere conducive to anticommunism. Miami being one of the earliest pockets of JBS support in Florida, Birchers were, as usual, present in the organization of the school. The Miami school drew five thousand people, which was becoming the regular turnout number. Shortly before the school opened, as he was interviewed once again by a *New York Times* journalist, Schwarz avoided any controversial statements but added, with defiance: "perhaps we'll have a big rally in Madison Square Garden soon."[33]

THE FULBRIGHT MEMORANDUM

On 13 June 1961, the investigation of General Edwin Walker, relieved from his command in Germany, submitted its conclusions. The inquiry cleared Walker of links with the John Birch Society but reprimanded him for making "derogatory public statements about prominent Americans," including former president Truman. Walker resigned from the army, making him the darling of conservatives, a victim of an alleged program of "muzzling the military." On 18 June, the *New York Times* headlined an article by Cabell Phillips revealing that many other high-ranking officers took part in programs based on "political theories resembling those of the John Birch Societies."

This was the first time the 1958 National Security Council directive pertaining to the military's participation in indoctrination programs was publicly mentioned, though its exact content remained classified. Phillips reported that only a handful of such programs had so far been conducted, such as a seminar held on the Naval Air Station Twin Cities (Minneapolis) in April 1961, during which the films *Operation Abolition* and *Communism on the Map* were shown after having been removed by the Pentagon from the list of acceptable material.[34]

Ten days later, J. William Fulbright, Democratic senator from Arkansas and chairman of the Committee on Foreign Relations, sent to President Kennedy a memorandum prepared by his staffers. Fulbright had learned that high-ranking officers had participated in a series of conferences held in Fort Smith, Fayetteville, and Little Rock, with speakers who included Robert Morris, George S. Benson, and Clifton L. Ganus of Harding College. Fulbright claimed to have uncovered instances of military involvement in programs dedicated to "right-wing radicalism" under the cloak of educational seminars, and he expressed his outrage that the military undertook education programs that stretched beyond its competence.[35]

The Fulbright Memorandum, as it would be called, warned the president that programs inspired by the 1958 NSC directive may "well become important obstacles to public acceptance of the President's program and leadership, if they are not already." Fulbright contended that the consequences of an outbreak of "this virus of right-wing radicalism" among the military could be horrendous, as was demonstrated by the recent revolt of the French generals against De Gaulle. The memorandum recommended the removal of the 1958 NSC directive and a transfer of all prerogatives pertaining to military education programs to the White House. Fulbright also recommended investigating the ties between the military and right-wing groups.[36]

For the Crusade, the most consequential passage in the document was an attachment containing a list of examples of military participation in educational seminars deemed of concern. Out of eleven entries from the years 1960 and 1961, more than four were related to Schwarz or the CACC. And yet Fulbright did not know the full extent of Schwarz's involvement with the military. He was unaware that the crusader had been sporadically lecturing before military personnel since the mid-1950s, that the military participated in the CACC school in San Diego in August 1960, or that, in early May 1961, Schwarz had spoken at the Minneapolis naval air station.[37]

Furthermore, the memorandum made no mention of a report that the ACLU had forwarded to Fulbright's office but that had remained confidential, perhaps in order to protect its anonymous source. It was based on the testimony of a man who presented himself as an ACLU member and naval reserve aviator at Glenview. The report claimed that, under the command of one Captain Isiah Hampton, the Glenview station had tried harder than most military bases to press anticommunist educational programs upon its personnel. The source had participated in the Education for American Security program in August 1960 and testified about a dinner he had had with the said officer and Schwarz. Both Hampton and Schwarz allegedly expressed views that considered civil liberties expendable in the anticommunist fight. Both men, the source added, had no problems with dictatorships, except those that were communist. The report ended with the source expressing his belief that neither Schwarz nor Hampton would oppose the establishment of a military dictatorship in the United States.[38]

Already, in April 1961, the Bay of Pigs fiasco had strengthened the Kennedy administration's determination to impose civilian control over the military. In May, still unaware of the 1958 NSC directive, Secretary of Defense Robert McNamara decided that no further policy statements would be made by army officials. In this context, the Fulbright Memorandum received a positive reading by both Kennedy and McNamara. However, in July, before the memorandum could be turned into policy, Pentagon officials revealed its existence to Democratic senator Strom Thurmond of South Carolina, a right-winger of Dixiecrat fame and former major general of the US Army Reserve. Thurmond burst into Fulbright's office, requesting a copy of the memorandum, but was turned down. On 21 July, some of the country's major newspapers disclosed the existence of the memo. Thurmond launched a series of orations on the Senate floor over this campaign that was "under way against the anti-Communist indoctrination of the American people and our troops in uniform" and that had been launched "by the Communist Party, U.S.A., in its official news organ, the Worker, and is now taking the form of a widespread movement from innumerable sources." On 2 August, under pressure to make the memorandum public, Fulbright reluctantly agreed to include it in the *Congressional Report*.[39]

Liberals widely approved the memo, and Fulbright's reputation among them ascended, an odd occurrence for a Southern Democrat with a long record of support for segregationist policies. On 10 August, Kennedy declared that Fulbright had "performed a service" by warning the administration of indoctrination programs. But conservatives, already angered by the Walker case, were most upset because their fears about the "muzzling of the military" had been confirmed. Thurmond called the memorandum an attack not only on the military but also "on the ability of the American people to understand the menace." In *Newsweek*, Ralph de Toledano saw the memorandum as stemming "from the philosophy prevailing in the new administration that the United States must get along with the Communists 'at all costs.'" *Human Events*'s Allan Ryskind spoke against this "brazen attempt" by New Frontier liberals, "who wax so eloquently about the guarantee of free speech in the First Amendment, to muzzle all those who disagree with the liberals." Robert Welch launched one of his letter-writing campaigns: Operation Fulbright Intimidation Binge.[40]

In July, after the controversy broke out but before the full disclosure of the memorandum on the Senate floor, the CACC was the subject of an article in the *Reporter*. In "Revivalism on the Far Right," an article that contained spoof drawings of medieval knights mocking the Crusade's name, journalist Philip Horton presented Schwarz and Strube as right-wing radicalism's recruiting agents, describing them as "having adopted techniques reminiscent of evangelists and patent-medicine salesmen," and warned that they should not be dismissed as marginal, considering "their growing influence in the schools and their prestige among certain elements of the armed forces." The Glenview seminar controversy illustrated "the manner in which these connections with the military can apparently grant a semi-official status to Dr. Schwarz and his forces."[41]

Before the end of the summer of 1961, Schwarz's relationship with the military was severed considerably. "Doors which had previously been open into military institutions were suddenly slammed shut," wrote Schwarz, who blamed the Fulbright Memorandum. People associated with the Crusade who had made speeches on military bases also found themselves out in the cold. Philbrick, who had been a popular lecturer over the years at military installations, found himself deprived of such engagements. In 1962, he explained in a letter that all military lecturing opportunities stopped with the memorandum.[42]

9

High-Water Mark: August–December 1961 and Crusade Spinoffs

"THE LARGEST ANTI-COMMUNISM RALLY IN AMERICA'S HISTORY"

By late summer of 1961, it was clear that it had been a frustrating year for the millions of Americans for whom the fight against communism was the frame through which most problems were viewed. Nineteen sixty-one had begun with the national press's agitation over the John Birch Society. In early August, California's attorney general Stanley Mosk announced there would be no investigation of the JBS, but he famously described its supporters as "wealthy businessmen, retired military officers and little old ladies in tennis shoes."[1]

Meanwhile, in the spring, the Kennedy administration's initial budget, which included a peacetime, non-recession deficit for the first time in years, confirmed that the president would continue to overextend the federal state. The fight over racial segregation, seen by many as proof that Communists were masterminding social strife, kept on raging. The summer of 1961 was dominated by the Freedom Rides, whereby civil rights groups attempted to test a Supreme Court ruling that, having declared racial discrimination in interstate passenger transportation unconstitutional, was organizing interracial rides throughout the South. The public across the nation, and the world, was shocked when the press, with gruesome pictures, reported on how the first Freedom Riders were assaulted in Alabama by KKK-led mobs.

The spring of 1961 saw the dual humiliation of the Bay of Pigs fiasco and the Soviet space flight. Then came the controversies over

General Walker and the Fulbright Memorandum. During the summer, the Soviets began to seal East Germany and build the Berlin Wall in order to curb the outflow of East Germans. In mid-August came the Fulbright Memorandum. It was against this backdrop that the CACC was preparing for its largest, most ambitious effort yet – the Southern California School of Anti-Communism, held at the Los Angeles Sports Arena (28 August – 2 September). In this non-election year, the anger of grassroots conservatives in Southern California was about to be channelled into Fred Schwarz's grand designs.[2]

Initially, Schwarz did not consider the project to be realistic: a second school in Los Angeles a year after a successful one, but this time with the week-long event being held at the recently built Los Angeles Sports Arena. This meant renting the building at the cost of $20,000 and finding a way to fill its sixteen thousand seats to capacity. The crusader was convinced of the feasibility of the project by William Brashears, a dentist from Fullerton who had chaired the Orange County school. However, the event was largely the brainchild of Patrick Frawley, who accepted the central chairmanship, coordinated the citizens' committees that sponsored the school, and hired a firm to advertise the event. Frawley also arranged for the LA Chamber of Commerce to organize a luncheon at which hundreds of businesspeople heard Schwarz. By the time the lecture ended, he could count on the support of an important part of the business establishment. The steering committee's eighty-seven members included industrialist Henry Salvatori, chairman of the oil enterprise Western Geophysical Co.; Alfred S. Bloomingdale, the inheritor of New York's Bloomingdale Department Stores; hotel mogul W. Barron Hilton; and John W. Dart, president of Rexall Drug Company.[3]

Having just recently completed his takeover of Technicolor, Frawley also managed to get Hollywood movie stars to appear at the school. One of them was the former president of the Screen Actors Guild, George Murphy, seen dancing alongside Shirley Temple in the 1938 hit *Little Miss Broadway*, and who had become a public relations executive for the film industry since his retirement from acting. Having become a Republican in 1939, Murphy was a fixture at GOP events and served as director of entertainment for Eisenhower's two inaugurations. Murphy agreed to serve as master of ceremonies for the school's evening sessions, and he appeared at the CACC school of San Francisco a few months later, where he spoke about his experience trying to root out Communists in Hollywood during his tenure at the Screen Actors Guild. Frawley later appointed Murphy vice-president of Technicolor.[4]

Ronald Reagan also appeared at the school. Ever since Murphy and Reagan had met while shooting Warner's 1943 musical *This Is the Army*, they had remained close. Murphy helped awaken Reagan's conservative views and paved the way for his peer by modelling a successful transition from Hollywood to conservative politics. In August 1961, Reagan had been the host of the TV and radio series *General Electric Theater* for eight years as well as the well-paid GE spokesman who toured the company's plants. His address disparaging the idea of the welfare state on the CACC school's third day was in the mould of his speeches of the late 1950s, when he regularly decried big government and communism. With Murphy and Reagan on board, fishing other big names among Hollywood Republicans was not hard. Singing cowboy Roy Rogers and his wife, actress Dale Evans (both already CACC life members); actor, singer, and Chevrolet spokesman Pat Boone; and actress Irene Dunn joined in. Hollywood legend John Wayne became a life-long CACC supporter. In a 1976 interview, Schwarz fondly recalled a recent $200 donation from Wayne. When Wayne died in 1979, Schwarz republished in his newsletter a letter he had once received in which "the Duke," having enclosed a $500 cheque, wrote: "I opened my big, fat mouth at our Annual Bull Sale in Arizona, and look what I got for you."[5]

Frawley also proposed that Schwarz give a series of prime-time televised lectures prior to the school. The crusader, who did not enjoy television and preferred live audiences, was cool to the idea but could not pass on such an opportunity. Air time was bought on KTTV-Channel 11, property of the Chandler family, an independent station fully owned since 1959 by Times-Mirror Company, which also owned the *Los Angeles Times*. KTTV, where air time was less expensive than on any affiliate of the "big three" national broadcasting corporations (ABC, CBS, and NBC), broadcast three half-hour sessions in which Schwarz lectured to a TV camera. The result was a cracking good one; indeed, Frawley's wife Geraldine told the crusader that those were the best talks she had heard from him. KTTV president Dick Moore suggested finding a sponsor who would televise the school's evening sessions. Such a sponsor appeared and threw in $30,000. The benefactor was the oil establishment incarnate, Charles S. Jones, head of the Richfield Oil Corporation since

9.1 | Roy Rogers and Ronald Reagan at Youth Night salute of the Southern California School of Anti-Communism, 1961. *Los Angeles Times* Photographic Archives.

1937. One of President Eisenhower's favourite golf and hunting partners, this sixty-five-year-old Texan was a big name among West Coast GOP fundraisers. After the CACC school in Orange County a few months earlier, a Richfield Oil representative bought the tapes of some of the lectures. "Finally," a journalist who detailed the story wrote, "he got the boss to listen to them. The boss was inspired by the messages and took up the cause."[6]

As preparation for the school was under way, not hundreds, but literally thousands of volunteers got involved, including three thousand Orange Countians who "attended and worked at the school during its five day stint," one journalist reported. The event was preceded by more than a month of preparatory rallies held in Greater Los Angeles cities, including Van Nuys, Pasadena, Anaheim, Whittier, Long Beach, and Santa Monica, attracting as many as seven thousand in some places. On 20 August, local newspapers ran a full-page advertisement announcing: "In Recognition of the So. California School of Anti-Communism: 41 Mayors Proclaim Anti-Communism Week." These included Los Angeles mayor Sam Yorty as well as mayors from almost all the important municipalities of the Greater LA area.[7]

Deep resentment towards the Kennedy administration clearly served as a catalyst for the event. During the preparatory meetings for the school, Schwarz tapped into this anger by speaking out against Kennedy's recently founded Alliance for Progress, a program aimed at containing Communism in Latin America through economic development. Before hundreds of clergy, he declared that "Communist leaders have apparently sold the West on the idea that communism springs from poverty and poor economic conditions." A few days later, before a hundred physicians, he accused the White House of working under a serious misapprehension. The best containment policy in Latin America, he said, was to recruit "a cadre of young South American intellectuals to go through the area's millions. For that is exactly what the Communists are doing."[8]

A few days later, the LA American Legion, which endorsed the school, suggested that the event's Youth Day feature a Marine colour guard. Representatives of the schools' Americanism Committee spoke to a Marine official, who assured them that the colour guard would be provided. The matter was passed on to the Marine Corps base in San Diego, but a ruling from Washington denied the request. GOP representative John H. Rousselot, an open JBS supporter, protested the decision and was quickly joined by many volunteers and sponsors. Secretary of Defense McNamara opted for appeasement and intervened to reverse the decision.[9]

The Fulbright Memorandum issue returned during the school's proceedings. Each mention of Fulbright's name fostered raucous booing. Retired admiral Chester Ward attacked Fulbright for the "gagging and smearing of the U.S. military," an initiative that he thought originated from the *Daily Worker* itself. Ward, a former navy judge advocate general, also spoke out against George

Kennan, Adlai Stevenson, and presidential advisers Walt Rostow, McGeorge Bundy, and Jerome Wiesner. During the Youth Day mass rally on the third night, Philbrick's call for a congressional investigation into the effort to "muzzle the military" earned him a standing ovation from the 17,500 present inside the Sports Arena and the few thousands outside.[10]

The school's "faculty" included the usual figures: Schwarz, Barnes, Colbert, Philbrick, Skousen, Sluis, and Strube. Walter Judd was originally announced as a speaker, but he called off his participation due to his busy House work in Washington. A high-tech solution was found: Judd's speech was to be broadcast from Washington on closed circuit television before the crowd at the Sports Arena. In this venture, the American Broadcasting Corporation (ABC) cooperated with KTTV. ABC officials later stated that "the request transcended competition with KTTV." A notable addition to the faculty was another politician: Democratic senator from Connecticut Thomas J. Dodd, who was given the responsibility of delivering the first televised lecture. Elected in 1958, Dodd was one of the Senate's most liberal members on domestic issues, but he was a hawk on foreign policy. Having served during the Nuremberg Trials as aide to Justice Robert H. Jackson, where he contributed to the sentencing of Nazi officials Wilhelm Keitel and Alfred Rosenberg, Dodd saw the USSR as tantamount to Nazi Germany.[11]

On Monday morning of 28 August 1961, Schwarz opened the school with his routine on communist philosophy, delivered before four thousand people. That evening came the first televised session. This was a critical moment as any hope to cover the school's mammoth costs hinged on the TV response. County commander of the American Legion Charles K. Wright read the pledge of allegiance. Master of ceremonies George Murphy introduced Dodd and Schwarz. Dodd's forty-five minute presentation dealt with how, after the Second World War, the United States had suffered "defeat after defeat" at the hands of the Communists, a situation that called for a new "national unity between Democrats and Republicans, liberals and conservatives, Catholics, Protestants and Jews." Schwarz then talked for an hour and a half, delivering what was the most watched speech he had made so far. The next evening, TV ratings soared, and, on Wednesday and Thursday evenings, the KTTV station, for the first time in its twelve-year history, topped all national broadcasters for two consecutive nights. KTTV president Dick Moore wrote to Walter

9.2 | Democratic Senator Thomas J. Dodd of Connecticut addressing the crowd at the Southern California School of Anti-Communism, 1961. *Los Angeles Times* Photographic Archives.

Judd that viewership figures were about 1 million, ranking the program first in viewers, with ABC's *The Untouchables* coming second. Newspapers were flooded by letters about the show. Schwarz was recognized by strangers in public places: "On several occasions people clapped when I entered a restaurant."[12]

On the second day, retired admiral Ward delivered a speech in which he offered a five-point "victory-over-the-Reds" program and criticized the inaction of Washington bureaucrats: "I am perfectly willing to pension all of them or put them in the housing administration." Skousen came onstage and expounded on his theories about Harry Hopkins's having given the A-bomb secrets to the enemy. The next day Skousen returned, this time speaking on "Communism, Psychiatry and Crime," and calling for an investigation of organized mental health programs

9.3 | Woman picket protesting an anticommunism school under way at the Los Angeles Sports Arena, 1961. *Los Angeles Times* Photographic Archives.

in the United States, which, he explained, were a smokescreen for communist propaganda, targeting "maladjusted personalities that lacked fundamental understanding or goals in life." This address drew an angry public reply from John Michel, president of the Los Angeles County Association for Mental Health.[13]

On Thursday, a conjunction of world events gave the school a particularly dramatic turn. On the same day that the Soviets announced they had resumed their nuclear tests the scheduled televised session was to feature a specialist on Cold War geopolitics, Major Alexander P. de Seversky, author of the classic Second World War treatise *Victory through Air Power*, which advocated the use of strategic air bombing. Within a solemn atmosphere, De Seversky explained that war was inevitable and that "it would be "national suicide" not to resume nuclear testing." The aviation pioneer spoke

9.4 | Dr Fred C. Schwarz, lower right, addresses the opening session of the Southern California School of Anti-Communism, *Los Angeles Times* Photographic Archives.

prophetically about the concept of an anti-missile shield. In order to survive, he said, the United States had to give priority to the development of the Nike-Zeus missile (an anti-missile missile), which he saw as the only way to protect the nation from the threat of intercontinental ballistic missiles. Walter Judd thereupon delivered his lecture from Washington on a closed circuit. After his talk, Murphy introduced Dr George M. Hollenback, former president of the LA County Dental Association, who displayed a $5,000 personal cheque he wished to give to the Crusade. "I want to see this movement sweep like a tidal wave across the country," said the seventy-four-year-old.[14]

A crowd of thirty-five hundred showed up at the Design for Victory Banquet at the Shrine exhibition hall, and two thousand more were

9.5 | Design for Victory Banquet of the Southern California School of Anti-Communism at the Shrine exhibition hall of Los Angeles, 1 September 1961. *Los Angeles Times* Photographic Archives.

turned away due to lack of seating. Strube gave a straight three-hour talk, which was relieved only by a five-minute break and a few songs from church singer Lee Childs. People donated dollar bills not by the thousands but by the tens of thousands. When the complete audit figures were released a month later, results were staggering. The school's disbursements were $96,496, but the revenues had been of more than $311,253, resulting in a net surplus of $214,496. When revenues are broken down into different categories, registration receipts were $109,615; contributions throughout the week were $92,699; and sales of books and records were $29,094. The closing banquet allowed the CACC to earn more than $69,745 in a few hours. In one week, the CACC raised almost as much money as it had during the whole of the preceding year (1960). The total attendance was about fifty thousand, ten times more than that at previous successful schools. The *Orange County Register* called the school "the largest anti-Communism rally in America's history," probably accurately so.[15]

Los Angeles Times entertainment columnist Hedda Hopper asked, "How about the Republican Party adopting this cause and putting this into every city in America?" In the same newspaper, former screenwriter-turned columnist Morrie Ryskind wrote, "At any rate, I can honestly say that in my 25 years in Los Angeles I have never known a local event that so completely captured the enthusiasm of the city." The *Los Angeles Examiner* editorialized: "The tremendous Los Angeles success of the School … now gives promise of its extension to other metropolitan centers." The *Orange County Register* congratulated Richfield Oil on sponsoring the show and claimed that the company "joins such other firms as Knott's Berry Farm, Cast Federal Savings, Dr. Ross, and Schick Razor in attempting to alert the people about the dangers to the American way of life from socialism and big government." A reporter contacted four Richfield Oil gas stations and was told that "hundreds of customers had paid their thanks for televising the sessions. During the week, sales pumped one-third, it was reported." During the three weeks following the school, Richfield received 6,545 letters about the show, of which only forty-four were negative. However, seeing Charles Jones sponsoring the whole venture made nationally known syndicated columnist Drew Pearson raise his eyebrow: "Mr. Eisenhower has denounced right-wing groups in vigorous language, but his friend Jones either doesn't read what the ex-President says or else doesn't agree with him."[16]

SPINOFFS

"There is no doubt whatsoever that there is a growing and spontaneous grass roots citizens' anti-Communist movement in the United States. A large part of the credit for this growth must be given to you and your colleagues," wrote public relationships specialist Marvin Liebman to Schwarz in 1962. However, Liebman warned, "Many individuals and organizations are attempting to utilize this growing national sentiment for various reasons and purposes – some highly motivated and responsible; others for personal profit either in terms of money, power or prestige."[17]

Any successful idea generates its share of offshoots and by-products, and CACC schools were no exception: "Dr. Schwarz, holds no patent on the school idea and lately he has begun to have imitators who may also become competitors." Thus wrote *Life Magazine*'s Keith Wheeler, commenting on the week-long seminars that were sprouting up in many states in 1961 and 1962. Sociologist Daniel Bell also noted "the fashionable spread of week-long seminars of anti-Communist 'schools' ... which swept sections of the country, particularly the Southwest and California." The same year, campaigning for re-election against Richard Nixon, California governor Pat Brown decried the "proliferation of right-wing groups and unlicensed anti-communist schools."[18]

The initial lookalikes were organized by CACC associates and featured some of the same speakers. In September 1959, an Austin anticommunism week was held in collaboration with the Austin Chamber of Commerce. It was chaired by Jack H. Sucke, a local insurance broker and one of Strube's acquaintances. During the week, which Sucke had Austin mayor Tom Miller proclaim "Anti-Communism Week," prominent local backers held two educational seminars and provided speakers before thirty civic clubs and five thousand junior or high school students. The second Austin school emulated the CACC model more closely. This time, it had day-long seminars organized that featured, among six speakers, Strube and Skousen (Philbrick was invited but could not attend). Presentations were interspersed with screenings of films such as *Operation Abolition.*[19]

After attending the 1958 CACC school of Long Beach, Walter Huss, pastor from Portland and leader of Freedom Center International (FCI), emulated the idea. In the summer of 1960, Huss's FCI sponsored its own school, featuring appearances by Schwarz, Skousen, and Arens. Philbrick was welcomed at the Portland airport by a flag-waving delegation. Hundreds attended the school held at the Multnomah School of the Bible (now Multnomah University), followed by two patriotic rallies at the local civic auditorium, the cumulative attendance of which reached four thousand people. This almost complete copy of the CACC formula ended with a Saturday night freedom banquet, where *Operation Abolition* was shown and fundraising pitches made for the FCI. As was the case with other CACC schools spinoffs, the FCI sold CACC material, thus acting as multiplier feeding the success of the Crusade. In November 1961, Cleon Skousen received news from his brother Leroy, from Portland, that Walter Huss was openly admitting that his project was an offshoot of CACC schools.[20]

The spinoff anticommunism schools peaked in 1961, with such events held nationwide throughout the year. On 11 March 1961, in Iowa, the Dubuque Soil Conservation District organized a seminar featuring local conservative speakers and a showing of – what else? – *Operation Abolition.* An eight-day program was organized in Oxnard, California, by retired army officer Carl Wilgus, consisting of lectures, opportunities to listen to recorded tapes of Schwarz, and the screening of anticommunism films. In May 1961, former intelligence officer Charles Woolery organized the four-day Greater Salt Lake City Anti-Communist Seminar, featuring big names (Cleon Skousen, retired Admiral Chester Ward, *National Review* collaborator Frank Meyer). In August 1961, in Illinois, a businessman named John Harrell and one hundred followers founded the Anti-Communist Christian Conservative Church, which set up a "permanent anticommunist school" on his eastern St Louis estate, but the venture ended when the FBI raided the school to arrest a deserting marine whom the congregation had been harbouring for some time. A month later, in Aurora, Illinois, the Copley Press organized a forum designed by its educational director Paul Terry and featuring George S. Benson and Skousen.[21]

Sometimes, a successful CACC school in a given location directly sparked local offshoots. The fifty-thousand-person extravaganza at the Los Angeles Sports Arena generated dozens of spinoff schools across Southern California. In the summer of 1961, shortly after the CACC school in Miami, a group of patriots set up the well-organized Fort Lauderdale Anti-Communism Crusade. Their chairman explained in a letter to Barry Goldwater that they set up headquarters in downtown Fort Lauderdale, where they organized study groups using films, books, and invited lecturers. In November 1961, they held the three-day Annual South Florida Anti-Communism Conference.[22]

The Project Alert program was one of a kind. It was founded by Walter Schindler, a former vice-admiral. In 1960, after his retirement from the military, he set up in Sarasota, Florida, a modest anticommunist educational initiative for which he received the backing of the local mayor. In September 1960, Schindler unexpectedly earned the support of George S. Benson. The National Education Program sent its executive vice-president Glenn A. Green to help Schindler organize a two-day seminar that, overnight, garnered the support of local right-wing groups, the city commission, and the county Chamber of Commerce. The first Project Alert seminar was so successful that a second one was organized two weeks later at the municipal auditorium, followed by dozens in Florida and throughout the country. Project Alert remained more a name for locally based events than a centralized organization. Its seminars nonetheless came to greatly resemble the CACC format. The transformation was almost complete in the fall of 1961, the only difference being that Project Alert events, the duration of which varied from one place to the other, were not yet held in single stretches.[23]

This difference disappeared when Project Alert organized a consecutive five-day school of anticommunism at Los Angeles's Shrine Auditorium in December 1961, three months after the CACC had organized its mammoth event at the LA Sports Arena. The Project Alert school featured more than nine CACC associates. This event was a carbon copy of a CACC school, only missing the official logo and Fred Schwarz himself, who declined any participation in the project. This seminar had gathered a large number of retired high-ranking military officers, and Schwarz was wary of unnecessarily stirring up criticism at a moment when there was widespread concern over the extent of military involvement in right-wing activities.[24]

The Project Alert school at the Shrine Auditorium was televised, which exposed to the wider public a few shades of lunacy. Paul Terry implied that President Kennedy had "Red, red-blooded Americans" as his advisors and called for the impeachment of politicians who were "soft on communism." Retired general Orvil Anderson deplored that "democracy has never been compatible with initiative in the military sphere." Colonel Mitchell Paige, Second World War hero, delivered a speech in which he claimed that, as far as Earl Warren was concerned: "impeachment is not the proper penalty but rather, it appears to me, a more deserved punishment would be hanging." This generated cheers and laughs from the audience. Paige later apologized, but the fuss that ensued took its toll on Project Alert, with attendance sharply dropped during the last two days, resulting in a net loss of $20,000. Los Angeles Methodist bishop Gerald Kennedy, who had on various instances criticized the JBS, wrongly claimed that Schwarz had advocated the hanging of Earl Warren, a comment he later refused to retract.[25]

The school movement began to recede by late 1962 but nonetheless continued until the mid-1960s. As late as 1965, a "freedom school" organized by libertarian activist William LeFevre and funded by South Carolina's textile mogul Roger Milliken held week-long courses each summer to expose socialism's pitfalls and teach the benefits of free enterprise. Fundamentalist leader Billy James Hargis organized his own five-day schools until the late 1960s, the first installment taking place in January 1962 in a motel in Tulsa, Arizona.[26]

The second major category of CACC spinoffs was the study group movement. Less visible than seminars, anticommunist study groups brought the anticommunist fight into the private sphere and gave anticommunist activists who wanted prompt action the possibility of mobilizing in partial or complete autonomy from multi-state or national movements. The CACC surely did not invent conservative study groups; an outgrowth of a long tradition of pre-television civic middle-class hobbies, they had appeared gradually among grassroots activists throughout the 1950s. Historian Michelle Nickerson notes that more than 123 such groups or political clubs already existed in Southern California by the mid-1950s, often founded by housewives and having a "distinct feminine style of political organizing." The CACC unsurprisingly tapped, and then considerably fed, this trend that infused politics into home life. Study groups provided numerous people a first shot in their lifetimes to unite in small groups, learn together about their common enemy, and then find ways to defeat its perceived manifestations in family, community, state, or national life.[27]

Study groups were a solution to two problems that were often acknowledged in both official CACC literature and in private correspondence between its collaborators. First, due to a lack of resources, no real effort could be made to directly coordinate local initiatives resulting from individual meetings or anticommunism schools. Philbrick once privately admitted that he wished someone could pick up where Schwarz left off in order to keep people involved after CACC schools. In 1962, Schwarz's hired adviser Marvin Liebman similarly suggested that, once Crusade events were finished, "a continuing organization – no matter how informal – should be in existence to continue educational work which would stimulate broader action." Another problem was the impossibility of organizing CACC schools in every location where the demand existed when the organization's mailbox began to overflow with proposals.[28]

A convenient idea came up in the April 1959 newsletter, which contained an ad for a handbook that was titled *Establish a Local Study Group*, and that was available for fifty cents. Written by Strube, the handbook offered a complete do-it-yourself method. In its preface, the fiery Texan conceived the study group concept as well adapted to the needs of the day: "If we are to learn from the lessons of our militia in war times, from 1776 until the outbreak of World War I, our combat bands must be tightly organized." In the 1960 handbook, Strube developed his method further:

> Madison Avenue public relations and sales techniques must be applied to "smoothly" develop interest. A dessert party, back-yard barbecue, or buffet dinner will entice friends that might not otherwise come ... AFTER the social festivities announce that you have a special surprise for them. Tell them you have procured an interesting historical film entitled "Communism on the Map" that you want them to see ... call for a show of hands of those that would like to meet regularly to listen to tapes and films to obtain more knowledge.[29]

Ten people was the recommended group size. The equipment consisted of only a tape recorder and a movie projector. Study group members were to each pay a suggested fee of two dollars for basic registration, plus one dollar for each meeting. "The clinic tapes," the handbook said, "cost $30.00 per set, and a 12 set of booklets cost $20.00, or a total of $50.00 is desirable for formation." Meetings, it was suggested, were to be held at least twice a month, with each covering a specific topic. Study groups were to be given names that enhanced the feeling of belonging. "Select a name such as 'Northside Study Group,' 'The Christian Cell,' 'Patrick Henry Brigade,' 'Paul Revere Lamp Lighters,' 'Americans for Freedom,' 'Youth for Victory,' etc. It is best not to pick up a city, county, or state name, as there will probably be other committees formed." The handbook also offered an extensive list of study material, including anticommunism films and more than two hundred recorded lectures given in the context of CACC schools.[30]

In June 1960, Schwarz announced that more than a thousand CACC-inspired study groups had been founded and that the movement was "spreading like a fire across the country." Barbara Hawkins, reporter from the *Lafayette Journal and Courier*, described the multiplying of small local study circles in Lafayette, Indiana, composed of "persons you may see on the streets any day of the year" and who have become dedicated "to learning, as thoroughly as possible, about communism." The article indicated that, "across the U.S., as you read this, are 1,000 similar study clubs composed of equally dedicated persons, Democrats and Republicans, Catholics, Protestants and Jews."[31]

Various conservative groups made up the movement. In Lafayette, activists used CACC material but also followed guidelines from the Cardinal Mindszenty Foundation, which, Hawkins reported, "supplie[ed] a list of documents and a series of discussion questions to be perused by the group." In Missouri, the Four Freedoms Study Group was designed specifically to orient people towards reading material from various organizations and authors. In January 1961, in Spokane, Washington, a dentist by the name of John Ghigleri designed, with his wife and six other couples, an eight-week course "composed of literature on Communism from government and private sources and recorded speeches by nationally-known anti-Communist authorities." In May 1961, Ghigleri's group had been incorporated under the name Freedom Fighters, Inc., with a few thousand people following the program on the West Coast. "Anti-communism study groups are sprouting everywhere," Idaho columnist John Corlett observed.[32]

The Crusade encouraged the formation of such groups. Schwarz reported that a young man from Chicago who attended only one session of the 1960 Milwaukee CACC school bought the tape recordings of all the speakers. Two months later, when the crusader returned to Chicago, he learned that the man "had established 13 study circles." Those who wrote to Barry Goldwater after attending the CACC school in Phoenix often mentioned the forming of several study groups in their community in the wake of the event. After the Orange County school in March 1961, a doctor from Garden Grove was credited for having founded more than forty-four study groups. In March 1962, when the movement was still at its peak, Jim Colbert told one journalist that he estimated that five thousand study groups had been founded, all of which followed the Crusade's lead. "In the wake of Dr. Schwarz's immense rallies and 'anticommunism schools' sprout militant 'study groups' that expand, subdivide and multiply like human cells," noted *Look* reporter Fletcher Knebel. A 1962 report from liberal watchdog Group Research indicated that the exact relationship these groups had with their respective patent organizations was impossible to determine. In fact, most of them became independent once they acquired the material necessary to function. There is much to suggest that most of these groups either disbanded once members had completed their "course" or continued to exist but switched their attention to other issues. The spontaneous, unmonitored, and decentralized nature of the study groups was entirely in keeping with Schwarz's dictum: "What we need is multiplicity, not unity." Strube echoed Schwarz when he claimed: "We must create ten thousand Anti-Communist organizations so that if one is smeared, there would still be 9,999 left."[33]

"HOLLYWOOD'S ANSWER TO COMMUNISM"

On 29 September 1961, the *Los Angeles Times* reported: "A giant rally at the Hollywood Bowl on Oct. 16 will present ... a follow-up on the Southern California School of Anti-Communism." This one-night event was again Pat Frawley's idea. The concept was simple: a televised rally at the Hollywood Bowl at which luminaries of the film industry would demonstrate their anticommunism. Pat Frawley could not help but ride the momentum he felt everywhere. Because Hollywood was often deemed a hotbed of liberalism by the right wing, because it was the main origin of American technicolored film spectacles, and because movie stars had had a great time at the Sports Arena three weeks before, an even bigger celebration was now possible. The show he envisioned was to feature some speakers of the Sports Arena school as well as other Hollywood personalities. It would once again be televised by KTTV-Channel 11 and sponsored by the Richfield Oil Corporation.[34]

"Hollywood's Answer to Communism" was scheduled for Monday, 16 October. A roster of Hollywood actors announced they would show up: Edgar Bergen, Pat Boone, Walter Brennan, Don DeFore, Andy Devine, Rock Hudson, Bill Lundigan, Jeanette MacDonald, Lloyd Nolan, Pat O'Brien, Gigi Perreau, Mary Pickford, Vincent Price, Gene Raymond, Ronald Reagan, Tex Ritter, Cesar Romero, Robert Stack, James Stewart, Marshall Thompson, John Wayne, and Van Williams. Several other personalities joined in: screenwriter and director Richard Breen, Nat King Cole, singer Connie

Haines, television personalities Ozzie and Harriet Nelson, producer Jack Warner, and two Hollywood directors – Walt Disney and John Ford. Once again, the master of ceremonies was George Murphy. The free-admittance show was planned to begin at 7:00 p.m. and to last for about three hours. This was almost like an Academy Award evening ceremony but featuring mostly known Republican or conservative Hollywood personalities.

Hollywood politics explained Frawley's success in finding participants. In 1960, blacklisted screenwriter Dalton Trumbo had received screen credits for the movies *Exodus* and *Spartacus*, to the great displeasure of many conservatives. Some blacklisted actors and writers had filed a suit against the Motion Picture Association of America and ten major film producers. In a context within which Hollywood appeared ready to turn the page on McCarthyism, the event provided an opportunity for conservatives of the motion pictures industry to reassert themselves. As *New York Times* reporter Murray Schumach noted, this was well understood by the industry's liberals, whose general attitude towards the Hollywood Bowl show "range[d] from suspicion to hostility," most of them noting that "leaders of this rally failed to recognize what liberals regard as a similarity between communists and such extreme right-wing groups as the John Birch Society."[35]

Frawley's Schick Safety Razor Company and Technicolor signed up with KTTV to sponsor the Hollywood Bowl show for the Los Angeles area, and Richfield Oil, which sponsored the show outside Los Angeles, sold the idea to thirty-five stations along the West Coast, stretching from Seattle to San Diego and including other western states such as Utah and Arizona. The whole US Pacific zone and a few other states aired the show on primetime. In a message sent to TV executives, Richfield specified that it was not planning a single commercial break during the three-hour broadcast, "with the exception of a short opening and closing statement plus occasional Richfield logo type supers." All in all, this "public service" cost the three sponsors (Richfield Oil, Technicolor, and Schick) nearly $50,000.[36]

Despite the success at the Sports Arena and the sponsorship by Richfield, many stations were apprehensive, particularly in areas where hard-hitting anticommunism was less fashionable. In Seattle, officials from the King Broadcasting Company, an NBC affiliate owning several local stations, expressed concern that the tone of the show would be tainted by what it called the "Birch Society approach."

Internal memos from the King Broadcasting Company show that the network only accepted the broadcast when Richfield Oil executives informed it that the oil company chairman, Charles Jones, understood and shared those concerns and that the event would be devoid of any emotional or unsubstantiated charges against individuals or institutions. In the end, the King Broadcasting Company executives decided that the show would be followed by the broadcast of a "serious" discussion panel on communism titled "The Threat." Interestingly, a State Department official, Roger Tubby, had an exchange with Lee Schulman from the King Broadcasting Company and was quite complimentary of the broadcaster's decision to air a high-brow discussion. Tubby even suggested that the discussion panel should include US attorney general Robert Kennedy.[37]

On 16 October 1961, the *Long-Beach Press-Telegram* announced that Fred C. Schwarz, "the summer season's most highly rated new television personality," would return with his crew "to compete with Fall fare." With no rain in the forecast, the show began at 8:00 p.m., with about fifteen thousand people flocking to the Bowl. For an hour the crowd was entertained by singer Connie Haines before the opening ceremony began. "Two hundred American Legionnaires served as ushers and 350 Boy Scouts formed a massive color guard," the *Los Angeles* Times reported, with Chinese, Japanese, and Hawaiian kids in the front ranks, projecting an image of tolerance and pluralism, a spectacle mocked by liberal columnist James Aronson who quipped that these kids' "unseen parents have unspoken trouble finding homes in Christian white American neighborhoods." George Murphy welcomed the live audience and TV viewers to "the largest anti-Communist rally ever held anywhere in the world." Producer Jack Warner gave a short speech, claiming that, twenty years before, "the Communists made Hollywood a prime target. Through domination of this vast media, they knew they could control a good percentage of our thinking." The show was peppered with Hollywood stars and personalities who took the stage for a few moments each.[38]

Thomas Dodd delivered the first of the night's four main addresses. The Democrat hawk warmed the audience by mocking the *New York Times* – the name of which generated spontaneous booing – for a recent piece in which he was mistakenly referred to as a Republican, though the rest of his speech kept a careful bipartisan tone and targeted communism. "Let's get Communism in true focus," Dodd insisted to a wildly applauding crowd. "Communism is total evil. It is all black. There is nothing gray about it."[39]

Following Dodd's speech, the unannounced appearance of C.D. Jackson brought the house down. The dashing, mustached, sixty-year-old former Eisenhower adviser and current *Life Magazine* publisher had just made a forty-eight-hundred-kilometre flight from New York. Jackson expressed what a great a privilege it was "to be here tonight to align *Life Magazine* with Sen. Dodd, Rep. Judd, Dr. Schwarz and the rest of these implacable fighters." Then, he apologized on behalf of Time-Life for a short, anonymous piece published in *Life* that had dealt with the CACC school and had been given at the LA Sports Arena the previous month. This article was titled "Far-Right Revivalists" and it described the Sports Arena event as a revival meeting "held with full hullaballoo and political portent." "Regretfully," Jackson said, "my own magazine recently published an oversimplified misinterpretation. I believe we were wrong and I am profoundly sorry." Though *Life* had received numerous letters of protest and subscription cancellations from its conservative readers over the article, Jackson's public apology would not have taken place without the behind-the-scenes initiative of Frawley, who called Henry Luce to complain about the article and later flew to New York to meet with him personally.[40]

Skousen took the stage for what quickly evolved into a more virulent presentation than either Dodd's or Jackson's. The Mormon outlined his program to end the Cold War, calling for an investigation into and a cleansing of the State Department, which he accused of having lost China, North Korea, Laos, Cuba, and, more recently, the Congo to Communists. He criticized the UN, using the term "world planner," and called for a redrafting of its charter – "or we get out of it." Skousen also demanded the outlawing of the CPUSA and the termination of all diplomatic relations with the Soviets as well as a Western embargo on shipments of food to countries of the Communist Bloc. Skousen's impassioned rhetoric, far from the moderate tone Richfield had promised broadcasters, drew the most applause of the night.[41]

Time was running out. C.D. Jackson's impromptu appearance and Skousen's harangue had eaten into the allotted time as Walter Judd took the stage. However, the Minnesota congressman ate a considerable amount of extra time himself. Judd lauded Schwarz: "Unfortunately I've been a poor salesman all these years of one main idea, the same idea that Dr. Schwarz has written about so brilliantly and convincingly in his book, *You Can Trust the Communists.*" He lauded Dodd: "We would welcome him in the Republican Party because he is the cream of the crop." He decried Communists: "They know they must conquer the world if they are to abolish private property. They must take children from their parents … They must bring up the children conditioned, as dogs were conditioned by Pavlov." He decried the State Department: "This is your State Department, in charge of your destiny. No wonder we've got to have a school in Washington."[42]

Left with a ridiculous ten minutes, the only thing Schwarz could do was announce upcoming CACC schools and make a prediction for the following spring: "Hold your breath," he said, "we invade the East – Washington D.C., and New York City." He called for a worldwide crusade against communism and announced that a permanent Latin American school would be launched to "flood South America with anti-Communist literature prepared by trained students on mobile printing presses." With so little time left, unable to build up the dramatic tension that characterized his polished speaking style, his speech appeared like the last minutes of a play and, as such, had a frantic, wound-up quality.[43]

Its glitches notwithstanding, "Hollywood's Answer to Communism" was the greatest triumph of Schwarz's career. Within a few weeks, despite the increasing glow of controversy surrounding its activities, the CACC had organized the largest single-issue anticommunist gatherings in the nation's history. Never before, or after, would the Australian be endorsed by so many big names, and C.D. Jackson's retraction almost served as a warning to those who would criticize the CACC. Estimates on the number of people who watched the show vary. The lowest was given by the *New York Times*, which estimated about 4 million people. Frawley's Technicolor company sheet gave a much higher figure of 7 million.[44]

Reruns of the show were made. Two weeks later, an edited version of the show, coupled with excerpts of the Sports Arena School, was broadcast in New York by the independent station WPIX-Channel 11 through the sponsorship of the Schick Safety Razor Company and Technicolor. With little advertising, the show managed to draw an average of 8.5 percent of New York viewers during the evening, with a peak of 12.5 percent. In December 1961, a copy of the telecast was bought by Roger Milliken, president of the Deering-Milliken

Company of Spartanburg, South Carolina (one of the country's textile giants), a JBS sympathizer and notorious union buster. Milliken decided thereupon to sponsor airing the show on the thirteen TV stations across the Carolinas and in Georgia, with limited audiences also being reached in Virginia, Tennessee, and Alabama. With these states still in the midst of the Southern Red Scare, the reaction was good. "Letters, telegrams and telephone calls exceeded 2,000. It is estimated the program was seen by 1,500,000 people," Milliken wrote in a promotional leaflet.[45]

By late 1961, Richfield Oil had received approximately fourteen thousand letters about the LA school and the Hollywood Bowl show, and they were overwhelmingly positive. George Murphy mentioned receiving about "13,000 pieces of mail" for Schick and Technicolor combined. Even in traditionally less conservative areas, the Bowl show had been well received. In Portland, Oregon, an *Oregon Journal* reporter wrote that, at KGMTV-Channel 8, "the switchboard was deluged with congratulatory calls. Messages have been coming in steadily since and all have been favorable." In Seattle, the King Broadcasting Company received numerous letters of praise; nonetheless, the minority of viewers who thought otherwise utterly despised the show. One wrote to King Broadcasting Company that he thought he saw a swastika on Schwarz's sleeve. A student newspaper from Stanford University compared Schwarz to Hitler. According to *Seattle Times* columnist C.J. Skeen: "grave doubts remain whether the emotional frenzy generated can be regarded as any real contribution to the cause advanced."[46]

The show depended on, but also fed, a popular wave that peaked in Southern California in the last months of 1961. The press reported daily anticommunist activities in the region, especially in the Greater LA Area. Highly attended patriotic meetings and rallies were held in schools, churches, and civic institutions. Suburbanites organized study groups using printed and recorded material from the CACC, the Cardinal Mindszenty Foundation, or other organizations that seemed to have spawned overnight. Politicians quickly joined the fray. The GOP from five Southland congressional districts held "an all-day 'Facts for Freedom' rally in Long Beach Municipal Auditorium," featuring Republican gubernatorial candidate for Texas Jack Cox and Crusade collaborator Robert Morris.[47]

In late October, *New York Times* journalist Bill Becker reported on the new "Rightist upswell" in Southern California, comparing the anticommunist appeal in the region to the America First movement that had preceded the Second World War. The trend, he wrote, "is considerable, and growing steadily," with some of its most immediately visible manifestations being the recent flurry of car bumper stickers ("with slogans like 'Americanism – The Only Ism for Me,' or 'Socialism Is Communism,' 'No On Red China'") and the proliferation of conservative bookstores such as the Heritage Book Shoppe in Van Nuys or Poor Richard's Book Shop in Hollywood. Becker identified more than twelve major "ultraconservative organizations" active in the Greater LA area alone.

But among all groups, Becker noted, the CACC had "supplanted the John Birch Society as the most popular group among Southern California Right-Wingers." The Crusade now had more than seventy thousand contributors (up from forty thousand four months before), of which a third lived in Southern California. As to the amount of money the CACC raised, Becker quoted Schwarz: "We should go over the $1,000,000 mark this year." The actual figure for 1961, as disclosed a few months later, was $1,273,492, which was more than the total amount for all previous years since the CACC was founded. Earnings came primarily from schools, which allowed the Crusade to raise a total of $494,726 across the whole year, when registration, fees, school donations, and banquet were included. The CACC had become a million-dollar business.[48]

The Hollywood Bowl rally was the CACC's high-water mark, but it also alarmed liberals nationwide. "If Schwarz could bring mighty *Life* to his knees, what else might he not do? Liberal magazines detected a Hitler in the making," historian William L. O'Neill writes. The Kennedy administration perceived that anticommunism was at risk of getting seriously out of hand. The Crusade, one of the groups that had been mentioned in the Fulbright Memorandum as politicizing the military, and that held rallies wherein the Kennedy administration's foreign policy was despised, was now holding televised events funded by large corporations and featuring Hollywood stars. "Kennedy," Rick Perlstein writes, "had a legislative agenda to pass, a foreign policy to manage – tasks complicated when the most powerful media institution in the country was joining forces with those who would declare both treasonous." While admittedly preoccupied by the situation, Kennedy also saw a political opening in the right-wing upsurge, one that would allow him to put the GOP on the defensive over the issue of extremism and that might help the

Democratic Party during the 1962 midterm election and the next contest for the presidency in 1964.[49]

The counterattack kicked off in the form of a series of speeches Kennedy delivered in the west. After stops in Seattle and Phoenix, Kennedy arrived in Los Angeles, where he spoke on 19 November at the Hollywood Palladium. Picketed by thousands of opponents outside the building, Kennedy attacked: "Let our patriotism be reflected in the creation of confidence in one another rather than in crusades of suspicion." He later criticized those who "find treason in our churches, in our highest court, and even in the treatment of our water." In a direct reference to the Fulbright controversy, he criticized those "who object quite rightly to politics intruding in the military, but are very anxious for the military to engage in their kind of politics." His speech received a rousing welcome from his audience.[50]

A few days later, Robert Kennedy breakfasted with Attorney Joseph L. Rauh as well as Walter and Victor Reuther, respectively, the head of the United Auto Workers (UAW) and his administrative assistant. Walter Reuther had been instrumental in Kennedy's victory in the 1960 Democratic primaries, notably by inciting Senator Hubert Humphrey to withdraw from the race and then recruiting his delegates to the Kennedy camp. During the presidential campaign in the fall of 1960, Kennedy included the UAW's labour policy proposals in his platform, and the union responded in kind, supporting the Democrats in many states. Like Robert Kennedy, the Reuther brothers were convinced that a show such as "Hollywood's Answer to Communism" should not be allowed to happen again, and they gave the president's brother a few suggestions to that end.[51]

At this point, the only mention found in the press about this impending counterattack was in an article by Ralph de Toledano, who reported in his *Newsweek* column that several meetings were being held between influential personalities in Washington "to plan the attack on the anti-Communists." De Toledano added that specific meetings were "scheduled to devise ways and means of discrediting the highly successful anti-Communist crusade being led by Dr. Fred Schwartz [sic]."[52]

10

World Ambitions

KERALA

While the CACC's fortunes and finances appeared to be growing limitlessly in 1960 and 1961, its leader's ambition to turn his organization into a major international player appeared to become a possibility at last. This was first seen in how the CACC responded more quickly than before to the requests it received for assistance. In 1960, Schwarz swiftly agreed to support the Conservative Baptist Foreign Mission Society, a fundamentalist missionary body active in Central Africa. Letters brought news of the situation in the Congo, where Belgium had granted independence to its former colony at the January 1960 Brussels Conference. The situation looked to be chaotic in the Congo, where riots in Leopoldville in late 1959 had alarmed Western governments, who feared that local and international Communists would exploit the crisis. The Baptist missionaries who wrote Schwarz mentioned that the security situation made their work difficult and that Christian missions were being targeted by radical leftist groups. Schwarz gave them copies of one of his pamphlets and paid for the printing of tracts in the Swahili language.

In 1961, the CACC also received an "urgent request" from Nigeria for thousands of copies of its literature (books, booklets, pamphlets) from the Pocket Testament League, another interdenominational evangelical mission, who planned to "flood an entire nation" with it. As one missionary wrote Schwarz, his agency would do its best to put this material in the hands of the right leaders: "Having worked all over Nigeria for three years we have a pretty good idea as to whom these people are." Before the year ended, the CACC had invested $4,000 in the project. Schwarz also launched an appeal to fund a Japanese student program, one that never came to be, but the sums amassed to that end – $12,500 – served to publish a Japanese translation of *You Can Trust.*[1]

However, Schwarz's most ambitious international project took place in the state of Kerala, located at the southern tip of India. On 10 March 1957, Kerala Communists won 36.5 percent of the vote in a state election, picking up sixty seats out of 126 in the state house, allowing them to form, with the support of five independents, one of the world's few democratically elected Communist governments. Kerala had India's highest population density – 13 million people in a territory as large as Switzerland – as well as its largest Christian community (one-third of the population), mostly composed of Syrian churches whose origin can be traced back to the first century. The growth of the Kerala Communist Party, implanted in the state since 1930, was based on successful outreach to rural areas. This phenomenon was furthered by Kerala's high literacy rates compared to the Indian average, which facilitated exposure to Western influences. The Kerala election result generated fear in Washington. The Eisenhower administration raised US assistance to India and mounted a CIA operation to fund political opposition groups. For Schwarz, a critical battle had begun: "The thought of the 400,000,000 of India added to the 900,000,000 already controlled by Communism is nightmarish."[2]

The man Schwarz considered up to the task was K. George Thomas, whom he had met in Seattle a few months after the Kerala election. India-born George Thomas was the son of a missionary from a conservative Christian movement, the Plymouth Brethren. On his mother's side, he belonged to the Pakalomattam family, one of the oldest Syrian Christian Kerali families. A dark-skinned, intelligent-looking man in his early thirties, Thomas had been lecturer in history and political science in a small college in Kottayam before receiving, in 1953, a scholarship that permitted him to complete his PhD in political science at the University of Washington in 1957. According to Schwarz, Thomas had been offered a job at the UN "and could have lived like a gentleman," but he decided to return home to manage the India Gospel Mission (IGM), a Brethren-based missionary group he had founded with his father. Upon his return to Kerala in 1957, the IGM began publishing a magazine called *Viswa Deepam* (lit. the light of the world), which published Christian and anticommunist articles in both English and Malayalam. In late 1957,

Schwarz recontacted Thomas and both men agreed that the CACC would send monthly sums of $250 to the IGM.[3]

Kerala's Marxist-Leninist premier E.M.S. Namboodiripad committed a series of missteps that doomed his government. Starting from a hard-line position, he freed Communist prisoners and cancelled their sentences before handing responsibility for public order to People's Committees, whose rule often led to abuse. The Kerala government proceeded with its program of popular education by announcing the nationalization of school textbooks, a measure that the important Kerala Christian community saw as a direct challenge to educational rights. One of Thomas's coworkers wrote to Schwarz: "we have organized thousands of volunteers willing and even ready to die, if need be, to withstand any attempt by the government to take the schools by force."[4]

In early 1958, Thomas wrote to his US sponsor that a wider circulation for his weekly magazine *Viswa Deepam* would require the acquisition of a second-hand printing press at the cost of $5,000. The request came at about the same time as the first big cheque from the Bradley Foundation, allowing Schwarz to send Thomas a cable authorizing the purchase of an entire printing establishment from a local printer in Kottayam. This permitted *Viswa Deepam* to be printed at a rate of ten thousand copies per month as well as allowing for the printing and distribution of a translated version of Schwarz's House Un-American Activities Committee testimony. By the end of 1958, the monthly sum George Thomas requested was $400, and the amounts sent to Kerala had already passed those allocated to Andhra.[5]

In 1959, the political crisis in Kerala deepened. The price of food rose, as did unemployment. The state was affected by multiple strikes and violence between public authorities and the opposition. Indian prime minister Nehru decided to use his constitutional powers to suspend the Kerala legislature. The Communist government of Kerala thus ended on 23 July 1959, after just two years. Kerala was subsequently directly run by India's central government until the special election of 1960. It was in this context that Thomas envisioned the printing of a daily Christian anticommunist newspaper. "The daily paper," Thomas wrote Schwarz, "will be the only mouthpiece of Christian evangelicals in India." But the project required about $50,000, which had to be invested quickly if the newspaper was to make some impact before the 1960 election. While Thomas sent Schwarz appeals for funds, warning that Communists were preparing their comeback, his sponsor tried, during the spring and summer of 1959, to find partners who could assist the CACC in this regard.[6]

Schwarz sought help from "one of the very large foundations in New York," the name of which remains unknown but which apparently showed interest in India. However, when they met, it was apparent that the foundation's officials had no understanding of Schwarz's grassroots approach. The crusader was irate:

> Can't you see what you are doing? You have told me yourselves that you have difficulty securing anyone to go to India representing your group unless you increase his salary by twenty-five per cent. When that individual with his increased salary gets to India, what does he do? Does he go out into the villages where the temperature may be 120 degrees in the summer, where the drinking water may be filled with dysentery, bacilli and amoebae? Or does he sit in an air-conditioned room at some hotel and write reports?[7]

Despite this setback, Schwarz was determined to help Thomas. In March 1959, the India Gospel Mission acquired a new facility, and five months later the newspaper published its first issue by using two second-hand presses working simultaneously. The new newspaper was called *Keraladhwani*, or "the Voice of Kerala." It required $5,000 to $8,000 a month to pay for its staff (ten reporters and over a hundred people in the printing plant) and the twenty-five tons of paper it used. In a September 1959 letter to Strube, Thomas claimed that *Keraladhwani*'s circulation of 21,800 copies made its launch one of the most successful kick-offs in the history of Malayalam language newspapers. Since the paper's revenues from advertising and subscriptions were negligible, any hope the CACC might have to alleviate costs rested on an increase in subscriptions and advertising, particularly on behalf of the Indian government. In a fundraising pitch, Schwarz compared his situation to that of a man expecting a baby but suddenly "blessed with triplets." Colbert visited Kottayam in late 1959 and testified as to the high quality of this paper compared to other Indian periodicals. By that time, Thomas had begun lobbying Schwarz for a rotary press, which could print as many as twenty thousand copies an hour but that would require another $50,000 investment. The press would have to be purchased from outside India and imported, and a licence would have to be obtained. Schwarz agreed, hoping that the press would help the paper become self-sufficient.[8]

On 5 February 1960, Kerala Communists were defeated at the polls. The Communist Party actually polled a million votes more than it had during the preceding election and increased its share of votes (43.3 percent), but it lost seats due to the formation of a united anti-communist front that included the Congress Party and the Muslim League. *Keraladhwani*'s headline read: "Democratic Government Re-Established in Kerala." The CACC newsletter's headline read: "From Tragedy to Triumph – Kerala, India." This development, however, did not halt the CACC's purchase of the rotary press or its acquisition of a new building and jeeps to transport the paper. When the rotary press came into use in November 1961, the newspaper project had already become a financial sinkhole for the CACC, which had spent $270,000 on it.[9]

Thomas reassured his American sponsors that *Keraladhwani*'s influence "and the position we have been able to secure in Kerala are far beyond our expectations," but the real impact of the whole Kerala enterprise was probably minor. The CACC newsletter's circulation figures for *Keraladhwani* varied from twenty thousand to twenty-nine thousand, and a text mentioned that each copy of *Keraladhwani* was read by about ten people. But even if these figures are accurate, *Keraladhwani*'s impact on the 1960 election, during which more than 8 million people cast their ballot, remained marginal. The official readership figures for *Keraladhwani* given by Thomas to the Indian authorities were 22,308 in 1961 and 21,121 in 1962. In 1964, after the Registrar of Newspapers for India conducted an investigation, Thomas was forced to acknowledge a lower figure of 17,821. Moreover, *Keraladhwani*'s readership probably consisted in great part of evangelical Christians, a minority among the Kerala Christian minority. Since relatively few Kerala Christians supported the Communist Party, the paper basically preached to the converted. Politically speaking, *Keraladhwani* probably did not swing voters so much as it contributed to energizing an already mobilized base. Another one of its impacts was assuredly that it provided subsistence to the people who benefitted, directly or indirectly, from the US money that poured in.[10]

The year 1961 marked the high point of CACC support of *Keraladhwani*, with a donation of $131,221, or one-tenth of the

CACC's overall budget during that year. The paper never became self-sufficient. The CACC kept on pumping money into it until at least 1965, at a monthly rate of about $5,000. This assistance became increasingly burdensome as the CACC's revenues began dwindling in 1962. In 1964, the situation in Kerala worsened once again with the disintegration of the anticommunist coalition. The Communists, having retained much of their rural base, stood a good chance of regaining power. But at this point, Schwarz had had enough and wished to sharply diminish his subsidy "and ultimately eliminat[e] it altogether." He pleaded with his supporters for a last contribution aimed at creating a fund whose interests would cover the paper's expenses. To this end, a fundraising banquet was held at the Hollywood Palladium in June 1964 with personalities that included Herbert Philbrick and Ronald Reagan.[11]

CACC support for *Keraladhwani* stopped not long after. Thomas, who had meanwhile helped to found the Kerala Congress Party, which split from the National Congress Party and was supported by Christians and the planters' class, closed the newspaper and was elected member of Parliament in the February 1967 elections. Kerala Communists, who had united in a coalition including pro-Moscow and pro-Beijing factions, returned to power by picking up 117 out of 133 seats at the Kerala legislature.

Little did Schwarz's supporters know that *Keraladhwani* had not only been unprofitable but also that some amounts sent to Kerala had been managed in a questionable way. In 1966, Thomas was arrested and briefly detained for fraud after a series of complaints on the part of *Keraladhwani* employees to the effect that they had not been regularly paid for long periods of time. The plaintiffs claimed that important amounts of money that were supposed to have been deposited in their employee fund had vanished. It also appeared that Thomas had not filed tax returns for sums he had received from the United States. An Indian journalist who commented anonymously on the case reported that there were rumours in Kottayam that the amount "that falls from heavens every month" on Thomas's mission was used for Thomas's personal expenses, that "a Chevrolet Impala car was negotiating the tortuous roads of Kottayam for some time. I was told that a great deal of landed property, particularly plantations, have changed hands lately in Kottayam." The same article quoted a newspaper editor who declared that Thomas's new interest in politics was suspect: "He has got to become Minister in order to survive. Or the income-tax wallahs will get him." Yet tax bureaucrats were in no rush to convict him "because, after all, the man was bringing in foreign exchange. Wonderful are the ways of the Lord!"[12]

This apparent reluctance on the part of Kerala authorities to convict Thomas dissipated in the early 1970s, when he was no longer a member of the Kerala legislature. Thomas was prosecuted for multiple violations of Kerala fiscal laws, notably for not having declared as income the sums deposited in the account of the Indian Gospel Mission that were used to fund *Keraladhwani*. Judge Gopalan Nambyiar's (High Court of Kerala) examination of Thomas's use of the sums of foreign money he had received mentioned, quoting the tax officer:

> household expenses -purchase [sic] of cow, payment of house rent of father, personal trips to Bombay, etc., purchase of property by [Thomas], providing loan facilities to [Thomas's] close relatives like father, brothers, etc., without interest. The personal expenses met out of these funds and the amounts utilised for the purchase of properties in the names of [Thomas] and his five brothers are claimed ... as loans taken by him in his individual capacity to be repaid in subsequent years.[13]

At first, Thomas successfully challenged these charges before the Kerala Income-Tax Appellate Tribunal by claiming that the US money he had received was not taxable as the deposits were "purely personal gifts and testimonials paid as a token of esteem and regard for the personal qualities of Dr. George Thomas, and [are] unconnected with any particular act or service." Yet the High Court of Kerala ultimately decided against Thomas in two rulings (July 1973 and February 1977) that upheld the penalties.[14]

For years, the Kerala project remained Schwarz's badge of honour, an example of a concrete anticommunist effort. Grilled by reporters at NBC's *Meet the Press* in 1962, Schwarz gave the Kerala project as the first example of one of the CACC's genuine successes in fighting Communism. Schwarz never wrote or commented publicly on the mishandling of some of the money the CACC had sent to India. However, this episode taught him a lesson and led the Crusade to adopt a low-cost, low-risk, and overall more effective international strategy.[15]

K. George Thomas died at the age of fifty-seven on 17 September 1993.[16]

SOUTH AMERICA AND THE ADVENTURES OF DR SLUIS

During its apex, the CACC pioneered the evangelical missionary movement based in Southern California, which, during the 1960s, began to massively interest itself in Latin America. Stimulated by the Cuban Revolution and the mounting importance of the Americas as Cold War battlefields, the CACC's activities in this part of the world reflected a broader dynamic involving numerous US evangelical churches and groups. Southern California became, in the second half of the twentieth century, the focal point of missions to Latin America, hosting scores of religious institutions that undertook programs to evangelize countries south of the Rio Grande and the Caribbean, attempting in the process to mobilize populations against communism. Not only was Southern California close to Latin America, but the region received, from the 1950s on, millions of foreign immigrants, many of them refugees from South American conflicts.[17]

The CACC's interest in Latin America can be traced back to Schwarz's appeals in 1958 and 1959 to fund the distribution of Spanish versions of the HUAC testimony. This first initiative came in response to incidents (most notably, a riot in Caracas, Venezuela) that marked Vice-President Richard Nixon's goodwill tour of South America in 1958, which alerted US officials and the general public to the growing anti-American sentiment in that part of the world. A more direct involvement came with a three-month trip Joost Sluis undertook in 1960. Visiting Mexico, Guatemala, El Salvador, Costa Rica, Panama, Peru, Ecuador, Colombia, and Jamaica, Sluis established contacts with educators, churchpeople, and businesspeople. He also managed to speak to student groups in universities, where he observed first-hand the influence of communism in the wake of the Cuban Revolution. Sluis reported that the majority of South American students had a very negative view of the United States, and three-fourths of those he personally met "were opposed to the American free enterprise system."[18]

Another sign of the CACC's mounting interest in Latin America was its school of June 1961 in Miami, then a growing hotbed of anti-Castroist activity. The school's chairman, William Hinson, a former local football star turned pastor of the Wayside Baptist Church, later became involved in Billy Graham's Latin American missions. An effort was made to reach out to the local Cuban exile population in Miami, already numbering twenty thousand people and growing at a rate of three hundred a day. The "faculty" featured the CACC's Cuban collaborator Dr Tirso Del Junco, and a Spanish Speaking Committee was set up. *Miami News* journalist Jack Oswald noted that many Cubans attended and that the front row of chairs "was furnished with headsets to enable Spanish-speaking people to hear simultaneous translations from the speaker."[19]

In 1961, the CACC sent about $44,000 to South America. The money was used to disseminate translated literature in various countries, including *You Can Trust* and the cartoon *Two Faces of Communism*, which in Mexico became *Si El Communismo Llega in Mexico*. In December 1961, a pastor from the Libreria Escogida, an evangelical mobile bookstore in Peru, wrote to Frank Ranuzzi, owner of a conservative bookstore in Los Angeles, that the CACC was sending him a great deal of English literature that he managed to give to important people in Peru. Also, the pastor wrote Ranuzzi, Colbert and Strube sent him recorded material, and Schwarz would soon help him to print Spanish material in Peru.[20]

Until 1964, the CACC showed a particular interest in Brazil. Despite the lukewarm relationship Schwarz had with State Department officials, the US Information Agency was interested in a limited collaboration. In 1961, the agency had subsidized an edition of *You Can Trust* in South Korea, the copies of which were distributed to a few hundred "leading citizens," and put the CACC in contact with a Korean publisher who produced thousands of copies of the book. In 1962 and 1963, the agency showed interest in a project to help the CACC distribute free Portuguese translations of *You Can Trust* in Brazil, which was experiencing political instability. In January 1963, Brazilian leader João Goulart (moderate left) won a referendum that installed him at the top of a new presidential system, but in the following year his regime could not control Brazil's deteriorating economy and it became alienated from local conservative forces. The US embassy in Rio put Schwarz in contact with a Brazilian publisher who showed interest in *You Can Trust* and proposed a print run of twenty thousand copies. In June 1963, the project was realized. In 1964, just as *You Can Trust* was beginning to be serialized in Brazilian newspapers, Goulart was overthrown by a coup that installed what was to be twenty years of military dictatorship. Schwarz rejoiced over this effort to "preserve the democratic life of Brazil from the spreading infection of Communism."[21]

The biggest focus of the CACC's Latin American activities in the 1960s was British Guiana, now known as Guyana. With a population of about 600,000, this colony, located in the northeastern tip of South America, was among the last remnants of the British Empire in the Americas. London still managed Guianese matters regarding law and order, the military, and foreign affairs, but, since 1953, elections for a colonial legislative assembly with limited powers had been allowed. However, the situation proved complicated for British authorities. The colony's strongest political force was the People's Progressive Party (PPP), a socialist party led by East Indian Cheddi Jagan, a former dentist trained in the United States who was highly popular among the East Indian majority. London wished to put an eventual end to colonial rule, but there was no question of the Colonial Office, of the US State Department, moving in this direction with Jagan in power. In 1953, the PPP scored a landslide electoral victory, but British authorities removed Jagan from power after 133 days in office. They suspended British Guiana's constitution and, for the next eight years, ruled the colony directly.[22]

New elections were scheduled for August 1961, but it looked like the PPP would again be victorious. This time, however, London decided it would allow Jagan, who had in the meantime moderated his program, to form a government should he win. But the Cuban Revolution had ensured that Washington would be preoccupied with this transfer of power in British Guiana. Decision makers feared the prospect of a British Guiana that would offer Cuba the use of its sea and airport facilities and thus weaken the US embargo. Thus, when the CACC began to be active in British Guiana in 1961, the US Central Intelligence Agency was already enmeshed in the colony's internal affairs.[23]

In May 1961, Schwarz wrote to his supporters: "Jagan must be defeated in his bid for total power ... A message must reach the Indian voters in the sugar and rice fields." The CACC quickly amassed tens of thousands of dollars to fund his strategy: Sluis would transform several trucks into mobile libraries. These vehicles would travel from village to village, enabling the distribution of literature, taped hearings, and films. Kerala Indians would assist Sluis: "There is a pool of Indians in Kerala who suffered under the lash of Communist government. They can be transported to tell the story."[24]

During the three months leading up to British Guiana's 1961 election, Sluis and his team, consisting of two other Americans and three Kerala Indians, went into Guianese rice and sugar plantations, conducted open-air meetings, showed propaganda movies, and distributed anticommunist literature. On 21 August 1961, Jagan's PPP won the election with 42.6 percent of the votes cast and secured twenty out of thirty-five parliamentary seats. The urban, African-based People's National Congress gained eleven seats, while four seats were won by the conservative United Force (UF), led by beer brewer Peter D'Aguiar, who mainly represented the white, Portuguese elite. Despite their victory, PPP officials were furious at the CACC's meddling in the election. Jagan's deputy premier Bradley H. Benn reported before the UN that the CACC "had openly supported UF and had admitted spending $BWI 176,000 during the campaign."[25]

Admitting the CACC "spent some money all right," Schwarz denied charges of meddling and declared that the Crusade had only been running an educational program. In November 1961, Democratic senator from Pennsylvania Joseph S. Clark asked the State Department if the CACC had violated the Logan Act, which prohibits private interference in relations between the US government and foreign governments. The inquiry was forwarded to the Department of Justice, but no evidence justifying an investigation was found. It is possible that PPP officials confused the CACC with another group, Americans Safeguarding Freedom, which was led by Schwarz follower Dr Carleton Campbell and which was reportedly also present in British Guiana. As the US consul in Georgetown wrote to Secretary of State Dean Rusk in March 1962, "Sluis is meddling (as other do-gooders have been in British Guiana during past year)." After the August 1961 election, the British allowed Jagan to form his government but, due to US pressure, chose to delay Guianese independence. Relations between Georgetown and Washington degenerated quickly. The Kennedy administration mounted a CIA covert operation aimed at financing the political opposition and organizing strikes by channelling money to Guianese unions through the AFL-CIO.[26]

In February 1962, protests against the Jagan government began in Georgetown, particularly in black areas. Protests turned into riots, and within days a third of Georgetown was burned to the ground. London sent troops and restored some order. A week after the riots, Guianese authorities told Sluis to leave the colony immediately, under threat of an order of expulsion. Sluis requested help from Everett Melby, the US consul, who cabled Secretary of State

Dean Rusk that he had discussed the matter with Jagan's police head, who had informed him that Sluis's presence, "who rightly or wrongly had been identified with Daguiar, who had instigated arson and looting in effort overthrow govt, was inimical to internal security." Melby continued, "Apart from responsibility for Feb 16 riots, however, there was no proof Sluis and his group had backed UF nor contributed to riots." He added that Sluis's deportation would have "immediate and violent repercussions" on US-Guianese relations. Rusk approved Melby's handling of the situation but also recommended that Sluis should be "aware [of the] possible consequences [of] his actions and avoid involving [the US government] officially in advising him what to do."[27]

State Department officials were irritated by the presence of a US-based vigilante whom they could not control but nonetheless had to protect. Not only was Sluis risking bringing scrutiny to bear on the ongoing operation to destabilize Jagan, but Washington also feared the domestic impact his expulsion would have. The US embassy in London reinforced this belief by advising the State Department that "deportation [of] Sluis could hardly escape attention [of the] press," both in Guiana and in the United States. Cables between Melby and Rusk show that the latter's prime concern was that Sluis should never have any basis to later claim that the US government in any way sought to hamper or interfere with his activities.[28]

But as Melby reported to Rusk, "Sluis seems well dug in, and rather enjoying role of hunted Galahad." This made the consul even more anxious to convince Guianese authorities that deportation would be a "panicky blunder." Yet the Guianese police head went forward with the deportation order. British governor Sir Ralph Grey refused to sign it, in keeping with his power to disregard ministerial advice in matters pertaining to foreign policy. "L'Affaire Sluis," as Consul Melby began calling it, was evolving into a constitutional quandary since this was the first time that the colony's governor had thwarted a ministerial decision.[29]

On 2 March, after a week spent in his hotel room in Georgetown under police surveillance, Sluis departed without notice for the nearby town of Berbice in the vehicle of a UF activist. He only returned to Georgetown later that day with a number of East Indians, who were dropped off at various locations. In the ensuing days, the police-monitored Sluis came and went from the homes of UF supporters but without carrying out any overt subversive activities. As

State Department officials saw it, Sluis wished to be arrested and deported without legal justification and thus cause a scandal. After a week, the Guianese police, without waiting for the deportation order to be signed, asked Sluis to leave the colony. Feeling that it was safer to do so, Sluis left British Guiana on 8 March 1962, under protests by UF leader D'Aguiar.[30]

Without a full deportation act being issued, Sluis retained the right to return to the colony. On 17 April 1962, Sluis was thus back in Georgetown, where he continued his activities. On 22 May, the British Guiana governor informed the US consul that, "after exhausting every delaying tactic possible, he … [was] obliged [to] sign [the] order prohibiting [the] entry" of Schwarz and Sluis. Two days later, Georgetown's newspapers announced that Sluis and Schwarz, "internationally known anti-Communist crusaders," had been classified as undesirable immigrants by the government and forbidden entry. Melby informed Rusk of the local reaction to the news, which was in fact quite moderate, apart from UF leader D'Aguiar's protesting and a "number of indignant editorials … exaggerating [the] international importance of Schwarz and Sluis." The State Department could only have been relieved that, apart from a few blurbs, the story was not picked up by the US press.[31]

Schwarz boasted that, thanks to Sluis, thousands of people in Guiana had been awakened to the threat of communism. Moreover, that he and Sluis were classified "illegal immigrants" was a "unique honor" conferred by Communists. Sluis concurred: "I am probably the only Harvard Medical School alumnus to have received that singular distinction and I wear it with pride and honor." The banning of Schwarz and Sluis did not completely stop Crusade activity in British Guiana. From California, Sluis maintained his connections in the British colony, sending them money and literature. In December 1964, Jagan lost his re-election bid to People's National Congress leader Forbes Burnham. In May 1965, Burnham lifted the ban on Schwarz and Sluis. The fear of a Communist takeover of British Guiana having decreased, London granted independence to the colony, which became a sovereign nation on 26 May 1966. In late 1967, Jagan, who had been invited on a speaking tour in the United States, was denied a visa by the State Department, leading to the tour's cancellation. "Today the tables have turned," Schwarz rejoiced, "and Cheddi Jagan is a prohibited immigrant to the United States."[32]

11

Crusaders

TRAJECTORIES

Dr Carleton Campbell graduated from the Long Island Medical College in 1925. He practised surgery for decades in Brooklyn, where he was born. By the late 1950s, he had developed a second practice in the affluent suburb of Wilton, Connecticut, where his family estate was situated. Staunchly meritocratic, Campbell associated his personal success with his strict Protestant work ethic. He was uninterested in culture, practised teetotalism, did not smoke, and had little use for hobbies. To a large degree, his social life was centred on Bridgeport's Black Rock Congregational Church, where he had developed a warm relationship with the young pastor Stanley R. Allaby.

On a Saturday night in June 1958, Campbell's wife persuaded him to accompany her to hear a visiting lecturer at the church. Campbell was not particularly interested. "Except for the pleasure of her company, I anticipated a wasted evening," he later wrote. But the speaker was Fred Schwarz, whose lecture on the Communist plan to overtake the United States affected Campbell with the regular mix of terror and revitalized sense of purpose. Reminiscing two years later, Campbell testified that he had previously been "enjoying an outlook on life in which the sky over America was mainly blue," but, after that evening: "I haven't been able to escape the challenge of the dark cloud in America's sky – the clouds alien to our heritage and that cast deep shadows over the structure of our cherished Freedom." He decided to act.[1]

A first meeting of interested people took place at Reverend Allaby's home. Allaby and Campbell invited as many people as they could.

Twenty-five showed up. Campbell was elected chairman and oversaw within a few days the birth of an anticommunist cell incorporated under the name Americans Safeguarding Freedom. Campbell organized numerous classes at the local church; arranged for the town's booksellers, libraries, and the school board to get material on communism; planned a series of newspaper and radio programs; and organized a second visit for Schwarz in Bridgeport.[2]

In the early 1960s, aside from his medical practice and his work with Americans Safeguarding Freedom, Campbell had started an eastern offshoot of the National Education Program's Freedom Forums called the National Freedom Education Center (NFED), which organized its own seminaries at King's College in upstate New York. Campbell's NFED featured household figures on the anticommunist speaking trail: Clarence Manion, Herb Philbrick, Walter Judd, and Schwarz, who came in May 1961. Campbell wrote that, because maintaining American freedom "is important enough to us, it will become evident in many different areas of our lives; I talk to my patients; to my colleagues in the hospitals; to as many school authorities as I can; to legislators; to ministers." One journalist noted that Campbell devoted "all of his free time" to his activities. His professional and family life were seriously affected by his political life by the late 1960s. He died in 1984.[3]

C. Ellis Carver was a gynaecologist-obstetrician and honorary Rotarian who first met Schwarz when he organized the crusader's lecture before the joint Rotary Clubs of Altadena and East Pasadena in December 1955. Carver began investing himself at a frenzied pace in anticommunist activities, notably by starting his own club in collaboration with the American Legion. After assuming the chair of the first CACC school of Los Angeles in 1960, he tried to refocus on his medical practice, but that proved anticlimactic. In 1961, he participated in the CACC schools in Orange County and at the LA Memorial Sports Arena. By the end of that year, a stroke compelled him to stop for good. In a letter to Skousen, he indicated that his doctors gave him strict instructions to cease activities that were not related to his profession.[4]

Walter Huss was leader of a fundamentalist congregation in Portland. He attended the Crusade school in Long Beach in December 1958. After such an event, he said, "life takes on different proportions." Huss founded an anticommunist Christian, pro-business group called Freedom Center International, Inc. In the 1960s and 1970s, Huss became, in the words of a political scientist, "the most visible Christian conservative in Oregon." He ran unsuccessfully for office twice: the first time in 1966, when he sought the GOP nomination for a Senate seat, and again in 1982, when he ran against incumbent GOP governor Vic Atiyeh. Despite these setbacks, Huss sought for years to attain power within the state GOP by convincing his followers to seek out positions in the local party, thus allowing him to be elected statewide party chairman in the late 1970s.[5]

Patricia Cullinane was one of those "down-to-earth, everyday people," as she called herself. This Newport Beach housewife saw an ad for the CACC school at the LA Sports Arena in summer 1961. Even though she was not particularly interested in politics, the event "spoke" to her. She called a baby-sitting agency and attended the school, resulting in her involvement in conservative politics. She got involved in the campaign to elect outspoken foe of progressive education and John Birch Society sympathizer Dr Max Rafferty to the position of state superintendent of public instruction in 1962. With help from a few friends and a mimeograph in her house garage, Cullinane formed Parents for Rafferty, which distributed 3 million pieces of literature in Los Angeles County alone and finished the race with a mailing list of about eight thousand people. On 7 November 1962, Rafferty won by a 52 to 48 percent margin over his liberal opponent Dr Ralph Richardson.[6]

Mrs R.B. ("Rusty") Feddersen was from West Covina, and she also attended the CACC event at the LA Sports Arena in the late summer of 1961. Wife of a structural engineer, Feddersen signed up for the Draft Goldwater Committee. Throughout the 1960s she remained involved in numerous initiatives, such as the one led by congressman and former CACC collaborator Captain Richard Barnes against obscene literature. In 1969, Feddersen was appointed to the GOP State Central Committee, a position she kept for four decades. In March 1979, she and her husband joined Dr Frank Rogers, a surgeon from Whittier, in organizing a "testimonial dinner" for Dr Fred Schwarz "in honor of his 25 years of faithful and courageous service." A year later, "Rusty" led a delegation of California Southlanders to the GOP convention that nominated Ronald Reagan for the presidency. "I'm celebrating – all week," she told a reporter.[7]

Their differences notwithstanding, these five individuals (Campbell, Carver, Huss, Cullinane, and Feddersen) shared an attraction to the CACC's message. They exemplified the characteristics to be found in the organization's base. Examining the CACC constituency not only reveals noteworthy details about the organization itself but also, and most importantly, provides a snapshot of the sociological structure of the "New Right."

Five main tools, or sources of data, can be used to analyze the CACC constituency. The first is the list of 540 persons who took out CACC life membership between 1956 and 1960, and whose names were displayed in the newsletter. The second consists of all the names available in Crusade school letterheads and informational leaflets, which often listed committee members. The third tool is the only available register of financial CACC contributors, a complete list of those who donated sums of $100 or more during the fiscal year of 1966, including their civic addresses and, in numerous cases, their occupations. All three of these tools, these sources of data, contain the names of people who gave important sums to the CACC or who were directly involved in its activities. As a result, they help to identify the core of the Crusade's support. However, they provide only limited information as to the CACC's sources of support in the general public and among those who did not qualify as political activists.

This gap is filled in great part by the fourth and fifth tools. The fourth consists of two survey studies conducted in 1962 by a team of academics under the direction of political scientist Raymond Wolfinger of Stanford University. Wishing to survey the CACC's rank-and-file followers as part of a project to assess the social sources of the right wing, Wolfinger and his students created a questionnaire to be distributed to attendees of the CACC school of San Francisco during the winter of 1962. Schwarz admitted the team from Stanford for free and allowed them to distribute their questionnaires, while warning them: "With one sentence, I could kill your whole project." The returned questionnaires numbered 308.[8] A few months later, Wolfinger's student Sheilah R. Koeppen, who had worked on the first study, ran a second similar study (167 questionnaires) at the CACC school in San Mateo in September 1962 and at two lectures given by Schwarz in Oakland. Both studies yielded similar results and can be considered part of the same project.[9]

The fifth tool consists of a poll conducted among the general public as part of the American National Election Studies (ANES), which is held each presidential election year by the Center for Political Studies at the University of Michigan.[10] In 1964, two questions on the ANES survey concerned the CACC. In the 1980s, political scientist Clyde Wilcox analyzed these results in a series of studies on what he referred to as the "Old Christian right."[11]

GENDER

At first sight, the crusaders were a boy's club. More than 61.6 percent of those who took the life membership between 1954 and 1961 were male, while 38.3 percent were female. More pointedly, less than half of the women in this group joined at the same time as did their husbands. Comparable proportions are found in the 1966 list of financial contributors of sums over $100.[12] Core crusaders were twice as likely to be male rather than female, reflecting a dynamic typical of postwar political organizations. The organization's leadership was male-dominated as well. Of the four officers and the twenty people who formed the Crusade's advisory council, all were men, as were all the local branch directors. Lecturers at CACC schools were almost always men.

However, the fact that one-fifth of the names on the life memberships' list are female remains high in an age when women earned three times less than men and sometimes did not earn anything at all by themselves. As a matter of fact, on the 1966 donors' list, the largest individual contributions were given by Mrs Elizabeth D. Lowe from La Mesa, California ($22,392), and Mrs Alarip Myrin from Kimberton, Pennsylvania ($9,895). Those two donations outstrip the amounts given by Missouri industrialist Menlo Smith ($6,000), by Mr and Mrs William P. Strube ($4,500), Roger Milliken ($2,500), and Walter Knott ($1,421.25).

Similarly, the prevalence of males on the list of organizers and sponsors for the thirty anticommunism schools held between 1958 and 1964 obscures the role played by women activists. Women were often overrepresented in some schools' organizing committees, where the tasks (often paper-pushing and phone-calling) were essential to making the event happen. For instance, in Phoenix and Orange County, women accounted for only a handful of names on the committees' lists but were concentrated in those ("Registration," "Literature," and "Banquet") that were fundamental to the organization. Also, for two schools, Milwaukee in February 1960 and Omaha in May 1962, the chair*man* was in fact a chair*woman*. In Milwaukee, in February 1960, this position was filled by Maxine Graham, wife of an executive of the Harnischfeger Corporation, who was also leader of the local JBS chapter. In Omaha, it was Mrs Truman S. Woods, a housewife who led the Gold for Goldwater fundraising drive in 1963 and 1964. Women would also welcome school registrants and attend to the formalities. The place of women in the CACC followed a pattern common to grassroots conservatism. Marjorie Jensen, former Bircher from Pasadena, once described the women's contribution to the JBS by saying that they did "the work" – that is, calling relatives to come or rounding up the crowds. Finally, conservative women were the key force behind the study group movement.[13]

The general postwar economic prosperity, coupled with a cultural and political environment that made it easier for women to engage in the public sphere, led many middle- and upper-class women to find, through conservative politics, a way to vent their commitment to embattled Americanism in an age of anxiety over the A-bomb, subversion, racial strife, and moral breakdown. What ignited this activism among women was often a perceived local threat, such as communist influence in the nearby school or in the church, both of which politicized women in light of their traditional gender role as defenders of family and community.

GEOGRAPHY

California, and especially Southern California, was the CACC's homeland. California accounted for a third of all lifetime members, and Southern California, in particular, for a quarter of them. When figures from California, Washington State, and Oregon are combined, a little less than half of the CACC's life members lived in the Pacific states, a finding that is in accordance with the geography of Schwarz's tours in the 1950s. The Midwest was home to the second largest number of crusaders, housing a quarter of the organization's lifetime members. While a fifth of the CACC's lifetime members lived in the South, they were overwhelmingly concentrated in Texas, which housed the organization's most active secondary branch in Houston.[14] Only a handful of lifetime members lived in the East. Similar data are found in the 1966 donors' list, which shows almost half of crusaders living in California, with four out of five people in that group living in Southern California. California was also the Crusade's financial base, the state accounting for more than 42 percent of all offerings on the 1966 donors' list, with Southern California comprising the lion's share with a third (33.4 percent) of the amount on the list.[15]

Perhaps more significant is the analysis of the specific kinds of residential areas in which crusaders lived, information that can be collected from the mail addresses on the 1966 donors' list. Crusaders were predominantly suburbanites: more than half lived in suburban areas, while a third lived in large cities, and only one in six could be considered a rural or small town resident. Yet this statistic conceals a major imbalance: there were in fact *two* Crusades – one in California and one in the rest of the country. In California, an outstanding 77 percent of crusaders were suburbanites, while only 14.5 percent lived in the Golden State's cities (Los Angeles, San Francisco, Sacramento, Fresno, and San Diego), and 8 percent lived in its rural heartland.[16] When the state of California is excluded, the CACC becomes an organization that existed markedly in large cities (51.7 percent) and not in suburbs (26.4 percent) or in rural/small town areas (21.8 percent). Therefore, the CACC's heart was located precisely where its Long Beach headquarters was situated: the bedroom communities of California and, more particularly, the suburban macrocosm that enveloped Los Angeles.

DEMOGRAPHY

Crusaders were, unsurprisingly, white. While about 12 percent of San Francisco area residents were non-whites, all respondents to Wolfinger's study were white. "In attending the school for five days, we saw no more than a handful of nonwhites," Wolfinger noted. Koeppen only saw whites during the meetings she attended. Among the ANES study's sample of blacks (about four hundred respondents), a third were familiar with the CACC, but only one in twenty were supporters. Crusaders usually came from long-established American families and were of Anglo-Saxon descent, with about nine out of ten born in the United States.[17]

Most CACC school attendees appear to have been middle-aged adults. While 45 percent of Wolfinger's respondents were over fifty, slightly higher than the percentage among Bay Area residents, Koeppen's respondents were exactly in line with regional data. Witnesses attending CACC schools indicated that participants were generally in their thirties. An observer at the Sports Arena school wrote: "The average age of the adults seemed to be in the middle thirties, a fact which surprised some of the observers. In addition, a great number of children were brought – some for every session."[18]

With respects to religion, crusaders were overwhelmingly Protestant (77 percent of Wolfinger's sample), while Catholics only amounted to 8 percent. Twenty-six percent of Wolfinger's Protestant respondents were "Baptists or members of minor fundamentalist denominations, compared to 13 percent of the white, college-educated Protestants in the San Francisco sample." Wolfinger also asked his respondents how they happened to come to the CACC. Fourteen percent answered that they arrived primarily through church influence. The researcher set aside this group (the "church group") and observed that several traits distinguished it from other crusaders: the "church group" respondents tended to be markedly fundamentalists, to attend church more regularly, and to have been raised on farms in greater numbers. Wolfinger thus identified two groups among crusaders: a fundamentalist minority, reminiscent of the CACC's origins, and a majority of more secularized white Anglo-Saxon Protestants (WASPs) that reflected the organization's larger outreach in the early 1960s.[19]

The ANES data are similar: they show the CACC being supported not only by a core of conservative Protestants but also by a majority of secular followers. Awareness of the CACC was only slightly higher among white conservative Protestants than among other whites (31 and 24 percent, respectively). Among supporters of the organization, only 29 percent belonged to an evangelical denomination. The religious indicators, Clyde Wilcox notes, were surprising not because of their strength but precisely because of their weakness.[20]

EDUCATIONAL AND PROFESSIONAL PROFILES

Wolfinger-Koeppen respondents were twice as likely to be professionals or businesspeople, or to be married to persons in such positions, than the Bay Area white population. Crusaders were also five times less likely to be blue collars or to work in skilled, semiskilled, and service jobs. Household incomes showed that they were predominantly an upper-class group, with more than 43.6 percent earning $10,000 or more in annual income before taxes and with more than a fifth in the upper bracket ($15,000). They were more educated than were average Americans. Four out of five had attended college. Yet the share of professionals and college graduates was lower among fundamentalist crusaders: more than half of Wolfinger's church group were clerical or manual workers, and the great majority belonged to households in which the annual income was lower than $10,000. This confirms that the CACC attracted two groups of supporters, one composed of predominantly upper-class professionals or businesspeople and another, smaller, group composed of conservative evangelicals of more rural background and lower social status. The fact that the CACC "did not seem to have much appeal to lower-status people, except for fundamentalists" was one of Wolfinger's significant findings, given that McCarthyism in the 1950s had a much stronger appeal "for people with less education."[21]

The role of health specialists is the most noteworthy aspect of the CACC constituency. To be sure, part-time activism in political parties, groups, lobbies, unions, or other groups was not rare for doctors. Overwhelmingly male, highly educated, and wealthy, medical specialists had the attributes associated with high rates of political participation. Doctors voted, contributed to political campaigns, read newspapers, and took leading civic roles in greater proportions than did the rest of the population. They were also more conservative. Poll studies during the 1940s and 1950s showed that physicians had a preference for the Republican Party that exceeded that of the upper class, with more than 70 percent voting for Eisenhower as presidential candidate in a poll by mid-decade and only 16 percent supporting Stevenson.[22]

The political involvement of health specialists in postwar anticommunist and right-wing activity was noted by social scientists of the day. In the late 1960s, three researchers who examined thousands of letters resulting from a JBS mail campaign noted that "there seemed to be an extraordinary number of doctors of medicine and doctors of osteopathy who wrote in protest." That 2.13 percent of medical professionals among letter-writers, the authors wrote, was "twenty-one times the number of M.D.'s and D.O.'s in the resident population." A greater proportion of medical specialists (3.3 percent) was noted among the authors of letters sent in 1962 in reaction to moderate GOP senator Thomas Kuchel's speech attacking the JBS. Three physicians were among the twenty-four members of the JBS's National Council in the mid-1960s.[23]

But the CACC's appeal to health specialists was unparalleled among postwar conservative groups. When the CACC's board of directors and advisory council had their joint meeting in Winona in 1956, of eleven people they included four MDs: Schwarz and Ypsilanti branch director George Westcott, plus two doctors from Southern California, John McLennan and Theo Moller. Among the 540 persons who took the CACC life membership between 1956 and 1960, more than thirty-five (or 6.4 percent) had medical degrees of some sort. An even higher proportion is found among the 1966 donors' list, of which sixty people out of 832 (7.2 percent) were medical professionals. Considering that the ratio was about one per one thousand with regard to this line of work among the general US population in 1960, this points to a presence of health specialists that was sixty-four times higher among crusaders than among the general population between 1956 and 1960, and seventy-two times higher in 1966. Political parties excluded, the CACC was probably the non-medical, conservative organization in which early 1960s US medical men were the most involved.[24]

Undoubtedly, the CACC's appeal to health specialists had much to do with Schwarz's personality. His status as a physician who gave up his medical career for the greater good made an impression on fellow doctors. Also, many medical professionals who joined the CACC were, like Schwarz, quite religious and were involved in their local churches, which allowed them to fuse the authority of two institutions: religion and medicine. Schwarz mobilized these socially conservative, engaged citizens by getting them to conceive of anticommunism as an extension of the medical service and the virtues associated with it. The nation was a patient, and they were its therapists.

Medical specialists involved in postwar right-wing activity were also influenced by debates regarding their professional status. Ever since it successfully mounted a lobbying effort against President Truman's project to enact a national health insurance system in the late 1940s, the American Medical Association (AMA) had been committed to blocking all trends towards socialized medicine or changes in private free practice. Despite the CACC's non-commitment on healthcare issues, some of the doctors who collaborated with Schwarz shared a common abhorrence for state medicine. George Westcott privately claimed that positive reports on the Soviet healthcare system were bogus. In 1964, in a speech before his AMA colleagues, Walter Judd stated: "our opposition to socialized medicine is not because it would hurt us, but because it would hurt the *public* [emphasis in original]."[25]

The AMA's opposition to all forms of interference with private fee practice reflected the individualistic, free-enterprise ethos of private fee practitioners, who formed its core membership. As opposed to medical specialists in teaching, research positions, or those working as salaried members of large medical institutions, the private fee practitioner enjoyed a professional autonomy denied to state employees while, at the same time, doing vital and distinguished work. Important to the AMA's ideology were such ideas as professional autonomy (which many doctors feared was threatened under health insurance schemes) and the need for an open medical market in which both doctor and patient enjoyed freedom of choice. Moreover, many believed that governmental control of medicine would bring to the medical field politics and all its evils: corruption, partisanship, and favouritism.[26]

By injecting anticommunism into their own fight for professional autonomy, doctors not only found a way to rally public opinion against state medicine projects but also a means to refurbish a status that they felt had been bruised by decades of attacks perpetrated on the medical establishment by politicians, journalists, and unions. In a 1964 lecture before his AMA colleagues, Judd claimed that medicine had entered an age in which doctors should play a leading role in public affairs in order to retain their professional freedom and to "ensure our future as human beings." This last objective included the fight against communism, which "behaves like other malignancies."[27] The major support the CACC drew from medical specialists was reinforced by its presence in California, a state that had pioneered the introduction of popular postwar health insurance programs. In reaction, the California state branch of the AMA was perhaps the country's most conservative and opposed any intermediaries (the state, politicians, employers, unions, insurers) between doctors and patients. Southern Californian medical specialists were involved in right-wing activity to a degree unseen elsewhere.[28]

CACC schools held in Southern California were particularly marked by the involvement of health specialists, several of whom remained involved in conservative politics. One example is Nolan Frizzelle, a Newport Beach optometrist who became involved in politics during a school board fight in Pasadena over progressive education before moving to Costa Mesa, Orange County. A few months after participating in the CACC school of Orange County, he helped found a local chapter of the California Republican Assembly (CRA), an activist group within the state GOP, which had long been endorsing centrist or moderate Republicans. Frizzelle sought to change that. As thirty-fifth district director of the CRA, he ran for the organization's state chair and turned to school members for help. "I started out in the Christian Anti-Communism Crusade and out of the 5,000 or 6,000 people that were there, there were 100 people that I came to know fairly closely in helping to organize that crusade," he recalled. He contacted Rufus and Peggy Pearce of Fullerton, with whom he had worked on the school's committees.[29]

Recruiting people one by one, Frizzelle's group overcame all opposition within the state GOP. On 17 March 1964, the *Los Angeles Times* reported that, after carrying the nomination by a two-to-one margin, Nolan Frizzelle, a "handsome Orange County optometrist who has argued that the federal income tax should be abolished is the new president of the California Republican Assembly," with Peggy Pearce being elected vice-president of the CRA. Frizzelle's first move as CRA head was to pledge support to Barry Goldwater for the GOP nomination, which proved essential to Goldwater's narrow victory during the primary of June 1964, allowing him to get a lock on the nomination. Frizzelle stepped down from the CRA presidency after Goldwater's defeat but remained an important GOP personality in Orange County and, in November 1980, in the wake of the Reagan landslide, was elected state representative for the 73rd District.[30]

Fullerton dentist William Brashears, chairman of the Orange County school, was the person who, in 1961, had convinced Schwarz that a school at the LA Sports Arena would be possible. Brashears later founded the Conservative Coordinating Council, designed to elect conservative candidates. In 1962, he and his group mailed thousands of sample ballots to Orange County voters listing the candidates they had endorsed, thus contributing to the unseating of Bruce Sumner, a moderate Republican who had enraged his constituents by voting for a fair housing act and for a fair employment practices bill. Brashears's name reappeared during the Iran-Contra hearings in 1987, when it was revealed that he had founded the Freedom Fighters International group, which raised money for Contra leader Edén Pastora.[31]

A Cuban native established in California, Dr Tirso Del Junco participated in several CACC schools, where he often testified about his university experience with Fidel Castro, whom he claimed had espoused communism for a long time. In early 1962, Del Junco founded the Committee to Free Cuba with people such as Skousen, Philbrick, Marion Miller, and Matt Cvetic. The good-looking Del

Junco was often invited to address civic clubs and GOP events. In 1964, he became head of Latin Americans for Goldwater. In 1968, Ronald Reagan, now governor of California, appointed him to the State Board of Medical Examiners, a position he would keep for several years. In February 1979, Del Junco, now an influential member of the Reagan machine in California, was elected vice-chairman of the CRA. In 1983, George Deukmejian, GOP governor of California, appointed him to the state Air Resources Board. Del Junco was later appointed to the University of the California Board of Regents and served a second tenure as chairman for the California GOP in the 1990s.[32]

Medical doctors were not the only professional group over-represented among CACC supporters. Even if the 1962 and 1964 survey studies did not contain information about participants' specific professions, the lists of CACC schools' sponsoring committees were consistently marked by the presence of the same subcategories. Besides medical specialists, two types of professionals participated in significant numbers: the clergy and retired military officers. For instance, the 132 names of the sponsoring committees of the Phoenix school for winter 1961 include, in addition to seven medical specialists, more than fourteen members of the clergy and fifteen retired military officers. Both of these groups, accounting for a small share of the general population and not highly represented among rank-and-file crusaders, were nonetheless important in leadership positions. While most members of the CACC's advisory council in the 1950s were pastors or theologians, religious professionals remained important contributors to the organization even after its appeal expanded beyond church networks.

Military officers who participated to the CACC did so on an individual basis, which explains why most of them were retirees, and could therefore associate with whatever cause seemed worthy to them. One CACC branch (San Diego) was led by a retired officer, Captain Barnes. In the early 1960s, this involvement of the professional military in right-wing politics interested fewer social scientists than it did journalists (Fred J. Cook's *The Warfare State*), novelists (Nevil Shute's *On the Beach*), and filmmakers (Stanley Kubrick's *Dr. Strangelove*). Sociologist Daniel Bell interpreted this involvement as a response to the challenges posed to the military establishment by the emergence of the new players in military affairs (atomic scientists, rocket engineers, strategic studies specialists). This resulted in a feeling of

11.1 | Dr Tirso Del Junco speaking in 1961. *Los Angeles Times* Photographic Archives.

dispossession among career soldiers, which reached its peak when Robert McNamara took over the Pentagon in 1961 and imposed the idea of civilian control over the military establishment. However, Bell was alone among social scientists of the time in noting the significance of this imprimatur given to right-wing ideas by members of the defence and national security establishment, a phenomenon that has markedly characterized the age of Reagan and the Bushes.[33]

Another important source of CACC support came from owners of small- and medium-sized businesses. More than 29 percent of respondents in the Wolfinger and Koeppen studies held a managerial position of some sort. Three of the organization's subsidiary branches (Seattle, Indianapolis, and Houston) were led by owners of small or average-sized businesses, and their role in the organization of CACC schools was central from the outset.[34] While the military's right-wing involvement drew little attention from social scientists, the presence of small- and medium-sized businesspeople was often noted, as they were the only middle- and upper-class professional group that had consistently supported hardline anticommunism since the days of Joe McCarthy.[35]

This support of right-wing politics was often seen by social scientists of the time as the expression of a "status concern," whereby right-wing behaviour expressed anxieties, most often resulting from the "disruptive effects of status shakeups in which older economic groups [were] displaced by younger, better educated workers," as Richard Hofstadter notes. Anticommunist activism was perceived as expressing businesspeople's resentment towards a changing world in which their status, hitherto valued by the legal and moral American tradition, was being challenged by the rise of big business, big labour, and big government. But this interpretation overlooks the fact that it was not only the owners of small- and medium-sized businesses who supported the right. In Dallas, Phoenix, Orange County, and Los Angeles, some important businesspeople supported CACC schools. While only a few moguls consistently backed the CACC over the long term, as opposed to the more durable backing it received from smaller businesspeople, this big business patronage of organizations such as the Crusade, the JBS, and George S. Benson's National Education Program was significant as it showed the continuing role of elites in shaping public discourse, which, to this day, constitutes one of the main sources of the right's longevity in US politics.[36]

POLITICAL AND IDEOLOGICAL PROFILES

That crusaders were conservative anticommunists is not surprising, but the extent to which they were so might be. More than 67 percent of the Wolfinger-Koeppen respondents were registered Republicans, 20 percent were Independents, and only 9.5 percent were Democrats. Almost all of them had voted during the 1960 presidential election (98 percent), and nine out of ten who did so supported Richard Nixon. Moreover, most belonged to the conservative wing of the GOP. At a moment when most Republicans nationwide supported Nixon's re-nomination as presidential candidate in 1964, with Barry Goldwater usually coming a distant second, Schwarz's base supported Goldwater by a two-to-one margin, even in Nixon's home state of California.[37]

Wolfinger-Koeppen's respondents considered internal Communism as either a "very great" or a "great" danger to the United States

(85.5 percent combined). Nine out of ten saw communists as having "a lot of influence" in colleges and universities; 55 percent saw a lot of such influence in the Democratic Party, and 20 percent even saw such influence in the GOP. They were divided as to whether "Communists live in my neighborhood": 36 percent agreed, 36 percent disagreed, and 28 percent admitted to not knowing. The crusaders' strong anti-statist inclination is revealed by their answers on domestic issues. Eighty-six percent of Wolfinger's respondents agreed that "the American people would have more get up and go if the government would stop giving them things." More than 60 percent were opposed to Medicare, 56 percent believed the unions did more harm than good, and a sizable minority (43 percent) opposed federal aid to education.[38]

Both the 1962 and 1964 surveys indicated that race issues were not important factors in drawing people to the CACC. To the question "What kinds of people in our country are most likely to be Communists?," only 7 percent of both Wolfinger's and Koeppen's crusaders answered "Minority groups." While crusaders were consistently conservative on most issues, Wolfinger classified their take on race as more liberal. "For instance, almost two-thirds [62 percent] of them are opposed to the southern position on segregation," while 35 percent approved of it. Koeppen included one question taken from a past national poll, "Negroes are as intelligent as white people." The proportion of crusaders who answered yes (73 percent) was comparable to that of white Northerners (77 percent).[39]

These trends held among CACC supporters in the general public. The 1964 ANES shows that they were slightly cooler than were other whites towards civil rights organizations such as the Congress of Racial Equality or the National Association for the Advancement of Colored People but were slightly warmer towards African Americans in general. Support for the CACC, Clyde Wilcox observes, "was not fed by anti-Catholicism, anti-Semitism, or racism." Among Wolfinger's "church group" (i.e., the most religious [and least-educated] of crusaders), rejection of segregation reached an impressive 92 percent. However, once this core of conservative Protestants is excluded, opposition to segregation among crusaders shrank from 65 to 52 percent. In other words, while higher education was almost always linked to support for race integration in national polls, this trend did not apply to Schwarz's base.[40]

Commenting on the CACC base's foreign policy outlook, Wolfinger called it "isolationist," in part because his respondents were systematically more likely to reject the idea of non-confrontational contacts with the Communist world (only 28 percent supported talks with the Soviets against 61 percent nationally). The ANES study's results among CACC supporters were similar. But were Schwarz's followers really isolationists? When Koeppen surveyed her respondents regarding whether they were concerned that the United States was too involved in world affairs, only 35 percent answered "yes," and only 41 percent believed the US should withdraw from the UN. An even lower figure among the combined Wolfinger/Koeppen respondents (34 percent) were against foreign aid for poor or neutral countries. While only 27 percent of Americans thought that a peaceful settlement with the Soviets was impossible, the proportion was 80 percent among Koeppen's respondents. In sum, within the Cold War context, CACC supporters were part of a minority of the American public who thought the US should act unilaterally and cut ties with the Communist world. They had a dim view of the UN, but were split on the idea of withdrawing from it. "Isolationism," in the case of the CACC base, should be substituted for terms such as "sovereignism," "unilateralism," or "conservative internationalism."[41]

"LIMITED BY ITS LACK OF MASS APPEAL"

> The typical supporter of Dr. Schwarz and his Christian Anti-Communism Crusade is a well-to-do businessman or professional man who wants to see Sen. Barry Goldwater in the White House … Although a college-trained man himself, he is certain that the main threat to the United States has to do with 'communist professors' and other 'intellectuals' to mislead the young.[42]

This kind of simplistic synopsis characterized newspaper reports on Wolfinger's findings upon their disclosure during the annual meeting of the American Political Science Association in September 1963. Wolfinger and Koeppen concluded that crusaders were an emerging conservative wing among the GOP that marked its political and ideological territory but that was condemned to remain a minority. "The political strategy of the radical right," Wolfinger stated, "is limited by its lack of mass appeal." Granting that more than "5,000 local study groups had been formed under their stimulus," he nonetheless observed that the CACC "probably reached the peak of its financial and popular success in the last half of 1961." He further concluded that the proliferation of right-wing activity nationwide was largely sparked by the election of a Democratic president. The Crusade's professions of political neutrality could not be taken seriously since it had "several characteristics that place[d] it on the radical right."[43]

Schwarz regretted having permitted the study at his school. Wolfinger's intentions, he stated, were unfriendly from the outset. "The motivation of the researchers," he said in a press conference, "is suggested by the fact that this report was released to the popular press. They knew that the full report would not be published but the more dramatic and controversial conclusions stressed." And these conclusions, he added, were "a prostitution of the scientific method." Schwarz acknowledged receiving "right-wing support" but insisted that the CACC was non-political. The study, he said, "could be described as sick comedy and should have been published in Mad Magazine."[44]

In 1967, Schwarz returned to the Wolfinger study on William Buckley's *Firing Line* television show. That his supporters were middle-class, conservative Republicans, he said, bore no significance. Had Wolfinger surveyed the audience of the San Francisco Symphony Orchestra, he added, his researchers would have noted that its clientele had a similar outlook. Buckley visibly found Schwarz's comments evasive. The TV host suggested that, "when one understands the seriousness of the international situation, one might be prompted to vote Republican." Buckley's reply revealed his understanding that the study did indeed have something interesting to say about the Crusade.[45]

Both the Wolfinger-Koeppen studies and the ANES showed that the Crusade appealed to two WASP constituencies. The first group was educated, upper- and middle-class, and composed of conservative (formerly Taft and now Goldwater) Republicans. By the late 1950s and early 1960s, this demographic formed the mainstay of CACC supporters. The second group, composed of conservative Protestants, constituted Schwarz's first followers when he stepped onto US soil in 1950. For these rather politically moderate (or otherwise apolitical) Bible-touting Christians, Schwarz's lectures, and the subsequent CACC mass events, were factors that reconnected them with the larger world, anticipating their mobilization as part of a new Christian Right. For these people, often of rural background, the CACC enabled their ideological integration into the cities or suburbs of the West, where they brought their conservative evangelicalism to the nation's fast-growing military-industrial complex. These two constituencies, brought together in the CACC schools, formed the armature of the future Reagan coalition, united under a broad-based anticommunist message.

In 1987, Clyde Wilcox compared Wolfinger's data on the CACC to the results of a mail survey of the membership of the Ohio Moral Majority conducted in 1982, noting that both groups appealed to a general mindset he referred to as "Christian Patriotism." They presented similarities, such as an almost identical sex and age distribution, and a much higher proportion of college graduates than displayed in national figures for white Northerners. Despite their much stronger emphasis on so-called "moral" issues, Moral Majority members were as concerned by communism as were the crusaders: "87% felt that Communists had a lot of influence on colleges and universities," about the same proportion as among the CACC, "and nearly three in four felt that Communists had a lot of influence on the Federal Government." The only difference was the more intensely religious outlook of the Ohio Moral Majority, whose members were more faithful in church attendance than Wolfinger's crusaders. Wilcox hypothesized, "Perhaps only communism provides the issue by which the Christian Right might appeal to the secular right without alienating its natural base among the evangelicals and fundamentalists." One slight misreading by Wilcox was his categorizing the CACC as a Christian Right organization. Though the CACC's religious dimension was still present in the early 1960s, its appeal had overflowed the evangelical world by that time.[46]

What prevented the crusaders from having constituted a more accurate representation of the future Reagan coalition was the low presence of some major subgroups, especially blue-collar whites, Catholics, and, to a lesser degree, ethno-cultural minorities. It remains unlikely that the CACC, or any other popular conservative group of that era, could have had the same broad-based appeal that the American Right incrementally built up during the following two decades. What made the transformation of the early 1960s "radical right" into a dominant force by the late 1970s were the shake-ups caused by the collapse of the Democratic South, the backlash against civil rights, the antiwar movement, and the counterculture – as well as ceaseless work on the part of right-wing activists.

Demographics and ideology aside, the Crusade still provides several hints about the long-term features that allowed the American

Right to survive the fading of most of its important organizations in the early 1960s and Goldwater's crushing defeat at the polls in 1964: the involvement of conservative women; the vitality of the right wing in Southern California, where the Reagan movement originated; and the growing prominence of suburbs, among other things. Equally vital was the ongoing support by elites: segments of the country's big business and many of the country's regional small- and medium-sized businesses, prominent members of the nation's military establishment, as well as numerous educated, established citizens, especially from the medical community, gave their seal of approval to right-wing conceptions. Insofar as elite involvement in the popular right wing is a legacy of groups such as the CACC, the social science of the early 1960s has perhaps erred by placing too much emphasis on status theories and by turning a blind eye to groups like the CACC and the JBS. A survey of some of the characteristics of the right from the late 1970s on suggests that, in various regards, the Radical Right of the New Frontier era was remarkably durable.

12

Troubled Times

THE LITTLE BROWN SCARE

In November 1961, still carrying the momentum of his triumphs at the LA Sports Arena and the Hollywood Bowl, Schwarz flew to Omaha for a rally designed to test the ground for a potential week-long school. This gathering was primarily the initiative of businessman and future mayor of Omaha, A.V. Sorensen, who wished to introduce him to the local establishment. The event consisted of a fundraising luncheon with selected citizens, followed by a free meeting held at the city's Music Hall. Nebraska's largest newspaper, the *Omaha World-Herald*, owned by publisher Henry Doorly, puffed the rally with front-page stories.[1]

Because of a snow storm, Schwarz's flight was delayed, but, by chance, Ronald Reagan, on a Midwestern promotional tour for General Electric, was not far away. Reagan agreed on short notice to host the luncheon and share his wit and wisdom in the service of the United States of America. Reagan held the fort before the crusader arrived to address an audience that included James Dworak and Don Lash, the mayors of Omaha and Council Bluffs, respectively. Later, a crowd filled the Music Hall's two thousand seats in fifteen minutes, forcing city officials to open the doors of the nearby Assembly Hall, where the lecture would be heard through monitors. However, with thousands still waiting outside, the City Auditorium was opened as well. Schwarz entered to a standing ovation that lasted nearly a minute and delivered his lecture before the three joint crowds. Women volunteers passed envelopes, allowing the CACC to net $6,000. Describing the whole thing as "amazing and unique in my experience for a first visit to any city," Schwarz decided to hold a CACC school in Omaha six months later, in May 1962.[2]

Six months later, the school took place. But it was far from the expected grand slam. Despite months of preparations, the *World-Herald*'s continuous support, and the $10,000 already purchased in ticket sales, the City Auditorium was only filled to capacity during the free sessions. The school ended up earning $20,000, but this was only three times what had been netted in a single night six months before. Most clergy approached for endorsements declined. Even Omaha's Mayor Dworak, who had supported Schwarz six months before, issued a statement in which, after dithering for a few days, he affirmed his neutrality.[3]

Moreover, a strong local opposition manifested itself. For the most part, it took the form of Omahans for Common Sense, which was organized primarily by local intellectuals and Catholic priests. "This is the first time our schools have experienced organized Catholic opposition as far as I know," Schwarz acknowledged. The group held a meeting in February, involving a local Jesuit philosopher, a history teacher, and a rabbi. "The Schwarz book," one reporter noted, "was labelled a work of careless scholarship, with a total lack of knowledge of the philosophical basis of communism or the historical facts of its foundation." Despite its small size, this group coordinated an effective opposition to the CACC and ensured that local newspapers covered their releases and activities.[4]

The Omaha school was one of many signs that the Crusade was about to enter a turbulent zone. Another sign was the mixed success the CACC met upon organizing a school in mid-December 1961 in St Petersburg, Florida, a retirement haven that was slowly emerging as one of the Sunshine State's conservative strongholds. In spite of good advance publicity and prestigious sponsors, the free-admittance youth event could not fill more than half of the fifty-five hundred seats of St Petersburg's Lang Field. For the first time, some school boards did not cooperate. The Women's Club of the local Democratic Party adopted a resolution against the event. A newspaper warned Suncoasters against "fear and hysteria" that could "weaken the underlying unity that makes America strong."[5]

While the CACC had for months appeared as a respectable counterpart to the John Birch Society, it was now increasingly lumped in the same group. On 16 December 1961, *Newsweek* published a special issue on the right wing, with General Edwin Walker displayed on the magazine's cover. The report "Thunder on the Right" named the JBS and the Crusade as the top "far-right-wing organizations that have sprung up recently." The article listed scores of conservative groups that had recently appeared, and it made them appear to be one single block. The report presented a description of "the fanatic fringe," describing Robert DePugh's Minutemen group, the existence of which had been revealed in October when it organized a guerilla warfare seminar in Illinois. The article established a link between the right wing of the early 1960s and that of the 1930s. It included an interview with sociologist David Riesman, contributor to the 1955 book *The New American Right*, in which he commented: "what is lacking is the kind of conservatism for which Senator Taft stood, which is reasonable, which looks at issues with discrimination."[6]

A few weeks earlier, a similar piece, by *Washington Post* editorialist Alan Barth, had appeared in the *New York Times Magazine*. Quoting another contributor to *The New American Right*, this time Richard Hofstadter, Barth qualified right-wingers as "pseudo-conservatives" since they were "much more in a rage to destroy than fervor to conserve." Barth made the unsubstantiated claim that a "close alliance" existed between "the White Citizens Councils on the one hand" and the JBS and the CACC on the other. Meanwhile, journalist Fred J. Cook ran an issue in the *Nation* on "The Warfare State." Cook drew on the Fulbright Memorandum to emphasize how the growth of the military-industrial complex, coupled with the marriage between the military and politics, was making possible a military coup on the part of war-mongering officers. The right wing, Cook added weeks later, had a "face bearing the marks of a sickness that could develop into fascism."[7]

Schwarz was not oblivious to the change in the general climate. On the same day the *Newsweek* article came out, he privately wrote Sluis:

> We are under thorough investigation by hostile forces desiring to discover something they can use to attack us. The things they are seeking are:
>
> 1 Links that can tie us to other organizations whom they classify as right-wing.
> 2 Attacks on individuals or other organizations.
> 3 Interference in political issues.
> 4 Over-simplified national programs.

> We must be careful to avoid giving them ammunition. If interviewed by a representative of the national press, it is wise to keep a tape recording of the interview. Avoid criticism of all individuals, organizations and government agencies such as the State Department. Please remove from our official recorded list literature of any other organization. Please do not officially show or advocate the films "Communism on the Map" or "Communist Encirclement."[8]

By the end of 1961, the most important forces of American liberalism (the Kennedy White House and Democrat-led governmental agencies, politicians, journalists, unions, and intellectuals) mobilized against what they deemed a danger for democracy. The fear of homegrown fascism, which had not been widespread since the Second World War, returned in a milder form and became an element of political debates of that era.

This period had a major historical precedent. Between the late 1930s and the end of the Second World War, the United States had experienced a "Brown Scare," which targeted various fascist-inspired movements that had grown up during the Depression years. Long before Pearl Harbor, the federal government had begun pushing for the repression of homegrown fascism. The founding of the House Un-American Activities Committee in 1938 was initially aimed at monitoring domestic far right activity. Meanwhile, the liberal press launched a campaign against pro-fascist figures and isolationists. During the Second World War, fascist sympathizers such as William Dudley Pelley, Gerald Winrod, and Gerald K. Smith were arrested and tried in sedition cases. The Brown Scare anticipated McCarthyism insofar as in both cases the extent of the domestic threat was exaggerated. With their small following and minimal exchanges with the Third Reich, racist demagogues such as Pelley and Winrod posed little threat to national security. Yet the Roosevelt administration made efficient use of the fear over Brown subversion to prosecute them and, more broadly, level the charge of un-Americanism against isolationists.[9]

By no means did the fear over homegrown fascism in the 1960s achieve the levels reached by the Brown Scare of the 1930s and 1940s. As opposed to the pro-fascist groups of the wartime era and the Communist Party of the Cold War, the right wing of the early 1960s, even in its most extreme forms (e.g., Robert DePugh's Minutemen or George Lincoln Rockwell's American Nazi Party), was not part of any hostile government-led international movement. Nobody was arrested, imprisoned, or tried for sedition. However, not since the Second World War had the threat of right-wing radicalism been on the minds of so many people and the object of so many discussions nationwide. In a reversal of the trends of the McCarthy era, liberal pundits, politicians, unions, churches, and other organizations across the country mobilized against the impending threat of homegrown fascism. For a brief period of time, throughout the year 1962, media coverage of the right wing reached unprecedented levels. Terms such as "Far Right," "Extremist Right," "Radical Right," and "Ultra-Right" came to be commonly used.

Most importantly, academics and pundits applied to the right wing of the early 1960s the conceptual framework used by Second World War social scientists to understand fascism. During the Second World War, a group of social scientists from the Frankfurt School (Max Horkheimer and Theodor Adorno, particularly) drew from Freudianism to elaborate a theory of the "authoritarian personality," whereby children raised in exploitive settings later tend to develop into people receptive to fascism. This theory, which turned right-wing radicals into an irrational "anthropological species," was the conceptual framework the group of New York intellectuals gathered around Daniel Bell and Richard Hofstadter used in 1955 for their seminal study on the origins of McCarthyism, *The New American Right*, and its 1962 update, *The Radical Right*, the latter having added new material in the context of the rise of groups such as the JBS and the CACC. Drawing directly from Adorno's work, "status anxiety" theories were elaborated to stress how psychological, not economic, factors were the prime force behind McCarthy's followers, thus depicting them as driven by an irrationality that set them apart from members of the older, nobler, conservative tradition. This had major consequences for the future of scholarship on conservatism since a theory originally designed to explain fascism was adapted by some of the nation's most gifted social scientists to understand the American Right, thus establishing an interesting, albeit debatable, continuum between two phenomena that grew out of very different circumstances. It refreshed the conceptualization of the right-wing as an irrational development. However, while the mindset and endeavours of groups such as the JBS seemed extreme, the great majority of right-wing groups failed to present the traits that met the generally agreed upon criteria for identifying fascism.

Historian D.J. Mulloy points out in his study on the JBS that Robert Welch was not "the fascist charismatic leader," that the society was not anti-Semitic, and that its opposition to civil rights legislation was primarily founded on its obsession with communism and the extension of federal power. Also, while the KKK, the Nazi movements, and other groups were actual threats to law and order, the JBS was not. Mulloy nonetheless points out that the general political and social climate made it "entirely understandable" that a sizable part of the American public grew worried about domestic fascism.[10]

This moment was an important one for liberal watchdog groups, who asserted their influence over national politics. Some were rather recent, such as the United Auto Workers-founded Group Research Inc. Established in early 1962, this investigative organization, led by Wesley McCune, was headquartered in Washington and tracked down right-wing groups, gathered information (membership, backers, activities), and published monthly reports. For the next three years, Group Research Inc. kept right-wing extremists in the news by providing press releases and reports showing they were apparently growing in strength. From 1962 on, the CACC's activities in the US were scrutinized by this group. A much older watchdog was B'nai B'rith's Anti-Defamation League (ADL). Founded in the early twentieth century with the goal of protecting US Jews from defamation, the ADL had gradually expanded its mission to fight all forms of bigotry and civil rights infringements, and it played no minor part in the CACC's woes.[11]

RUMBLE ON THE WEST COAST

In late 1961, Schwarz arrived in San Francisco for two months of preparatory rallies for the San Francisco School of Anti-Communism, held between 29 January and 2 February 1962 at the Oakland Auditorium Theatre. In contrast to Florida, where the recent experience had been disappointing but where Schwarz's organization was not solidly established, the CACC had a local branch in San Francisco headed by Sluis.

But negative press coverage of the Radical Right had been intensifying in the previous weeks. In January 1962, Robert Welch came to San Francisco to speak before a luncheon of the Commonwealth Club of California. During the question period that followed his address, he claimed: "Many of our members help to set up Dr.

Schwarz's schools … and we frankly do our best to take the people who have been stirred up and awakened and alarmed by him to get them together in the John Birch Society." This intensified questions about the JBS each time Schwarz spoke to the press. As before, the crusader sidestepped the issue with statements such as "I don't know much about the society," but this fence-sitting was becoming difficult to maintain. Only one San Francisco newspaper, the *Oakland Tribune*, owned by the Knowland family, endorsed the school. Admitting he faced greater opposition than expected, Schwarz pre-emptively ordered films and literature from Harding College and the National Education Program to be removed from the list of CACC-recommended material.[12]

Growing anxiety among liberal churches about the potential effects of CACC schools manifested itself. Eight religious leaders voiced their opposition to the event and made public a letter they had sent to churches and synagogues in the Bay Area calling on religious leaders to oppose it. The group's spokesman, Dr Robert D. Bulkley, from the United Presbyterian Church in the USA, deemed the CACC guilty of spreading "suspicion of American institutions, particularly the churches and the schools." Schwarz replied that he had never seen "such cowardice masquerading as Christianity." To his relief, the day after, representatives of thirty-five churches of the Bay Area Conservative Baptist Association released a statement expressing their "wholehearted support" of the school, followed ten days later by the local National Association of Evangelicals branch, representing about one hundred churches.[13]

More fuss erupted over the anticommunist weeks that were proclaimed by the mayors of almost all Bay Area cities (fifty-five in all). In Mill Valley, the City Council, in the absence of Mayor Robert Huber, voted to disclaim the proclamation; in Fairfax, Mayor Kenneth Edgar denied he had ever signed it. The mayor of Fremont, George Demmel, said he signed it "as a perfunctory matter – the same as I might proclaim Alcoholics Anonymous Week." In San Rafael, Mayor John F. McInnis told a journalist that he signed the proclamation reluctantly after one of the school's emissaries told him that "mayors throughout the Bay Area were signing and that anyone who didn't sign obviously had communist leanings." San Jose mayor Paul Moore said his signature had been obtained by "misrepresentation." Republican San Francisco mayor George Christopher distanced himself from the crusader: "I merely signed an Anti-Communism Week proclamation. I did not endorse Dr. Schwarz." One of California's foremost liberal figures, Attorney General Stanley Mosk, amidst his campaign for re-election as attorney general, stated: "I am profoundly shocked that public officials should sign endorsement resolutions for the benefit of fly-by-night school promoters." Mayor Christopher responded that these remarks associated him unfairly with right-wing extremism.[14]

Mosk continued to pound the CACC in his speeches, describing the group as a money-making scam. Challenged by Schwarz to substantiate his accusations, Mosk replied during a televised broadcast on KTVU-Channel 2. He criticized CACC schools for not being licensed under any state educational law and listed the amounts netted by the organization during its schools in Los Angeles, Phoenix, and Oakland. He then attacked the CACC's message, using carefully selected generalities that blurred the distinction between declarations by CACC schools and those by other right-wing personalities. Schwarz requested, through an attorney, that he be allowed to see Mosk's sources: they were all second-hand reports on the right wing containing unreliable evidence (and nothing on the CACC itself). Afterwards, Mosk admitted privately that he would consider retraction should any statement of his be proven wrong. Negotiations between him and the CACC were still ongoing three years later, by which point Schwarz's time limit for legal action had expired and Mosk had ended all discussion.[15]

Only three hundred people showed up at the CACC school's opening session in Oakland, but the number increased to one thousand for most sessions, with a peak of twenty-one hundred during the evening events, which were televised on local stations. Nonetheless, not once were the Oakland Auditorium's five thousand seats all filled. Even the free event for young people could not draw more than half the auditorium's capacity. About 13,600 people attended at least one school session – the banquet that closed the event netted about $30,000. One year before, these numbers would have been considered astonishing. This time, they were disappointing.[16]

Controversies raged throughout the school's duration. Three days after it began, a full-page advertisement appeared in newspapers, paid for by the Citizen's Committee to Protest the Christian Anti-Communism Crusade. Signed by hundreds of names displayed in small print, the document condemned the CACC for emulating the methods of Joe McCarthy and the JBS. As the school was under way, on short notice Stanford University organized a conference at which intellectuals, politicians, and clergy discussed how to defend democracy against the threat of the "Ultra-Right."

On the school's fourth day, on Tuesday, 2 February, homemade bombs damaged two San Fernando Valley houses. The two targeted persons were Reverend John G. Simmons from the St Matthews Lutheran Church of North Hollywood and Reverend Brooks R. Walker of the Emerson Unitarian Church of Canoga Park. The bombs, the *Los Angeles Times* reported, projected "jagged metal chunks" that "gouged holes in the exterior of their houses," shattering windows and striking a baby's crib, but did not injure either cleric or their families. Simmons and Walker were liberal pastors who had been vocal opponents of the right wing, and this had earned them numerous threats and anonymous phone calls. The case was made even bigger by the fact that a third person participating in the panel that night was television and film actress Marsha Hunt, long-time liberal activist who had been blacklisted in the 1950s. A member of the American Association for the United Nations (AAUN), Hunt told one journalist that her home escaped the bombings "because the terrorists were unable to find out" where she lived. The police later revealed that the bombs were identical to one that had failed to detonate two months earlier at the Los Angeles headquarters of the AAUN.[17]

The bombers were never arrested, but the right wing was put on the defensive. Syndicated columnist Drew Pearson wrote that this was perhaps only the beginning of a rash of violence spreading nationwide, "for when people in high places endorse hate gatherings such as Southern California and Texas have witnessed in recent months, it's impossible to predict what extremists will do in their wake." The JBS condemned the bombings. "I don't know what the significance is ... but we are against it with every breath of our body," Schwarz stated. When Los Angeles mayor Sam Yorty contacted Reverend Simmons, asking what he could do for him, he got a stern reply: "You can take back that statement you made approving [Schwarz] and his Christian anti-Communist Crusade ... You and 44 other California mayors can take back the blessing you gave this hate movement."[18]

If Schwarz and his collaborators expected the storm to die down in time for the opening of the next school, the Puget Sound School, at Seattle's Olympic Hotel from 12 to 16 February 1962, they were disappointed. The previous weeks had crippled the efforts of the CACC's advance team to get endorsements from the mayors of western Washington. A few days before the event began, Schwarz was scheduled for a radio debate with Communist Party of the USA leader Gus Hall. The debate, however, was cancelled without reason. Labour organizations, much more powerful in Washington State than in the Southwest, took offence at the fact that one of the school's corporate sponsors was Boeing, which had for years been leading anti-union "right-to-work" campaigns in several states. Twenty-one leading Protestant and Jewish religious leaders joined the movement. The fifteen hundred seats of the Olympic's grand ballroom were never filled to capacity. The free youth event drew only twelve hundred young people, who came to hear Schwarz and George Murphy at Seattle's Civic Ice Arena. The school's closing banquet enabled the Crusade to net $10,000, enough to cover the expenses of the event.[19]

The topic of right-wing extremism kept making headlines throughout the winter and spring of 1962. William Buckley excommunicated Bob Welch from "responsible" conservatism in a *National Review* editorial. Welch, Buckley wrote, "persists in distorting reality and in refusing to make the crucial moral distinction ... between, 1) an active *pro-Communist*, and 2) an *ineffectually anti-Communist liberal* [emphasis in original] ." Buckley's editorial came after other important figures of the right (Russell Kirk, Walter Judd, Fulton Lewis) had voiced similar criticism. Richard Nixon, whose gubernatorial campaign in California was undermined by the extremist issue, suggested that conservatives should leave the JBS. The general climate took its toll on the JBS: from its reported peak of 100,000 in early 1961, its national membership dropped to about twenty-four thousand by mid-1962. Meanwhile, CBS broadcast a program called "Thunder on the Right," which focused on thriving "right-wing extremism" across the nation. The one-hour report dedicated ten minutes to the CACC, where it mixed footage taken at a CACC school with an extract showing rifle-toting Minutemen searching for communists on the Mississippi River. The material on the Crusade came from footage a CBS team had recorded with Schwarz's approval during the CACC school in St Petersburg in late 1961. The crusader protested that the footage had been spliced into the documentary, thus producing "the most effective 'forgery by film' I have ever seen."[20]

Schwarz's associates began to feel the heat as well. Invited to NBC's *Meet the Press*, Thomas Dodd was forced to justify his participation in anticommunist events and to defend his speech at the Hollywood Bowl rally. He later admitted that responsible anticommunists should distance themselves from right-wing extremism. Walter Judd received regular complaints from people, often his own supporters, who disapproved of his participation in Crusade activities. Philbrick received similar letters. In a reply to one of these messages, he explained that, since he began working with Schwarz, sales for the book version of *I Led Three Lives* had increased and that he would not discontinue his work with the CACC merely because communists slandered it.[21]

In late May 1962, during the annual meeting of stockholders and management of Technicolor, Inc., 250 stockholders fired a barrage of questions at Patrick Frawley. Their concern was largely over the 14 percent drop in the value of Technicolor stock since Frawley had taken over the company a year before, but some questions also concerned right-wing politics and the appointment of George Murphy as vice-president. After the meeting, a reporter wrote, "one stockholder cornered George Murphy ... and asked him about reports that Mr. Frawley was a member of the John Birch Society."[22]

THE REUTHER MEMORANDUM

On 19 December 1961, US attorney general Robert F. Kennedy received from Victor Reuther a memorandum outlining a strategy against the right wing. The twenty-three-page document, titled *The Radical Right in America Today*, offered a battle plan: it assessed the enemy's strengths and weaknesses, and made suggestions on how to take the offence. The Reuther Memorandum remained secret for years. Part of its contents was leaked to the press in late 1963, but the full report was disclosed only in 1976. Robert Kennedy denied that he had ever read the document. In 1964, he stated that he and the president never considered the right wing as anything more than an amusing "pain in the butt." The actions of the Kennedy administration, nonetheless, suggest otherwise.[23]

"The Radical Right," the report said, "includes an unknown number of millions of Americans of viewpoints bounded on the left by Senator Goldwater and on the right by Robert Welch." Even if only a minority among them were active militants, right-wing groups were "growing in strength and there [was] no reason to expect a turning of the tide." The report called for "deliberate Administration policies and programs to contain the Radical Right from further expansion." One recommendation was to curb the flow of money that funded right-wing groups by way of targeting tax-exempt groups and finding proper grounds for revoking their exempt status. A complete audit of right-wing groups, the report read, should be made to that end.[24]

The IRS had been monitoring the CACC even before the memorandum. During the days that followed the 1961 event at the LA Sports Arena, letters began pouring into the Exempt Organizations Branch of the IRS in Washington about possible breaches of the exempt-status regulations. Thus, at the very outset of the operation launched by the IRS in the wake of the Reuther Memorandum, the CACC was considered a priority case. As John Andrews III writes in his study of the politicization of the IRS, "Nowhere were the pressures from Congress on the IRS with respect to ideology more evident than in its investigation of Dr. Fred Schwarz's Christian Anti-Communism Crusade."[25]

In early 1962, the IRS secretly launched its Ideological Organizations Project (IOP), which singled out organizations it deemed justified a special tax audit. This was unprecedented: the IRS had almost never conducted such large-scale, time-consuming, and difficult audits, which rarely resulted in more tax revenues. Moreover, agents trained to undertake quantitative inspections also had to learn how to do qualitative ones, which meant "an analysis of books and pamphlets published by the organization … [as well as] the monitoring of telecasts and broadcasts and the examination of hundreds and in some cases thousands of speeches." The first phase of the IOP was only completed in May 1963. More than 75 percent of the groups audited were right wing. In July 1963, the White House received the preliminary IOP report and was delighted by the results.[26]

Yet, perhaps due to the delays that had bogged down the whole process, and anticipating congressional hearings on the IRS and tax-exempt organizations in 1964, President Kennedy urged the IRS to narrow its focus to the most important exempt organizations. The IRS thus singled out twelve groups that it considered "the anti-communist complex or radical right as it is sometimes known," which included, apart from the CACC, the Cardinal Mindszenty Foundation, the Christian Echoes Ministry (Billy James Hargis's media network), Edgar Bundy's Church League of America, the Life Line Foundation, and the National Education Program.[27]

In February 1963, even before the White House pressured the IRS to act more swiftly, IRS commissioner Mortimer Caplin had received a report recommending revocation for two groups: the CACC and the Life Line Foundation, H.L. Hunt's broadcast funder. The CACC's case was based on the examination of its books for the years 1959 through 1961, which detailed a series of alleged infringements on tax regulations, the most serious being the amounts sent overseas. The CACC had distributed "substantial sums of money to its officers for use in foreign countries without requiring adequate substantiation of actual expenditures," and it had made a contribution to a private individual, George Thomas in India, "for use in acquiring and operating a daily newspaper." Moreover, both in India and British Guiana, the CACC had meddled in local politics. The sums piped to Australia also posed a problem. Between 1954 and 1960, the CACC channelled more than $40,000 to Australia, most of which ($28,266) was sent between 1958 and 1960, the period scrutinized by the IRS. This money was allocated to the CACC's Sydney branch. Per IRS documents, Schwarz's wife Lillian earned a $450 monthly salary and "performed little apparent work for CACC." Tax-exempt status could not be revoked solely on these grounds, but the IRS was confident that a revocation could be successfully defended before the Tax Rulings Division.[28]

The IRS's problem, however, was twofold. First, no solid legal precedent existed as to whether a prohibition against domestic political engagement for tax-exempt organizations also applied outside of the United States. Also, IRS auditors had to work with fragmentary evidence on the CACC's international activities and, for the most part, relied on information provided by the organization itself. A passage from the report on the CACC indicates that, even if its foreign activities "do raise serious problems with respect to whether the organization's exemption should be continued," recommendation was made to question the organization about these activities "before issuing a notice of revocation."[29]

The circumstances served the CACC well. IRS staffers, already overwhelmed by the colossal size of the IOP, apparently did not conduct an extensive search of the CACC's international activities. While the audit was taking place, the organization had just been expelled from British Guiana and was gradually withdrawing its support to George Thomas in Kerala, thus removing two irritants for the IRS. Moreover, during the period covered by the IRS investigation, the Australian CACC had hired a new director, Elton Wilson, one of Schwarz's former patients and friends in Australia. In November 1959, Wilson was introduced in the CACC newsletter as a "young business man" who was "planning to surrender his business and devote his full time to rallying Australians to wholehearted commitment in this battle for Christian liberty." This undoubtedly complicated any plan the IRS might have had to show that no Australian CACC genuinely existed, even though the Australian CACC was admittedly a far cry from its US counterpart. It always remained a small-scale, close-knit operation run by Schwarz's relatives in Sydney and Brisbane. It conducted episodic radio broadcasts, distributed pieces of literature, and organized rallies and talks. The Australian CACC was apparently not profitable. In a fundraising letter from 1965, Wilson wrote: "the ordinary American people, who are our main supporters in the United States, are subsidizing the Australian Crusade's attempts to keep Australia free."[30]

What initially appeared a solid case against the CACC was weakening. Also, the assumption that had been at the very core of the Reuther Memorandum – that right-wing groups were almost by definition violating their tax-exempt status – appeared increasingly shaky. Despite the early hopes of the Kennedy administration, the IOP was able to mount a serious case for revocation against only one group: Billy James Hargis's Christian Echoes Ministry. In late 1964, on the grounds that Hargis had used his organization as a front for political activities, the IRS revoked his tax-exempt status. In 1965, the IRS shut down the IOP almost entirely, perhaps as the consequence of a belief that the defeat of Barry Goldwater in the 1964 presidential election had discredited right-wing groups.[31]

The IRS was not the only federal bureaucracy that confronted the CACC. The Reuther Memorandum had recommended that the Federal Communications Commission (FCC) curb the visibility of right-wing groups by eliminating the free (or reduced-rate) radio and TV time they often got across the country as a public service. Though the CACC was not using radio or television broadcasting on a regular basis, the Hollywood Bowl rally in October 1961 had alarmed FCC officials, who had questions for the broadcasters. In Seattle, affiliates of the King Broadcasting Corporation received letters from the FCC voicing the concerns of groups such as the American Association for the United Nations. The company justified the airing of the show as a public service announcement.[32]

The FCC's concern with offering "differing viewpoints" was rooted in the Fairness Doctrine, which, since its introduction in 1949, had been more of a general guideline than a systematic policy. The Kennedy administration was the first one to politically exploit the doctrine, almost a decade before the Nixon administration similarly used it to its ends. Kennedy's assistant secretary of Commerce, Bill Ruder, declared decades later that the doctrine was used "to challenge and harass right-wing broadcasters and hope the challenges would be ... costly to them." An IRS report mentions that when Kennedy asked IRS commissioner Mortimer Caplin to step up his campaign against right-wing groups in 1963, he also stated that this request was part of a larger program. "The President's interest in combating extremism," the report read, "apparently also manifested itself in the reemphasis by the Federal Communications Commission of its 'fairness doctrine,' requiring broadcasters to afford reasonable opportunities for the presentation of contrasting viewpoints on any controversial matters the broadcasters decide to cover." Fulton Lewis Jr, for instance, received threats in early 1962 from the Senate Subcommittee on Freedom of Communications that his conservative radio broadcast could be barred for violating the doctrine. In 1963, when the IOP's second phase was under way, the FCC ruled that H.L. Hunt's broadcasting empire Life Line had to give free time to "bonafide groups that wish to oppose 'Life Line' on the air." Broadcasters and sponsors who wished to air right-wing material were also pressured by private groups that wished to curb the visibility of right-wing rhetoric. When the Hollywood Bowl rally was aired on the East Coast in early 1962, the ACLU wrote to the FCC and broadcasters to request air time for speakers who had different opinions than those expressed during the show.[33]

Later in the year, when the CACC came to New York to organize a rally and a school, Schwarz realized that it was almost impossible for him to buy television time. Five stations refused to sell any time, forcing the crusader to secure three half-hours on the small independent WOR-TV. Two years later, he could not find a single broadcaster from whom he could buy air time for his school in Washington. He later accused the FCC of having followed the guidelines of the Reuther Memorandum.[34]

The Reuther Memorandum also recommended that the FBI monitor right-wing groups, though its authors admitted to not knowing "the extent to which the [FBI] ha[d] planted undercover agents inside the radical right movement as it ha[d] inside the Communist Party and its allied organizations." In fact, before the document was drafted, FBI director Edgar Hoover had tried to respond to White House concerns by increasing the surveillance of right-wing groups, even though the Bureau's work focused much more on groups such as the KKK than on political organizations.[35]

The FBI had begun following the activities of the CACC and the JBS even before Kennedy took office in January 1961. As opposed to the early JBS, the CACC was not a secret organization, and the FBI never treated it as subversive. But, by the late 1950s, the Bureau had a sizable file on the CACC because, since 1953, it had been receiving requests for information on it. While the FBI replied to these inquiries that it was not its mission to provide evaluations of private organizations, it kept note of CACC activities whenever it could.

In September 1960, the personal view FBI officials had of Schwarz and the CACC became negative after the CACC school in Dallas. For that event, organizers tried to invite J. Edgar Hoover as a speaker; he was unavailable, but a lecturer from the Bureau, special agent Arbor W. Gray, was sent. Gray reported on the event to his superior W.C. Sullivan, the FBI's chief inspector and the main official responsible for the Bureau's anticommunist affairs. Sullivan expressed displeasure that Schwarz used his lectures to promote his own writings and decided that the FBI would no longer collaborate with the CACC. In a memo, Sullivan blamed people like Schwarz for "misinforming people and stirring them up emotionally to the point that when FBI lecturers present the truth, it becomes very difficult for the misinformed to accept it." From then on, the FBI denied any requests from the Crusade to use its printed material. "The Bureau," internal FBI memos indicate, "has been discouraging requests for publications from persons who are under the influence of Dr. Schwarz since he obviously is capitalizing on our reprint material." This policy not only applied to the CACC but also to individuals and/or groups associated with it. In October 1961, Hoover handwrote on the cover of a report on the CACC: "We should have nothing to do with Schwarz."[36]

Perception of the Crusade worsened when the Bureau became aware of Skousen's role. Skousen sought the GOP gubernatorial nomination in Utah in 1960 by presenting himself as "Administrative Assistant to J. Edgar Hoover during World War II." The FBI received inquiries about this claim, which angered Hoover not only because he did not want his organization to be "injected into political matters" but also because the FBI never had such a position. In 1961, in the wake of Skousen's lecturing activities, the Bureau received inquiries regarding the story Skousen told about Harry Hopkins smuggling uranium to the Soviets; however, the FBI had nothing in its files that could support this charge. In September 1961, the FBI deleted Skousen from its mailing lists.[37]

Letters about Skousen's claims kept coming, displeasing FBI officials. "Apparently," Hoover's deputy, C.D. "Deke" DeLoach, wrote to Administrative Affairs handler John P. Mohr in October 1961: "Skousen, Schwarz et al are becoming more and more irresponsible and have apparently succumbed to the philosophy that the ends justify the means." In January 1962, the Bureau was contacted by an official of the Florida State Department of Education, who expressed doubts about the use of Skousen's *The Naked Communist* in Florida schools. In a memo, Chief Inspector W.C. Sullivan reminded Hoover's assistant: "during the past year or so, Skousen has affiliated himself with the extreme right-wing 'professional anti-communists' such as Fred Schwarz, who are promoting their own anticommunism for obvious financial purposes." Six months later, Schwarz contacted Sullivan himself to invite him to appear at the New York CACC school in late August 1962. "Needless to say," Sullivan wrote in an FBI memo, "I declined the invitation. Dr. Schwarz was rather persistent and wanted to know whether some other Bureau representative would accept. I gave him no encouragements." Hoover handwrote at the bottom of the memo, "Absolutely no."[38]

"BETTER RED THAN FRED": NEW YORK

In late 1961, Frawley convinced Schwarz that the CACC was ready to take on the East Coast now that the West Coast had been stirred up. Skousen noted in his diary that Frawley, Murphy, and Charles Jones from Richfield Oil intended to organize an event at the Madison Square Garden with a projected TV audience of 50 million. In April 1962, Schwarz arrived in New York with his secretary Ella Doorn and Jim Colbert for a three-month stay designed to prepare the CACC's most ambitious bid yet. In mid-April a free tentative rally was held at the Manhattan Center. The results were encouraging: three thousand people showed up. The CACC thereupon issued a statement announcing a bigger rally at Madison Square Garden two months later, on 28 June 1962, and a full-fledged school by late summer.[39]

The degree to which the national mood had changed between late 1961 and mid-1962 made this project a risky idea. But this motivated Schwarz, convinced as he was that a successful school in the lion's den would debunk misperceptions about his group. Of this project, he stated in May 1962: "In the life of every man and movement there comes a time when choice must be made. We made a choice which will profoundly affect the entire work of the Christian Anti-Communism Crusade and can affect the future of mankind." The crusader chose New York for various reasons. It was the headquarters of the UN, where world leaders were exposed to the press and news media of New York; it was the headquarters of the CPUSA; it was the metropolis where hundreds of colleges and universities were concentrated within a short radius. It was also the nerve centre of the media and the publishing business.[40]

Murphy put Schwarz in contact with Marvin Liebman, head of Marvin Liebman Associates, Inc., which, at the time, was the nation's foremost conservative public relations firm. Liebman was a brilliant Brooklyn nerd of Jewish background. He was in his late thirties and was considered a pioneer of fundraising and direct mail campaigns. A closeted homosexual who was discharged from the US Army during the Second World War when his superiors became aware of his sexual orientation, Liebman had been involved in the 1930s with left-wing groups before shifting rightward, largely because of the Soviets' mistreatment of their Jewish population. In the late 1950s, he had become involved in the China Lobby and served as secretary of the Committee of One Million against Communist China's admittance to the UN. In the letter introducing Schwarz to Liebman, Murphy said that Liebman was the most suited guide to New York culture, a subject upon which he thought the Australian needed a great deal of advice.[41]

Liebman sent Schwarz a memo in which he warned the crusader: "attacks on the Crusade will be stronger here than, perhaps, any other section of the country." Liebman made a series of suggestions aimed at broadening the CACC's base by reaching out to all religious and political creeds – for instance, by dropping the word "Christian" from the organization's promotional literature in New York (which was done) – so as to transform the organization into something more than "an expression of … [Schwarz's] individual personality and ideals." Schwarz hired Liebman's firm for $3,000 per month for the duration of the New York project. Liebman's Madison Avenue office became the CACC's New York headquarters. Until the end of the summer, this New York bid cost the CACC thousands of dollars each month, excluding the costs of renting the Madison Square Garden and maintaining other regular activities across the country.[42]

The CACC only had a limited number of supporters in the East. Yet Liebman claimed to have a list of about 100,000 names constituting the lists of *National Review* (current and expired), Young Americans for Freedom, his own lists, and other smaller ones from anticommunist or conservative organizations. As for the program, he gave top priority to the enlistment of a bipartisan roster of speakers. He wished to place Schwarz and Judd alongside at least two prominent Democratic figures. Apart from Dodd, he suggested Senator Henry "Scoop" Jackson, George Meany, and HUAC chairman Francis Walter, but none accepted.[43]

As the preparatory period got under way, the crusader could tell that things would not be easy in New York. At his first press conference, Schwarz was submitted to the now-usual barrage of questions on the JBS. He later appeared at Princeton University to address a colloquium titled "The Rise of the Right Wing," an invitation he had refused until organizers of the event allowed him to choose his own topic (the communist threat), but he found himself picketed by students with signs that read "Aussie Go Home," and "Better Red Than Fred."[44]

Schwarz and Colbert arranged a meeting with executives of WPIX-Channel 11, which had broadcast "Hollywood's Answer to Communism" on the East Coast in late 1961. Both men were told that, in spite of the impressive public response to the show, WPIX would not sell air time for the Madison Square Garden rally. Schwarz was taken aback and lost his temper. He left the building saying that with friends like these, "I pray the Lord will give us a few enemies." Decades later, he expressed regrets: "I failed to realize that they legitimately feared the loss of their license because of the Democratic administration's hostility." The story repeated itself with four other local TV stations. After much difficulty, the CACC secured air time on the independent WOR-Channel 9.[45]

Similarly antagonistic to the CACC was the *New York Post*, which, prior to its acquisition by Rupert Murdoch in 1976, was known for its liberal leanings. *Post* columnist James Wechsler described a CACC event that he attended as "a journey from the real world to a remote universe of fantasy and pathology." Another *Post* columnist,

Murray Kempton, ridiculed Schwarz in several of his columns. In May, Liebman was quoted in a *Post* article as saying, "Fred Schwarz says everybody will be happy when we kill off all Communists." Liebman wrote in protest to the *Post* that he had never made such a remark. Schwarz apparently believed Liebman's explanation since both men continued their association, but this incident worsened relationships with the New York press.[46]

The intense hostility Schwarz faced from George Sokolsky, syndicated columnist for the Hearst-owned papers since 1940, took everybody by surprise. A Jewish New Yorker and staunch anticommunist, Sokolsky was well acquainted with many people associated with Schwarz. Since 1961, he had led the American Jewish League against Communism (AJLAC), whose main committee included Ida Kohlberg, widow of Alfred Kohlberg; Los Angeles-based syndicated columnist Morrie Ryskind; and Liebman, who was acting secretary. The record of "Sok," as his friends called him, had always been flawless in right-wing circles. In his column, Sokolsky had extolled the virtues of his friends Joe McCarthy, Roy Cohn, and J. Edgar Hoover (he once praised McCarthy for exposing the State Department as "a nest of homosexuals"), and he followed the line of the Republican right on most issues. Sokolsky's antipathy towards Schwarz first led to a crisis at the AJLAC in late 1961. Upon learning that the AJLAC's Los Angeles chapter, led by Ryskind and Rabbi Max Merritt, had accepted money from Pat Frawley, Sokolsky fired Merritt and then wrote Frawley, stating that the league did not accept money from non-Jews and that he would report him to the IRS.[47]

Sokolsky also began taking on Schwarz in his syndicated column. In late 1961, in a text decrying what he saw as the climate of hysteria the liberal media had created regarding the right wing, he dismissed both the JBS and the CACC as a waste of ink: "It is not to be assumed that Bob Welch or even Dr. Fred Schwarz, an Australian who operates out of Long Beach, California, could stand up in an intellectual discussion on Marxism." Fusing the respectable Schwarz with the Wild Bill Hickok figure of Welch struck many as incomprehensible. Philbrick privately asked the columnist why he was attacking his "friends," urging him to get acquainted with Schwarz's writings and to later publish a clarification. Schwarz tried to have his corporate supporters pressure the Hearst Corporation to get Sokolsky to apologize for his remarks. But Sokolsky would not budge. "It angers Dr. Schwarz's followers to question his intellectual prowess, they believing that he is the greatest living authority on [communism]," he added in his next column. Sokolsky was further displeased when he learned that his acquaintances George Murphy and Marvin Liebman were collaborating with Schwarz.[48]

Schwarz and Liebman always claimed not to know why Sokolsky was so hostile. The most direct explanation lies in an internal FBI memo summarizing a phone conversation Sokolsky had in March 1962 with an assistant of FBI director J. Edgar Hoover, himself one of Sokolsky's long-time friends. Sokolsky claimed that Schwarz "was formerly a member of the Jewish faith but dishonored his faith and later became a Baptist and he, Sokolsky, did not trust Schwarz." According to the memo, Sokolsky also stated that the CACC's name itself was "an insult to the Jewish faith." This was why Sokolsky had refused to let the AJLAC accept any money from Frawley, whom, he claimed, wanted to fuse the AJLAC with the CACC. Also, Sokolsky was perhaps aware of the FBI's low opinion of the Australian.[49]

Fred Schwarz was not an apostate Jew; his father, Paulus Schwarz, was. But that Sokolsky still privately made that false claim in March 1962 – months after his first column on Schwarz – is nonetheless noteworthy. The first article in which Sokolsky attacked Schwarz in late 1961 indicates that, from the outset, the columnist had serious misgivings about Schwarz's conservative Protestant creed, a background that was sometimes associated with anti-Semitism (evangelical leaders such as J. Frank Norris, Billy James Hargis, Gerald K. Smith, and William Bell Riley embodied this line of thought). His column criticized those "who do not understand the Hebrew Bible but demand that every word of it translated into post-Elizabethan English be accepted as truth." These people, he wrote, are "anti-Semites devising numerous concepts to justify their confusions." Echoing Liebman's recommendation to drop the "Christian" from the CACC's letterheads, another of Schwarz's collaborators, Arthur McDowell, once suggested that they change the organization's name, which he suspected was especially off-putting to many Jews, who "simply bogle [sic] at everything in connection with communism that uses the word Christian, because it has been so typically exploited by the racists and other extremists along the line." This situation was worsened by the confusion of the CACC's name with Billy James Hargis's Christian Crusade.[50]

"Before I had the opportunity to meet with Dr. Schwarz," Liebman wrote Sokolsky, "I was inclined to agree with a good deal of your evaluation. However, after meeting with Dr. Schwarz and his colleagues, I find myself in total disagreement with you. Dr. Schwarz is not an anti-Semite. His colleagues are not anti-Semites." But Sokolsky's impression of Schwarz was shared by many others. Schwarz later wrote that, on his arrival in New York, "I quickly realized that the delusion that I was anti-Semitic was widespread." One of the CACC's rare corporate sponsors in New York, Chesebrough-Ponds, had one of its representatives interview several members of the Jewish community to inquire if its sponsorship would present any problem. Many of those interviewed said Schwarz was anti-Semitic.[51]

In spite of his father's Jewish origin, Schwarz, who did not enter a synagogue before the age of forty, never showed any particular interest in Judaism. He had worked or befriended a few Jews in the past, such as Alfred Kohlberg, and his record was clear of any anti-Semitic activity, as evidenced by internal reports from organizations such as the Anti-Defamation League, which noted in 1959 that he had no known record of "harmful activities." When the Jewish Federation Council of Greater Los Angeles (JFCGLA) monitored a CACC school in 1961, it did not register any anti-Semitic content. In 1961, under a false identity, white supremacist Gerald K. Smith wrote to Schwarz to ask if he agreed that communism was a Jewish plot, but Schwarz dismissed the idea. Ironically, this intensified Smith's suspicion that Schwarz might be a closeted Jew, a perception Smith shared with James Madole, leader of the National Renaissance Party, a neo-fascist group that denounced the so-called "Jewish Leadership of the Conservative Movement" (Barry Goldwater, Roy Cohn, and Fred Schwarz) and whose members picketed some CACC meetings, accusing Schwarz of being a "phony Jewish conservative" trying to infiltrate Gentile ranks.[52]

Liebman contacted Benjamin Epstein and Arnold Forster, co-directors of the Anti-Defamation League, and proposed that they meet Schwarz. Considering the ADL's strong liberal leanings and ties to the Democratic Party, Liebman's hopes were probably that such an encounter would clear up misunderstandings and improve Schwarz's image among liberals. However, the meeting was never to be. Epstein and Forster were also close friends of Sokolsky, and their view of Schwarz was the same as his. Moreover, both considered Liebman's proposal a trap, assuming that such a meeting would be seen as an endorsement, while a refusal to meet could be presented as persecution. The ADL did not answer the request and gave no explanation for not doing so. Weeks later, Liebman tried for a second time to bring together Epstein, Forster, and Schwarz. Informed by Forster of Liebman's initiatives, Sokolsky phoned Liebman. "For half an hour," Liebman privately wrote, "he berated me as I have never been berated. Among other things, I was a crook, dishonest, disloyal, a potential anti-Semite, and 'with no authority to telephone Forster.'" Liebman thereupon submitted to Sokolsky his resignation from the American Jewish League against Communism and ended his firm's handling of AJLAC's public relations.[53]

New York's prime conservative personality, William F. Buckley, weighed in at this point in Schwarz's favour. He privately informed Sokolsky that *National Review* considered Schwarz's work to be perfectly endorsable, partly because it digressed from *National Review*'s highbrow discussions on communism. Buckley also contacted Forster at the ADL to ask for an explanation for its refusal to meet Schwarz. Forster replied that he had no need to meet the crusader and was under no obligation to explain why. Buckley lamented the whole situation in a *National Review* editorial, in which he criticized this tendency to "brand as anti-Semitic anyone associated with an explicitly Christian undertaking who is also a tough anti-Communist or conservative," and he took offence at Forster's refusal to meet the crusader. The ADL, "staffed by political Liberals," was encouraging the "continued circulation of invidious rumors" about Schwarz. Two of Buckley's Jewish collaborators, Eugene Lyons (*Reader's Digest* editor) and Ralph de Toledano (*Newsweek* columnist), also decried the ADL's attitude. Arnold Forster replied, dismissing Buckley as an "eighteen-century egg-head and a quixotic beatnik in a Brooks Brothers suit."[54]

These squabbles were hurting any momentum the New York project may have had. Not more than two hundred persons showed up to do volunteer work for the Madison Square Garden rally. Schwarz and Colbert begged attendees to help them mail the envelopes for the meeting. "If you can come," Colbert said, "we'll have cookies, coke, and we'll have fellowship while you're working." In a letter sent to his supporters, Schwarz admitted to having underestimated the obstacles he would face in New York, decrying the opposition, which was "operating in semi-secret" and threatened every businessperson susceptible to supporting him with "financial strangulation." In addition to sending an urgent plea for funds, the CACC also implored supporters across the country to come to New York to help fill the seats of the upcoming school. On 29 May, Prentice-Hall, under pressure from several of its school textbook customers, asked that mentions of its collaboration with the Crusade be removed from CACC material.[55]

In March 1962, the Schick sales management received a letter protesting Schick's sponsorship of the Crusade. C. Irving Dwork, president of Franlee Distributors, a toiletry furnisher and vice-chairman of the American Jewish Congress, said he would not contribute to "support such a vicious gospel through the profits on … [his] sales." Dwork, a *New York Times* journalist wrote, "then began removing Schick razors and blades from the shelves of the 400 supermarkets" that Franlee supplied in and around New York. Dwork, along with Irving Feldman, president of the Zelart Drug Company (another toiletry furnisher), proceeded to organize opposition to Schwarz's lecture before the Toiletry Merchandisers' Association in Miami Beach in April. This caused a commotion at Eversharp, whose president, Thomas J. Welsh, who opposed Frawley's ventures in politics, organized a meeting of the board of directors and succeeded, over Frawley's head, in obtaining a resolution stating that Schick would no longer buy television time for Schwarz. "We still think very highly of Dr. Schwarz," a statement read, "but our plans do not call for sponsoring any such thing in the future." Schwarz's most proactive business supporter was out of the picture for an indefinite period.[56]

Throughout the summer, the ADL went on the offence. Arnold Forster publicly attacked Schwarz as "one of today's foremost practitioners of a philosophy of despair and gloom," and Benjamin Epstein called for mobilization against "anti-democratic radical right groups …, [which he saw as] a threat against the Jewish community." Other segments of the Jewish community joined in. Nathan Mironov, county commander of the Jewish War Veterans, called for a boycott of the Crusade. In Minneapolis, a week before the Madison Garden rally in New York, eight hundred rabbis from the Central Conference of American Rabbis issued a pronouncement against the "radical and rampageous Right."[57]

On 28 June 1962, the CACC held its Greater New York Anti-Communism Rally at Madison Square Garden. Only one newspaper, the conservative *New York Daily News*, plugged the show. Only eight mayors of the New York suburbs agreed to endorse the event, and one of them withdrew his support before the rally. The list of speakers fell short of expectations. Judd and Dodd were occupied by their duties in Washington. Schwarz had to rely on himself, Philbrick, Eugene Lyons, singer Pat Boone, and a new contact he had recently made: Arthur G. McDowell, long-time executive of the Upholsterers' International Union and a rare outspoken anticommunist liberal personality. Two hundred people from the Anti-Fascist Youth Committee picketed a Madison Square Garden that was not even half full: more than ten thousand of its eighteen thousand seats were empty. There was an admission fee, but many had been offered free entry at the last moment when organizers became desperate to fill the seats.[58]

Colbert, acting as master of ceremony, first introduced Philbrick, "one of the nicest guys I know," who received a standing ovation as he entered to attack those who had criticized Schwarz. He was followed by Eugene Lyons, who stressed the importance of distinguishing the Russian and Chinese people from their rulers. Arthur McDowell proved to be a bad speaker. He hailed the rally as "the largest anti-slavery movement" since Lincoln's address at Cooper Union, followed by an endless monologue devoid of structure, which addressed, successively, slavery, freedom, being an anticommunist union man, King George II, Edmund Burke, Hitler, Lenin, and Mussolini. People began shouting "We want Schwarz!" before it ended.[59]

Schwarz was unable to fully re-energize the crowd during his address, leaving Pat Boone in charge of wrapping things up. Boone explained how his business pals had warned him not to "type" himself and appear alongside Schwarz, but "there comes a day when we must all put the interest of our beloved country above personal interest." He then repeated the same thought that he had expressed at the LA school eight months before: he would rather see his four little girls "lined up against a wall and shot than for them to grow up in a communist America" and have "those poor kids blown in [sic] hell by nuclear weapons than [sic] taught into hell by communism."

The rally was a bust. The speeches were ineffective, the message moderated to the point of meaninglessness for both friends and foes, and the attendance disappointing. McDowell consoled Schwarz by telling him that he was actually lucky to get such a turnout "in the imperial Babylon of Communist and ultraliberalists strength after less than two months of preparation."[60]

A delighted Sokolsky, meanwhile, continued his series of tirades against the "Schwarzites," emphasizing the "small audience" at the

Garden and the "dull and uninspired" speeches. He ridiculed Pat Boone, whose "greatest contribution to the cause of anti-Communism was his promise to blow up his four daughters if the Communists captured them." In another column, Sokolsky attacked Schwarz for not becoming an American citizen. To the press, Schwarz put on a brave face, framing the rally as a victory achieved against insurmountable odds. Though the New York project was "far in the red," as a journalist reported, Schwarz described the project as a mere "investment," putting all hopes on the weeklong CACC school coming in late summer.[61]

The hard reality was that Carnegie Hall had already been booked for a week for the school, and cancellation was not an option. Schwarz and Liebman spent the rest of the summer trying to pick up the pieces. However, the financial reserve the CACC had accumulated since late 1961 had already evaporated before the Garden rally. Throughout July and August, the CACC repeated fundraising pleas to its supporters and Schwarz was compelled to make a series of impromptu round-trips in a search for money. In mid-August, he toured Tyler, Dallas, Los Angeles, and St Louis. In each city he spoke to overflowing halls, allowing him to return to New York with $10,000.[62]

Schwarz's last gamble was his appearance on NBC's *Meet the Press* the day before the school began. The crusader was to be interviewed on primetime national television by Richard Clurman (*Time*), William Rusher (*National Review*), James Wechsler (*New York Post*), and NBC's Lawrence Spivak. For most of the show Spivak, Wechsler, and Clurman grilled Schwarz. Spivak set the tone early on by focusing on a statement Schwarz had made about the need to achieve a "miracle" to secure the USA's freedom, asking him: "What kind of a miracle do you think you can achieve teaching or speaking to maybe 500, 600 or 1,000 people?" Schwarz answered that disseminating knowledge on communism in New York, "the center of communication media for the United States and the world," could indeed produce a miracle that would lead to freedom. Spivak then pressed Schwarz regarding what his organization actually did to fight Communism. When Schwarz gave the example of the Kerala newspaper, Spivak brushed this argument aside. "Dr Schwarz, you have been going for almost ten years. Is this the most thrilling story that you can find after ten years? You have gotten off a printing press for someone in India?"

Wechsler, who had already criticized the CACC in his *Post* column, pounded his guest about the JBS. The crusader gave his usual answer: "I don't feel competent to sit in judgment on the John Birch Society because I don't know too much about it." Expecting this reply, Wechsler asked Schwarz if he agreed he should inform himself more thoroughly about the JBS, prompting the Australian to say that the CACC's goal was "a very limited one ... we don't claim to be experts in every area." Clurman picked up where Wechsler left off, listing some of those who had condemned the JBS, including Buckley and *National Review*, and asked his guest to comment once more on the JBS's work. He received a similar answer, though Schwarz added: "If you would like to ask whether I think President Eisenhower is a Communist, I think that is a totally inaccurate and ridiculous statement." Clurman then confronted Schwarz with Bob Welch's statement that the crusader was a good recruiting agent for the JBS. Schwarz said again that he was not "in a position to adjudicate every organization that ha[d] members attending [his] schools." This led to the following exchange:

> MR CLURMAN: Sir, we are not asking you to adjudicate every organization. The John Birch Society has been virtually drummed out of respectable political conservatism. It has been renounced and denounced by the most distinguished Americans. Yet you equivocate on the question.
> DR SCHWARZ: I am not in the drumming-out business, and I have enunciated a principle. I propose to stand by that principle. I think it is important.
> MR CLURMAN: May we assume that you welcome John Birch members –
> DR SCHWARZ: No, you may not assume. That is a totally false assumption. You may assume that we have a principle that I do not sit in judgement of other organizations or individuals."[63]

Reactions to the interview were mixed. TV commentator Harriet Van Horne said: "Though he maintained the pious air of the one who has sown wheat and somehow reaped thorns, the Australian spellbinder was repeatedly thrown off side. He squirmed, he equivocated – and now and then he snarled." *Newsday*'s Len Chaimowitz thought the crusader seemed hard put at moments. Siding with Schwarz, gossip guru Walter Wintchell observed that the members of the press panel "were demolished from start to finish." Though NBC received hundreds of letters from the audience that criticized

Spivak and his team for what was seen as rudeness towards their guest, most of those letters came from the CACC's geographical bases (California, Texas, Missouri) rather than from New York.[64]

When the school began at Carnegie Hall that Monday morning, 28 August, 250 people showed up. No free event for the youth was planned. Only five hundred people showed up at the Commodore Hotel for the fundraising banquet, where the hat was passed, allowing for a collection of $12,210. The crusader was in a bitter mood. "New York can be proud – they did two third as well as Omaha," he said before taking to task local businesspeople "who said they opposed communism but weren't willing to help pay for the fight against it." The whole New York project resulted in a monumental deficit of about $75,000. Still, the crusader claimed, the school had been "great" despite the financial fiasco. "But we've had to spend western money to do it – and Midwestern money." He finally announced that the CACC would go back to the West Coast, "where we've got our friends."[65]

This five-month New York venture was the multilayered disaster that put an end to Schwarz's hope of building a truly national movement and becoming part of the cultural and political mainstream. The aura of efficiency and respectability the crusader had carefully cultivated over a decade's time had been tarnished. New York marked the beginning of the end of the CACC's brief prominence on the American national public scene.

A few weeks later, on 14 December 1962, George Sokolsky died of a heart attack.

"DANGER ON THE RIGHT"

On the evening of 6 November 1962, as the results of the US congressional elections began pouring in, it appeared that the Kennedy administration had been able to shield itself from the typical pattern of midterm elections losses. The number of Democratic representatives dropped by only four, allowing them to retain a comfortable majority in the House. In the Senate, there was a net increase of three new Democratic senators. Three main factors can explain these results: first, the good standing of the US economy; second, Kennedy's handling of the Cuban missile crisis, which took place at the end of the campaign (15–28 October); and third, more than a year and a half of controversy over right-wing extremism across the country.

While groups such as the JBS had hoped that their letter-writing campaigns would translate into electoral support, the elections proved them wrong. Almost all openly pro-JBS candidates were defeated, including H.L. Richardson (future founder of Gun Owners of America in 1974) and Jack Seale, former mayor of Amarillo, Texas. The JBS also lost its two strongest supporters in the House: Representative John H. Rousselot, from Southern California, and Edgar Hiestand, from Illinois. Two foes of the right wing were easily re-elected: Senator Thomas Kuchel, moderate GOP senator of California, and William Fulbright of Arkansas, whom Billy James Hargis had tried to unseat. One exceptional right-wing success was the election of K.W. Stinson, a Washington State Republican who had endorsed the CACC's school in Puget Sound. For columnist Walter Lippmann, the election showed there was nothing "to suggest that there [was] a Republican majority, much less a popular majority, for Sen. Goldwater and those to the right of him."[66]

The most consequential race for anticommunist militants and for the CACC took place in Minnesota, where Walter Judd was facing an uphill fight. In the spring of 1962, his congressional district had been gerrymandered to include the heavily Democratic city of Minneapolis. He had initially announced he would not seek re-election, appalling conservatives nationwide and causing a flood of calls and letters imploring him to reconsider. Judd changed his mind but found himself under fire for his associations with anticommunist figures. Judd's Democratic opponent Donald Fraser particularly decried his link with Schwarz and the CACC. As the pressure mounted, Judd, against the advice of his advisors, refused to turn his back on Schwarz, "a person above reproach personally, perhaps the most thorough student of Communism as a disease of human behavior." On 5 November, on the eve of the vote, Judd was still defending his ties to Schwarz. "Show me one bit of evidence against him," he said, "and I will not be associated with him." Given the circumstances, Judd did well at the polls but still lost by a 52 to 48 percent margin.[67]

Before the New York fiasco, CACC schools had already been planned in San Mateo and Cleveland in the fall of 1962, but the timing was bad. Money reserves were shrinking and the costs of maintaining the staff the CACC hired in 1961 put a strain on the organization. The midterm elections campaign monopolized the press's attention as well as the energy of most of the CACC's supporters.

Moreover, after the controversies of San Francisco, Seattle, and New York, the opposition had worked out the formula. In San Mateo and Cleveland, the ADL, the American Jewish Committee, and Group Research traded data and fed local oppositions information weeks in advance of the opening of the schools. They also began filing requests for the CACC's tax returns to get the names of sponsors and then put pressure on them. They sent local media lists of embarrassing questions reporters could ask Schwarz (e.g., "Why do you try to disassociate yourself from extremists on your program by saying that your so-called 'faculty' has academic freedom when you know that your so-called 'schools' are not accredited schools and can have no faculty?").[68]

Both the San Mateo and Cleveland events incurred financial losses. In San Mateo, attendance never surpassed a few hundred. The only moment that attracted some attention occurred when labour leader Harry Bridges appeared at the school uninvited, denouncing Schwarz as "a fraud and a charlatan." Schwarz challenged his fellow Aussie to a debate, which took place in the latter part of October at the San Francisco Commonwealth Club, crowded with 1,250 people. Both men traded insults, charges, and countercharges. Bridges accused Schwarz of being a racketeer, a union-buster, a race-hater, and, referring to Schwarz's medical background, a quack. When Bridges challenged Schwarz to sue him, the crusader replied, "The statements are utterly false, completely false, totally false, and you don't sue a skunk for stinking."[69]

The school in Cleveland, in October 1962, was in Schwarz's own words, "the worst of all." The CACC faced the hostility of the political machine of Democratic senator Stephen Young of Ohio. On the US Senate floor, Young affirmed that schoolchildren should not "waste valuable time listening to ... a Fascist-minded leader of the lunatic rightwing fringe, now in this country playing his profitable rabble-rousing." On opening day, about fifty people were scattered among the hundreds of seats in Cleveland's Hanna Theatre. "Schwarz appears to be tired, exhausted, haggard and irritable," indicated a report sent by an FBI informant to J. Edgar Hoover's deputy C.D. "Deke" DeLoach.[70]

CACC schools subsequently went on a five-month break, the longest since 1959. While the idea of a week-long school in Southern California had to be dropped because of the political climate, a fund-raising rally in December at Los Angeles's Shrine Auditorium hosted by Roy Rogers and Dale Evans was attended by five thousand people and netted $10,000. In a letter to Philbrick, Schwarz expressed his relief that the events of the past year had had little impact on the support the CACC enjoyed in its heartland. Meanwhile, fundraising pitches were momentarily facilitated by the Cuban missile crisis, which put Communism back in the news. By the end of 1962, the CACC had raised $633,207, making 1962 the second highest-grossing year in its history, but these revenues were down by almost half since 1961 and were outstripped by expenses of over $100,000. The Long Beach office staff was reduced from its peak of thirty in late 1961 to only a few people by the end of 1962. The same occurred at the Houston office, where the staff was reduced from fifteen to five. Still, the CACC's brief Golden Age had given it a base of supporters that guaranteed yearly revenues of about half a million dollars for the following two decades.[71]

This extended break from organizing schools gave Schwarz the opportunity to distance himself from W. Cleon Skousen. Schwarz had already avoided inviting Skousen to the Madison Square Garden rally, despite his initial plans. In November 1962, McDowell, acting as Schwarz's eyes and ears in the liberal world, warned him that Skousen was a highly polarizing figure on communism who spoiled attempts at reconciling conservative and liberal anticommunists. When CACC schools resumed in February 1963, Skousen was no longer present. In 1965, Wes McCune, from Group Research, asked Joost Sluis about Skousen's association with the CACC. The conversation summary reads: "Said Skousen has not been used by Schwarz for several years and implied it was because Skousen was too far out."[72]

The 1963–64 period saw the end of the classic CACC school formula after the failure of the last four events, organized in San Diego, Sacramento, Indianapolis, and Washington, respectively. Particularly difficult was the failure of the October 1963 school in Indianapolis, where the CACC had a branch. The Lilly Endowment, headquartered in Indianapolis, granted $5,000 to organize the event. Schwarz wrote Philbrick before the school began that the only opposition was coming from labour unions and that he expected it would dissipate. But the school met strong opposition not only from the local AFL-CIO but also from the Catholic diocese of Indianapolis. Moreover, Judd cancelled his appearance, disappointing the Lilly Endowment sponsors. Attendees never grew to more than four hundred during the week, and the school ended with a deficit of $4,000.

"Fred was completely unprepared for it," McDowell wrote to one of his correspondents. Schwarz had no choice but to fall back on lecturing tours. While he never went back to his frantic schedules of the 1950s, he averaged about two hundred lectures a year for the next several years.[73]

Still, the controversial aura still lingering over the CACC would not easily dissipate. Just after the New York fiasco in the summer of 1962, any hopes that the opposition from the Jewish community might cool off were dashed when George Sokolsky, in one of the last columns before his death, claimed that Schwarz had gone on an anti-Semitic rant during a speech in Tyler, Texas, in August 1962. Sokolsky quoted one man who attended Schwarz's lecture: "Boy, I tell you, [Schwarz] spells out a death struggle with the Jews. … Schwarz said 'New York is controlled by them,' that is, by Jews. He said the thing is divided down the middle, Christians and Jews." The ADL dedicated its entire late 1962 report sheet to Schwarz and described the Tyler speech as Schwarz spelling out, "in meeting halls, crowded with rightwing extremists, his battle with the Jews of New York." In private exchanges, Schwarz affirmed that his Tyler speech was not anti-Semitic, though he had admittedly criticized the Jewish War Veterans, the ADL, and the American Jewish Congress president C. Irving Dwork for his boycott of Schick's products during the previous spring. Schwarz sought advice from William Buckley, affirming that the ADL was trying to pigeonhole him as an anti-Semite and that he was tempted to hire a Jewish lawyer. Buckley advised against such an action, as did Dr Solomon Andhil Fineberg, a Reform rabbi whom the crusader had befriended and who recommended appeasement.[74]

Schwarz did not sue the ADL, but he decided to take legal action against whoever might call him an anti-Semite. The opportunity presented itself quickly: on 15 April 1963, James F. Droney of the *Boston Herald* wrote a column calling the Australian "another of the nation's top anti-Semites." This time, Schwarz sued, encouraged by Philbrick and supported by Pat Frawley, who covered the legal fees. The five years it took for the court to hear the case ultimately destroyed Schwarz's hopes as, in the meantime, the US Supreme Court delivered a ruling – *New York Times Co. v. Sullivan* – whereby a plaintiff in a libel suit who was a public figure had to prove that the defendant knew that his libelous statement was false. Unable to prove that Droney knew his statements about Schwarz to be untrue, the crusader lost his case after a Massachusetts court finally heard it in October 1968.[75]

Books published in 1963 and 1964 by various muckrakers of the right wing added to Schwarz's woes. *The Far Right*, by journalists Donald Janson and Bernard Eismann, covered the Crusade alongside the JBS and Billy James Hargis's Christian Crusade, calling Schwarz "essentially, a peddler of phrases" who had "perfected the use of ambiguity." *Men of the Far Right*, by Richard Dudman, placed Schwarz alongside Strom Thurmond, Barry Goldwater, Robert Welch, Billy James Hargis, and the entire military-industrial complex. In late 1964, the ADL's co-directors Forster and Epstein released a more sophisticated piece with *Danger on the Right*, which, as Richard Gid Powers summarizes, "tied one organization to the next until it created an overall impression of an unbroken network of dangerous right-wingers ranging from anti-Semites, racists, [and] Birch Society paranoids to mainstream figures like Barry Goldwater and William F. Buckley, Jr."[76]

At the end of 1963, the assassination of President Kennedy once more put the American Right on the defensive. Some accused the right wing of having created the climate in which the assassination took place. Many conservatives took comfort when it was discovered that Lee Harvey Oswald had been an avowed Marxist and that he had attempted to kill General Edwin Walker shortly before shooting the president. Despite the hard time the Kennedy White House had given him, Schwarz, blaming Oswald's Communist ties for the assassination, expressed his "shock, sadness, horror and anger."[77]

The year 1964 saw, with the Goldwater movement, the coalescing of various strains of the American Right into a more coherent national structure. It resulted in an intense, if brief, resurgence of CACC activities, during which Schwarz was joined by a unique and colourful character. While lecturing in Columbus, Ohio, he met a businessman called David Greenroos, who told him about his wife Janet, a television and music personality. In a subsequent event, Janet Greenroos, known by the stage name Janet Greene, came to hear the crusader. An Ohio native, Greene (born Marcum), who married at seventeen, began performing folk music in Cincinnati clubs and eventually got a television job, portraying Cinderella on a weekday musical morning show. She was fired after refusing sexual advances from the TV station's manager. The Greenrooses relocated to Columbus, where WTVN, a local station, put Janet in their own *Cinderella* show.

Greene recalled of Schwarz: "I thought he was an excellent speaker. In fact, he was comedic, too ... You know, I had never even been to high school or college, so I was taken in by that." Schwarz asked her to become the CACC's new "Musical Director," which included a $500 weekly package and the opportunity to come and live with her husband (who would become a CACC staffer) and their three kids in Long Beach in a rented house. By her own admission, Janet Greene's main motivation in joining the CACC had less to do with patriotism than with living in Southern California, though in due course she released a statement saying that the "American heritage and Christian religion are in great jeopardy." At a press conference, Schwarz said that he had "taken a leaf out of the Communist book." Communists, he stated, were "undoubtedly involved in folk singing, but by all means that does not mean all folk singers are communists." "You'd be amazed," he added, "at how much doctrine can be taught in one song." His aim was to create anticommunist folk music. "Every great movement throughout history," he wrote in the newsletter, "has expressed its inspiration in music."[78]

During CACC rallies, Greene's function was to warm up the crowds by singing the national anthem and a few satirical, folksy tunes that she had composed based on Schwarz's writings. Greene often drew more applause than Schwarz. Her presence balanced out the crusader's cut-and-dry lectures, making rallies more family-friendly, while also tapping into the growing popularity of folk music in the USA. One Group Research infiltrator of a Crusade meeting in 1965 mentioned in his report: "Mrs Greene is very pretty and sings well. Her presence considerably enlivens the meeting." Greene conferred upon CACC meetings a distinctively feminine presence. This turn had been long overdue for the organization, particularly in an era of profound transformation pertaining to women's social, cultural, and legal status. It reflected the crusader's attempt to diversify his offering in a context within which touring was once again an important part of his activities. "Through Greene's activism," historian Eileen Luhr notes, "the anti-communist message could extend into female-dominated civil organizations such as the school, church, and home."[79]

In 1965, eight of Greene's songs were included in a four-record package of lectures by Schwarz titled *What Is Communism?*" A song titled "Commie Lies," based on the melody "Jimmy Crack Corn," had the following chorus: "Be careful of the commie lies / Swallow them and freedom dies / The U.S.A. must realize / That she is the biggest prize." Another song, "Inch by Inch," rationalized the Vietnam

12.1 | Janet Greene, Fred Schwarz, and Herbert Philbrick at an anticommunist press conference in Los Angeles, California, 1964. *Los Angeles Times* Photographic Archives.

War by arguing that the Communist strategy of world conquest hinged on the US not defending small nations. "The Hunter and the Bear" told of the pitfalls of negotiating with Communists, illustrated by the tale of a hunter who succumbs to a bear's soft soap in the forest. "No matter what you say," Greene said, "if it has a beat people will listen and not feel resentful." Once, a few beatnik-styled young people who picketed a CACC meeting sent a note to Greene telling her that her singing was "the best." "They have nothing against me as long as I sing," she said.[80]

Greene was part of the magic of a smaller Crusade show, centred on Schwarz, herself, and Philbrick, the latter reluctantly back on the lecturing trail after various unsuccessful business ventures. This reduced line-up was convenient and relatively inexpensive. Greene warmed up the audiences, Schwarz delivered his routine on Marxism-Leninism, and Philbrick told his infiltrator's tales. The event wrapped up with Schwarz making his fundraising pleas over Greene's songs. This trio toured the nation's cities and small towns, organizing meetings that attracted a declining press attention, even if audiences sometimes numbered several thousand people.

In 1964, the Schwarz-Greene-Philbrick roadshow toured amidst the Goldwater movement. During the GOP primaries of 1964, the Goldwaterites won the primaries in a cluster of big states (Florida, Illinois, Texas) where the primary election system made it easier to defeat the Republican establishment with a grassroots push. The single most important moment of the nomination process came in early June, when Goldwater won the California primary over Nelson Rockefeller, thus eliminating his only remaining serious contender. Still, dark clouds were looming over the GOP. The convention of July in San Francisco that nominated Goldwater exposed the bitter divisions among Republicans. Rockefeller was booed when he took on the Birchers in a speech, while Goldwater delivered the words that later haunted him: "I would remind you that extremism in the defense of liberty is no vice. And let me remind you also that moderation in the pursuit of justice is no virtue."[81]

Though the CACC was committed to a non-partisan stance, politics were never far away. In 1964, George Murphy ran for Senate as GOP candidate against incumbent Pierre Salinger in California. As soon as Murphy announced his candidacy, pundits rightly predicted that his association with Frawley and Schwarz would be a liability. During a debate, Salinger questioned Murphy's decision to participate in CACC events, but Murphy neither denied his participation nor distance himself from the Crusade. Salinger lost to Murphy's fund of goodwill among the public.[82]

More importantly, the 1964 surge of conservative mobilization created a wave of popular enthusiasm that benefited Schwarz, Greene, and Philbrick. California evangelicals, an important part of Schwarz's clientele, were at the vanguard of the 1964 conservative mobilization, enlisting "their churches, schools, associations, and ministries on Goldwater's behalf," Darren Dochuk writes. In the electoral context of the late summer and fall of 1964, attendance at the Schwarz-Greene-Philbrick rallies was high. In March 1964, Schwarz agreed to let Greene participate in several Goldwater events, such as the one held at Knott's Berry Farm, where she sang the anthem before a few thousand people, with Ronald Reagan and John Wayne acting as masters of ceremonies. The trio later held a series of meetings in Northern California that looked like campaign rallies. In August, the trio came to Indianapolis, where a crowd of one thousand greeted them at the Clowes Memorial Hall. Schwarz told a local journalist that the mere mention of Goldwater's name drew a crazy response: "I've never seen anything to equal this pure devotion to a candidate." He then came as close as he ever did to endorsing Goldwater, saying: "The Communists are hysterically afraid of Senator Goldwater. They believe he is a threat to their plans of world conquest and they will do anything to attempt to defeat him." Schwarz's positive view of Goldwater was apparently no longer reciprocated. In 1961, Goldwater had praised the CACC school of Phoenix and, in private, spoke well of Schwarz. But in February 1962, as press coverage of the Crusade became increasingly negative, Goldwater was reported by a private citizen to have replied to a question on the CACC during a meeting that he merely saw Schwarz as a businessman whose goal was to make money. Luckily for the crusader, if this ever happened, no journalist was present.[83]

On 3 November 1964, Johnson was re-elected in a landslide victory, winning in all states except Goldwater's home state of Arizona and the Deep South (Louisiana, Mississippi, Alabama, Georgia, and South Carolina), where the GOP elected its first members of Congress since Reconstruction, laying the groundwork for the region's realignment into the Republican fold in the following decades. By helping reorient the national conversation away from Communism, the 1964 election was an important factor in the Crusade's ongoing marginalization.

"THE MOST IMPORTANT SINGLE FACTOR IN THE RIGHTIST REVIVAL"

In April 1962, in a rare Australian interview, conducted as he was taking some rest in his native country, Schwarz let loose his irritation: "I'm sick of being tied with crazy American right-wing groups ... I get a very raw deal from the American press. They write their articles ... before they send their reporters out to hear me speak and then they just quote one or two words to make it sound real."[84]

The crusader's irritation was understandable: countless times between 1961 and 1964 he and the CACC were either tied to groups and figures with which they had no links or were the object of false information. Moreover, Schwarz's speeches were void of the most hare-brained schemes that permeated the grassroots conservative subculture, such as the ones involving fluoridation, the establishment of a world government through the UN, the communist infiltration of high-level government positions, communism being a Jewish plot, or black-red theories. Having seen in Australia a socialist government crushing a Communist-led strike in 1949, and having a few liberal acquaintances, Schwarz was aware that the whole left-of-centre spectrum could not be lumped in one single group.

But the fall from grace also had a lot to do with the CACC itself. First, the CACC's contribution to the right-wing upsurge carried the seeds of its own demise. The visibility of right-wing groups had increased throughout the late 1950s, and the CACC was at the cutting edge of this phenomenon. By late 1961, it had become the highest-grossing anticommunist group in the United States, drawing support from some of the country's most important corporations. Its impact on the bubbling right wing was real. In his *Look* article on the right wing in early 1962, reporter Fletcher Knebel affirmed in his segment on the CACC that he was convinced, "after more than 100 interviews on the ramparts of the Right, that the Christian Anti-Communism Crusade [was] by far the most important single factor in the Rightist revival." In early 1962, the FBI received information that, after securing the support of Richfield Oil, Schwarz was trying to get the financial backing of the Standard Oil Company of California: "Some officials of this huge corporation are beginning to be concerned by Schwarz's extremist activities and his ability to get financial backing from responsible businessmen." Needless to say, the Kennedy administration shared these concerns.[85]

With the memory of McCarthyism still fresh, the CACC's most serious foes had good reasons to think that the organization was fueling hazardous popular fears over Red infiltration and leading the way towards a new climate of hysteria. A common critique pertained to the after-effects of the week-long schools and other initiatives. In his *Look* report, Knebel described how the Crusade was stirring up the citizenry and then leaving "a vacuum into which missionaries of the far Right promptly pour[ed].” While the CACC appeared in some regards to be more moderate than many other organizations, the people it mobilized went “on to find Communists in the White House, the income tax sapping America for a Communist coup[,] and Red plots behind such proposals as countywide government for municipalities.” Urban Whitaker, liberal professor of education at the San Francisco State College, whom Schwarz publicly debated on the topic of the benefits of CACC schools in early 1962, castigated these events for leaving in their wake “increased right-wing attacks on schools, churches, labor unions and spokesmen for liberal causes.” After the LA Sports Arena school, one Presbyterian reverend wrote to Judd to express his concern about the problems caused by CACC supporters who, he said, after such events, tended to accuse members of their congregations of being Communists. Another member of the clergy, from San Francisco, wrote in a similar fashion to Philbrick in November 1961, airing his discontent over the attacks on the churches that were reported following each CACC school.[86]

Schwarz discharged himself of any responsibility for what his supporters did independently from him, even when it had become commonplace to label him the “far right’s recruiting agent.” When questioned on the subject, his usual response was to say that if people did not want Welch or other extremists to take advantage of his awakening of the masses, then local institutions had to step in and direct fighters as to where they should focus their attention. To *Look*’s Knebel, he affirmed that “churches should guide the study groups to keep the extremists from gaining control.” But this position only corroborated the general sentiment that the crusader was tapping into public fears while not assuming any of the potential consequences of doing so.[87]

By 1962, the CACC already had a record of having held numerous events at which the patriotism and loyalty of some of the nation’s most important institutions and individuals had been questioned. Echoing many other detractors of the crusader, in early 1962, the *San Leandro Morning News*’s Dana McGaugh criticized the ambiguous “academic freedom” policy of the CACC’s schools, noting that, while any lecturer delivering a speech contrary to the organization’s etiquette would not be re-invited, so far “no lecturers ha[d] been dropped from the faculty, despite their engagement in political debates and criticism of the United States government, United Nations, Supreme Court decisions and foreign aid.” Here again,

Schwarz had thought that the "academic freedom" policy was more than enough to shield him and his organization from being held accountable for statements uttered during CACC schools.[88]

This strategy failed, primarily because the crusader never established where academic freedom ceased to apply. Skousen was the only "faculty" member the crusader ever decided to let go on these grounds, and he did so only after more than three years of collaboration. In the meantime, Skousen had been allowed primetime participation during the televised sessions of the second CACC school in Los Angeles and at the Hollywood Bowl. While Schwarz was permanently concerned with being perceived as an extremist and was ready to adopt a more moderate stance when it became necessary (as he did in New York), he does not appear to have been personally disturbed either by the continuous barrage of controversy-prone statements made at his schools or by the fact that most speeches were designed for a right-wing audience (indeed, Schwarz's own view of the social order made it obvious that he himself was no beatnik). He came to realize that this was a problem at the same time as the school formula was losing its steam. In 1963, to the interview question "Have you read any valid criticism of your schools?," he replied, "Well, yes, I think there's some truth to the criticism that the faculty of my schools doesn't represent a sufficiently wide political spectrum."[89]

Some controversies were just ill-managed. The Australian waited for about two years before criticizing Welch's statement about Eisenhower's being a Communist, and he took too much time to realize the damage caused by his costly feud with the ADL and the Jewish community, let alone to fully gauge what, in his rhetoric, program, and methods, made him suspicious to those circles of American society highly sensitive to bigotry.

To be sure, the Australian had an understanding of the complexities of the world that exceeded that of many of his collaborators. Yet, in many regards, his message continued to bear the mark of intransigence, especially in its unchanging, monolithic view of Communism and in its lack of concern for civil liberties should they be considered to be standing in the way of the good fight. To this should be added his own sporadic inclination for unsubstantiated statements, as seen in *You Can Trust*'s passages on brainwashing or on the alleged Communist influence over US churches and universities worldwide, writings that were available for anybody to read. In sum, many of Schwarz's foes found enough reasons in his work to brush aside those elements that distinguished him from Robert Welch and other "peddlers of hysteria."

Finally, the school formula, based as it was upon collaboration with local institutions, was highly vulnerable to any controversy and boycott. Although, by Schwarz's own admission, Billy Graham's revivals provided the organizational model for CACC schools, the Australian never mastered Graham's ability to pre-emptively defuse local criticism, which he did through the masterful use of his Southern charm, meeting his detractors one by one and with humility. Quite the opposite, Schwarz's tendency to respond to criticism with counter-criticism and challenges to public debate often ensured that it was unlikely that his detractors would change their minds.[90]

However, in the wake of the Goldwater defeat, the national mood shifted away from concern over homegrown fascism. The monitoring of right-wing activities by groups such as the ADL and Group Research continued, but their releases attracted much less attention, and press coverage on the right subsided. During the 1966 gubernatorial race in California, Ronald Reagan's opponent Pat Brown tried to use Reagan's ties to Schwarz, Frawley, and right-wing organizations to discredit the former actor and future president, but the attack fell flat. This led journalists Robert Novak and Rowland Evans to proclaim: "the Birch issue is dead." This created a much quieter climate for the CACC. While the Crusade never again reached the level of success it had achieved in the early 1960s, the following decades would see it redesign its strategies and, to some extent, enjoy a resurgence.[91]

13

Resilience, Revival, and End

OUT OF SYNC

During the years that followed the Goldwater defeat, the United States underwent fundamental changes. It was not in the first but, rather, in the second half of the "Turbulent 1960s" that the "turbulence" actually took place: the counterculture; the urban race riots; the splintering of the civil rights movement with the emergence of the Black Power movement and the assassination of Martin Luther King, Jr; the large-scale American presence in Vietnam and the growth of the antiwar movement; the student unrests; the rise of a new feminist movement and the gay rights movement; and the stormy 1968 presidential election marked by Robert Kennedy's assassination and the George Wallace campaign.

Within such a context, the Cold War East-versus-West paradigm was increasingly condemned to irrelevance. For the Christian Anti-Communism Crusade, this period was marked by a struggle for public visibility in the United States as the organization's base shrank. Supporters were turning their attention to issues other than communism; some were demobilized by the easing of Cold War tensions (détente between the US and Soviet worlds; US recognition of the People's Republic of China). In the wake of Nixon's trip to China in 1972, Schwarz lamented to Judd that his supporters believed that the global situation rendered anticommunist activism outdated. One of the marked changes was the gradual decline in church support. "The Crusade owes its existence, particularly in its early years, to the support received from individual Christians and individual churches ... Regrettably, as the Crusade has grown, we seem to have become more isolated from the churches," Schwarz editorialized. Individual believers continued to support the CACC, but institutional support was gone. The changing context made conservative churches far more inclined to focus on culture wars than on Communism.[1]

Schwarz lost some of his most important collaborators, beginning with the CACC's two major liberal allies. In October 1966, Arthur McDowell died in a car crash on the Pennsylvania turnpike. Senator Thomas Dodd had been re-elected in 1964 but received continuous criticism for his regular appearances at Crusade events. In 1967, Dodd was the first US senator since Joe McCarthy to be censured by the Senate after revelations that he had transferred some campaign funds to his own bank account. In 1970, he lost the nomination for his senatorial seat. Dodd died one year later from a heart attack.[2]

In 1966, Bill Strube closed the CACC's Houston branch and retired, though he remained a financial backer of the Crusade. He and his wife bought a former casino in Missouri City, Texas, which became their seventy-two-hundred-square-foot retirement house. They became involved in Bill Bright's Campus Crusade for Christ as well as other Christian groups. Strube also became a writer of Christian comic books and, in the late 1970s, developed an interest in health and self-improvement, proposing a blend of evangelicalism, esotericism, and alternate body detoxification therapies.[3]

Joost Sluis remained an active CACC member longer than Strube, keeping its San Francisco branch alive. In December 1965, he departed for Vietnam, where he worked as a civilian surgeon for a few months. After a few weeks spent as part of a navy medical team in the Gulf of Siam, he was transferred to a town in the Mekong Delta, where he practised medicine among Vietnamese civilians. During this time, Sluis was the only fully trained orthopaedic surgeon in the entire Mekong Delta and, as such, was the object of much security. His contact with Vietnamese civilians shocked him. Due to contaminated water, problems such as ascariasis, worms, typhoid fever, and bubonic plague were common. He was appalled by the US troops' lack of understanding of communism. Thus, from 1965 to 1970, the CACC launched a drive to send copies of *You Can Trust* to the greatest possible number of troops in Southeast Asia. The only way to get the list of names and addresses of service personnel was to stalk newspapers, where such information was often printed (e.g., during Christmas, a time when the public was encouraged to write to the troops). In March 1966, the CACC newsletter announced that these lists had helped to send "several thousand books" to the troops.[4]

Sluis visited Southeast Asia a second time in 1967. He was introduced to South Vietnamese officials, who showed an interest in *You Can Trust*. About eighty thousand copies of the book were distributed to students in the five universities of South Vietnam and to US service personnel in 1969. Sluis also visited Thailand and met the minister of foreign affairs and the undersecretary of state (Thanat Khoman and Netr Khemayodhin, respectively). A minor program to spread literature in Thailand cropped up in the following years. In 1967, this led to a heated televised exchange between Schwarz and African American journalist Louis Lomax, who told the crusader that "the man in Thailand right now, under his own government, cannot even vote. He does not have a constitution ... In other words, what are you going to do to save him?" Schwarz replied: "If the threat of Communism diminishes, his opportunities will increase. There is not an equality of evil. Some systems are bad, other systems are worse."[5]

Sluis closed the San Francisco CACC branch and left the organization in 1970, though he continued to support its work. In 1972, he launched his own group, Christian Cause International, aimed at keeping the USA's Christian foundations alive. Schwarz's influence continued to be visible in most of his writings. Sluis ended his activist's career in oblivion.[6]

In mid-1967, Janet Greene left the Crusade. She had decided that the time had come to move on. "I was tired from all of the traveling ... It's strange because sometimes I'd be in Detroit one night and then I'd be in Denver the next night and I'd forget where I was [laughs]." Moreover, her husband "would try and tell people how to do their jobs and that would not go far with Dr. Schwarz." Greene divorced her husband in 1979 and returned to her native Ohio in the late 1990s. Schwarz's friend and part-time recording technician, Dr George Westcott, closed the CACC branch of Ypsilanti and resumed his activities as a medical missionary in the Congo. In 1981, he died of cancer.[7]

The CACC's important financial backers also disappeared. F. Gano Chance retired in 1971; Charles Stewart Mott died in February 1973. Walter Knott died in 1981 at the age of ninety-one. Patrick J. Frawley died in 1998, but his association with Schwarz had been severed long before. In 1970, it was disclosed that George Murphy had been on Technicolor's payroll for the previous five years (at $20,000 a year), despite his election as senator in 1964. Before long, Frawley faced an all-out revolt from Technicolor's shareholders, who managed to oust him from the company. The scandal cost Murphy his Senate seat, which he lost to a Democratic opponent. Frawley, however, had managed to defeat his opponents within Schick. But in 1970 he also resigned as the head of Schick and lost interest in politics, instead devoting his time to fighting alcoholism, which had afflicted him since he was young. To that end, he founded the Schick hospitals and clinics for addiction treatment. He died in 1998 at the age of seventy-five.[8]

J. Howard Pew died in 1971, though this had no immediate effect on Glenmede Trust Company's support of the CACC since Glenmede remained under the control of Allyn Bell, Pew's long-time aide who had served in 1960 as chairman of the CACC school in Philadelphia. During the last years of his tenure at Glenmede, Bell provided a surge of support for the CACC, which peaked at about $100,000 in 1977. The Pew Freedom Trust provided what was apparently the last financial help the Crusade received from Glenmede foundations, a $15,000 gift in 1978. Bell retired thereafter and financial help from Glenmede ceased. The only new major business sponsor the CACC had during the three decades prior to Schwarz's retirement was Harry Casey, brother of United Parcel Service (UPS) founder James Casey. The octogenarian Casey once came to one of Schwarz's meetings in Seattle. Before long, he began frequently making $1,000 contributions, and, in 1984, he gave a $100,000 cheque, the single largest personal donation in CACC's history (inflation notwithstanding).[9]

While the CACC managed to keep its annual revenues at about half a million dollars throughout the 1960s and 1970s, the inflation rates that afflicted the US economy during this period decreased the value of these assets. Schwarz accordingly increased his own salary: by the mid-1970s, he was taking home $25,000, up from $5,000 ten years before. The CACC's financial situation was a constant obsession in its newsletter. In October 1967, Schwarz sent a letter to his supporters, informing them that income was running about $60,000 lower than it had been at the same time the previous year. With no financial response, he sent his supporters a stronger statement: "My natural desire to return to my home and family is strong and growing." This argument apparently worked as the financial situation improved in the months that followed.[10]

Some of Schwarz's collaborators insisted the CACC should rebrand itself. In late 1965, after a newspaper from Oregon had published one of many texts confusing Schwarz's group with Billy James Hargis's Christian Crusade, McDowell pushed for a change, claiming in a letter to Sluis that the CACC's name was a huge liability. Philbrick concurred, adding that this change would be justified because the need to distinguish the CACC from other organizations that included "Christian" in their names. Philbrick suggested names such as the "International League of Freemen" and the "World Alliance of Freemen (WAF) for Peace with Liberty," while McDowell suggested simply adding a subtitle emphasizing peace as well as civil and religious liberty. However, Schwarz refused each option. In fact, in the early 1960s, the crusader had declined an offer from a supporter to donate $100,000 if the word "Christian" was removed from the name.[11]

With the world confronted with new problems that could hardly be addressed through the CACC's bipolar proposition, Schwarz devoted an ever-increasing amount of energy to contemporary issues. A good example is the issue of moral decline. In 1972, he opposed the decriminalization of marijuana, which, he believed, would "be followed by an orgy of commercialization and epidemic usage." In 1975, as the national campaign led by Phyllis Schlafly against the Equal Rights Amendment was in full swing, Schwarz took on "women's libbers," whom he claimed wanted to remove the male from "his role as provider for the family" and, therefore, would cause his regression to "the primitive masculine role of 'hunter and fighter,'" which, among other things, would lead to "the dramatic increase in the numbers of the victims of rape." A journalist who attended a meeting of Republican women in California, where Schwarz delivered the keynote address, reported that, during the ensuing question period, the crusader identified the ERA as part of the effort to "demoralize America." And he drew enthusiastic applause from the seventy-five attending women when he described himself sarcastically as "an unabashed, unashamed male chauvinist supremist [sic] who believes in the absolute superiority of women."[12]

Though Schwarz never went so far as to claim that the culture wars were masterminded by Communists, for him there was a threefold connection between communism and moral decline. First, internal demoralization was aiding Communists. Second, communism and moral degeneracy shared a common root in godlessness. Atheism not only generated communism but also caused this great "social pathology" that was threatening the United States: sexual promiscuity, drug and alcohol consumption, family disintegration, the "sanctification of sodomy," and individualistic hedonism. Third, according to Schwarz, in their analysis of the superstructure (i.e., the institutions) that supported capitalism, Communist authors were promoting immorality. Here, Schwarz drew primarily on Marx and Engels's call in the *Communist Manifesto* to abolish the "bourgeois family" (i.e., the nuclear family). Similar ideas were found in Engels's *The Origin of the Family, Private Property and the State*, in which the author attempts to explain how the institution of the family is not rooted in the state of nature but in the historical evolution of human societies.[13]

Ironically, one of the key features of Soviet propaganda and policy throughout the Cold War was its portrayal of the Communist Bloc as a bulwark against the "decadent" West, whose higher levels of moral permissiveness, as well as its consumerist culture, were represented as markers of cultural degeneration. Sexual education in the USSR was highly conservative. While the production and consumption of pornography became widespread in the West by the early 1970s, it remained forbidden by Soviet authorities until the USSR's collapse in 1991. Schwarz tried to fit these facts into his analysis by arguing that such policies were applied dialectics: Communists were sheltering themselves from cultural degeneracy while letting the West self-implode.[14]

Schwarz found the link connecting communism and moral degeneracy in the writings of Herbert Marcuse, which became popular among the New Left by the mid-1960s, and especially in the synthesis of Freudianism and Marxism in Marcus's 1955 book *Eros and Civilization*. Assuming that capitalist societies domesticated the working class through consumption, thus impeding revolutionary sentiment, Marcuse's theories sought to "deenergize" this process through a countercultural transformation that would unleash repressed sexual energy. In Marcusian appeals for a sexual revolution that would tear down bourgeois society, the link between Marxism-Leninism and immorality came full circle. "Herbert Marcuse," Schwarz wrote, "is a remarkable hybrid, a Freudian Marxist. Marx has given him the imperative to destroy society; Freud has shown him a practical method by which to do this." The crusader elaborated the

"Revolutionary Bomb" theory: "The Marcusians, the anarchists and the Communists – with about 30,000 hard-core members altogether – are at the heart of forces threatening this country." While their numbers were limited, these groups were comparable to the explosive device forming the core of a bomb. Around them, like a mass of flammable material, lay the "surrounding body" of the bomb, those "3 million needy individuals who may be stimulated to violence" given the proper circumstances (i.e., student organizations, radical civil rights groups, hippies).[15]

In 1970, an opportunity to confront Marcuse presented itself. The University of California at San Diego, where Marcuse was a professor, invited Schwarz to participate in a debate with Marcuse as part of a credited course on political conservatism. However, Marcuse decried the university's initiative and refused to debate Schwarz. Marcuse's decision was scorned by many, including some who had little appreciation of Schwarz. Columnist Jack O'Brian said sarcastically that Marcuse had fought to "permit racist Eldridge Cleaver and admitted Communist Angela Davis to teach and lecture at the U. of Calif. – but fought even more ardently to keep conservative Dr. Fred Schwarz from being granted his right to speak." A cartoon from a student newspaper ridiculed Marcuse. The *Los Angeles Times* editorial asserted that "Marcuse's right to teach ... has been nobly defended by the university ... but it was not at all surprising that Marcuse would deny another man the privilege he himself has been afforded."[16]

Marcuse's crusty reaction provided his opponent with the moral high ground. Schwarz showed up for the debate that Marcuse's absence turned into a one-man show that was assured high attendance due to the controversy. When he got word that two hundred students were picketing against him outside the Scripps Auditorium and, further, that they were protesting the four-dollar admittance fee, Schwarz announced that the CACC would cover entrance costs for all of the remaining empty seats, thus allowing forty-four picketers to be admitted. The violence that some feared did not occur, and the crusader got to lecture to an attentive audience. Schwarz proudly related this non-encounter with Marcuse in his second book, *The Three Faces of Revolution*, published in late 1972. Ignored by the press, this book consists primarily of texts Schwarz had published in the late 1960s and early 1970s.[17]

RIOTS AND RACE

In July 1964, race riots erupted in Harlem after a black teenager was shot dead by a police officer. In August 1965, riots burst out in the Los Angeles ghetto of Watts, leaving, after a week, thirty-four people dead and more than a thousand injured. In 1966 and 1967, the disturbances spread nationwide. While the passage of the Civil Rights Act (1964) and the Voting Rights Act (1965) had given the impression that race relations were heading in the right direction, the riots exposed the deep-rooted problems that afflicted racial minorities: racism, poverty, and the existence of ghettos. The civil rights movement fractured. Led most notably by Martin Luther King Jr and the Southern Christian Leadership Conference, whose moderate wing promoted an incremental approach based on the eradication of poverty, groups such as the Student Nonviolent Coordinating Committee and the Black Panthers took a more radical approach to the problem. Meanwhile, a growing weariness with the civil right issue was perceptible nationwide, as revealed in the US midterm elections of 1966 (in which the Democrats experienced severe losses) and the presidential election of 1968 (which was marked by the George Wallace campaign and the election of Richard Nixon).

The CACC office was located only a few kilometres from the Watts neighbourhood where the riots erupted in August 1965. The havoc extended for a brief period to Long Beach, where many downtown stores were burned or looted. Schwarz wrote: "[The CACC] is grateful for the protection provided by the police ... Civil disobedience is the thin edge of the wedge that leads to the rupture of society, rioting, revolution and tyranny." Schwarz maintained this "law-and-order" stand throughout the years, and his praise for law enforcement authorities often drew spontaneous applause at his meetings.[18]

While until this point he had turned a blind eye to the race issue, he now addressed the problem directly.

> The general conditions in these so-called ghettos is housing standards are low, houses are overcrowded, and unemployment is substantial. Vice and crime are rife and there is a great deal of illegitimacy and breakdown of family life. These frustrations generate hostility and it is human nature to blame nature for whatever predicament prevails. While others may be partly to

> blame, there is always an area of individual responsibility and individual failure. The trick of the demagogue is to direct the attention of the people away from their own responsibility and focus the blame upon someone else.[19]

This passage encapsulates the elements that constituted Schwarz's position on racial strife over the following years. Poverty problems, he said, were real and had to be dealt with, if only to reduce subversion. To that end, "antipoverty programs" were necessary. After the Detroit riots, he restated that it was "imperative that injustice be fought and that every effort should be made to provide employment, decent housing, adequate education, and physical security for all citizens including the Negroes." These declarations suggest that he approved of the war on poverty, which was one of the cornerstones of President Johnson's Great Society program. This leaning, uncommon for a conservative personality, was probably not popular among Schwarz's base: an observer affiliated with a liberal group who attended one of his meetings in 1965 noted that the audience remained still during his entire lecture on the theme of racism and that the first applause of the evening came when the crusader said, "Thank God for the Police!"[20]

However, according to Schwarz, addressing racial minorities' material needs would not root out racism, the origins of which lay in human flaws and not merely in the economic environment. This was well illustrated by the 1967 Detroit riot, which was considered as the "model city" in the war on poverty. "The mayor of Detroit, Jerome P. Cavanagh, was elected with large Negro support ... 28 redevelopment projects were underway at a cost of $180 million of which $112 million is Federal funds." True to his conception of human nature, he reminded his readers that racism, being universal, would always appear wherever people of different ethnicities or nationalities were "living in quantity and proximity." Since the conditions prevailing in the ghettos had existed for decades, the logical explanation for the riots was that a new factor was at play: "The new element is the professional agitator urging violence and rebellion to the Negro youth. These agitators are usually influenced, if not fully controlled, by the Communists."[21]

For a while after the Watts riot, Schwarz blamed the unrest on the activism of the Progressive Labor Party (PLP), a group born in 1961 when it splintered from the CPUSA. This group was inspired by Maoism and promoted a radical, aggressive strategy of class warfare. In 1964, the PLP made headlines when the FBI indicated that it bore responsibility for encouraging the Harlem riots. Schwarz told one journalist that he was convinced that the PLP, and the Chinese Communists behind it, were involved since Beijing had been interested in the African American issue for years and had tried, in particular, to draw a parallel between the civil rights movement and the Viet Cong. Schwarz's theory became more complex after a conference organized by black nationalists was held at Lincoln University, during which PLP members and the Nation of Islam discussed how to overthrow capitalism, colonialism, and "the white supremacy system." This convinced Schwarz that Communists and black Muslims were forging an alliance, which fit within a long-standing pattern whereby Communists exploited any potential group or grievance to their own ends.[22]

During the summer of 1967, former SNCC president and radical black leader Stokely Carmichael travelled to Cuba to participate in a Latin American Solidarity Organization conference, and the *Worker*, the CPUSA's official paper, published articles that celebrated the riots as an experience of "liberation" for the proletariat. Thus, rioting, Schwarz wrote, was all about terrorizing the "majority of Negro citizens and ... convinc[ing] them that the law cannot protect them from the groups of violent and criminal extremists so they had better pay up and keep their mouths shut." Schwarz praised the "moderate Negro civil rights leadership" (Martin Luther King Jr, Roy Wilkins) for condemning the riots and for keeping the black population at a distance from radical groups. To that end, the CACC, by late 1967, raised money to send a copy of *You Can Trust* to "every Negro minister" in the United States. When news of King's assassination spread in 1968, in a letter to Philbrick he described the event as a tragedy that could spark riots throughout the nation (which it did).[23]

Schwarz's newly publicized black-red beliefs were shared by many. In 1967, J. Edgar Hoover, testifying before Congress, claimed that "Communists and other subversives and extremists" had been active in riots in Chicago, Harlem, Watts, and Cleveland. President Eisenhower came out from retirement to declare that "it looks like there is some kind of pattern" to the riots, which perhaps resulted from a "national planning system." Opinion polls showed that a sizable share of the American public was receptive to these theories. In 1967, 40 percent of respondents to a nationwide Harris poll blamed the riots on "outside agitation." The same year, a *Congressional Quarterly* poll had 40 percent of Southern Democrats thinking that "Communist agitation" was at play in the riots, while 20 percent of Republicans nationwide thought the same.[24]

To be sure, some radical leftist groups do seem to have been involved in the riots. Apart from FBI and HUAC material, Schwarz relied mainly on the testimony of Philip Abbott Luce, a former PLP leader who broke with the left and was now with the Young Americans for Freedom (YAF). Luce appeared at CACC events and published a few texts in the newsletter, in which he testified that the PLP had been stockpiling arms and promoting race riots. One of the PLP leaders, a Maoist named Bill Epton, was sentenced to prison for inciting violence during the Harlem riots of 1964. However, radical activity was at best a marginal factor in the riots. The report from the Kerner Commission, mandated to examine the causes of the 1967 riots, concluded that the primary causes of the disorder were the social and economic conditions in which racial minorities lived.[25]

Furthermore, Schwarz's bête noire, the PLP, could not be considered part of a coherent bloc due to its bad relationships with other radical groups in the late 1960s. Just as the PLP vanished, the late-1960s emergence of the Maoist-inspired Black Panther Party (BPP), which reached the height of its influence in 1969–70, appeared to be another link between racial strife and Communism. In particular, the crusader warned that the de facto establishment of "no-go zone" ghettos policed by armed BPP members was one of the greatest threats to the United States. But the BPP began collapsing in 1970 due to internal splits, the incarceration of its leaders, its involvement in illegal activities, and defections, leaving the crusader with no main suspect on the racial front, which progressively vanished from his interest.[26]

TARGETING THE YOUTH

In late 1964 and early 1965, student protesters, under the banner of the Free Speech Movement, clashed with the University of California at Berkeley and local police over the school's policy of prohibiting political advocacy on the campus. In March 1965, the "teach-in" movement began, the first major manifestation of the antiwar movement, which rapidly spread across the nation's campuses. Coupled with the continuing involvement of students in civil rights demonstrations, these campus activities signalled the coming of age of the baby-boom generation, which saw the greatest increase in the student body in history. The organization that came to be an icon of 1960s student activism, Students for a Democratic Society, was originally founded in 1962 and expanded substantially until 1968, before a series of internal splits resulted in its collapse.

As he often did, Schwarz saw the participation of a few Marxist-influenced groups and individuals as evidence of a plan to manipulate non-Communist activists. His response to the rise of radical student activism was swift. Six months before the Berkeley confrontations, Schwarz had developed a new type of CACC school formula, initially tested in June 1964 in Washington. Because it was primarily aimed at a student audience, its religious elements were muted and its format modified to make it appear more academic. Individual lectures were followed by panel discussions in which the public was invited to participate. Besides Schwarz and Philbrick, the speakers were CACC collaborators with extensive academic backgrounds, such as Eugene Lyons, Edward Rozek, and John Drakeford. This change was noted by the watchdog groups that still monitored CACC activities.[27]

The objective was no longer to attract as many people as possible and use the crowds for fundraising opportunities; rather, the CACC solicited its supporters to help finance the new formula and, more particularly, to cover the "tuition" fees so that young people could attend free of charge. After sending advertising to the mailing lists of young conservative groups, the CACC received eleven hundred replies showing interest, from which about half were selected for the "scholarship." A *Washington Post* journalist who came to Washington school in June 1964 reported that about five hundred students "from 49 states and five countries" followed a "no-nonsense 12 hour daily schedule" in a studious atmosphere. "The key was low, the interest was intense and the intelligent quotient was high and ivy-clad." The infiltrators sent by Group Research and the ADL concurred. One noted: "The audience ... was almost entirely made up of young people – probably college students, with a number of young adults. There were a great many YAF and Goldwater buttons in evidence." Another commented: "The turnout was disgustingly good, and the audience not the senile, retired folksy types one would expect from the previous TV programs about the Far Right; this audience was comprised ... of fresh-faced, alert college students who seemed to know what they wanted." The only time things became topsy-turvy was when forty enthusiastic young crusaders organized an impromptu demonstration before the Soviet embassy. Schwarz later scolded them, explaining that the CACC remained non-political and that such actions put the organization at risk of losing its tax-exempt status.[28]

In December 1964, as the confrontation continued on the Berkeley campus, Schwarz announced that the CACC would launch a "great offensive" in the form of schools specifically oriented towards students, starting in Berkeley in February 1965. In order to respond to what was deemed an urgent situation, this Berkeley school was put on a fast track, with a reduced team of volunteers and no assurance that expenses ($15,000) would be covered. The event took place at University House, Berkeley, near the university campus, and was attended by more than two thousand students, half of whom were admitted free.[29]

With the successes of the Washington school of June 1964 and the Berkeley school of February 1965, the CACC abandoned the mass rallies that had characterized its prime years and took a decisive turn towards youth and student outreach, illustrated by the appearance of the Anti-Subversive Seminars, which were held over a period of eight years. The transition from one formula to the other was not immediate.[30] The CACC continued to organize events known as Schools of Anti-Communism, with more than a dozen being held between 1965 and 1968. In July and September 1968, events in this format were called Leadership Training Schools of Anti-Communism. It was in 1969 that two events, at Fordham University in New York and at the Hotel America in Washington, were advertised as Anti-Subversive Seminars (ASSs). The emphasis was now almost exclusively on recruiting students, to whom "scholarships" were often given, along with a small amount for their accommodation and food.[31]

Between 1969 and 1976, about twenty ASSs were held, at a yearly rate that varied from one (in 1974) to six (in 1972). While former CACC events had lasted a week, the new formula lasted about three or four days. In part because the CACC paid for the admission and accommodation of many attendees, these seminars were designed to attract not more than a few hundred people. Reporter Bob Greene, present at the ASS of Chicago in February 1974, quipped: "There were about 250 persons there. In the early 1960s, Schwarz used to rent Madison Square Garden for his talks, but he seemed pleased to come into the room and see this turnout."[32]

Apart from Schwarz, Philbrick, Colbert, and Judd, over the years ASSs featured political scientists Henry Paolucci, David Rowe, Joseph Dunner, and James David Atkinson from St John's University, Yale, Yeshiva, and Georgetown universities, respectively; Charles Lowry, Oxford-trained philosopher; Reed Irvine, economist and media watchdog; Raymond Alcide Joseph, anthropologist from the University of Chicago who later became ambassador of Haiti in Washington; Richard Bertsch, attorney and member of the Presidential Commission on Obscenity and Pornography; Charles Rice, professor of law at University of Notre-Dame; Rus Walton, columnist and author; and M. Stanton Evans, *Human Events* editor. A few speakers, such as Juanita Castro and Phyllis Schlafly, were less associated with the academic world.[33]

Schwarz once described the ASSs's goal as the articulation of the positive qualities of free enterprise, limited constitutional government, and individualism. While communism remained paramount, the inclusion of several other themes revealed an evolution towards a broader approach. One of these themes was moral decline, present in such lectures as Drakeford's "The Great Sex Dwindle" and "Sex, Education and Morality," and Richard Bretsch's "The Presidential Commission on Obscenity and Pornography… Magna Carta for the Pornographer." A greater emphasis was also put on extolling the American constitutional and economic system, with lectures such as Benson's "The Wealth Machine" and Paolucci's "Government and the Constitution."[34]

A notable difference from previous schools was the emphasis on a practical type of training, with many addresses such as "How to Speak," and "How to Organize Campus Discussion." In 1977, the last recorded Crusade seminar took place in Washington under a new appellation: the Washington, DC, Conference of Workers against Communism. This event focused almost exclusively on practical knowledge, with workshops such as "How to Gain Access in the Media," "How to Write Effectively," "How to Form and Finance an Organization and Secure Tax Deductible Status for It," and "How to Secure Speaking Engagements." The pioneer of conservative direct-mail fundraising, Richard Viguerie, came to participate in sessions titled "The Message via the Mails" and "How to Be Effective in Politics."

A good number of students who attended ASSs were selected from the mailing lists of conservative organizations. In 1969, Jim Colbert initially wished to run advertising in student newspapers based in institutions near where the events were being held, but the idea was dropped in order to limit the number of hostile infiltrators. This decision compelled the CACC to use either its own mailing lists or those of the YAF.[35]

This being the case, many attendees had previous right-wing affiliations. Observers at ASSs pointed out that participants wore YAF, patriotic, or "Jesus Saves" pins. "Some small number represented groups at home." An ADL observer noted a "teenager who won a scholarship to attend from his church in Kentucky. A few were recruiting for their own churches or groups. A representative from 'The United Family' was recruiting interested people. The organization is in D.C. and wants to put 'Christ back into family life.'" A *Washington Post* journalist interviewed a husband and wife who came with their son, a University of Notre Dame student, because, as the father said: "[the professors] are too liberal-minded and are advocating socialism to be perfectly honest."[36]

Most attendees were YAF types (described by a reporter as "neatly-dressed, with short, well-combed hair"), though the crowd also sometimes contained a mishmash of elderly Republican women; foreign students from the Caribbean, Asia, or Africa; or curious citizens of all ages. In 1972, many participants in Washington were liberal students who attended primarily, Schwarz wrote, "to have a weekend at a hotel in Washington with their living expenses paid." However, he added, most "who came to scoff remained to listen with interest and respect."[37]

The switch from a policy of charging fees for each individual admission to a policy of paying each individual to attend made ASSs projects costly. When the expenses of paying the "faculty," renting a hotel hall, and other logistical elements were added, a seminar could cost as much as $50,000, as did the one held in Hotel Sonesta in Washington in June 1970, although most cost about half this sum. In 1975–76, during the final seminars, attendance was reduced to about three hundred to four hundred people, with the CACC not spending more than $10,000 to $12,000 on "scholarships," and each student receiving thirty-five dollars to attend. As long as they were held, the seminars absorbed about half of the Crusade's yearly finances.[38]

Observers described these seminars as markedly efficient. An ADL infiltrator sent to the first ASS in 1969 noted:

> I have never seen as fine a presentation. Every speaker was magnetic and his information presented both clearly and emotionally. The schedule was followed and all sessions were recorded for sale after the seminar. The propaganda skill that was used in preparing this seminar is beyond equal. There was not a single word said that could be used by a critic to show that the group is anti-Semitic or antidemocratic.[39]

ASSs were tightly controlled. Entering the seminar room, participants were given a copy of *You Can Trust*, the *What Is Communism? Study Book*, and a notepad. Another watchdog infiltrator, in 1970, mentioned the "non-humor, intent listening, [and] determination in the faces of everyone." Attendance was compulsory for those on a scholarship. In fact, they had to punch a card. At the end of a first seminar day, Schwarz insisted "that there be no partying that night, that everyone keep quiet, and preferably go to bed early." During the breaks, groups such as the YAF were allowed to distribute their literature to participants, but organizers carefully supervised the material so disseminated.[40]

Small-scale and mostly preaching to the converted, ASSs were less influential in the long term than were the early 1960s schools. Still, Schwarz wrote that some former ASSs attendees "came to occupy responsible positions in government, education and religion." Those young anticommunist activists whom Schwarz met during the ASSs period include Dana Rohrabacher, libertarian and president of the California YAF chapter, who later became one of Ronald Reagan's speechwriters and served from 1989 through 2019 as Republican representative for California's 42nd District (which encompasses Orange County). Another example is Anthony Dolan, another "YAFer," who became a journalist and, from 1981 on, President Reagan's main speechwriter. In March 1983, Dolan wrote the presidential speech in which Reagan famously referred to the Soviet Union as "the evil empire." Schwarz wrote Dolan to tell him that he felt pride and exaltation when reading the speech, and this prompted Dolan to send the crusader a copy of the speech with the note, "I thought you might like to see the oak tree that has grown from the acorn which you planted so many years ago."[41]

"A NEW ERA OF OPPORTUNITY"

In November 1964, Schwarz, Philbrick, and Janet Greene were touring in Michigan. The trio began a series of gigs with a stop before a full-capacity crowd at Michigan State University's Erickson Hall. In the midst of a speech, Schwarz collapsed. He was brought to a nearby hospital where he was diagnosed with tachycardia. He was quickly released from the hospital, but the heart problem reappeared during the following years, in particular when he gave public addresses. Schwarz continued to deliver numerous individual talks before small or medium-sized audiences between the mid-1960s and the mid-1970s, but his pace slowed.[42]

In 1967, the crusader appeared on William Buckley's *Firing Line* television show, the title of this particular program being "The Decline of Anti-Communism." Though the one-hour exchange remained cordial and Schwarz delivered his message with his usual aplomb, he seemed to have difficulty in convincing Buckley that his ideologically based analysis of Communism was in sync with the mood of the day. The crusader only minimally acknowledged that there were some differences between Stalin, Khrushchev, and Alexei Kosygin (the top Soviet leader until the early 1970s), stating that they only differed as to the means whereby they wished to apply communism towards the goal of world conquest. As for the fact that Kosygin had been trying since 1965 to implement economic reforms based on the introduction of market measures to stimulate the Soviet economy, Schwarz, as always, saw the initiative as a mere dialectical sidestep. He added that the Sino-Soviet split risked making Communism even stronger since competition encourages innovation and resourcefulness.

In May 1972, Schwarz participated in the last important public debate of his career, and probably his easiest win, at the College of the Sequoias in Tulare, California. His opponent was Roger McAfee, a raisin farmer who had made headlines when he covered the $102,000 bail for Angela Davis, a Black Power militant and former UCLA instructor who had been arrested for her alleged involvement in the abduction and murder of a California judge. Before a crowd of three thousand people, McAfee pointed out that Schwarz had never travelled to any country of the Communist Bloc and challenged him to disclose the source of his knowledge. "I studied at the University of Queensland in Australia, and they taught me to read,"

13.1 | William Buckley, C. Dickerman Williams, and Fred Schwarz on *Firing Line*, 29 June 1967.

Schwarz replied, generating laughs. One journalist reported: "It was evident McAfee came out on the short end. Against the advice of the panel moderator and Schwarz, he demanded a 'demonstration vote of confidence' by a show of hands – it was a hands down victory for the anti-communist crusader."[43]

In 1974, Schwarz appeared before the US Senate Subcommittee to Investigate the Administration of the Internal Security Act and Other Internal Security Laws, led by Southern stalwarts James Eastland and Strom Thurmond. This testimony took place amidst the 1974 events that saw a new left-wing urban guerrilla group, the Symbionese Liberation Army, making headlines for kidnapping the nineteen-year-old media heiress Patty Hearst, who announced in an audiotape two months after her abduction that she had joined that organization Schwarz testified as an expert witness on radical movements, but he also lectured on the issue of brainwashing, which he considered pertinent to the Hearst case. His recommendations for curbing radical violence in the United States included a program of education aimed at exposing the falsity of anti-imperialist, anti-capitalist rhetoric in order to halt the recruitment of guerrilla members on campuses. Unlike Schwarz's HUAC appearance seventeen years before, this testimony drew no media attention.[44]

In May 1976, the tachycardia problem reappeared on a graver scale, compelling the crusader to further reduce his speaking engagements. In a 1977 interview, he said he still made about ten speeches a month, but in early 1978, he wrote Judd that he was now taking the drug Inderol, one of whose side effects was a reduction in energy. After almost three decades and thousands of talks (perhaps twenty thousand, as was once suggested at a dinner held in Schwarz's honour in the 1980s), the crusader abandoned the speaking trail. In 1982, he received an invitation from Carl McIntire to address the delegates of the next Congress of the International Council of Christian Churches. Schwarz declined the invitation, explaining that his ministry was now comprised primarily of writing and research, in part due to his heart problem.[45]

In 1977, Schwarz wrote to Philbrick that he now had an "apprentice," Dr Marvin Olasky. Twenty-seven at the time, Olasky was the first person whom the crusader praised in this way. This Boston Jewish native had studied journalism at Yale University and became a Communist. He attended the University of Michigan, where he earned his PhD in American culture in 1976. He then became a born-again Christian and later joined the CACC. For a few months, Olasky lectured at CACC activities and wrote in the newsletter. Yet, in October 1977, after only five months, the "apprentice" left to become public relations handler for DuPont before accepting the position of professor of journalism at the University of Texas at Austin. He later became one of the USA's most influential social conservatives. He had an important impact on Republican social policies in the 1990s and 2000s due to his 1992 book *The Tragedy of American Compassion*, in which he argued that churches and private charities should reclaim from the state the responsibility for welfare.[46]

Schwarz also continued to scrupulously follow the international scene, which monopolized a great amount of space in the CACC newsletter, where he continued his strong advocacy for pure realpolitik. For instance, he supported the September 1973 military coup in Chile, which overthrew elected socialist premier Salvador Allende. Schwarz hailed the "courageous" actions of the Chilean armed forces, though he acknowledged that Chile's move towards democracy had unfortunately been interrupted.[47]

However, these were disappointing times for anticommunist activists. In the early 1970s, Nixon initiated the policy that led to the United States's diplomatic recognition of Communist China, which Schwarz compared to British prime minister Chamberlain's Munich Agreements with Hitler in 1938. In a letter to Philbrick, Schwarz, who had in the past defended Nixon, said of Nixon's decision that it was as bewildering as a reversal of the law of gravity. Judd expressed similar feelings in a letter exchange: "One can only wonder if the President has lost his mental balance ... Has he developed delusions of grandeur that he has become the Almighty? ... If so, it is hard to see how the US can ever be trusted again, or persons like myself, who worked for his election, ever to hold up their heads again."[48]

Outrage continued over the US-Soviet process of détente, initiated under Nixon with the Strategic Arms Limitation Talks (SALT) agreements and retained under Gerald Ford. Equally concerning was the support détente was receiving among an increasingly dovish public, as evidenced by the widespread rejection of President Ford's last-minute 1975 request to Congress for funds to stop the collapse of South Vietnam. Schwarz gave a no-confidence vote to the entire US political class, criticizing the growing number of elected officials who approved of détente solely because doing so was popular with the public. Commenting on the televised debate during the 1976 presidential campaign, the crusader criticized both Gerald Ford and Jimmy Carter. The former was blamed for his controversial statement that the USSR did not control Eastern Europe and the latter for his desire to see a regime change in Chile.[49]

The only leader the crusader found trustworthy was Ronald Reagan, though Schwarz waited until his friend's arrival in the Oval Office to praise his politics. In January 1981, Schwarz ridiculed pundits for not having predicted the GOP wave of November 1980. Even those who did, he added, "were surprised in most cases by the ease and magnitude of that victory, and I know of no professional pollster who predicted the defeat of so many 'liberal' Democratic senators that the control of the Senate will pass to the Republicans." Pollsters could not understand the outrage caused by "a liberal elite dominating the political process and destroying traditional moral values." He added, "A new era of opportunity has opened, but the opportunities must be seized." Reagan's first foreign policy statements, outlining a new confrontational approach towards the Communist Bloc, were deemed "refreshing" by Schwarz, who from that point on extolled the president. He never wavered from his support for Reagan, even when the latter agreed during his second term to engage in talks over peace and arms control with Mikhail Gorbachev, who, by 1985, had assumed supreme powers in the USSR.[50]

During the last two decades of his career, pursuing a trend that began in the mid-1960s, the crusader often commented on moral issues, in particular abortion and homosexuality. Schwarz first saw an abortion performed in medical school in Queensland in 1943. A group of students were permitted to watch a surgeon perform the operation by Caesarean section on a woman who was six months pregnant. "We watched as the surgeon incised the abdomen and the uterus and removed the writhing, crying child. He handed it to an attendant to dispose of it in the trash. Since that day I have never doubted that an abortion terminates a human life." From the moment abortion was decriminalized throughout the United States, with the 1973 *Roe v. Wade* Supreme Court ruling, Schwarz crucified those who considered the procedure acceptable. He qualified the legal framework as an "insane system" for making it possible to destroy an unborn baby while making it a capital crime to kill a born child.[51]

His comments on abortion pale, both in proportion and virulence, in comparison to those on homosexuality, which he considered with utter contempt – "an aberration, an excrescence," and a "social pathology." In 1977, his praise of singer and activist Anita Bryant, famous for her opposition to a law in Florida banning discrimination on the basis of sexual orientation, became the springboard for a discussion of homosexuality:

> By any rational standards, homosexuality is an undesirable life style; by Christian standards, it is an abomination. One method of determining the quality of an attitude is to consider what would happen if that attitude became universal. In the case of homosexuality, the answer is clear: It would mean national suicide. A world without children would be a horrible place … Homosexuality is the ultimate immorality.[52]

This attitude intensified with the outbreak of AIDS in the early 1980s. AIDS, Schwarz theorized, "has been in existence for an indefinite period of time," but the epidemic resulted from the development of conditions that facilitated its spread, such as the growing tolerance for "male promiscuity." Sodomy, he wrote, was "comparable to swimming in water containing raw sewage. Indulgence for this conduct often causes debilitating and deadly diseases."[53]

THE INTERNATIONAL SWITCH

In the late 1970s, for the first time in almost two decades, the CACC's financial resources began to improve, despite the loss of many of its important backers. The political and cultural setting of the 1980s, with its reinvigorated conservatism and Cold War polarization, pushed the CACC out of the doldrums. With GOP's fortunes increasing, several former crusaders reached prominent positions in politics, which translated into more contributions. In 1982, Schwarz wrote that he often received calls from the White House. "Mind you," he added, "it is never the President personally, but one of his staff. Or the introduction may be: '*I am calling from the office of Senator ____. The Senator asked me to call and see if you can help us secure authentic information on ____.*'"[54]

The CACC also benefitted from the rise of its life-long supporters to social prominence as well as from inheritances from some who had died. In October 1980, Schwarz wrote that, with $510,000 earned, the amount netted was $90,000 higher than that netted in the corresponding period in 1979. By 1982, revenues had reached $883,799. Schwarz thus began pleading with his supporters to help the CACC reach the $1 million mark. The following year, 1983, was the first time since 1961 that the Crusade's earnings hit a seven-digit figure – $1,060,417. This sum was worth less than it would have been twenty years earlier, but a symbolic threshold had been reached. The CACC's revenues remained stable until the Cold War ended.[55]

With the reduction and, ultimately, termination of major domestic projects, much of these sums was invested in international initiatives. The CACC evolved into an international anticommunist agency, with its leader more than ever convinced that the Vietnam debacle had proven him right: the Cold War would primarily be won by winning the hearts and minds of peoples around the globe. In 1982, he wrote to Judd how it was amazing that so few people understood that military actions were much more costly than trying to prevent the recruitment of Communist guerillas. The same year, the CACC spent $698,940 overseas, more than 75 percent of its total expenditures for the year, an increase of more than 40 percent for the international budget compared to the organization's prime years in the early 1960s. For this last outburst of global initiatives, the CACC did not initiate ambitious projects like the newspaper in Kerala or Sluis's mobile library in British Guiana; rather, it operated through a cluster of small-scale initiatives that allowed it to spread its resources more efficiently. As Colbert once wrote, there was now a strict policy whereby no CACC branch should be formed in Third World countries; rather: "we encourage the formation of local organizations with which we cooperate by providing teaching, training, literature and whatever financial support we are able to give."[56]

These last hyperactive years on the international front were also characterized by a decision to operate independently after a short-lived involvement with the World Anti-Communist League (WACL). In September 1967, Schwarz announced in his newsletter that an "Anti-Communist International ha[d] been formed to coordinate plans to fight communism throughout the world" and that Colbert would represent the CACC at its first conference in Taipei. Colbert was part of a delegation that represented a handful of US-based groups. About 250 delegates from seventy-two countries participated in the conference, half of them from Asia, and an eighty-year-old Chiang Kai-shek delivered the keynote address. The WACL was neither entirely private nor entirely a state organization. The South Korean and Taiwanese states were involved in its founding, with representatives of the political and military establishments of both countries holding key positions. Other Asian regimes, including Thailand and the Philippines, participated. Private groups were highly varied and came from several countries. Apart from political groups such as the CACC, there were conservative businesspeople and bankers from Hong Kong, Macao, and Singapore as well as anticommunist church groups, including the Unification Church of South Korean guru Sun Myung Moon.[57]

The WACL's activities had a public facet, which mainly involved holding conferences based on the model of the one in Taipei in 1967. This was apparently the only set of WACL initiatives in which the CACC was involved. In December 1968, the WACL's second conference was held in Saigon, where representatives of about fifty countries and thirty organizations met. Colbert attended as well and forged new contacts among high-ranking representatives of South Vietnam, Thailand, and Indonesia, all three countries in which the CACC disseminated its literature in the following years. In July 1971,

Schwarz went to Manila, where he addressed the WACL convention and established contacts with local churches and national security bodies. In August 1972, Judd invited Schwarz to participate in the sixth WACL conference in Mexico, but the crusader could not attend and, instead, sent some money and Colbert.[58]

Though, unlike Asian states, the US government refused to affiliate itself with the WACL, a meeting of American WACL supporters was held in February 1970 at Washington's Mayflower Hotel. The main force behind this meeting was Lee Edwards, one of Young Americans for Freedom's founding members, now turned political organizer and fundraiser. Among the participants with some CACC affiliation were Schwarz, Herbert Philbrick, Walter Judd, George Benson, Anthony Bouscaren, Robert Morris, Stefan Possony, David Rowe, and Fred Schlafly. As the meeting got under way, it became clear that attendants were reluctant to become affiliates of an international body controlled by foreigners. The American Council for World Freedom was thus formed, the official goal of which was to facilitate the "communication and cooperation" of anticommunist organizations "active in the field of international affairs." It was as a member of the American Council for World Freedom that the CACC participated in WACL activities from 1970 on.[59]

However, beneath its institutional front, the WACL had another side that had little in common with conferences. The league was also an apparatus through which much of the financial and material support for right-wing groups worldwide was channelled. The WACL evolved into an employer and dispatcher of graduates of the Political Warfare Cadres Academy, based in Taipei, which was originally designed to train Kuomintang military officials. However, in the 1970s, it turned into a global supplier of mercenaries. A multitude of right-wing groups, many of which were fascist and anti-Semitic, or had ties with organizations with such tendencies, associated themselves with the WACL. The entire Latin American branch of the league, the Confederación Anticomunista Latinoamericana, connected with a web of right-wing groups in multiple countries, sprang up largely through the effort of the "Tecos," a Mexican ultra-Catholic and anti-Semitic secret society with neo-Nazi ties. In 1972, in reaction to rumours of extremism in the WACL's Mexican branch, Stefan Possony was sent to investigate. His report confirmed that the WACL Mexican branch was a smokescreen for the "Tecos," which he deemed not only anti-Semitic but also anti-American and standing in opposition to most of the goals supported by the American Council for World Freedom.[60]

Possony's report prompted the American Council for World Freedom to hold a special meeting in Washington. According to the minutes, Schwarz's first gesture was to step down from the council's board of directors, invoking his busy schedule. Several members begged the crusader to change his mind, to no avail. Schwarz told the meeting participants that it was essential for the survival of the WACL that the organization purge itself of its anti-Semitism. This generated an extended discussion that resulted in a resolution stating: "Anti-Semitism is incompatible with enlightened, civilized conduct, and we condemn the communist states for the practice of it." Schwarz's decision to step down from the council's board was wise insofar as the league would become increasingly embroiled in controversial covert activities. By the mid-1980s, it had become one of the world's largest weapons suppliers to right-wing paramilitary groups.[61]

Working independently of the WACL did not impede the CACC from becoming part of a complex web of private agencies that was active in the worldwide anticommunist fight through the use of "low intensity conflict" (LIC) strategies, increasingly prominent in the US's foreign policy in the wake of the Vietnam debacle. LIC strategies were "war at the grassroots," referring to the use of economic, political, and psychological warfare rather than pure military force to run effective countersubversive measures. During the 1980s, the United States's LIC strategies often involved the use of religious groups that meshed humanitarian and evangelistic objectives with an aggressive anticommunist agenda. This "privatization" of US foreign policy became one characteristic of the Reagan era.[62]

As it became an informal element of US Cold War strategy, the CACC, as never before, found easy access to the resources of the local military and political establishments in the countries in which it operated. Hence, the case of Taiwan – where the Crusade, continuing its long-lasting relation with the Kuomintang, translated and distributed its material in schools and universities throughout the 1980s – was no longer the exception but the rule.[63]

From the mid-1970s on, one leading figure of the CACC international projects was John Whitehall, considered by Schwarz as his foster son. Whitehall had become a medical missionary and had done humanitarian work in South Vietnam, South Africa, and Rhodesia (Zimbabwe) before developing a particular interest in East

Timor. Part of the Indonesian archipelago, East Timor was one of the last remnants of the disintegrated Portuguese empire, where a brief civil war in 1975 resulted in the victory of the Fretilin, a socialist-inspired party popular among the Timorese people. During the unrest, Whitehall travelled twice to East Timor. In December 1975, under the pretext of preventing a Communist takeover, the Indonesian army invaded East Timor. Despite Schwarz's ongoing hardline approach, the CACC did not support the Indonesian invasion. Whitehall had forged relations with the Fretilin leaders, whom he considered "simple and untutored nationalists." The CACC's position was well-advised, considering that the Indonesian army committed acts of genocide against the Timorese, resulting in 100,000 to 200,000 deaths between 1976 and 1980. Whitehall briefly envisioned the founding of a group that would provide medical and dental help to the poor in association with an anticommunist program. His vision was incorporated into the CACC.[64]

In 1980, Whitehall made his first trip to the Philippines, where he was invited to speak at two Filipino theological colleges that held lectures on Communism. Whitehall made at least fifteen visits to that country between 1981 and 1987. The Philippines were governed by President Ferdinand Marcos, whose regime had grown increasingly authoritarian by the late 1960s. Marcos oversaw the country's rapid economic growth, but a lack of civil liberties, wealth inequality, and endemic corruption fuelled Communist movements, notably the New People's Army (NPA), a Maoist guerrilla group established in the rural areas of the largest islands (Luzon and Mindanao) that reached the height of its power during the early 1980s.[65]

In 1981, Schwarz's other son David, who was an airline pilot by day, "surveyed communist activity" in the archipelago and met with "a wide spectrum of Filipino anticommunists, including high government officials, the Archbishop of Manila, Cardinal Sin, and humble Baptist pastors in isolated rural areas." For his part, Whitehall organized a seminar in Iloilo (Panay Island), where he met Jun Alcover, Baptist pastor and member of the Armed Forces of the Philippines (AFP), who became the CACC's main Filipino contact. A former Communist, Alcover had been commander in the NPA before his conversion to Christianity led him to become an AFP agent in 1976. Developing contacts with the local public authorities, and the AFP in particular, allowed the Crusade to benefit from a high level of intelligence and protection. While in several countries the CACC operated by subsidizing its operations through local church bodies and individuals who handled the fieldwork, in the Philippines its involvement was more direct.[66]

In 1981, Whitehall, accompanied by Jim Colbert and Australian CACC director Elton Wilson, returned to the Philippines to organize a series of seminars, each attended by several hundred people under AFP protection. During another tour he made in 1983, Whitehall conducted nine seminars in fourteen days, speaking to thousands in Luzon and Mindanao. The seminars were advertised on the radio and took place in many of the areas where Communist guerillas were active. During a 1986 tour, Whitehall addressed thousands of people, including "governors, mayors, trade union officers, government employees, nuns, seminarians, students and soldiers." Groups formed, and the CACC supplied them with educational material and equipment. The CACC returned the AFP's favour. It did this first by defending the Marcos regime and, in 1985, by having Schwarz criticize the tendency in the US media "to assume that any regime that replace[d] it [would] be an improvement."[67] Second, it "reviv[ed] the credibility of the AFP propaganda," at least according to a 1987 report by a group of churches that relied partially on the CACC's Philippine activities. The same report mentioned that the CACC's local contacts participated "in AFP operations, as informants, guides, and even combatants." It continued: "It is a matter of public record that Jun Alcover carries arms issued by the Region 7 Command, and that he is a member of the AFP, working to build anti-Communist and vigilante groups." In early 1986, a coup forced Marcos into exile and installed Corazon Aquino, who lifted martial law, adopted a new constitution, and liberalized the regime. Nonetheless, the early Aquino years saw the high-water mark of the involvement of US-based private groups, including the CACC, in countersubversive activity in the country.[68]

In July 1986, according to the same report, a conference was held with Whitehall and General Fidel Ramos, chief of staff of the Armed Forces of the Philippines and, from 1992 on, president of the country. In February and March 1987, the CACC organized a speaking tour in the United States for Alcover, who went to Washington to address the Heritage Foundation and meet the staff of North Carolina senator Jesse Helms, senior Republican on the Foreign Relations Committee. Alcover also visited the Pentagon, where he met generals, CIA officials, and made contact with retired general

John L. Singlaub, director of the US Council for World Freedom, the US affiliate of the WACL. Singlaub's group was the main US private group involved in the Iran-Contra scandal, which broke out around the same time.[69]

In early 1987, the "Pacific CACC," based in the Sydney suburb of Toongabbie, was established with Whitehall as director. The PCACC published its own English newsletter, with a circulation of about twenty thousand copies per month. According to the Human Rights desk of the officials of the National Council of Churches in the Philippines, the PCACC newsletter was published in the Philippines "with the backing of businessmen from the Visayan city of Cebu." That Whitehall and the CACC had managed to draw the support of conservative Filipino businessmen might account for the presence of criticism in the newsletter directed towards some labour unions in the Philippines. In 1986, Whitehall made a presentation before the Australian Parliament's Joint Committee on Foreign Affairs and Defence, where he claimed that the Kilusang Mayo Unio, an anti-Marcos and militant anti-US trade union, was a Communist front. According to sociologist and attorney Sara Diamond, Whitehall's testimony before the Australian Parliament was printed in a booklet that was "intended to look like an official Australian government document" and was later distributed in the Philippines.[70]

The Aquino years saw the Philippine government regain ground over the NPA insurgency. By late 1987, Whitehall noted that the Filipino masses were turning against Communists and that the economy, which had stagnated during the final Marcos years, was improving. Due to these developments, CACC projects in the Philippines declined by the late 1980s. Despite limited resources, Whitehall had mounted an effective countersubversive operation that reached out to both the elites and the grassroots. It is no small wonder that in January 1988 it was announced that the NPA had put Whitehall on its list of those to be assassinated. In 1989, replying to an article by a Canadian liberal church group that accused him of having been part of the dirty LIC war in the Philippines, Whitehall stated that his Philippine initiatives had been a "privilege" and that Communists were to be blamed for sparking the LIC war.[71]

Meanwhile, in the 1980s, as part of what Schwarz called the "worldwide truth campaign," for which a million-dollar "truth fund" was raised, the CACC shipped large quantities of material to distributors around the globe, particularly in the Caribbean and Latin America

(Belize, Chile, Colombia, Costa Rica, El Salvador, Guatemala, Jamaica, Mexico, Panama, Argentina, Dominican Republic, Brazil, Ecuador) but also in several African countries (Kenya, Nigeria, Ghana, Tanzania, Cameroon, South Africa, and Uganda).[72]

Most of this material consisted of literature, including translations of Schwarz's last pamphlet, *Why I Am against Communism* (1981). Colbert became a permanent globe trotter during this period, embarking on a series of trips not only to supervise these programs but also to organize seminars targeting the local elites. Until his declining health compelled him to halt his travels in the early 1990s, Colbert organized dozens of events each year worldwide. Colbert travelled several times to Africa, most notably to Kenya and Nigeria, where the presence of well-established evangelical churches provided an important pool of local supporters. When Colbert arrived in Kenya in late 1986, he was greeted by the national director of the Kenya National Evangelism Fellowship, who had arranged his entire itinerary in rural Kenya. Of his 1988 trip in Nigeria, Colbert wrote that each meeting had "overflow crowds which ranged from 1,000 to 1,600. After the meetings, the people almost mobbed us."[73]

Latin America, where the CACC was most active apart from the Philippines, was the primary focus of Colbert's work. Between 1981 and 1990, Colbert travelled at least nine times to El Salvador and Costa Rica; six times to Honduras; five times to Mexico; four times to Guatemala, Belize, and Peru; three times to Venezuela; and twice to Bolivia, Argentina, and Panama. This emphasis on Latin America reflects an era when this region was one of the world's most intense zones for proxy wars, marked by the Nicaraguan Revolution of 1979, the short-lived Communist takeover of Grenada in 1983, and other leftist insurrections. The CACC also rode the wave of the spectacular growth of the evangelical population in all Latin American countries between 1960 and 1990. El Salvador and Costa Rica, the two countries most visited by Colbert, saw their evangelical populations quintuple during those three decades.[74]

Most of Colbert's operations in Central America were carried out by a team consisting of himself, Reverend John Korszyk (a Paraguayan native and graduate of the Fuller Theological Seminary in Pasadena), and Reverend Peter (Pedro) Padro. In 1983 in Honduras, Colbert met Miguel Alvarez, president of the National Evangelical Ministerial Alliance, who guaranteed him hours of speaking time before an upcoming national conference that would be attended by the country's various denominations. In 1984, Colbert and Padro were given the opportunity to address the largest evangelical church in El Salvador.[75]

While evangelical churches remained the CACC's primary foothold, the organization also succeeded in reaching public authorities in Latin America. In 1983, the governments of Guatemala and El Salvador agreed to distribute its literature to school, college, and university students, and to the personnel of their respective armed forces. In 1984, in Costa Rica, Colbert's team spoke in churches and on the radio and notably met "the Minister of Education, and the Archbishop of Nicaragua in exile in Costa Rica." In the same country, where an important portion of the anti-Sandinista exiles was established, Colbert met Contra leaders and set up programs for local security forces. In Honduras, the CACC organized a series of lectures at the Aviation Military Academy. In Paraguay, in 1985, the Ministry of Education helped organize a seminar by Colbert's team. In 1989 in Colombia, the team addressed the senior officers of the Colombian armed forces at their National War College. The Crusade had recreated in the developing world the broad alliance of elites of its prime years in the United States.[76]

THE END

In 1990, while Communist regimes were collapsing in Eastern Europe, Schwarz celebrated the fortieth anniversary of his crusading life at a banquet at the Beverly Wilshire Hotel in Beverly Hills, where his fiftieth wedding anniversary and his seventy-seventh birthday were also honoured. This was not the first time the crusader's life and work were celebrated with pomp. In March 1979, a silver jubilee banquet had been held in Los Angeles, where present and past collaborators came to testify to the Australian's accomplishments. A few months later, the Council against Communist Aggression, a lobbying group of which Schwarz had been an individual member since the mid-1960s, offered him a life achievement award. In 1987, Schwarz was honoured by the Council for National Policy, an organization that regrouped some of the country's most influential conservative businesspeople and Christian Right leaders (including Nelson Bunker Hunt, brewer Joseph Coors, Jerry Falwell, and Pat Robertson).[77]

Yet, more than the other events, the 1990 banquet looked like an end-of-career commemoration. Relatives, conservative personalities (Bill Buckley, James Dobson, Eleanor Schlafly, Reed Irvine,

Dale Evans, Roy Rogers, Patrick Frawley, Fred Rogers, and John Stormer), and politicians (Jack Kemp, Dana Rohrabacher, Bob Dornan) presented testimonies on how the Australian affected their lives and American politics. Ernie Kell, mayor of Long Beach, presented an honorary plaque with the seal of the city. Ronald Reagan sent a letter: "Fred, you're to be commended for your tireless dedication in trying to ensure the protection of freedom and human rights, and I know you join me in special satisfaction in the recent events in Eastern Europe."[78]

Schwarz kept crusading for eight more years. When the USSR collapsed in late summer 1991, he expressed his satisfaction: "The lesson of the collapse of the Soviet Union is that Marxism is an unstable edifice of deadly delusions, while Leninism is maniacal banditry." But with over a billion people still living under communism, there was no question of stopping. Besides, his supporters would not let him. Three years earlier, in December 1987, he had mailed them a questionnaire, asking whether or not they wished him to retire. The response: 1,817 respondents urged him to continue his leadership, a 97 percent vote of confidence.[79]

Those last crusading years were primarily devoted to publishing the newsletter. Schwarz continued to monitor the activities of radical groups as well as to follow the activities of Communists worldwide. Moral issues such as abortion, homosexuality, and AIDS remained uppermost in his thinking. Meanwhile, the CACC saw its last collaborators vanishing. In May 1992, George Murphy died, followed by Fred Schlafly and Herbert Philbrick, both in August 1993. In February 1994, Walter Judd died at the age of ninety-five. In 1996, Jim Colbert, Schwarz's collaborator of forty-three years, died at the age of seventy-nine. "Every day the mail contains the sad news that some of our friends and supporters have died," Schwarz noted. Colbert's death basically reduced the CACC's operations to Schwarz's writings. In 1996, the crusader published his memoirs *Beating the Unbeatable Foe: One Man's Victory over Communism, Leviathan, and the Last Enemy* (Regnery).[80]

In April 1998, Schwarz informed his supporters that he was finally resigning and returning to Australia, where he and his wife planned to spend time together with their children and grandchildren. For some time, despite his general good health, the eighty-six-year-old crusader had short-term memory difficulties: "I can quote from memory hundreds of poems, including some that I learned in grade school. Sadly, when I now learn a new poem, I have forgotten it within 15 minutes." He announced that the CACC would continue its work under his "spiritual son," Reverend David A. Noebel, president of Summit Ministries, located in Manitou Springs, where the CACC headquarters were moved. Announcing that he would take over what was left of the CACC (basically, a name, a newsletter, and a mailing list), Noebel announced that the CACC newsletter would be renamed the *Schwarz Report*.[81]

David Noebel, in his early sixties then, had first met Schwarz four decades before during his junior year at Hope College, Michigan, where the Australian had been invited to talk to the students. In the early 1960s, after his graduation, Noebel founded Summit Ministries, a leadership centre the goal of which was to train conservative Christians to fight against such modern trends as secularism, humanism, and atheism. Noebel remains notorious for his works of the 1960s, *Communism, Hypnotism, and the Beatles* (1965) and *Rhythms, Riots, and Revolution* (1966). Both argue that rock music has a Communist origin. "Throw your Beatle and rock and roll records in the city dump. We have been unashamed of being labeled a Christian nation; let's make sure four mop-headed anti-Christ beatniks don't destroy our children's emotional and mental stability and ultimately destroy our nation," Noebel wrote in *Communism, Hypnotism, and the Beatles*.[82]

Noebel was an intriguing choice for Schwarz's successor. These men were not known to have publicly collaborated beforehand. While Noebel was in line with Schwarz's conservative views, his eagerness to address all types of hot political issues with a tone and perspective much more typical of the Christian right wing of the Moral Majority era than of his predecessor marked a clear break. "This was," Laura Jane Gifford rightly asserts, "an ironic choice for a man who had spent so many years attempting to differentiate his organization from unambiguously right-wing fundamentalists, but likely it reflects his increasing concerns about contemporary social trends." In 2010, Noebel released a new edition of *You Can Trust*, updated with chapters of his own, under the title *You Can Still Trust the Communists: To Be Communists, Socialists, Statists, and Progressives Too*.[83]

Schwarz returned to Australia and spent his last days in Elderslie (New South Wales). He concluded his life surrounded by his family, which, aside from himself, now included more than seven medical doctors. As time went on, the old crusader's memory deteriorated to the point at which he could not recognize people or recall his own identity. His amnesia cleared occasionally, notably when he was able to recite long verses of poetry. He also suffered from speech difficulties, which sometimes left him wordless for days. On 24 January 2009, he died not long after his ninety-sixth birthday. Very little information could be found in the local media concerning his death. However, his family received, in the following weeks, scores of letters of sympathy from people around the world, mostly Christian leaders who testified to the influence Schwarz had had on their lives. Bill Muehlenberg, columnist for the online Australian evangelical magazine *Christian Today*, lamented: "While Australia has many heroes – especially sporting figures and movie stars – perhaps the greatest hero to arise from Australia in recent times has been totally overlooked by our secular, leftist media."[84]

Epilogue

The Christian Anti-Communism Crusade was a minor organization in the history of the American Right. Nonetheless, during its heyday in the late 1950s and early 1960s, it anticipated many themes that came to dominate conservative political discourses until at least the 2010s: patriotism, distrust of intellectual elites, antistatism, anticollectivism, muscular foreign policy, moral conservatism, and individualism, all packaged in a colour-blind fashion. This was so because opposition to communism swept across the whole right-of-centre spectrum, inspiring activists of all stripes to unification and mobilization. It spurred a generation of postwar conservative militants to engage in promoting and defending their values, regardless of creed or social standing. This movement cut across classes and united grassroots activists, small and large businesspeople, professionals, military personnel, clergy, and movie stars in what was to be a dress rehearsal for the Reagan years. Many of those who constituted the backbone of the American Right during the 1980s and 1990s underwent their political awakening in the anticommunist subculture before maturing and taking up whatever issues spoke most clearly to them. Their consequent involvement in right-wing politics grew out of their youthful convictions as the experiences of their formative years continued to tint the glass through which they viewed reality.

In effect, what was dismissed in the early 1960s as the Radical Right became in time the American Right. The persistence of anticommunism in the conservative imagination testifies to the importance and durability of communism as the United States's prime antagonist during the mid-twentieth century. "Isn't our choice really not one of left or right, but of up or down?," Ronald Reagan asked during his speech at the Republican National Convention, where he was re-nominated for the presidency in 1984. "Down through the welfare state to ... more government largesse accompanied always by more government authority, less individual liberty and, ultimately, totalitarianism, always advanced as for our own good. The alternative is the dream conceived by our Founding Fathers, up to the ultimate in individual freedom consistent with an orderly society." Eight years later, during his 1992 Republican convention speech, fundamentalist leader Pat Robertson linked the "dark cloud" of communism to the "more benign but equally insidious plague [that] has fastened itself upon the families of America" – bureaucratism, regulation, and centralized government. In the early twenty-first century, although to a lesser extent, the Red bogeyman was still present in the rhetoric of figures of the Tea Party movement, which conceived of all forms of state intervention as Marxist or socialist-inspired, revealing the continuity of the American Right.[1]

Conservative historian and activist Lee Edwards once stated that the personalities who built contemporary American conservatism can each be categorized in the one of the "four Ps." There were the "philosophers" like Russell Kirk, who conferred on the movement its intellectual respectability; the "popularisers" like William F. Buckley, who spread conservative ideas; the "politicians" like Goldwater or Reagan, who attempted to actualize these ideas in the political realm; and the "philanthropists" like J. Howard Pew, whose wealth made the other categories possible. To Edwards's four Ps the category of "propeller" can be added, of which Schwarz was an excellent example. Propellers do not provide long-term guidance; rather, they are catalysts and teachers of political involvement. While it remains true that "ideas have consequences," as the maxim says, the way ideas are presented, argued, and, perhaps more importantly, *experienced*, matters as much as their actual content. In this regard, Fred Schwarz's contribution to four decades of conservative mobilization is worthy of reflection.[2]

Rooted in evangelicalism and its emphasis on a personal encounter with the truth, Schwarz's projects were permeated by the conviction that only direct experience could provide the foundation for meaningful commitment. Schwarz once stated, "Theoretically, all Americans are anti-Communists, but they don't practice it in their daily lives." Thus, for Schwarz, battling communism was a cause to which more was due than lip service. He was a dynamo of ongoing projects, and his uneven writings and rhetoric were combat material. Through his rallies, schools, study groups, and seminars he had the capacity to transform anticommunism from an abstraction into a concrete reality in a manner that left a permanent impression on many people. He set an example in this regard by his own life story. Even though the idealized portrait of Schwarz as a man who forfeited native country, family, life, and career for the sake of his cause has to be nuanced, his detractors' frequent implication that he was primarily interested in personal profit misses the mark: his life and that of his family would have been far easier (including money-wise) had he remained a physician in Australia and not turned professional anticommunist in the United States.[3]

The CACC's legacy, most particularly its schools and study groups, has similarities with its perennial rival partner – the John Birch Society – in that it provided conservatives one of the first opportunities to join a grassroots movement. As Jonathan Schoenwald points out about Robert Welch in a logic equally applicable to Schwarz, the JBS founder might never have conceived of his organization as grassroots-oriented even though its members believed that it "personified grassroots activism, where groups of ten or fifteen people pursued agendas to bring change to their communities and country." Beyond their respective differences in styles, tones, and belief systems, Welch and Schwarz, as well as other figures of the early 1960s Radical Right, provided outlets for those who demanded and needed direct, immediate, and concrete actions against communism (or what they perceived as such). By this time, popular anticommunism reflected the urgency numerous people felt regarding the direction the nation was taking (though its virulence and rising visibility shocked many). Schwarz, whose organization greatly contributed to – and reaped the benefits of – this late 1950s conservative anticommunist impetus became an irresistible target when the Radical Right came under attack. That Schwarz had tried to keep his distance from more controversial right-wing figures and groups, and did not personally condone or adhere to the most outrageous popular conspiracies of the day regarding communism, did little to appease his critics. They understood, perhaps much better than he did himself, that the Crusade was more than what he pretended it was, and that its activities were an important enough factor in the anticommunist surge to justify a proper response. They also grasped one of the Crusade's existential dilemmas: although it differed in some ways from the

JBS and other controversial right-wing groups, to a large extent it appealed to the same supporters – sometimes desperately so.[4]

Both the CACC and the JBS have been the subject of renewed interest in the twenty-first century. However, substantial differences between Schwarz and Welch were such that in the decades following their mutual heyday the former's long-term imprint on the right has been more visible than the latter's. Due to his individual-based conception of social action, Schwarz provided little direction as to what the born-again anticommunist should do once he or she had been enlightened regarding the dangers of the threat, while Welch, for his part, always tried to keep close control over his followers. Moreover, since Schwarz understood that communism meant many things to many people, he always maintained a somewhat ambiguous posture so that many people could read many things into his words. As a result, his followers tended to go off in different directions.

The JBS's identity is more perceptible today in light of the turn taken by the early twenty-first-century American Right – particularly by the Tea Party movement and President Donald Trump's supporters – towards anti-establishment conservatism, populism, and a rhetoric riddled by varying degrees of conspiratorial overtones "transforming otherwise legitimate political disputes into fevered charges of betrayal and treason" in a manner that resonates well with Richard Hofstadter's "paranoid style" of American politics. By contrast, the very nature of Schwarz's politics – that is, that of an expatriated Australian conservative who integrated into his creed very little, if any, of the various ideas and schemes promoted by his American collaborators and supporters – prevented the CACC from making a comparable impact to that of the JBS as far as partisan politics are concerned. Other factors include the crusader's greater concern for his respectability among the elites as well as his desire to retain tax-exempt status with the IRS.[5]

But the CACC's more discrete imprint mitigates neither its influence on rank-and-file conservatives nor the fact that a good number of Schwarz's more "talented" students contributed to reshaping American politics by the late twentieth century. Examples abound in this regard, but two messages Schwarz received twenty years apart stand out. In 1978, as the Reagan era was about to begin, Schwarz received this message from Samuel G. Campbell, editor of the *Orange County Register*: "Just for your information, let it be recorded that the tax-limitation amendment so overwhelmingly adopted at the

California polls on June 6, 1978, was both a proximate and indirect consequence of your efforts in Southern California two decades before. The forces and friendships then formed still are working. I thought you would like to hear a report. Moral: There's more than one way to skin a conspiracy." In 1998, a retiring Schwarz received this other note from Tom Phillips, publisher of *Human Events*: "You educated both the leaders and the grassroots. You taught all ages from young to old your message about freedom, Communism, and God. Many of this youth you taught in the 1950s and 1960s have become the intellectuals and political leaders of the 1990s, and they are carrying on your work and your message."[6]

Moreover, the CACC's role in the evangelical anticommunist mobilization dwarfs that of the great majority of Radical Right groups of the late 1950s and 1960s, including the JBS. While observers who wrote about Schwarz sometimes wondered whether the CACC fitted more with the Radical Right or with fundamentalist Christianity, the truth is that it fitted with both, thus constituting a missing link in the origins of Reagan's "New Right." Here lies one of the main features of the CACC's long-term significance: its increasing appeal to secular conservatives in the late 1950s only came after years of gradually building a following among the Protestant conservative churches, which it rallied against the threat of communism and atheism, often presented as two faces of a single antagonist.

Schwarz was part of this group of fundamentalist leaders (others being Carl McIntire, Billy James Hargis, and Edgar Bundy) who not only redirected the evangelical psyche towards a strong identification with anticommunism but, as Ruotsila points out, also saturated the churches "with their claim that the Protestant mainline had become in essential ways un-Christian, un-American, and 'Other' because of the stances that many of its leaders took on free enterprise and Communism and later on moral issues." But while, throughout their respective careers, other "Old Christian Right" leaders appealed mostly to an evangelical base, Schwarz's scope was broader and regularly embraced the secular sphere, notably allowing him to turn down the religious component of his message whenever necessary, particularly in his relationships with politicians and the academic world. This led the CACC to collaborate with anticommunists of various creeds both in the United States and worldwide, including Catholics, thus paving the way for the interdenominational collaboration that, by the late 1970s, had become a common feature of the Christian Right. In spite of the shortcomings of "status anxiety" theories developed by social scientists who tried to explain right-wing behaviour in the postwar era, some of them, most notably Bell and Hofstadter, correctly identified the major role played by evangelical anticommunists in the conservative mobilization of the 1950s and 1960s.[7]

The CACC's most original trait, however, remains its global perspective. The internationalist outlook was not a rarity among the American Right. The foreign policy promoted by Buckley's *National Review* and the emergent neoconservative movement during the 1950s and 1960s aggressively pushed for a worldwide confrontation with communism, often coupled with a nationalist, unilateralist vision highly distrustful of the UN and liberal internationalism that paralleled Schwarz's. The crusader's twist was to reject the top-down approach saddling Western states with the main, if not sole, responsibility of containing and rolling back communism; rather, he adopted a bottom-up strategy aimed at challenging communism wherever possible with counter-propaganda disseminated through home-grown networks. Here again, this vision reflected the idiosyncrasies of an Aussie evangelical transplanted to the United States of America whose motivation, almost unaltered by his prolonged contact with US conservatives, remained his dream of building an "International" of anticommunist Christians loosely coordinated and funded by the United States, conceived not as the free world's undisputed leader but simply as its geographically and militarily unassailable stronghold. As a fragment of a global, faith-based subculture, the CACC advocated an approach that blended influences from the evangelical missionary tradition with its founder's skills as a rigid, yet efficient, counterrevolutionary propagandist. This approach was unique among postwar US anticommunist or conservative groups, the great majority of which focused mostly, if not exclusively, on domestic subversion.

For Laura Gifford, the Crusade's internationalism carried the seeds of an interesting prospect, the potential of which ultimately remained unfulfilled. "Had Schwarz chosen to repudiate affiliation with internal-subversion advocates and instead grounded the CACC's approach wholly in the international sphere," Gifford assesses, "his organization could have represented a uniquely Christian approach toward understanding of – and intervention in – the struggle for control and authority around the world." This characterization of the Crusade as a missed opportunity to build a

Christian anticommunist "International" is fascinating. It suggests that Schwarz could have discharged himself from most militant anticommunist figures, groups, and institutions and found support for his overseas schemes elsewhere, such as in mainline churches, moderate conservatives, liberals, or a combination of these groups. In light of the strong divide that had become entrenched between the right and the left over hard-hitting anticommunist activism by the late 1950s, one might wonder if this was a possibility. Also, the fact that the CACC could only deploy its international programs when its reputation was quickly ascending among the right wing in the late 1950s suggests that both phenomena were inexorably connected. The crusader's strategy, based as it was on the assumption that international Communism should be rolled back and that governmental initiatives alone were not enough to achieve this end – thus empowering individuals with the responsibility to conduct the fight both in the United States and globally was in harmony with that of his supporters. This approach actually became part of US foreign policy during the Reagan years.[8]

Even though the CACC's international initiatives were admittedly a drop in the ocean in the big picture of the Cold War, they absorbed a significant proportion of the organization's budget (and, from the late 1970s on, almost all of it). From an outsider's perspective, these projects reflected Schwarz's own unwavering, but sometimes ill-advised, commitment since they involved investing great effort in raising substantial amounts of US money to send overseas with apparently little (and sometimes nothing) to be gained in return. Yet the Crusade's effectiveness should not be evaluated according to business standards, nor it should be compared to that of faith-based institutions or church bodies whose earthly successes hinged on conversions, membership, and donations. Schwarz was primarily a teacher, and his Crusade was conceived as a non-profit educational institution. His core ambition of educating the peoples of the world regarding the ills of communism from a Christian, evangelical perspective required almost limitless resources – and these his organization never possessed and never could have possessed. Seeing the nature of his goal and his group's finite resources sheds a different light on the CACC's international projects. Over four decades, despite a limited budget, the CACC managed, through US money, to assist local anticommunist forces in more than twenty countries where proxy wars, which were part of a worldwide power struggle, took place.

In the early 1950s, Carl McIntire and Billy James Hargis collaborated in a much-publicized stunt to fly balloons carrying Bibles over the Iron Curtain, but otherwise they devoted much of their energy and resources to denominational feuds, partisan or political issues, and internal communism. By comparison, a few years later, Schwarz spent more than a third of his organization's budget to assist evangelical and missionary groups in spreading anticommunist material in various countries of Asia, Africa, and Latin America, and the Crusade's collaborators conceived of themselves as fighting on the frontlines of a global power struggle for freedom.

The development of the Crusade's international programs took place against the backdrop of a major expansion of the fundamentalist missionary movement throughout the second half of the twentieth century, which often came with an anticommunist outlook. What was particular about the CACC was that its strategy was based on providing tools conceived primarily as educational and only secondarily as evangelical, and not the other way around. Further research would be necessary to unveil fully the impact his strategies had in countries other than the United States. But there is much to suggest that the CACC's influence on anticommunism, conservatism, and the Christian Right was truly transnational.

The crusader admittedly did not live to see the disappearance of Communist regimes. And, like other figures of the Christian Right, he could not impede world cultures from evolving in directions (e.g., secularization, erosion of "traditional" morality, changing gender roles, expanding female and homosexual rights, etc.) he loathed and deemed fertile ground for communism and radicalisms of all sorts. But he sure tried to reach these goals, and he sought for decades to convince people across the globe that they should, too.

And yet, Frederick Charles Schwarz's actions have tended to stay under the radar of pundits and historians, both in the United States and elsewhere. His successor David Noebel decried: "As I have said numerous times Dr. Schwarz should be an authentic American hero, but alas the liberal/leftist/humanistic forces in place in this nation cannot afford a Christian anti-Communist hero." Obscurity, however, is often the fate of grassroots fighters, even global ones.[9]

Notes

ABBREVIATIONS USED IN NOTES

ACCC-ICCC	American Council of Christian Churches and International Council of Christian Churches Collection, the Historical Center of the Presbyterian Church in America, St Louis, Missouri
ACLU	American Civil Liberties Union Records, 1947–95 (bulk 1950–80), Seeley G. Mudd Manuscript Library, Princeton University
AKP	Alfred Kohlberg Papers, Hoover Institution Archives, Stanford University
ARDF	Anthony R. Dolan Files, Ronald Reagan Presidential Foundation and Library, Simi Valley, California
BMGP	Barry M. Goldwater Papers, Arizona State University, Archives and Special Collections, Charles Trumbull Hayden Library, Tempe, Arizona (formerly stored at Arizona Historical Foundation, Tempe, Arizona)
CACCN	Christian Anti-Communism Crusade Newsletter (all texts and fundraising letters by Schwarz unless specified; all online issues viewed between 2007 and 2011).
CMP	Carl McIntire Papers, Special Collections, Princeton Theological Seminary (unprocessed during research)
ChiTri	Chicago Tribune
CWCP	Conservative Women of California Project (directed by Michelle Nickerson) Center for Oral and Public History, California State University, Fullerton

DMP	Donald McNeil Papers, Archives Division, State Historical Society of Wisconsin, Madison, Wisconsin
DSBP	Dorothy Stimson Bullitt Papers, University of Washington Libraries Special Collections
FBIF	Federal Bureau of Investigation Files, material retrieved (through Freedom of Information Acts) and made accessible by Ernie Lazar. Available online at https://archive.org/details/lazarfoia?and%5B%5D=mediatype%3A%22collection%22
FRP	Florence Ranuzzi Papers, Manuscript Collections, Huntington Library, California
GHGH	Gordon Hall and Grace Hoag Collection of Dissenting and Extremist Printed Propaganda, John Hay Library, Brown University
GKSP	Gerald K. Smith Papers, Michigan Historical Collections, Bentley Historical Library, University of Michigan
GRIR	Group Research, Inc., Records, Rare Book and Manuscript Library, Butler Library, Columbia University, New York
HPP	Herbert Philbrick Papers, Manuscript Division, Library of Congress, Washington, DC
IRS-EOD	Internal Revenue Service – Exempt Organization Determination, Department of the Treasury, Cincinnati, Ohio (Form 4506-A Request) – Requested 30 July 2008
JFKP	John Fitzgerald Kennedy Papers, John F. Kennedy Presidential Library, Boston, Massachusetts
JHPPP	J. Howard Pew Personal Papers, Manuscript and Archives Department, Hagley Museum Library, Wilmington, Delaware
JLRP	Joseph L. Rauh Papers, Manuscript Division, Library of Congress, Washington, DC
JLSM	"John L. Shover's material relating to his article on Fred Schwarz' Christian Anti-Communist Crusade," Bancroft Library, University of California, Berkeley
JWFP	James William Fulbright Papers, Special Collections, University of Arkansas Libraries, Fayetteville
LAE	*Los Angeles Examiner*
LAT	*Los Angeles Times*
LSP	Lawrence E. Spivak Papers, Manuscript Division, Library of Congress, Washington, DC

MKP	Mary Koenig Papers, manuscript collection, Huntington Library, California
MLP	Marx Lewis Papers, Hoover Institution Archives, Stanford University
MLieb	Marvin Liebman Papers, Hoover Institution Archives, Stanford University
NARA	National Archives and Record Administration, College Park, Maryland
NYT	*New York Times*
PJSP	Peter J. Stram Papers, manuscript collection, the Historical Center of the Presbyterian Church in America, St Louis, Missouri
PRAA	Political Research Associates Archives, Political Research Associates Library, Somerville, Massachusetts
PSC	Phyllis Schlafly Collection, Communism series, Eagle Forum Library and Archives, St Louis, Missouri
QSA	Queensland State Archives, Runcorn, Brisbane, Australia
SFE	*San Francisco Examiner*
TJDP	Thomas J. Dodd Papers, Archives and Special Collections, Thomas J. Dodd Research Center, University of Connecticut Libraries, Storrs
TTSP	T.T. Shields Papers, Jarvis Street Baptist Church Archives, Toronto
WashP	*Washington Post*
WCNP	William C. Norris Papers, Control Data Corporation Records, Charles Babbage Institute, University of Minnesota
WCSP	W. Cleon Skousen Papers, Private Collection, Skousen Family, Salt Lake City
WFBP	William F. Buckley Jr Papers (MS 576). Manuscripts and Archives, Yale University Library
WHJP	Walter H. Judd Papers, Hoover Institution Archives, Stanford University, copyright Stanford University
WHJU	Walter H. Judd Papers, Collections, Minnesota Historical Society
WSP	William E. Simon Papers, Special Collections and College Archives, Skillman Library, Lafayette College, Easton, Pennsylvania

Newspaper articles are anonymous unless specified otherwise.
Fundraising letters are written by Schwarz unless specified otherwise.

INTRODUCTION

1 Fred Schwarz, *Beating the Unbeatable Foe: One Man's Victory over Communism, Leviathan, and the Last Enemy* (Washington: Regnery, 1996), 209; "Anti-Red Youth Night Draws Overflow Crowd at Arena," *Independent*, 31 August 1961, A4.

2 KTTV, *Hollywood's Answer to Communism*, TV Special 1961-10-16, University of California at Los Angeles, Film and Television Archive, 2 videocassettes of 2 (VHS), 180 min. (extracts only); report on the LA CACC school, GRIR, box 299, f. "Sluis, Joost."

3 "Youth Prime Red Target, Reagan Says," *LAE*, 31 August 1961, 2; Louis Fleming, "Probe into 'Muzzling' of Military Asked," *LAT*, 31 August 1961, B1.

4 GR report on the LA CACC school, GRIR, box 299, f. "Sluis, Joost."

5 R. Moore to W. Judd, 5 September 1961, WHJP, box 48, f. 4, copyright Stanford University.

6 Bill Becker, "Right-Wing Groups Multiplying Appeals in Southern California," *NYT*, 29 October 1961, 43.

7 Daniel Bell, "The Dispossessed (1962)," in *The Radical Right: The American Right, Expanded and Updated*, ed. Daniel Bell (New York: Doubleday, 1962), 4–5.

8 From *NYT*: Tom Wicker, "Kennedy Asserts Far Right Groups Provoke Disunity," 19 November 1961, 1; "Rightists Picket Kennedy Speech," 19 November 1961, 54. Bell, "Dispossessed (1962)," 1; Craig Schiller, *The (Guilty) Conscience of a Conservative* (New York: Arlington House, 1978), 29.

10 Eisenhower qtd. in "Farewell Message Has Sober Warning," *Spokesman-Review*, 18 January 1961, 4; Stephen Whitfield, *The Culture of the Cold War* (Baltimore: Johns Hopkins University Press, 1996), 231.

11 Ellen Schrecker, *Many Are the Crimes: McCarthyism in America* (Princeton, NJ: Princeton University Press, 1998), 360–9. See also David M. Oshinsky, *A Conspiracy So Immense: The World of Joe McCarthy* (New York: Oxford University Press, 1983), 507; Doris Kearns, *Lyndon Johnson and the American Dream* (New York: Harper and Row, 1991), 252. On the effects of anticommunism on the civil rights agenda, see John T. McCartney, *Black Power Ideologies: An Essay in African-American Political Thought* (Philadelphia, PA: Temple University Press, 1992). On US domestic policy, see Michael Reisch and Janice Andrews, *The Road*

Not Taken: A History of Radical Social Work in the United States (Philadelphia, PA: Brunner-Routledge, 2001).

12 Richard Gid Powers, *Not without Honor: The History of American Anticommunism* (New York: The Free Press, 1995), 272; Daniel Bell, "Interpretations of American Politics (1955)", in *The Radical Right: The American Right, Expanded and Updated*, ed. Daniel Bell (New York: Doubleday, 1962), 49.

13 Lisa McGirr, *Suburban Warriors: The Origins of the New American Right* (Princeton, NJ: Princeton University Press, 2001), 35–6; Darren Dochuk, "Evangelicalism Becomes Southern, Politics Becomes Evangelical: From FDR to Ronald Reagan," in *Religion and American Politics: From the Colonial Period to the Present*, ed. Mark Noll and Luke Harlow (New York: Oxford University Press, 2007), 300. The nature of this dynamic has started to be detailed more closely by these studies tracing the social roots of the contemporary right.

14 Donald Critchlow, *Phyllis Schlafly and Grassroots Conservatism: A Woman's Crusade* (Princeton, NJ: Princeton University Press, 2006), 309n3; Phyllis Schlafly to Fred Schwarz, attached to fundraising letter to CACCN readers, July 1998, PRAA, f. "Schwarz, Fred C." Don Critchlow uses the term "grassroots conservatism" so as to "distinguish local activists from the Republican Establishment and conservative intellectuals and writers."

15 George Marsden, *Fundamentalism in American Culture: The Shaping of Twentieth-Century Evangelicalism, 1870–1925* (New York: Oxford University Press, 1979), 210; Angela Lahr, *Millennial Dreams and Apocalyptic Nightmares: The Cold War Origins of Political Evangelicalism* (New York: Oxford University Press, 2007), 203.

16 Geisler qtd. in David Noebel, "Frederick Charles Schwarz, January 15, 1913–January 24, 2009," *Schwarz Report* 49, 3, (2009): 2; Dobson qtd. in Schwarz, *Beating*, xviii; Gary North, "It All Began with Fred Schwarz," *LewRockwell.com*, http://www.lewrockwell.com/north/north145.html; Gary North, *Healer of the Nations: Biblical Blueprint for International Relations* (Fort Worth, TX: Dominion Press, 1987), vi.

17 Joel Carpenter, *Revive Us Again: The Reawakening of American Fundamentalism* (New York: Oxford University Press, 1999), 184.

18 Laura Jane Gifford, "Girded with a Moral and Spiritual Revival: The Christian Anti-Communism Crusade and Conservative Politics," in *The Right Side of the Sixties: Reexamining Conservatism's Decade of Transformation*, ed. Laura Jane Gifford and Daniel K. Williams (New York: Palgrave Macmillan, 2012), 162.

CHAPTER ONE

1 Schwarz, *Beating the Unbeatable Foe: One Man's Victory over Communism, Leviathan, and the Last Enemy* (Washington, DC: Regnery, 1996), 15–17; "Organizations: Crusader Schwarz," *Time* 79, 6 (1962): 18.

2 Schwarz, *Beating*, 16, 495; F. Schwarz to A. McDowell, 23 June 1962, MLP, box 1, f. 2.

3 Fundraising letter, 1 July 1979; "Organizations: Crusader Schwarz," 18; Schwarz, *Beating*, 494.

4 *Immigration: Federation to Century's End, 1901–2000* (Belconnen, Canberra: Statistics Section, Department of Immigration and Multicultural Affairs, Australia, 2001), 16; A.G.L. Shaw, *A Short History of Australia* (New York: Frederick Praeger, 1969), 142–7; Brittany Trubody, message to author, 7 February 2011. Because of their indispensable role in Queensland's economy, especially the sugar cane and sugar refining industry, Asian workers continued to land unimpeded after the Immigration Restriction Act, 1901, which was designed to curb the flow of immigration from Australia's neighbouring countries.

5 William Lawton, *The Better Time to Be: Utopian Attitudes to Society among Sydney Anglicans, 1885–1914* (Sydney: University of New South Wales Press, 1990); Margaret Dunn, *The Dauntless Bunch: The Story of the YWCA in Australia* (Clifton Hill, Melbourne: YWCA of Australia, 1991); Alison Holland, "Feminism, Colonialism and Aboriginal Workers: An Anti-Slavery Crusade," *Labour History* 69 (November 1995): 52–64; R. Howe, "The Australian Student Christian Movement and Women's Activism in the Asia Pacific Region, 1890's–1920's," *Australian Feminist Studies* 36 (2002): 311–24.

6 D. Woodbury, "From Mustard Seeds," *Hallelujah: From Small Beginnings – The Story of the Salvation Army in the Western South Pacific* 1, 1 (2007): 32; Brian Dickey, "Evangelical Anglicans Compared: Australia and Britain," in *Amazing Grace: Evangelicalism in Australia, Britain, Canada and the United States*, ed. George Rawlyk and Mark Noll (Montreal and Kingston: McGill-Queen's University Press, 1994), 219, 235–6; D.W.B. Robinson, phone interview with author, 15 December 2007. The Salvation Army has been in Brisbane since the 1890s.

7 A. McDowell to S. McNail, 18 July 1962, MLP, box 1, f. 2; Brooks Walker, *The Christian Fright Peddlers: The Radical Right and the Churches* (New York: Doubleday, 1964), 56–8; "How Atheism and Its Followers Sabotage the Church," *CACCN*, 1 February 1982, 2. The only

article of belief he did not take a position on was the premillennial return of Christ.

8 Fundraising letter, 1 January 1970; Fred Schwarz, "Will the Kremlin Conquer America by 1973?," *Freedom Forum Presentation* (Searcy, AR: National Education Program, 1959), 26; Fred Schwarz, "Communism Training I," in *What Is Communism? Part V–VIII*, Chantigo Records, 1965 (recorded lecture); Peter Coleman, "Crusader Fred Schwarz," *Sydney Bulletin*, 7 April 1962, 18; Donald Baker, "Old Pros of Anti-Communism Lecture on 'Real Enemy,'" *WashP*, 2 July 1972, B9; Schwarz, "Will the Kremlin Conquer America by 1973?," 31; Peter Loveday, "The Liberals' Image of Their Party," in *Australian Conservatism: Essays in Twentieth-Century Political History*, ed. Cameron Hazlehurst (Canberra: Australian National University Press, 1979), 240.

9 "Classism and Classicide," CACCN, 15 May 1972, 1; Schwarz, *Beating*, 479.

10 Schwarz, *Beating*, 494; "Debate on Marcuse," CACCN, 15 January 1972, 2.

11 Schwarz, *Beating*, 16; "Sunday School – Examination Results," *Brisbane Courier*, 3 November 1928, 26. In 1928, he was awarded a prize when coming in at the sixth rank of his class with a result of 96 percent at the Sunday School examination conducted by the Young People's Department of the Queensland Methodist Conference.

12 Fred Schwarz, *The Heart, Mind and Soul of Communism* (Waterloo, IA: Evangelize America Program, 1952), 10–11; Fred Schwarz, "Births and Babies: Address Delivered in Angelus Auditorium, October 10, 1952," *Foursquare Magazine* 25, 1 (1952): 19–23; Fred Schwarz, "The Deadly Disease: Communism," CACCN, 1 December 1997, 1; Fred Schwarz, *You Can Trust the Communists (to Be Communists)* (Long Beach, CA: Chantico Publishing Co., 1966), 123. Schwarz's outlook was similar to the Baconian ideal so long promoted by Protestant philosophers. Yet, in a 1952 sermon (see *Foursquare Magazine* above), he decried that, "in this modern day of apostasy," belief in miracles was ridiculed.

13 Schwarz, *Beating*, 17; Keith and Gladys Hunt, *For Christ and the University: The Story of the InterVarsity Christian Fellowship of the USA, 1940–1990* (Downers Grove, IL: InterVarsity Press) 32, 56–9; Stuart Piggin, "The Challenging But Glorious Heritage, Difficult But Joyful Birth, and Troubled But Triumphant Childhood of the Melbourne University Evangelical Union, 1930 to 1940," paper presented during the MUEV's 75th anniversary, 14 May 2005, 2–5. The IVF initially grew out of the Cambridge Inter-Collegiate Christian Union (CICCU, pronounced Kick-U), founded in 1877.

14 Ian Breward, *A History of the Churches in Australia* (New York: Oxford University Press, 2001), 255; Schwarz, *Beating*, 17.

15 Stuart Piggin, *Evangelical Christianity in Australia: Spirit, Word and World* (Melbourne: Oxford University Press, 1996), 80; Schwarz, *Beating*, 17–18; Joy Parker, *A Vision of Eagles: Fifty Years of the Crusader Union of New South Wales* (Sydney: The Crusader Union of NSW, 1980), 7; Stuart Braga, *A Century Preaching Christ: Katoomba Christian Convention, 1903–2003* (Sydney, Katoomba: Christian Convention Ltd., 2003), 72; John and Moyra Prince, *Tuned in to Change: A History of the Australian Scripture Union, 1880–1980* (Sydney: Scripture Union of Australia, 1979), 113. The Crusader Union's statement of beliefs was typically fundamentalist. Schwarz's involvement in the Crusader Union was appreciated, despite some members' distaste for Pentecostalism and their knowledge of his association with it.

16 "The Medical School of the University of Queensland," *Science* 91, 2362 (1940): 331; "The Supply of Practitioners for Australia," *British Medical Journal* 2, 4150 (1940): 5; Editorial, *Trephine: The Journal of the Queensland Medical Students' Association* 3 (1942): 5; Schwarz, *Beating*, 21.

17 Schwarz, *Beating*, 18–25.

18 A. Donald Macleod, *C. Stacey Woods and the Evangelical Rediscovery of the University* (Downers Grove, IL: InterVarsity Press, 2007), 17–21; Ad for Schwarz lecture, *Semper Floreat*, 8 May 1942, 4; "Shocking Bedside Manners: Meds at Variance," *Semper Floreat*, 1 April 1943, 3. Meanwhile, in 1944, several American evangelicals met at Plymouth Rock to form the Plymouth Conference for the Advancement of Evangelical Scholarship.

19 Louise Overacker, "The Australian Labor Party," *American Political Science Review* 43, 4 (1949): 678–9; Stuart Macintyre, "Dealing with Moscow: The Comintern and the Early History of the Communist Party of Australia," *Labour History* 67 (1994): 130–3; David McKnight, "The Comintern's Seventh Congress and the Australian Labor Party," *Journal of Contemporary History* 32, 3 (1997): 401–7; Stuart Macintyre, *The Reds: The Communist Party of Australia from Origins to Illegality* (St Leonards, NSW: Allen and Unwin, 1998), 389–411.

20 Schwarz, *Beating*, 22; Fred Schwarz, "The Greatest Murderers of Mankind – Adolf Hitler," *Schwarz Report* 38, 11 (1998): 2; "Abner Lets Hair Down," *Semper Floreat*, 3 May 1940, 3; Ad, *Semper Floreat*, 10 May 1940, 3.

21 Fred Schwarz, "What Makes Students Susceptible to Communist Seduction?," *Schwarz Report* 38, 6 (1998): 4; Jonathan Herzog, *The Spiritual-Industrial Complex: America's Religious Battle against*

Communism in the Early Cold War (New York: Oxford University Press, 2011), 45.

22 Schwarz, *Beating*, 23–4, 135–6. Lillian Schwarz qtd. in "Organizations: Crusader Schwarz," 18.

23 "Medical Graduation," *Semper Floreat*, 15 June 1944, 1; Ronald Wood, "Conflict, Conciliation and Conditions of Service: A Pioneering Medical Industrial Court Action in 1944," in *Some Milestones of Australian Medicine: A Centenary Book for the Queensland Branch of the Australian Medical Association*, ed. John Pearn (Brisbane: Amphion Press, 1994), 60–2; Schwarz, *Beating*, 29; Memorandum qtd. in Fred Schwarz, "Resident Medical Officers and the New Sociology," *Trephine: The Journal of the Queensland Medical Students' Association* 5 (1944): 45; "RMOs Demand Justice: Arbitration Only Solution," *Semper Floreat*, 3 August 1944, 1; James Gillespie, *The Price of Health: Australian Governments and Medical Politics, 1910–1960* (Cambridge: Cambridge University Press, 2002), 68–9. By contrast, a first-year dentist made £466 per year for a forty-hour week.

24 Ad, "List of Office Bearers, 1941," *Trephine: The Journal of the Queensland Medical Students' Association* 2 (1941): 5; "News from Herston: New Blood in U.Q.M.S.," *Semper Floreat*, 5 August 1943, 1.

25 Wood, "Conflict, Conciliation and Conditions of Service," 61; Schwarz, *Beating*, 32. The BMA had long fought against nationalized or socialized medicine, and the prospect of doctors being involved in such a labour conflict within a state-run institution was something it viewed with distaste.

26 All exchanges taken from *Resident Medical Officers of the Brisbane General Hospital v. Crown and the Brisbane and South Coast Hospital Board*. Available in QSA, TK1716, box 496, 1944 "Mixed," item ID 7888360, SRS 4508 /4/496, 1.

27 "Social Justice Triumphs," *Semper Floreat*, 26 October 1944, 3; Derek Meyers, "Obituary: Frederick Charles Schwarz," *Medical Journal of Australia* 190, 7 (2009): 368; Schwarz, *Beating*, 32. Even some conservative medical professionals were pleased: J.G. Wagner, president of the Queensland BMA, who had implored RMOs to cease their action, sent Schwarz a letter of congratulations.

28 Schwarz, *Beating*, 33–4; Elton Wilson, obituary speech at Schwarz's funeral, 29 January 2009, DVD recording provided by the Schwarz family; Meyers, "Obituary: Frederick Charles Schwarz," 71; "Questions and Answers on KHJ-TV, Los Angeles, Monday, March 22," *CACCN*, 1 April 1965, 2. In 1965, Schwarz estimated that his net annual income would have been US$20,000 if he had not given up medicine.

29 Drakeford (1914–2004) became pastor upon completing seminary studies at the New South Wales Theological College. In 1954, he came to the United States, where he completed his PhD in psychology at the Southwestern Theological Seminary.

30 F. Schwarz to C. McIntire, 16 April 1950, CMP, f. "Dr. F. C. Schwarz – Alvalea – 142 Concord, North Strathfield, Australia" (hereafter "Dr. (etc.)"); Schwarz, *Beating*, 39–40. Jack Murray, "Newsrelease: The Beloved Physician. Dr. F. C. Schwarz, B.A., B.Sc., M.B., B.S.," *TTSP*, box. 7, 1950, f. "S"; "Another Debate Proposed on Communism," *Canberra Times*, 25 September 1948, 4.

31 Coleman, "Crusader Fred Schwarz," 18.

32 Kenneth Woodward, "What Qualifications for a Crusader? Fred Schwarz on Communism," *Catholic Reporter*, 1 February 1963, 15; "Deeds and Vision," CACCN, 15 November 1982, 1.

33 "Deeds and Vision," 1; Coleman, "Crusader Fred Schwarz," 18.

34 Herzog, *Spiritual-Industrial Complex*, 47; Nicholas Klepinin, "The War on Religion in Russia," *Slavonic and East European Review* 8, 24 (1930): 514–32. In 1941, only about five hundred Orthodox churches remained in the USSR, down from fifty-four thousand during the First World War years.

35 Walker, *Christian Fright Peddlers*, 62; Schwarz, *Beating*, 310.

36 Walker, *Christian Fright Peddlers*, 65–6.

37 Karl Marx, *Capital: A Critique of Political Economy* (Toronto: Penguin Classics, 1990), 103. This was in the postface of the second edition of Marx's *Capital*.

38 Schwarz, *Beating*, 48; Schwarz, *You Can Trust the Communists*, 8.

39 Schwarz, *Beating*, 66.

40 Edward Rozek, phone interview with author, 23 January 2008; *Firing Line* with William F. Buckley Jr, Program 062, "The Decline of Anti-Communism (1967)," Hoover Institution Archives.

CHAPTER TWO

1 David McKnight, "The Moscow-Canberra Cables: How Soviet Intelligence Obtained British Secrets through the Backdoor," *Intelligence and National Security* 13, 2 (1998): 159–70; Stuart McIntyre, *A Concise History of Australia* (New York: Cambridge University Press, 1999), 204; David Lowe, *Menzies and the "Great World Struggle": Australia's Cold War, 1948–1954* (Sydney: University of New South Wales Press, 1999), 11. The historiography still reflects the Cold War divide.

2 Robin Gollan, *Revolutionaries and Reformists: Communism and the Australian Labour Movement* (Surrey: The Richmond Publishing Col., 1975), 221; Derek Meyers, message to author, 18 January 2010. The BMA's general secretary, J.G. Hunter, wrote a pamphlet in which he linked the Labor Party's plan to Lenin, who "once proclaimed socialised medicine 'the keystone of the arch of the Socialist State.'" Meyers did not recall Schwarz taking a public stance on the issue.

3 Derek Meyers, message to author, 18 January 2010; F. Schwarz to W. Judd, 16 July 1975, WHJP, box 226, f. 5, copyright Stanford University; Coral Bell, "Review," *International History Review* 23, 1 (2001): 202; Fred Schwarz, "Control the Unions," *Schwarz Report* 40, 12 (2000): 3; Eric Bodin, review of *Beating the Unbeatable Foe* by Fred Schwarz, "One Man's Victory over Communism," *Citizen*, 28 April 1997 10; "Another Debate Proposed on Communism," *Canberra Times*, 25 September 1948, 4; F. Schwarz to C. McIntire, 16 April 1950, CMP, f. "Dr. F.C. Schwarz – Alvalea – 142 Concord, North Strathfield, Australia" (hereafter "Dr. (etc.)"); Fred Schwarz, *Beating the Unbeatable Foe: One Man's Victory over Communism, Leviathan, and the Last Enemy* (Washington, DC: Regnery, 1996), 39. He kept private his views on socialized medicine. Still, in a 1975 letter to friend and fellow MD Walter Judd – after Australia's first universal healthcare system had been introduced – Schwarz was rather critical of Premier Gough Whitlam's Labor government.

4 "Fred C. Schwarz M.D.," *CACCN*, November 1955, 1.

5 Phillip Deery, "Chifley, the Army and the 1949 Coal Strike," *Labour History*, 68 (1995): 80.

6 Fred Schwarz, "The Communist Blueprint for the Conquest of Canada," *Gospel Witness and Protestant Advocate* 29, 23 (1950): 7–8.

7 Phillip Deery and Neil Redfern, "No Lasting Peace? Labor, Communism and the Cominform: Australia and Great Britain, 1945–1950," *Labour History* 88 (2005): 63–72.

8 "No Decision in Debate on Communism," clipping, CMP, f. "Dr. (etc.)"; "Australian Tells Reds' Progress 'Down Under,'" *LAT*, 14 June 1950, A13.

9 Schwarz qtd. in St Louis Civil Liberties Committee, *Communism on the Map (Complete Text of the Tape-film Strip) and The Greater St. Louis School of Anti-Communism – April, 1961 (Selected Quotations)*, St Louis, 1962, 18–19; "Schwarz and Mandel in Quiet Debate," *Oakland Tribune*, 27 January 1962, 1, 3.

10 Editorial, *CACCN*, November 1955, 1.

11 Stephen Crocco and Robert Benedetto, "Carl McIntire: Creeds, Councils, and Controversies," paper presented at the Annual Meeting of the

American Theological Library Association, Kansas City, 18 June 2004; C. Allyn Russell, *Voices of American Fundamentalism: Seven Biographical Studies* (Philadelphia, PA: The Westminster Press, 1976), 155–6.

12 Carl McIntire, *The Rise of the Tyrant: Controlled Economy and Private Enterprise* (Collingswood, NJ: Christian Beacon Press, 1945), xiii.

13 C. McIntire to T.T. Shields, 3 November 1949, TTSP, box 6, 1949, f. "McIntire."

14 "A Fateful Visit," *CACCN*, 1 March 1978, 2; Fred Schwarz, "What Shall the End Be? According to Joseph Stalin," *Gospel Witness and Protestant Advocate* 29, 13 (1950): 7. From CMP, f. "Dr. (etc.).": F. Schwarz to C. McIntire, 4 and 13 April 1950; C. McIntire, letter of introduction for US customs, 18 December 1950.

15 Stanley Allen, "Australian Party to Begin American Tour," *Christian Beacon* 15, 13 (1950): 1; C. McIntire to F. Schwarz, 27 March 1950, CMP, f. "Dr. (etc.)."

16 From *Christian Beacon* 15, 17 (1950): "Australian Visitors Welcomed in Hawaii," 1–7; "John C. Bennett of New York's Union Seminary Speaks in Hawaii on Communism: Dr. Schwarz of Australia Sends Answer to Newspaper," 2.

17 David Bebbington, "Evangelicalism in Modern Britain and America: A Comparison," in *Amazing Grace: Evangelicalism in Australia, Britain, Canada and the United States*, ed. George Rawlyk and Mark Noll (Montreal and Kingston: McGill-Queen's University Press, 1994), 211.

18 Sydney Ahlstrom, *A Religious History of the American People* (New Haven: Yale University Press, 2004), 952.

19 Ibid., 952–3; Dean Kelley, *Why Conservative Churches Are Growing: A Study in Sociology of Religion* (New York: Harper and Row, 1972), 17–36.

20 Richard Fried, *Nightmare in Red: The McCarthy Era in Perspective* (New York: Oxford University Press, 1996), 87; Eugene Wittkopf and James McCormick, "The Cold War Consensus: Did it Exist?," *Polity* 22, 4 (1990): 630–1; M.J. Heale, *American Anticommunism: Combating the Enemy Within, 1830–1970* (Baltimore: Johns Hopkins University Press, 1990), 155.

21 Schwarz, *Beating,* 43; Jack Murray, "Newsrelease: The Beloved Physician. Dr. F. C. Schwarz, B.A., B. Sc., M.B., B.S.," TTSP, box 7, 1950, f. "S"; Stanley Allen, qtd. in Carl McIntire, "Schwarz-Inglis Party Praised in California," *Christian Beacon* 15, 19 (1950): 1, 8; S. Allen to *Beacon*, 14 June 1950, CMP, f. "Dr. (etc.)." After the first lectures in California, ACCC's California executive Stanley Allen wrote to the *Christian Beacon*

team in Collingswood that ACCC pastors should feel absolutely comfortable in booking the Australian in their churches.

22 From *Christian Beacon* 15, 23 (1950): "He 'Foresaw' Korean War: Australian Visiting Here Crusades against Reds," *Grand Rapids Press*, 7 July 1950, 2, 7 (repub.); "Australian Asks Church to Clean Itself of Reds," *Courier-Post* (PA), 13 July 1950, 2, 7 (repub.); Carl McIntire, "Australia Team Receives Splendid News Coverage in U.S. Papers," 2; "Time Favors the Russians, Australia Authority Says: Schwarz Calls Outlook Gloomy," *Pittsburgh Press*, 20 July 1950, 15–16 (repub.).

23 "Australian Tells Reds' Progress 'Down Under,'" A13; "Schwarz Party in West Starts Towards Midwest," *Christian Beacon* 15, 18 (1950): 1; "Favorite Radio Programs over Three Major Networks," *Oelwein Daily Register* (IA), 12 July 1947, 9.

24 F. Schwarz to T.T. Shields, 22 July 1950, TTSP, box 7, 1950, f. "S." Jarvis Church had 1,258 seats but could accommodate up to 1,700 people.

25 Schwarz, "What Shall the End Be?," 9.

26 T.T. Shields, "Dr. F. C. Schwarz and Mrs. Clarice Inglis in Jarvis Street Last Weekend," *Gospel Witness and Protestant Advocate* 29, 13 (1950): 1.

27 "Communism Debate at U.M. Is Cancelled: Lane Requests Byrd to Withdraw Permission for Auditorium," clipping, 8 August 1950, 18, 28, CMP, f. "Dr. (etc.)."

28 C. McIntire, "Income," "Expenses," in CMP, f. "Dr. (etc.)." In particular, he could save on accommodation expenses by having a reliable pool of contacts. The account of his expenses that Schwarz submitted to McIntire at the end of his trip indicates very little cost for lodging, which means that the Australians were welcomed in several towns by private citizens.

29 T.T. Shields to C. McIntire, 8 June 1950 and T.T. Shields to C. McIntire, 15 July 1950, TTSP, box 7, 1950, f. "McIntire"; Schwarz, *Beating*, 44; Transcript (Schwarz's speech), ACCC-ICCC, RG 01, box 466 B, file 8, f. 1; Markku Ruotsila, "Transnational Fundamentalist Anti-Communism: The International Council of Christian Churches," in *Transnational Anti-Communism and the Cold War: Agents, Activities, and Networks*, ed. Luc Van Dongen, Stéphanie Roulin, and Giles Scott-Smith (New York: Palgrave Macmillan, 2014), 237; D. Hedegard, *De Oecumenische Beweging en de Bijbel* (Amsterdam: Internationale Raad van Christelijke Kerken), 1959, 197–201. In the wake of the Geneva event, ICCC-affiliated denominations increased from sixty-one to eighty-three.

30 Fred Schwarz, "Blood Transfusion," *Gospel Witness and Protestant Advocate* 29, 20 (1950): 1–4; Schwarz, "Communist Blueprint for the Conquest of Canada," 5–9; From TTSP, box 7, 1950, f. "S": F. Schwarz to

T.T. Shields, 16 September 1950; T.T. Shields to F. Schwarz, 18 September 1950. See also F. Schwarz to C. Oakley, 20 September 1950, CMP, f. "Dr. (etc.)."

31 From CMP, f. "Dr. (etc.)": F. Schwarz to C. McIntire, 12 December 1950; C. McIntire to F. Schwarz, 15 December 1950.

32 Charles Sheldon, "Public Opinions and High Courts: Communist Party Cases in Four Constitutional Systems," *Western Political Quarterly* 20, 2 (1967): 353–4; From CMP, f. "Dr. (etc.)": C. McIntire to F. Schwarz, 2 March 1951; F. Schwarz to C. McIntire, 27 March 1951; C. McIntire to F. Schwarz, 2 April 1951; F. Schwarz to C. McIntire, 5 May 1951; F. Schwarz to C. McIntire, 2 October 1951.

33 C. McIntire, "A Letter from Dr. McIntire," *Gospel Witness and Protestant Advocate*, 30, 35 (1951): 11. From *Christian Beacon*: "Manila Conference Gives Testimony to the Faith: Christian Manifesto Adopted," 16, 44 (1951): 8; "Australian Lay Leader to Give Message at Manila," 16, 35 (1951): 1–8; "Communism Defined by Schwarz at Manila," 16, 44 (1951): 5, 8.

34 From CMP, f. "Dr. (etc.)": C. McIntire to L. Brown and C. Bunzel, 11 March 1952; C. McIntire to F. Schwarz, 22 April 1952; D. Corwith to C. McIntire, 24 April 1952; A. Slaght to R. Trato, 29 April 1952 and 13 May 1952; F. Schwarz to R. Trato, 22 May 1952.

35 From CMP f., "Dr. (etc.)": R. Trato to M. Wenger, 27 March 1952; R. Trato to F. Stroud, 27 March 1952; R. Trato to M. Wenger, 21 April 1952; F. Schwarz to R. Trato, 28 April 1952.

36 J. Allen to F. Schwarz, 30 October 1952, pub. in Schwarz, *Beating*, 204; R. Shuler, "To Whom It May Concern," 28 April 1952, CMP, f. "Dr. (etc.)"; Darren Dochuk, "Evangelicalism Becomes Southern, Politics Becomes Evangelical: From FDR to Ronald Reagan," in *Religion and American Politics: From the Colonial Period to the Present*, ed. Mark Noll and Luke Harlow, 301–7 (New York: Oxford University Press, 2007); "Missionary Student to Be Heard at Rally," *LAT*, 4 October 1953, 35; *2 Anticommunist Meetings, Sunday May 1 and 8, 2:00 pm*, CACC pamphlet, 1964; James Gregory, *American Exodus: The Dust Bowl Migration and Okie Culture in California* (New York: Oxford University Press, 1991), xiv–xv; Michael Engh, "'A Multiplicity and Diversity of Faiths': Religion's Impact on Los Angeles and the Urban West," *Western History Association* 28, 4 (1987): 487. When Schwarz arrived in California in the early 1950s, natives from the South, especially its western portion (Oklahomans, Arkansans, Texans), formed about 13 percent of California's population.

37 From CMP, f. "Dr. (etc.)": F. Golden, "To Whom It May Concern," 25 June 1952.

38 From CMP, f. "Dr. (etc.)": C. McIntire to L. Brown and C. Bunzel, 11 March 1952; C. McIntire to F. Schwarz, 22 April 1952; "Golden Opportunity," *Rotarian*, July 1948, 53A.

39 Erling Jorstad, *The Politics of Doomsday: Fundamentalists of the Far Right* (Nashville: Abingdon Press, 1970), 70. From CMP, f. "Dr. (etc.)": F. Schwarz to C. McIntire, 13 April 1950 and 12 December 1950. See also ICCC 3rd Plenary Congress, 03-12-1954, PJSP, RG 01, box 409, file 39, 1-2. From CMP, f. "Dr. (etc.)": C. McIntire to F. Schwarz, 20 December 1982; F. Schwarz to C. McIntire, 13 May 1983; and "Fred C. Schwarz – Christian Anti-Communism Crusade." However, nothing suggests that Schwarz ever disapproved of the ACCC's theological conservatism.

40 Markku Ruotsila, *Fighting Fundamentalist: Carl McIntire and the Politicization of American Fundamentalism* (Oxford Scholarship Online, 2016), 105, DOI: 10.1093/acprof:oso/9780199372997.001.0001; C. McIntire, "Letter from Dr. McIntire," 11; "A Christian Manifesto on World Communism and the Christian Church," *Christian Beacon*, 16, 44 (1951): 1, 8.

41 Ruotsila, *Fighting Fundamentalist*, 138; W. Strube to W. Judd, 18 May 1956, WHJP, box 224, f. 4, copyright Stanford University; "Summer School," *CACCN*, July–August 1956, 3. Other names included Dr Vance Webster, G.A. Weniger, Reverend Bond Bowman, Dr Charles C.T. Walberg, and Reverend Gordon Peterson. In 1956, World Vision printed one of Schwarz's pamphlets: Fred Schwarz, *Communism: Diagnosis and Treatment; The Story of Brainwashing – How Communism Conquers the Minds of Men* (Los Angeles: World Vision, Inc., 1956).

42 "Rally to Hear Red Foe," *LAT*, 31 May 1952, 5; F. Schwarz to R. Trato, 22 May 1952, CMP, f. "Dr. (etc.)."

43 From AKP, box 155, f. "Fred C. Schwarz, –1955": A. Kohlberg to F. Schwarz, 9 June, F. Schwarz to A. Kohlberg, 17 June 1952; F. Schwarz to A. Kohlberg, 23 June 1952; A. Kohlberg to F. Schwarz, 24 June 1952; A. Kohlberg, "Invitation," 29 August 1952. Ad, "America in Peril: Hear Dr. Fred Schwarz from Sydney, Pennsylvania," *Lebanon Daily News*, 21 June 1952, 3.

44 Joseph Keeley, *The China Lobby Man: The Story of Alfred Kohlberg* (New Rochelle, NY: Arlington House, 1969), 10–11. W. Judd to S. Bride, 19 March 1971, WHJP, box 59, f. 1, copyright Stanford University; A. Kohlberg to R. de Toledano, 16 March 1955, RDTP, box 19, f. "K."

Kohlberg openly used the expression "China Lobby," while Walter Judd claimed such a lobby never really existed.

45 Information on Kohlberg from Keeley, *China Lobby Man.*

46 Michael Miles, *The Odyssey of the American Right* (New York: Oxford University Press, 1980), 71–118; Jack Samson, *The Flying Tiger: The True Story of General Claire Chennault and the U.S. 14th Air Force in China* (Guilford, CT: Lyons Press, 1987), 302–3; Thomas Bodenheimer and Robert Gould, *Rollback: Right-Wing Power in U.S. Foreign Policy* (Boston: South End Press, 1989), 68; Matthew Frye Jacobson, *Barbarian Virtues: The United States Encounters Foreign Peoples at Home and Abroad, 1876–1917* (New York: Hill and Wang, 2000), 3–9, 111–47. Though more generally connected to the GOP's eastern wing, Luce had a special interest in China.

47 "Portions of speech by Dr. Fred C. Schwarz of Sydney, Australia at New York, Sept. 5, 1952," AKP, box 155, f. "Fred C. Schwarz, –1955."

48 From AKP: F. Mason to A. Kohlberg, 9 September 1952; A. Kohlberg to F. Schwarz, 8 October 1952; 15 October 1952; 20 January 1953; 23 January 1953, box 155, f. "Fred C. Schwarz, –1955"; A. Kohlberg to Madame Chiang Kai-shek, 23 January 1953; Madame Chiang Kai-shek to A. Kohlberg, 8 February 1953, box 28, f. "Generalissimo and Madame Chiang Kai-shek."

49 Fred Schwarz, *The Heart, Mind and Soul of Communism* (Waterloo, IA: Evangelize America Program, 1952), 9.

50 "Evangelist Comes Sunday," *Hammond Times*, 8 September 1933, 14; "Bible Conference to Be Held Here during Week-End," *Times Record of Troy*, 4 February 1944, 10; "Crusader against Reds: Fred Charles Schwarz," *NYT*, 29 June1962, 5.

51 "NEWSFRONT- Convention," *Foursquare Magazine* 26, 2 (1953): 17; James Colbert, "Director of Missions," CACCN, September 1958, 5; "The Life and Death of Rev. James Colbert, 1914–1996," CACCN, 1 July 1996, 1–2; Larry Eskridge, "'One Way': Billy Graham, the Jesus Generation, and the Idea of an Evangelical Youth Culture," *Church History* 67, 1 (1998): 85.

52 "To Incorporate Anti-Red Group," *Waterloo Daily Courier*, 27 May 1953, 30; CACC incorporation form, 05/12/1953, *IRS-EOD*."

53 Schwarz, *Beating*, 106; Fred Schwarz, "Will the Kremlin Conquer America By 1973?," *Freedom Forum Presentation* (Searcy, AR: National Education Program, 1959), 24.

54 Ad, "Kiwanis Club of Long Beach," *Independent Press-Telegram*, 8 April 1953, C9. From *Long Beach Press-Telegram*: "What Ministers Say in Long

Beach Pulpits," 11 April 1953, A5; "Australian to Speak at Breakfast Forum," 14 April 1953, B2; "Communism Like Cancer in Workings, C of C Told," 15 April 1953, B2; "Red Conquest Blueprint to Be Discussed," 18 April 1953, A5.

55 Lisa McGirr, *Suburban Warriors: The Origins of the New American Right* (Princeton, NJ: Princeton University Press, 2001), 29–30. See also Manuel Perez and Richard Watson, "The Long Beach Story: A California City Repositions Itself," in *International Urban Planning Settings: Lessons of Success*, ed. Jack Williams and Richard Watson (Oxford: Elsevier Science Ltd., 2001), 132–3.

56 Schwarz, *Beating*, 109; W. Pietsch, "Dear Fellowship Member," CACCN, November 1954, 1.

57 Schwarz, *Beating*, 110, 481; Brad Altman, "Dr. Schwarz's Bank Roll Has Red Lining," *Independent Press-Telegram*, 12 September 1976, B1; Fred Schwarz, Christmas card, 2 December 1968; John Schwarz qtd. in CACCN, 15 April 1990, 7.

58 From AKP: A. Kohlberg to F. Schwarz, 28 June 1955; F. Schwarz to A. Kohlberg, 4 March 1959; A. Kohlberg to F. Schwarz, 18 March 1959; editorial, CACCN, April 1955, 3; W. Strube to W. Judd, 18 May 1956, WHJP, box 224, f. 4, copyright Stanford University. From CACCN: W. Pietsch, "W.E. Pietsch, D.D., President," July–August 1956, 9; "Dr. Pietsch Goes 'Home,'" March 1959, 3.

CHAPTER THREE

1 E. Doorn to H. Philbrick, 30 March 1971, HPP, box 66, f. 6. Janet Greene, phone interview with author, 29 July 2009.

2 First issues of the newsletter were unfortunately unrecoverable. Apart from the newsletter, four booklets were published by Sackett's printing.

3 Arnold Forster and Benjamin Epstein, *Danger on the Right: The Attitudes, Personnel and Influence of the Radical Right and Extreme Conservatives* (New York: Random House, 1964), 54.

4 From AKP: box 155, f. "Fred C. Schwarz, –1955": F. Schwarz to A. Kohlberg, 8 June 1954; F. Schwarz to A. Kohlberg, 25 June 1955. Editorial, CACCN, 1 September 1956; Charles Grutzner, "Reports of Dr. Schwarz's Anti-Communist Crusade Show $1,273,492," *NYT*, 24 June 1962, 9; Schwarz qtd. in Brooks Walker, *The Christian Fright Peddlers: The Radical Right and the Churches* (New York: Doubleday, 1964), 59.

5 From JHPPP: box 3, f. "Christian Anti-Communism Crusade – Dr. Fred C. Schwarz, 1959": F. Schwarz to J.H. Pew, 28 March 1959; J. Colbert to

J.H. Pew, 10 April 1959; "Itinerary for Dr. Schwarz"; J.H. Pew to E. Daly, 3 April 1959; E. Daly to J.H. Pew, 13 April 1959; R. Johnson to J.H. Pew, 13 April 1959. "Anti-Communism School," CACCN, October 1957, 6. See, for instance, Colbert's work before the crusader's visit to Philadelphia in spring 1959. Colbert contacted oil millionaire J. Howard Pew, whom Schwarz had once met, to help fill the touring schedule. The Australian quickly found himself booked in local churches and civic clubs. Pew also managed to book him for a talk before students of Villanova University.

6 From CACCN: editorial, February 1955, 2; editorial, November 1955, 2, 5. L. Judd to F. Schwarz, 11 October 1955, pub. in Fred Schwarz, *Beating the Unbeatable Foe: One Man's Victory over Communism, Leviathan, and the Last Enemy* (Washington, DC: Regnery, 1996), 207. Also see editorial, CACCN, April 1955, 1; editorial, CACCN, April–May. 1956, 1–2.

7 CACC incorporation form, 05/12/1953, IRS-EOD; W. Pietsch, "Dear Friend and Member," CACCN, January 1955, 2; M. Liebman to F. Schwarz, 4 April 1962, MLieb, box B11, f. "Fred Schwarz."

8 Ellen Schrecker, *The Age of McCarthy: A Brief History with Documents*, 2nd ed. (New York: Palgrave Macmillan, 2002), 16. From FBIF: W.C. Sullivan to A.H. Belmont, 3 March 1961, f. "Sullivan, William C.-5"; C.D. Brennan to W.C. Sullivan, 5 July 1967, f. "CACC-Fred Schwarz HQ-7." Schwarz qtd. in *Firing Line* with William F. Buckley Jr, Program 062 "The Decline of Anti-Communism (1967)," Hoover Institution Archives.

9 Richard Gid Powers, *Not without Honor: The History of American Anticommunism* (New York: The Free Press, 1995), 93; "Talk Isn't Cheap," *Tuscaloosa News*, 20 August 1967, 3; Herbert Packer, *Ex-Communist Witnesses: Four Studies in Fact Finding* (Stanford, CA: Stanford University Press, 1962), 124; Ellen Schrecker, *Many Are the Crimes: McCarthyism in America* (Princeton, NJ: Princeton University Press, 1998), 44–5. From NYT: John Finney, "Senators Oppose White House Curb: Balk at Limiting Authority to Make Commitments," 2 November 1967, 9; Ad, "Benjamin Mandel" (Obituary), 10 August 1973, 34.

10 Schrecker, *Many Are the Crimes*, 196–200.

11 Fred Schwarz, qtd. in Paul Harvey, "Slow Boat to Siberia by 1973 Unless We Shake Off Torpor," *ChiTri*, 8 January 1958 (n.p.; clipping sent to author); Walter Lippman, "Prohibitive Cost of Nuclear War Forces Acceptance of Coexistence," *St Petersburg Times*, 22 December 1954, 6.

12 Erling Jorstad, *The Politics of Doomsday: Fundamentalists of the Far Right* (Nashville: Abingdon Press, 1970), 64; Billy Graham, *Christianity*

vs. Communism (Minneapolis: The Billy Graham Evangelistic Association, 1951), 2; Andrew Hartman, *Education and the Cold War: The Battle for the American School* (New York: Palgrave Macmillan, 2008), 2, 71–2; William Conklin, "Eisenhower Says Farewell to Columbia University: Eisenhower Takes Leave on Columbia," NYT, 17 January 1953, 1; W. Kern to F. Schwarz, 22 October 1955, pub. in CACCN, January–February 1956, 2–3.

13 Numan Bartley, *The Rise of Massive Resistance: Race and Politics in the South during the 1950's* (Baton Rouge: Louisiana State University Press, 1997), 187–8; Jeff Woods, *Black Struggle Red Scare: Segregation and Anti-Communism in the South, 1948–1968* (Baton Rouge: Louisiana University Press, 2004), 98–9; Donald Critchlow, *The Conservative Ascendancy: How the GOP Right Made Political History* (Cambridge: Harvard University Press, 2007), 37.

14 "Urge Schools to Teach Reds," *Gettysburg Times*, 8 October 1956, 9; Powers, *Not without Honor*, 477; "Education News: Varied Activity on the Campus and in the Classrooms," NYT, 4 May 1958, E9; Jonathan Zimmermann, *Whose America? Culture Wars in the Public Schools* (Cambridge: Harvard University Press, 2002), 105–6; Joint Committee of the National Education Association and the American Legion, *Teaching about Communism: Guidelines for Junior and Senior High School Teachers* (Indianapolis: American Legion, National Emblem Sales, 1962).

15 Richard Steele, "Schwarz – Historian, Not Red-Baiter," *Minnesota Tribune*, 4 April 1956, 17.

16 From *Bridgeport Post*: "To Address Exchange," 12 June 1958, 31; "Baptists Will Hear Dr. Fred Schwarz," 14 June 1958, 6; "Group Sends Thanks for Lecture Coverage," 20 November 1958, 24; "Correction," 21 November 1958, 14. From CACCN: editorial, November 1954, http://www.schwarzreport.org; editorial, January 1955; editorial, April 1955, 1, 3; editorial, May 1955, 1–8; editorial, January 1956, 1–6; "Fred C. Schwarz, MD," September 1956, 1; "Winona Lake School," September 1956, 1; "Dr. Schwarz's Itinerary," May 1957, 2–3; Untitled, October 1957, http://www.schwarzreport.org/uploads/schwarz-report-pdf/schwarz-report-1957-10.pdf; "Future Schedule," September 1958, 6; "Future Schedule," November 1958, 6; "Schedule," March 1959, 6; "Universities and Colleges," April 1959, 5; "Schedule," April 1959, 6; "Dr. Schwarz's Schedule," September 1959, 4; "Dr. Schwarz's Schedule," January 1960, 4; "Dr. Schwarz's Schedule," March 1960, 4; "Dr. Schwarz's Schedule," April 1960, 6; L.L. Smith to Fred Schwarz, 11 June 1956, pub. Sept. 1956, 2; Marshall S. Roth to Fred Schwarz, 10 August 1956, pub.

September 1956, 2; John S. Wimbish to Fred Schwarz, 24 September 1956, pub. January–February 1957, 2; Merlin G. Smith to Fred Schwarz, 1 October 1956, pub. January–February 1957, 2. From *ChiTri*: "Charges Reds Mark 33 1/3% in U.S. for Death," 20 November 1953, 2; Ad, "Religious Services," 21 November 1953; Ad, "The Moody Church," 2 January 1954, 6; "D.A.R. Groups to Hear Talk on Communism," 21 February N1; Richard Philbrick, "Notes on News in Religion," 14 July 1956, 16; Ad., "Hear Dr. Fred Schwarz," 10 October 1958, E7; "Notes on the News in Religion," 14 March 1956, 10. From *Eugene Register-Guard*: "Club Speaker Tells of Commie Threat," 6 July 1955, A8; "Communism Talks Set," 19 October 1957, 3. From *Fresno Bee*: "Australian Doctor Will Speak in City on Communism," 30 May 1953, A4; "City News in Brief," 31 January 1956, B6; "Activities in Brief," 16 March 1957, A4; "Australian Plans Three Talks in Fresno Churches Tomorrow," 23 March 1957, A5; "Will Address Optimists," 24 March 1957, A15; Ad., "8-Solid Hours Radio Marathon by Dr. Thos. Wyatt," 28 March 1958, 11-A. From *LAT*: Ad, "South Gate Municipal Auditorium: Guest Speaker – Dr. Fred Schwartz, in Person," 29 August 1953, A3; "Missionary Student to Be Heard at Rally," 4 October 1953, 35; Ad, "Untitled," 15 January 1956, A12; Ad, "Untitled," 18 January 1956, 10; "Psychiatrist Will Address Harbor Club," 26 March 1957, A2; "Missionary to Speak," 8 December 1957, 37; "Leader of Anti-Red Crusade Will Speak," 26 July 1958, 10; Ad., "Eagle Rock Baptist Church," 6 September 1958, 10; Hedda Hopper, "Chimp Will Monkey around Disney," 21 April 1959, C7; "Psychiatrist to Discuss Communism," 15 May 1960, WS3. From *Lodi News-Sentinel*: "Psychiatrist to Speak on Reds," 18 December 1954, 6; "Dr. Schwarz to Talk in Lodi," 24 December 1954, 8; "Dr. Schwarz Will Talk Here Tonight on Communism," 28 December 1954, 8. From *Long Beach Independent*: "Anti-Communist Slated for Two Lectures Sunday," 22 August 1953, 4; "Luncheon and Service Clubs," 6 September 1953, A9; "Australia Speaker Says U.S. Sole Bar to Red World Rule," 10 September 1953, 26; "Dr. Schwarz Speaks," 12 September 1953, 6; "Youth to Be Spotlighted at Services," 26 September 1953, 4; "Brain Washing Topic at Forum," 29 November 1953; "Anti-Red Crusader to Talk to L.B. Clergy," 7 December 1953, 2; "Officers to Be Installed in L.B. Churches Sunday," 9 January 1954, 4; "What Ministers Say in Long Beach Pulpits," 1 January 1955, 4; "What Ministers Say in Long Beach Pulpits," 8 January 1955, A4; Ad, "First Brethren Church," 36 March 1955, 7; "Director of YFC Speaking in Texas," 2 April 1955, 6; "Foe of Reds Will Speak Here Sunday," 13 June 1959, A6; "Foe of Reds Will Speak at Assembly,"

24 October 1959, B5; "Anti-Red Crusader to Speak," 27 February 1960, A7. From *Long Beach Press-Telegram*: Ad, "North Long Beach Nazarene: Techniques of Brainwashing: Dr. Schwarz of Sydney, Australia," 22 August 1953, A5; "What Ministers Say in Long Beach Pulpits," 22 August 1953, A4; Ad, "Revival Center Church – Dr. Fred Schwarz of Australia, Outstanding Authority on Communism," 2 September 1953, A4; "What Minister Say in Long Beach Pulpits," 26 September 1953, A4; "Forum Told of Red Plot," 3 December 1953, B15; "Nazareres to Hear Expert on Commies," 8 January 1955, A5; Ad, "First Assembly of God," 12 November 1955, A5. From *NYT*: "Psychiatrist Preaches: Calls Communism 'Disease of Mind, Body and Spirit,'" 1 October 1956, 22; "Australian Warns on [sic] Reds in Hawaii," 17 April 1957, 17; Ad., "Religious Services," 16 May 1959, 15; Ad., "Manhattan Baptist," 16 April 1960, 21. From *Oakland Tribune*: "Aussie Doctor to Speak Here on Red Menace," 12 March 1954, E31; "Expert on Communism to Speak on Wednesday," 14 March 1954, A59; "Rotarians Hear World Lecturer," 15 March 1954, E5; "What's Up in the Bay Area," 16 March 1954, E9; "What's Up in the Bay Area," 24 March 1954, E37; "Men's Club Will Hear Expert on Communism," 6 June 1954, A62; Ad, "Foothill Blvd Baptist Church," 25 September 1954; Ad, "Praise the Lord, for the Lord Is Good," 30 April 1955, 9; "Her Children Rise Up and Call Her Blessed," 7 May 1955, 9; "Let the People Praise Thee, O God," 14 May 1955, 11; "Youth Rally to Hear Doctor," 20 January 1956, D23; "Lutheran Speaker," 27 November 1958, 44; Ad, "Melrose Baptist," 29 November 1958, B9; "Australian Will Deliver Anti-Red Talks," 5 August 1959, S3; "NGDW Will Open 74th Convention," 15 June 1960, 30. From *Oshkosh Daily Northwestern*: "Communism to Be Topic of Lecturer," 30 September 1958, 3; "Australian to Give Talk on Communism," 9 October 1958, 5; "Speaker Says Complacency Hurt Nation," 16 October 1958, 33. From *Pasadena Star-News*: "Doctor to Tell Communism Ills," 21 July 1958, 1; Ad, "Speaks Tomorrow," 22 July 1958, 24; Ad, "Immanuel Baptist Church," 20 July 1957, 4. From *San Mateo Times*: Times County News Service, "Anti-Communist Speaker for S.S.F.," 3 March 1954, 5; "CIC Agents Alumni to Hear Dr. Fred Schwarz," 25 April 1955, 4. From *Spokesman Review*: "Books, Comics Red Weapons," 4 February 1956, 5; "Schwarz Warns of Red Hordes: Speaker Says Commies Plan to Conquer U.S.," 6 February 1956, 5. From *WashP*: "Anti-Communist Rally to Hear Dr. Schwarz," 9 June 1956, 26; Kenneth Dole, "News of the Churches," 12 April 1958, C9; "Returned Missionaries Will Report on Work," 3 May 1958, A13; Mary McNair, "Town Topics: 'Labor' Prevents A Party

Quorum," 27 April 1959, B3. From *Waterloo Daily Courier*: "Anti-Red to Speak Monday at Churches," 19 August 1953, 5; "Dr. Schwarz of Australia to Be Guest Speaker," 14 August 1953, 9; "Dr. Schwarz Is Guest Speaker Sunday Evening," 13 September 1953, 13; "Clubs This Week," 20 September 1953, 22; "Anti-Communist Group Sponsors Two Speakers," 28 March 1954, 1; Courier Special Service, "Anti-Red Rally Sunday at Junior High Auditorium," 1 April 1954, 19; Ad, "Christian Anti-Communism Rally," 4 April 1956. From *Van Nuys News*: "Dr. Fred Schwarz to Discuss Communism at Church Here," 4 December 1958, 18D; "Dr. Fred Schwarz to Be Speaker at Church in Valley," 5 February 1959, 12B; "Dr. Fred Schwarz Will Speak Here," 11 June 1959, 27D. From others: "Communism Lectures at Foursquare Church," *Cedar Rapids Gazette*, 4 June 1953, 3; "Rule of World by Reds Seen: Chances Are 100-1," *Milwaukee Journal*, 29 December 1953; "Anti-Communist Speaks at Baptist," *Daily Review*, 6 March 1954, 9; Ad, "Tonite Hear Dr. Fred Schwartz of Sydney, Australia," *Muscatine Journal and Daily News-Tribune* (IA), 30 April 1954; "Attended the Farm Bureau Institute," *Fergus Falls Daily Journal* (MN), 20 January 1955, 9; Connie Gee, "Auxiliary Warns Music Publishers," *Miami Daily News*, 12 October 1955, C2; "World Authority on Communism to Lecture Here," *Albuquerque Journal*, 6 January 1956, 25; "Schedule Set for Australian," *Spokane Daily Chronicle*, 28 January 1956, 5; "Bethel Conservative Church," *Walla Walla Union Bulletin* (WA), 24 August 1956, 2; "Should Teach Red Creed in Schools," *El Paso Herald-Post*, 6 May 1958, 10; "Truth Urged to Combat Red Threat," *Hartford Courant*, 27 October 1958, 4; "Dr. Fred Schwarz to Preach Friday," *Norwalk Hour* (CT), 6 November 1958, 7; Jay Hanlon, "1,500 Told Magnitude of Red Menace," *Manchester Union Leader* (NH), 8 April 1959, 1, 7; "Expert on Communism Faith Baptist Speaker," *Chester Times* (PA), 2 May 1959, 5; "Anti Communist Doctor Will Be Local Speaker," *Modesto Bee and News Herald* (CA), 11 June 1959, B1; "Dr. Fred Schwarz to Speak at Open Meeting on Monday," *Independent Record*, 9 December 1959, 4; "Crusade Speaker to Appear Here," *Odessa American* (TX), 15 February 1960, 23; "Speaks Here," *Hobbs Daily News-Sun* (NM), 10 May 1960, 1. From Schwarz, *Beating*: R. Reynolds to F. Schwarz, 2 September 1953, pub. at 205, indicating lectures for Christian Far Eastern Broadcasting; J. Pillion to F. Schwarz, 4 June 1957, pub. at 137–9, 156; Fred Schwarz, *Address on the Disease of Communism, Given to the Texas Legislature by Dr. Fred Schwarz* (Houston: CACC, 1959); "Communists Are Madmen Speaker Tells Students," *Hartford Courant*, 7 April 1959, 32. From AKP:

F. Schwarz to A. Kohlberg, n.d., box 155, f. "Fred C. Schwarz, 1956–1957"; Fred Schwarz to A. Kohlberg, 2 February 1958; 25 March 1958, and 2 April 1960, box 155, f. "Fred C. Schwarz, 1958–1960." From JHPPP: F. Schwarz to J.H. Pew, 29 March 1959, box 3, f. "Christian Anti-Communism Crusade – Dr. Fred C. Schwarz, 1959"; "Itinerary for Dr. Fred C. Schwarz," box 3, f. "Christian Anti-Communism Crusade – Dr. Fred C. Schwarz, 1959." "Bob Siegrist and the News, WLS–WGEZ," PSC, Communism series, box 1, f. 2, box 9, f. 16. Schwarz's use of unscheduled touring makes it impossible to know with exactitude the number of lectures he delivered between 1953 and 1960. Naturally, what remains possible is to identify those engagements that were explicitly described, mentioned, or acknowledged in the available documentation: newspapers, advertising, newsletters, private correspondence, and reports from other organizations' respective archives. Sources referring to lectures not used elsewhere are listed above.

17 "Researchers Find Iowans Not Too Optimistic about Avoiding War," *Milford Mail*, 3 January 1963, 8; Clyde Wilcox, "Popular Backing for the Old Christian Right: Explaining Support for the Christian Anti-Communism Crusade," *Journal of Social History* 21, 1 (1987): 122; Clyde Wilcox, "Sources of Support for the Old Right: A Comparison of the John Birch Society and the Christian Anti-Communism Crusade," *Social Science History* 12, 4 (1988): 435. The Northeast is the region in which the CACC's visibility remained significantly lower than elsewhere, though the same could be said of most grassroots conservative groups that emerged during the 1950s.

18 Clyde Wilcox, *God's Warriors: The Christian Right in Twentieth-Century America* (Baltimore: Johns Hopkins University Press, 1992), 72–3. Sporadic addresses were also made before various audiences: professional associations, private businesses' staffs, chambers of commerce, governmental institutions, and political meetings.

19 Robert Horwitz, *America's Right: Anti-establishment Conservatism from Goldwater to the Tea Party* (Cambridge: Polity Press, 2013), 73–7; Schwarz, *Beating*, 107–8. By Schwarz's own account, most churches were "evangelical and small."

20 Editorial, CACCN, November 1954, http://www.schwarzreport.org; Dobson qtd. in David Noebel, "Frederick Charles Schwarz, January 15, 1913 – January 24, 2009," *Schwarz Report* 49, 3, (2009): 2.

21 Walker, *Christian Fright Peddlers*, 61–2; Robert Wuthnow, *The Restructuring of American Religion* (Princeton, NJ: Princeton University Press, 1987), 52.

22 Schwarz, *Beating*, 310; David Danzig, "The Radical Right and the Rise of the Fundamentalist Minority," *Commentary*, April 1962, 292; John Wicklein, "Christian Group Aims at Politics: Conservative Protestants to Work at Precinct Level," *NYT*, 1 February 1962, 23; Darren Dochuk, *From Bible Belt to Sunbelt: Plain-Folk Religion, Grassroots Politics, and the Rise of Evangelical Conservatism* (New York: W.W. Norton and Company, 2011), 230; Jonathan Herzog, *The Spiritual-Industrial Complex: America's Religious Battle against Communism in the Early Cold War* (New York: Oxford University Press, 2011), 207.

23 "The Churches and Communism," CACCN, 1 February 1969, 6. These findings are consistent with those of a survey the Crusade conducted in a later period of its history (1969). In a questionnaire, Schwarz inquired about the denominational affiliation of the churches that received his newsletter. Out of 308 replies, 111, or 36 percent, were Baptist, with the rest of the sample being constituted by a wide array of different traditions. This reflected an age of rising ecumenism.

24 Wuthnow, *Restructuring of American Religion*, 182–3.

25 From CACCN: C. Julian to R. Azzara, 27 April 1955, pub. May 1955, 2–3; H. Culver to R. Azzara, 27 April 1955, G.L. Rose to R. Azzara, 30 April 1955, pub., 3–5; pub in "Semantic Sabotage," November 1958, 1–3.

26 Charles Wright and Herbert Hyman, "Voluntary Associations and American Adults: Evidence from National Sample Surveys," *American Sociological Review* 23, 3 (1958): 287. From CMP, f. "Dr. F.C. Schwarz – Alvalea – 142 Concord, North Strathfield, Australia" (hereafter "Dr. (etc.)"): F. O'Brien to F. Schwarz, 8 May 1952; F. Schwarz to C. McIntire, 12 June 1952; editorial, CACCN, February 1955, 2.

27 Schrecker, *Many Are the Crimes*, 61–2; William Pencak, *For God and Country: The American Legion, 1919–1941* (Boston: Northeastern University Press, 1989), 265–76.

28 M.J. Heale, *American Anticommunism: Combating the Enemy Within, 1830–1970* (Baltimore: Johns Hopkins University Press, 1990), 172–3; "Wisconsin Town Goes Red for Day," *Eugene Register-Guard*, 1 May 1950, 1.

29 "Reds Would Slay Throngs, Visitor Tells Legionnaires," *Albuquerque Journal*, 21 November 1952, 28. From CACCN: editorial, February 1955, 2; editorial, May 1955, 6; editorial, May 1955, 2. Pencak, *For God and Country*, 296. On still another occasion, he flew to Austin after receiving a proposal to address the American Legion Auxiliary, a legion offshoot for women founded in 1944.

30 Jeffrey Charles, *Service Clubs in American Society: Rotary, Kiwanis, and Lions* (Champaign: University of Illinois Press, 1993), 4; Alan Raucher,

"Dime Store Chains: The Making of Organization Men, 1880–1940," *Business History Review* 65, 1 (1991): 149–55.

31 Maurice McQuillen, "N.H. Vets Endorse Schwarz Rally," *Manchester Union Leader* (NH), 31 March 1959, 10.

32 Schwarz, *Beating*, 108; editorial, CACCN, January 1955, 4. J. Colbert to J. Howard Pew, 10 April 1959, JHPPP, box 3, f. "Christian Anti-Communism Crusade – Dr. Fred C. Schwarz, 1959"; F. Schwarz, "The University Front," CACCN, June – July 1959, 2. From May 1953 to May 1956, thirty-five of forty-seven of Schwarz's identified engagements in educational settings took place in high schools.

33 From CACCN: editorial, January 1955, 4; editorial, May 1955, 3; "Hawaii," April–May 1956, 2.

34 "CPI Inflation Calculator," http://www.in2013dollars.com/us/inflation/1955?amount=2800; "U.S. Inflation Calculator," https://www.usinflationcalculator.com/; fundraising letter attached to the May 1955 CACCN; Form 990A: Return of Organization Exempt from Income Tax, box 364, f. "CACC General and Financial"; Schwarz, *Beating*, 108; Notes on CACC Tax Exemption Application, 10/17/62, GRIR, box 364, f. "CACC General and Financial," 3; M. Rogovin to H. Swartz, 27 October 1965, WSP, File Internal Revenue Service Study of Ideological Organizations, 31 December 1965, f. "G," 2.

35 "Asia Sees Korea as Victory for China, Says Red Expert," *Long Beach Independent*, 3 September 1953, 6; Helen Wood Birnie, *The Story of Helen and Kate: A Story in Contrast* (Tulsa. OK: Christian Crusade, 1965), 4–5, 7.

36 *Information on Helen Wood Birnie, Ex-Communist Party Leader of Long Beach, California*, flyer, GRIR, box 37, f. "Birnie, Helen Wood"; Helen Wood Birnie, *The Broken Wall* (Waterloo, IA: CACC, 1955); "AntiCommunist Group Sponsors Two Speakers," *Waterloo Courier*, 28 March 1954, 13; "A Political Profile," *People's Voice*, 2 May 2 1960, 21; Ed Christianson to Mr Patterson, 18 November 1959, GRIR, box 37, f. "Birnie, Helen Wood"; Alan McIntosh, "Asiatics Being Trained as Executioners of U.S. Boys and Girls, Says Anti-Red Fighter," *Minnesota Farms Bureau News* 34, 7 (1955): 1; "Ex-Communist Slurs Farmers and Boy Scouts," clipping, 1955, GRIR, box 37, f. "Birnie, Helen Wood." Committee on Un-American Activities, *Investigation of Communist Activities in the Chicago Area – Part 2*, US House of Representatives, Washington, United States Government Printing Office, 83rd Congress, 2nd session, 16 March 1954, 4231-4243. In 1954 she testified before HUAC (see last reference above).

37 Editorial, *CACCN*, April 1955, 1; "Farm Union Attacks Farm Bureau as Sponsor of Anti-Communism Crusade: Here Is Typical List," clipping (1955), GRIR, box 37, f. "Birnie, Helen Wood," 3; Michael W. Flamm, "The National Farmers' Union and the Evolution of Agrarian Liberalism, 1937–1946," *Agricultural History* 6, 3 (1994): 54–5; William Pratt, "The Farmers Union, McCarthyism and the Demise of the Agrarian Left," *Historian* 58 (1996): 336–41; "Jammed Hall in New Ulm's Answer When Anti-Communism Crusader Is Refused Hearing in Bernadotte," *Minnesota Farms Bureau News* 34, 7 (1955): 10; editorial, *CACCN*, April 1955, 1.

38 Notes on CACC Tax Exemption Application, 10/17/62, GRIR, box 364, f. "CACC General and Financial"; W. Pietsch to A. Kohlberg, 9 July 1955; W. Pietsch to A. Kohlberg, 9 July, AKP, box 33, f. "CACC"; H. Swartz to CACC, 18 September 1956, IRS-EOD.

39 Ad, "Christian Anti-Communism Rally: Local Churches – Youth for Christ – Citizens Cooperating," *Waterloo Daily Courier*, 2 April 1956, 9; J. Milton to R. Owings, 19 January 1960, GRIR, box 37, f. "Birnie, Helen Wood."

40 H. Swartz to CACC, 18 September 1956, IRS-EOD, 2.

41 Irving Leibowitz, "Dr. Schwarz Takes the Stand," *Indianapolis Times*, 2 October 1963, 17 (regarding Schwarz's unwillingness to give up his Australian citizenship).

42 Fred Schwarz, "How Long 'Til Joseph Stalin Is President of the United States?," *Freedom Club News*, October 1952, 3–7.

43 F. Schwarz to A. Kohlberg, 8 June 1954, AKP, box 155, F. "Fred C. Schwarz, –1955"; *CACCN*, editorial, November 1954, 2; Peter Coleman, "Crusader Fred Schwarz," *Sydney Bulletin*, 7 April 1962, 18; G.K. Smith to W.F. Buckley, 4 June 1962, GKSP, box 55, f. "B." Fundamentalist leader Gerald K. Smith was angry over Schwarz's use of the word "anarchist" in reference to McCarthy.

44 Passages of this letter were published in *CACCN*, May 1955, 7.

45 A. Satyanarayana, "Rise and Growth of the Left Movement in Andhra, 1934–1939," *Social Scientist* 14, 1 (1986): 31–4; William Taubman, *Khrushchev: The Man and His Era* (New York: W.W. Norton and Company, 2003), 354; "Fred Schwarz," *CACCN*, January–February 1956, 1; A.A. Fursenko and Timothy J. Naftali, *Khrushchev's Cold War: The Inside Story of an American Adversary* (New York: W.W. Norton and Company, 2006), 81. Ironically, Khrushchev was himself unimpressed by Indian Communists: he found their propaganda to be quite unappealing and believed that their hard-line approach towards the Nehru government risked undermining emergent Indo-Soviet relationships.

46 From CACCN: "Indian Work," July–August 1956, 3; "Our Indian Project," September 1956, 1.

47 Schwarz, *Beating*, 132; editorial, CACCN, January–February 1957, 1.

48 Schwarz, *Beating*, 133. From CACCN: editorial, May 1957, 1; "Positive Programs," October 1964, 8; editorial, January–February 1957, 1; "What a Family?," 4 September 1967, 7; D. Rao to F. Schwarz, pub. 1 October 1969, 8.

49 Michael Bergunder, *The South Indian Pentecostal Movement in the Twentieth Century* (Grand Rapids, MI: William B. Eerdmans, 2008), 15. From CACCN: D. Pushpanadham to F. Schwarz, pub., September 1958, 5; "Andhra," November 1958, 5.

50 "Anti-Communism School Scores – More Old-Fashioned Patriotism Needed, Declares Dr. Schwarz, Noted Red Fighter," *Van Nuys News*, 1 December 1961, 2A; Report, 10/15/1965, GRIR, box 363, f. "CACC Notes on Individual Meetings." "It would appear," he lamented in 1961, "that in some areas of our present society, old-fashioned patriotism has gone the way of cigar store Indians and unconditional guarantees."

51 "The New China Policy," CACCN, 15 November 1971, 1; Schwarz, caption from CACCN, April 1964, 3. Markku Ruotsila, *The Origins of Christian Anti-Internationalism: Conservative Evangelicals and the League of Nations* (Washington, DC: Georgetown University Press, 2008), 2; Robert Morris, "The Spirit of Socrates," CACCN, July 1964, 6–8; "Unconscious Surrender to Kremlin Cited," LAE, 30 August 1961, 5. Schwarz's collaborator W. Cleon Skousen once called UN veto clauses a "legal monstrosity." In 1971, apprehensive of the potential "catastrophe" that would be the inclusion of Red China in the UN, he wrote that one of the options left to the United States would be simply to withdraw from the organization.

52 A. Kohlberg to G. Benson, 13 August 1952; J. Bales to A. Kohlberg, 24 February 1954, AKP, box 76, f. "Harding College"; Mark Sherwin, *The Extremists* (New York: St Martin's, 1963), 83; Richard Thomas Hughes, *Reviving the Ancient Faith: The Story of Churches of Christ in America* (Grand Rapids, MI: W.B. Eerdmans, 1996), 156; William Hixson, *Search for the American Right Wing: An Analysis of the Social Science Record, 1955–1987* (Princeton, NJ: Princeton University Press, 1992), 69; L. Edward Hicks, *"Sometimes in the Wrong, but Never in Doubt": George S. Benson and the Education of the New Religious Right* (Knoxville: University of Tennessee Press, 1994), 57. In the 1950s, Benson was on the list of pro-Nationalist China supporters Kohlberg fed with information.

53 George Benson, "Looking Ahead," *Evening Independent* (OH), 31 October 1951, 15; editorial, CACCN, May 1955, 6; George Benson, "The Truth about Communism," *National Program Letter*, June 1955, 1; Dochuk, *From Bible Belt to Sunbelt*, 230; Benson editorials from *Evening Independent* (OH): 25 May 1955, 35; 9 June 1955, 24; 15 June 1955, 22. Benson reproduced extracts from Schwarz's first speech in the NEP newsletter and devoted three issues of his syndicated column to the crusader.

54 Fred Schwarz, *Communism: America's Mortal Enemy* (Long Beach: CACC, 1956), 1–29. First use of the encirclement axiom was in March 1966: "A Visit to the University of California at Berkeley," CACCN, 4 April 1966, 2. Rick Perlstein, *Before the Storm: Barry Goldwater and the Unmaking of the American Consensus* (New York: Hill and Wang, 2001), 115. As Rick Perlstein describes, coexistence-era communists were increasingly perceived as wishing to slip "the noose over a people through steady and subtle propaganda, colonizing their very minds."

55 Schwarz, *Communism: America's Mortal Enemy*, 28; Fred Schwarz, *Insurance against Communism* (Houston, TX: CACC, 1960), 16–17; editorial, CACCN, October 1957, 2.

56 From AKP: box 155, f. "Fred C. Schwarz, 1956–1957": A. Kohlberg to G. Benson, 31 July 1956; A. Kohlberg to F. Schwarz, 31 July 1956.

CHAPTER FOUR

1 Phyllis Schlafly, private invitation, 13 March 1956, "Midwestern Residential Seminar on the Techniques of Communism – June 1-2-3 1956, Père Marquette Lodge, to be Conducted by: Louis Budenz," PSC, Communism series, box 3, f. 1. In 1954, Budenz published a textbook, *The Techniques of Communism*, and in 1955 he initiated an educational program on communism in a few Eastern cities.

2 Fred Schwarz, "Five Basic Steps to Communism," *American Mercury* 84, 397 (1957): 143–6; Fred Schwarz, "Communism – Murder Made Moral," *American Mercury* 84, 399 (1957): 92–6; Robert Muccigrosso, "American Mercury, 1924–1980," in *The Conservative Press in Twentieth-Century America*, ed. Ronald Lora and William Longton, 243–6 (Westport, CT: Greenwood, 1999).

3 F. Schlafly to F. Schwarz, 18 May 1957, pub. in Fred Schwarz, *Beating the Unbeatable Foe: One Man's Victory over Communism, Leviathan, and the Last Enemy* (Washington, DC: Regnery, 1996), 162–3.

4 Fred Schwarz, "Will the Kremlin Conquer America by 1973?," in *Freedom Forum Presentation* (Searcy, AR: National Education Program, 1959), 25.

5 Ibid., 25–6; Fred Schwarz, *Beating*, 165; Peter Coleman, "Crusader Fred Schwarz," *Sydney Bulletin*, 7 April 1962, 18.

6 David O'Connor, "The Cardinal Mindszenty Foundation: American Catholic Anti-Communism and Its Limits," *American Communist History* 5, 1 (2006): 40.

7 Robert Horwitz, *America's Right: Anti-establishment Conservatism from Goldwater to the Tea Party* (Cambridge: Polity Press, 2013), 97; Patrick Allitt, *Catholic Intellectuals and Conservative Politics in America, 1950–1985* (Ithaca, NY: Cornell University Press, 1995), 60; Jonathan Herzog, *The Spiritual-Industrial Complex: America's Religious Battle against Communism in the Early Cold War* (New York: Oxford University Press, 2011), 67–8.

8 Matthew Sutton, *American Apocalypse: A History of Modern Evangelicalism* (Cambridge: Belknap Press of Harvard University Press, 2014), 311–12; Phyllis Schlafly, interview with author, 8 December 2008 and 23 January 2009. In 1951–52, the project of President Truman – who believed in interfaith collaboration against communism – to establish a permanent US embassy in the Vatican was dropped after drawing the ire of Protestant churches and leaders.

9 Donald Critchlow, *Phyllis Schlafly and Grassroots Conservatism: A Woman's Crusade* (Princeton, NJ: Princeton University Press, 2006), 67; P. Schlafly to F. Schwarz, attached CACCN, July 1998, PRAA, f. "Schwarz, Fred C."

10 Editorial, CACCN, June 1957, 1; "Hawaii Studied," *Amarillo Globe-Times*, 21 May 1957, 20. From *NYT*: "Australian Warns on [sic] Reds in Hawaii," 17 April 1957, 17; "Hawaii Discounts Reds as a Menace – Inquiry Shows Absence of Publications and Fronts – Dock Unions 'Strongholds,'" 16 March 1959, 15. Schwarz saw the ILWU's power in the fact that it endorsed eighteen of thirty members of the Hawaii House.

11 James Daniel, "Russian Blueprint for World Conquest Open to Public View," *El Paso Herald-Post*, 27 February 1953, 21; David Aikman, *Billy Graham: His Life and Influence* (Nashville: Thomas Nelson Publishers-Business, 2007), 80; Steven Miller, *Billy Graham and the Rise of the Republican South* (Philadelphia: University of Pennsylvania Press), 2009, 72–3. Bushby was later Liberal state senator and member of the CACC international board. Schwarz's Detroit trip had probably been designed only to meet Graham. Soon, he was back to the Southwest.

12 Schwarz, *Beating*, 154–5; Miller, *Billy Graham*, 72–3.

13 William Barnard, *Dixiecrats and Democrats: Alabama Politics, 1942–1950* (Tuscaloosa: University of Alabama Press, 1984), 56–7; Carl Grafton and

Anne Permaloff, *Big Mules and Branchheads: James E. Folsom and Political Power in Alabama* (Athens: University of Georgia Press, 2008), 79; Fred Schwarz, *The Communist Interpretation of Peace* (Waterloo, IA: CACC, 1953), 8.

14 Eleanor Nance, "Guest of State Congressmen: Australian Doctor's Talk Stirs Capital to Red Threat," *Tuscaloosa News*, 3 March 1953, 7, 16; Schwarz, *Beating*, 155–6; Notes on CACC Tax Exemption Application, 10/17/62, GRIR, box 364, f. "CACC General and Financial," 2. From *CACCN*: editorial, May 1955, 5–6; "Legislatures," April–May, 1956, 6.

15 "Report – Washington," *CACCN*, July–August 1956, 2–3; E.T. Wooldridge to F. Schwarz, 11 June 1956, pub. in Schwarz, *Beating*, 199.

16 Lee Edwards, *Walter H. Judd: Missionary for Freedom – The Life and Times of Walter Judd* (New York: Paragon House, 1990), 34; William Buckley, "Red China Lobby Tries New Track," *Washington Evening Star*, 9 October 1967, taken from WHJP, box 29, f. "William F. Buckley"; Robert Herzstein, *Henry R. Luce, Time, and the American Crusade in Asia* (New York: Cambridge University Press, 2005), 63–70. Letters between Judd and Benson, Hoover, Chiang, and Rhee available at Hoover Institution, copyright Stanford University. On links between Judd, Kohlberg, and Luce, see Herzstein above.

17 W. Judd to W. Strube, 27 June 1956, WHJP, box 224, f. 4, copyright Stanford University; Hedda Hopper, "Chimp Will Moskey around For Disney," *LAT*, 21 April 1959, C7; Marie McNair, " 'Labor' Prevent a Party Quorum," *WashP*, 27 April 1959, B3; Schwarz, *Beating*, 350. Unfortunately for Schwarz, at the last moment, more than ten senators dropped out from the 1959 luncheon.

18 "Hawaii Statehood Opposed as Red Group," *NYT*, 15 February 1955, 14; J. Pillion to F. Schwarz, 4 June 1957, pub. in *CACCN*, June 1957, 2; Schwarz, *Beating*, 157.

19 "3,000,000 Aliens Seen Illegally in U.S.," *Christian Science Monitor*, 20 August 1951, 7; Schwarz, "Will the Kremlin Conquer America by 1973?," 28. Arens served as director of the Senate Immigration Subcommittee (1947–52), the Senate Internal Security Subcommittee (1952–56), and HUAC (1956–60).

20 Committee on Un-American Activities, *International Communism (The Communist Mind)*, Staff Consultation, US House of Representatives, Unites States Government Printing Office, 85th Congress, 1st session, 29 May 1957, doc. 92964, repub. by CACC.

21 Schwarz, "Will the Kremlin Conquer America By 1973?," 16; Vladislav Zubok, "'To Hell with Yalta!' – Stalin Opts for a New Status Quo," *Cold War International History Project Bulletin* 6–7 (1995–96): 24, 29.

22 Daniel Bell, "The Dispossessed (1962)," in *The Radical Right: The American Right, Expanded and Updated*, ed. Daniel Bell (New York: Doubleday, 1962), 10–12; Richard Mitchell, *Dancing at Armageddon: Survivalism and Chaos in Modern Times* (Chicago: University of Chicago Press, 2002), 141–3; George Michael, "Blueprint and Fantasies: A Review and Analysis of Extremist Fiction," *Studies in Conflict and Terrorism* 33, 2 (2010): 150–5.

23 Schwarz, *Beating*, 159, 168; Schwarz, "Will the Kremlin Conquer America by 1973?," 16; Oleg Hoeffding, "The Soviet Seven Year Plan," *Rand Corporation Bulletin*, 2 February 1959, P1607, 2.

24 "Red Plan World Domination in '73," *Progress-Index*, 16 June 1957, 2; editorial, CACCN, June 1957, 1; Schwarz, *Beating*, 181–2.

25 From AKP: box 155, f. "Fred C. Schwarz, 1956–1957": F. Schwarz to A. Kohlberg, 25 July 1957; A. Kohlberg to F. Schwarz, 10 September 1957; F. Schwarz to A. Kohlberg, 14 September 1957. The State Department received a copy on 9 September 1957.

26 Untitled, CACCN, March 1958, 2; W. Strube to J. Cowles, 3 February 1958, WHJP, box 225, f. 1, copyright Stanford University. The text appeared notably in the *Chicago Tribune*, the *Dallas Morning News*, the *Detroit Free Press*, the *Los Angeles Examiner*, the *New York Herald Tribune*, the *Pittsburgh Post Gazette*, and the *Wall Street Journal*. Beasley had begun his journalistic career in 1907. James O'Neill, former national commander of the American Legion, encouraged him to show Bradley the document.

27 "Harry L. Bradley, 80, Dies: Industrialist in Milwaukee," *NYT*, 24 July 1965, 21; "Allen-Bradley Co. Elects Arloe W. Paul President," *Wall Street Journal*, 30 June 1967, 16; Michael Zitz, "Back in Broadcasting: Bob Siegrist Return to Roots – Behind a Microphone," *Free Lance-Star*, 4 February 1998, 1, 4; Harry Bradley, *Harry L. Bradley: An American Story* (Milwaukee, WI: Rockwell Automation, 2003), 8–58, 105–7; John Gurda, *The Bradley Legacy: Lynde and Harry Bradley, Their Company, and Their Foundation* (Milwaukee, WI: The Lynde and Harry Bradley Foundation, 1992), 103; John Micklethwait and Adrian Wooldridge, *The Right Nation: Conservative Power in America* (New York: Penguin Press, 2004), 79; A. Kohlberg to F. Schwarz, 24 February 1958, AKP, box 155, f. "Fred C. Schwarz, 1958–1960."

28 W. Strube to J. Cowles, 3 February 1958, WHJP, box 225, f. 1, copyright Stanford University; Untitled, *CACCN*, March 1958, 1–5; F. Schwarz to A. Kohlberg, 17 February 1958, AKP, box 155, F. "Fred C. Schwarz, 1958–1960."

29 A. Kohlberg to F. Schwarz, 24 February 1958, AKP, box 155, f. "Fred C. Schwarz, 1958–1960." From *CACCN*: Untitled, March 1958, 2; "The Allen-Bradley Company," May 1958, 2.

30 Schwarz, *Beating*, 158; "Bob Siegrist and the News, WLS–WGEZ," 23 April 1958; "Bob Siegrist and the News, WLS–WGEZ," 25 April 1958, PSC, Communism series, box 9, f. 16; "Operation Testimony," *CACCN*, September 1958, 1, 5; George Megow to Marcia Gordon, 18 December 1962, GRIR, box. 3, f. "Allen-Bradley Co." Bradley began supporting institutions such as Benson's Harding College and the Freedom Education Center of Valley Forge. He strongly backed Goldwater in 1964.

31 From *CACCN*: "Operation Testimony," June–July 1959, 1–4; "Operation Testimony," May 1958, 1–4. See also "Dr. Fred Schwarz to Speak at Open Meeting Monday," *Helens Independent Record*, 9 December 1959, 4; F. Schwarz to A. Kohlberg, 4 June 1958, AKP, box 155, f. "Fred C. Schwarz, 1958–1960"; W. Strube to J. Cowles, 3 February 1958, WHJP, box 225, f. 1, copyright Stanford University; editorial, "An Outrage," *Criterion* 4, 14 (1964): 4. Robert Smith of the *Minneapolis Star* criticized Schwarz for having no real strategy, drawing an angry letter from Strube. In 1964, a veterans association wanted to distribute it in Indianapolis schools, but the local Catholic Archdiocese opposed it.

32 From *CACCN*: "South America," March 1959, 5: Wang Shih-Ping to F. Schwarz, 5 September 1958, pub. September 1958, 6; "Formosa," July 1958, 4; "'Round the World in Twenty-Eight Days," January 1960, 1–2. See also CACC income and expenses (fiscal years 1958 and 1959), GRIR, box 364, f. "CACC General and Financial."

33 Denny Roy, *Taiwan: A Political History* (Ithaca, NY: Cornell University Press, 2003), 60–77; Steven Phillips, *Between Assimilation and Independence: The Taiwanese Encounter Nationalist China, 1945–1950* (Stanford, CA: Stanford University Press, 2003), 40–114; Murray Rubinstein, *The Protestant Community on Modern Taiwan: Mission, Seminary, and Church* (Armonk, NY: M.E. Sharpe, 1991), 33, 35; "Asian Clerics Tell Tortures," *Milwaukee Journal*, 1 June 1959, 9. The Chinese CACC's secretary, Wang Shih-Ping, travelled to Washington in 1959 and testified before HUAC.

34 Min Ye, "China, 1946–1949," in *Civil Wars of the World: Major Conflicts since World War II*, ed. Karl DeRouen and Uk Heo (Santa Barbara, CA:

ABC-CLIO, Inc., 2007), 251–2; "Formosa," *CACCN*, July 1958, 2–4. Schwarz met "the Foreign Minister, the Minister of Education, the Speaker of the Provincial Assembly, and the Provincial Governor of Taiwan."

35 Willie Morris, "Houston's Superpatriots," *Harper's*, October 1962, 52.

36 George Benson, "Looking Ahead," *Evening Independent* (OH), 18 June 1958, 17; "Featured Film to Be Shown at Rally Saturday," *Sheboygan Press* (WI), 3 October 1958, 4; "County Youth for Christ Rally Scheduled Saturday," *News-Palladium* (MI), 18 December 1958, 2; "Dr. Schwarz, Foe of Reds, Speaks Sun," *Long Beach Independent*, 7 February 1959, A8; caption, "Dr. Schwarz Exposes Red Plot," *Manchester Union Leader* (NH), 8 April 1959, 1; F. Schwarz to H. Philbrick, 11 April 1960, HPP, box 65, f. 10. In April 1960, a patriotic group presented Schwarz with the "Freedom Book Award." Past recipients included Ed Hunter, Budenz, and Philbrick.

37 Schwarz, *Beating*, 98, 168; Norman Nygaard, *Walter Knott: Twentieth-Century Pioneer* (Grand Rapids, MI: Zondervan Publishing House, 1965), 67–85; Richard Harris, *Early Amusement Parks in Orange County* (Charleston, SC: Arcadia, 2008), 17.

38 Allan J. Lichtman, *White Protestant Nation: The Rise of the American Conservative Movement* (New York: Grove, 2008), 74–5; J.H. Pew to W.M. Hart, 18 November 1959, JHPPP, box 64, f. "H." Schwarz might have been recommended to Kershner by James Fifield, a CACC advisory council member whose group, Spiritual Mobilization, also benefited from Pew's protection. Pew called Robert Welch a friend (see 18 November 1959 letter).

39 Fred Schwarz, *Beating*, 191; Richard Pierard, "J. Howard Pew: Reaction's Inconspicuous Patron," *Reformed Journal*, March 1972, 6; John Ingham, "Pew Family," *Biographical Dictionary of American Business Leaders, N-U* (Westport, CT: Greenwood, 1983), 1081–4. From JHPPP: R.E. Ells to J.H. Pew, 4 November 1958, box 3, f. "Christian Anti-Communism Crusade – Dr. Fred C. Schwarz, 1959"; F. Schwarz to J.H. Pew, 31 October 1958; box 187, f. "The Glenmede Trust Co. 1961–1965." The Pew family fortune came from its oil empire Sun Oil.

40 Robert Grimm, "Pew Family," in *Notable American Philanthropists: Biographies of Giving and Volunteering*, ed. Robert Grimm (Westport, CT: Greenwood, 2002), 248.

41 Schwarz, *Beating*, 192; Russell Adams, Jr, *King C. Gillette: The Man and His Wonderful Shaving Device* (Boston: Little, Brown and Co., 1978), 230.

42 Richard Match, "Things You Never Knew about Your Fountain Pen," *Popular Science* 169, 3 (1956): 167; "Patrick Frawley, Jr. Named Top

Executive at Eversharp," *Wall Street Journal*, 14 January 1958, 10; "Frawley Chief at Technicolor," *LAT*, 7 February 1961, C11; Frawley qtd. in Wallace Turner, "Coast Millionaire Upset by Publicity and Politics," *NYT*, 14 July 1970, B47; Leo Rennert, "Murphy's Right-Wing Boss Spends Millions to Sway Public," *Modesto Bee* (CA), 13 March 1970, A8; Report, 12/10/65, GRIR, box 138, f. "Frawley, Patrick J.," 3; Peter Gall, "Battling Blade Man: Patrick Frawley Mixes Ideology and Business with Few Ill Effects," 24 June 1966, 1, 15; William Turner, *Power on the Right* (Berkeley, CA: Ramparts Press, 1971), 172.

43 Schwarz, *Beating*, 190, 194. From HPP: A. Bell to H. Philbrick, 20 October 1960; H. Philbrick to A. Bell, 25 October 1960, box 55, f. 11; A. Bell to H. Philbrick, 11 November 1960; R. Farmer to H. Philbrick, 11 November 1960, box 3, f. 8. The Philadelphia school chairperson was Glenmede Trust president Allyn Bell, who hired an advertising agency.

44 From GRIR: box 364, f. "CACC General and Financial," notes on Pew Freedom Trust Tax Exemption Application, 8/7/63; box 268, f. "Pew Memorial Trust"; notification document on the Crusade's finances for 1958–59 fiscal years. See also Schwarz, *Beating*, 192; Deborah Huntington and Ruth Kaplan, "Whose Gold Is behind the Altar? Corporate Ties to Evangelicals," *Contemporary Marxism* 4 (1981–82): 84; GRIR, Form 990A: Return of Organization Exempt from Income Tax, box 364, f. "CACC General and Financial," 18–19. The CACC also received shares of Sun Oil from Pew's sister Mabel.

45 Frawley qtd. in Phil Kerby, "Anti-Red Crusade Seen Expanding across U.S.," *WashP*, 7 November 1961, A4. From GRIR: Report, 12/10/65, box 138, f. "Frawley, Patrick J.," 2; Form 990A: Return of Organization Exempt from Income Tax, box 364, f. "CACC General and Financial," 18–19. The tax returns available for the year 1966 indicate that the CACC received a $5,000 grant from Technicolor, approved by Ettinger, and another one of the same amount from Schick, bringing the total to $10,000.

46 Kim Phillips-Fein, *Invisible Hands: The Businessmen's Crusade against the New Deal* (New York: Norton and Norton, 2009), 2–25.

47 Gail Hollander, *Raising Cane in the 'Glades: The Global Sugar Trade and the Transformation of Florida* (Chicago: Chicago University Press, 2008), 76, 121–2. From *NYT*: "Ask Congress End of Union Boycotts," 13 March 1946, 41; Arthur Krock, "In the Nation: Immunity of Labor from Anti-Trust Laws," 8 December, 1955, 36; "2 Companies Lose on War Tax Issue," 23 January 1957, 56.

48 Mark Pinsky, *The Gospel According to Disney: Faith, Trust, and Pixie Dust* (Louisville, KY: Westminster John Knox Press, 2004), 235–6.

CHAPTER FIVE

1 D. McNeil, notes from CACC Phoenix school, DMP, box 1, f. 1-3, 1.
2 From BMGP: Mr and Mrs Tomlinson to B. Goldwater, 3 March 1961, MF 34, box 011_REEL023_0003, pdf. 452; Mrs L. Speers to B. Goldwater, 6 March 1961, MF 38, box 011_REEL031_0007, pdf. 467; W.V. Ellsworth to B. Goldwater, 30 March 1961, MF 38, box 011_REEL031_0004, pdf. 177; R. Brown to B. Goldwater, 14 March 1961, MF 38, B. 011_REEL031_0007, pdf. 467; Barry Goldwater, "Good News from the Home Front," *LAT*, 14 March 1961, B4.
3 "St. Louis School a Success," *CACCN*, May 1958, 2.
4 F. Schwarz to A. Kohlberg, 4 June 1958, AKP, box 155, f. "Fred C. Schwarz, 1958–1960"; Fred Schwarz, *Beating the Unbeatable Foe: One Man's Victory over Communism, Leviathan, and the Last Enemy* (Washington, DC: Regnery, 1996), 163; "St. Louis School a Success," 2; "Attention Citizens of St. Louis," *Counterattack* 12, 9 (1958): 1; Peter Meyer Filardo, "Notes and Documents: The Counterattack Research Files on American Communism, Tamiment Institute Library, New York University," *Labor History* 39, 2 (1998): 189–91.
5 Schwarz, *Beating*, 160; "Anti-Communism School," *CACCN*, January 1958, 7; Fred Schwarz, "Will the Kremlin Conquer America by 1973?," in *Freedom Forum Presentation* (Searcy, AR: National Education Program, 1959), 21.
6 Kenneth Woodward, "What Qualifications for a Crusader? Fred Schwarz on Communism," *Catholic Reporter*, 1 February 1963, 16.
7 "Schwarzism," *Kingsport News* (TN), 1 April 1958, 4; "St. Louis School a Success," 1; William Henderson to Fred Schwarz, pub. in *Beating*, 163.
8 From *CACCN*: "St. Louis School a Success," 2; "Schools for Anti-Communists," March 1959, 3. Branch leaders are Joost Sluis (San Francisco) and Charles Sarvis (Seattle).
9 Sydney Ahlstrom, *A Religious History of the American People* (New Haven, CT: Yale University Press, 2004), 957; Deborah Hart Strober and Gerald S. Strober, *A Day in the Life of Billy Graham: Living the Message* (Garden City, NY: Square One Publishers, 2003), 9–10; F. Schwarz to M. Liebman, 13 February 1963, *MLieb*, box 11, f. "Fred Schwarz." Much of the promotional strategy of each school hinged on displaying the names and professional backgrounds of endorsers.

10 Schwarz, *Beating*, 166; "Banquet," CACCN, July 1958, 2.

11 J. Sucke to H. Philbrick, 8 December 1959, HPP, box 3, f. 5. From CACCN: Harold Handley, "Proclamation for Indiana's Anti-Communism Week," 27 September, 4 October 1959, repub. November 1959, 2; "The Indianapolis Anti-Communism School," 2. The idea came from Austin, where, a few weeks before, a group of prominent anticommunists held an event for which Mayor Tom Miller was solicited to proclaim an "Anti-Communism Week."

12 Dennis Lythgoe, "Political Feud in Salt Lake City: J. Bracken Lee and the Firing of W. Cleon Skousen," *Utah Historical Quarterly* 42, 4 (1974): 316; J.B. Lee to E. Laine, 8 August 1960, FBIF, f. "Skousen, W. Cleon – 1"; W. Cleon Skousen, *The Naked Communist* (Salt Lake City, UT: Ensign Publishing Company, 1962), 166–8.

13 D. Jensen to H. Philbrick, HPP, box 175, f. 5. Philbrick was also a good friend of Richard Arens. R. Arens to H. Philbrick, 8 November 1957, HPP, box 2, f. 7. D. McNeil, notes from CACC Phoenix school, DMP, box. 1, f. 1–3, 4. Philbrick had never met the Australian before but he had read Schwarz's *The Heart, Mind and Soul of Communism.*

14 From HPP: G. Greene to H. Philbrick, 1 November 1957, box 2, f. 2; H. Philbrick to W. Strube, 7 November 1960, box 185, f. 1; H. Philbrick to I.B. Bell, 15 February 1960, box 243, f. 5; H. Philbrick to Mrs C.F. Ashley, 12 October 1959, box 3, f. 3.

15 "Milwaukee Anti-Communism Schools [sic]," CACCN, March 1960, 4; CACC leaflet, "Faculty and Class Sessions," *School for Anti-Communists, Milwaukee, February 9th-13th*; James Peale Jr, "Review: A Guide to Anti-Communist Action," *Military Library* 23, 4 (1959–60): 223; "Author Warns of Danger of Brain-Washing," *Milwaukee Sentinel*, 11 February 1960, pt. 2, 3; "Results of the Schools," CACCN, December 1960, 2; T.H. Masters qtd. in Fred Schwarz, "Milwaukee Anti-Communism Schools [sic]," 4; Edmund Lambeth, "Anti-Communist Groups Here Show Big Increase in Activity," *Milwaukee Journal*, 4 June 1961, 1.

16 "The Lord Hath Done Great Things For Us," CACCN, April–May 1961, 1. The figure was $603,591, excluding a fund for foreign expenditures ($28,046). Total expenditures: 1958 ($87,355), 1959 ($202,980), and 1960 ($288,022).

17 William Strube, *What Is the Christian Anti-Communism Crusade?* (Houston: CACC, 1961), 4–7. CACC income and expenses (fiscal years 1962 and 1963), GRIR, box 364, f. "CACC General and Financial."

18 E. Richard Barnes, "First Newsletter from the San Diego Branch," CACCN–*San Diego*, May 1961, 1; D. McNeil, notes from CACC Phoenix school,

DMP, box 1, f. 1-3; CACC income and expenses (fiscal years 1958, 1959, and 1960), GRIR, box 364, f. "CACC General and Financial." Branch leaders were: a trained reverend (Long Beach), a restaurant-owning businessman (Seattle), a retired military officer (San Diego), a civil engineer (Indianapolis), a generalist MD (Ypsilanti), an orthopaedic surgeon (San Francisco), and an insurance broker (Houston).

19 "Projects," CACCN, May 1959, 5. From *Lewiston Morning Tribune* (ID): "Anti-Red Movie Booked," 1 February 1961, 6; "Speaker Scheduled," 4 February 1961, 6. From WHJP, box 226, f. 4, copyright Stanford University, J. Elmer to R. Hightower, 2 April 1962; R. Hightower to W. Judd, 7 May 1962. *The Greater New Orleans School of Anti-Communism*, CACC pamphlet; "Warns of Crime Crimp to Army," *Milwaukee Sentinel*, 12 February 1960, 2; E. Richard Barnes, "Source Material – Study Group Helped," CACCN–*San Diego*, August 1961, 1.

20 "Floyd Edward Burroughs, 85, Headed Civil Engineering Firm," *Indianapolis Star*, 1 February 2000, D6; Schwarz, *Beating*, 185–6.

21 "George Westcott, M.D., 1903–1981," CACCN, November 1981, 2. A CACC brochure distributed by Westcott in Haiti was titled *If Communism Comes to Haiti – What?*.

22 Joost Sluis, "On the China Card," edited and authored by Joost Sluis, MS, MD, accessible in the WCNP, CB180, box 19, series 9, f. 293, 3; "Eight Modestans Are Given Navy Releases," *Modesto Bee* (CA), 29 May 1946, 3; Joost Sluis, "An Alumnus and the Christian Anti-Communism Crusade," independent reprint from the *Harvard Medical Alumni Bulletin*, Spring 1963, 1–2. From *Oakland Tribune*: "Understand Marxism, Rotary Told – Physician Warns Ignorance of Reds Aids Their Drive," 21 October 1959, E17; "Lions Club Speaker," 13 January 1960, D30.

23 Saul Friedman, "Crusade against Commies Grows: Scores Spreading Message to Other Cities and States," *Houston Chronicle*, 5 July 1961, 1–14; Strube qtd. in Willie Morris, "Houston's Superpatriots," *Harper's*, October 1962, 52; William Strube, "W. P. Strube, President, Mid American Life Insurance Company, Houston, Texas," CACCN, September 1956, 2.

24 Friedman, "Crusade against Commies Grows," 14; "Houston Office Opened," CACCN, May 1958, 4; Morris, "Houston's Superpatriots," 52; Philip Horton, "Revivalism on the Far Right," *Reporter*, 20 July 1961, 26; CACC income and expenses (fiscal years 1962 and 1963), GRIR, box 364, f. "CACC General and Financial"; "Strube, William B., Jr. – 6-6-62", GRIR, box 305, f. "Strube, William P. – General, 1959–1973"; "Hitchcock Men to Hear Strube on Communism," *Galveston Daily News*, 8 November 1959, 3B ; W. Strube to H. Philbrick, 6 September 1960, HPP, box 185, f.

3; Morris, "Houston's Superpatriots," 52. In 1962, IRS audit documents show that Strube was earning $6,000 annually as the Crusade's vice-president.

25 Friedman, "Crusade against Commies Grows," 1–14. From HPP, box 185, f. 3: Strube postcard to Philbrick; W. Strube to H. Philbrick, 2 February 1961. Strube qtd. in Morris, "Houston's Superpatriots," 52; "Study Circles," CACCN, June 1960, 3; Friedman, "Crusade against Commies Grows," 14.

26 William Strube, *Double Talk*, Houston, CACC, 1961; William Strube, *Two Faces of Communism* (Houston: CACC, 1961); Hamilton Stone, "Speech given by Hamilton Stone – San Diego Grocers Association," WCSP, binder: Hollywood's Answer to Communism, 16 October 1961. Before the San Diego Grocers Association, advertising mogul Hamilton Stone urged grocers to sell this material in super-markets.

27 From HPP, box 185, f. 3: W. Strube to H. Philbrick, 15 December 1959; W. Strube to H. Philbrick, 2 February 1961. Bill Strube, "Houston Anti-Communism School Attended by over 1000," CACCN, June 1960, 3; Fred Schwarz, "Address by Dr. Fred Schwarz," *Texas House Journal*, Proceedings, Texas House, 56th Legislature, regular session, Austin, Texas, 25 March 1959, 1064–9; F. Schwarz to J.H. Pew, 28 March 1959, JHPPP, box 3, f. "Christian Anti-Communism Crusade – Dr. Fred C. Schwarz, 1959."

28 Numan Bartley, *The Rise of Massive Resistance: Race and Politics in the South during the 1950s* (Baton Rouge: Louisiana State University Press, 1997), 83–4, 120.

29 Don Carleton, "McCarthyism in Houston: The George Ebey Affair," *Southwestern Historical Quarterly* 80, 2 (1976): 163–76; Don Carleton, "McCarthyism in Local Elections: The Houston School Board of 1952," *Houston History* 3, 1 (1981): 168–77; Debbie Z. Harwell, message to author, 25 February 2014. As of 1961, neither Rice University nor the Shamrock Hilton, where the CACC held events, were integrated.

30 Dan Smoot, "Our Race Relations," *Dan Smoot Report* 8, 41 (1962): 327; Mary Dudziak, *Cold War Civil Rights: Race and the Image of American Democracy* (Princeton, NJ: Princeton University Press, 2000), 120–9; 159–62; "The Near East," CACCN, November 1958, 3; Gregg Brazinsky, *Winning the Third World: Sino-American Rivalry during the Cold War* (Chapel Hill: The University of North Carolina Press, 2017), 150–5.

31 Stephen Garton, "Sound Minds and Healthy Bodies: Re-Considering Eugenics in Australia," *Australian Historical Studies* 26, 103 (1994): 163–4. The eugenic movement had little impact in Australia.

32 Michael Emerson and Christian Smith, *Divided by Faith: Evangelical Religion and the Problem of Race in America* (New York: Oxford University Press, 2000), 78; Matthew Sutton, *American Apocalypse: A History of Modern Evangelicalism* (Cambridge: Belknap Press of Harvard University Press, 2014), 306–7. The idea that people are saved "one heart at a time" creates a strong bias against the idea that social structural influence can be the determining factor in any human problem. The world's fundamental problem is seen as the individual's "broken" relationship with God, of which the race problem is seen as one manifestation among others.

33 From CACCN: "Debate on Marcuse," 15 January 1970, 2; "The Attractive Face of the United States," 18 September1967, 1; "Communism and Race Riots," 24 August 1967, 4; "Racism and Classicism – The Deadly Twins," 1 December 1985, 1; "Bishop Tutu and His Message," 15 January 1985, 3. Woodward, "What Qualifications," 15.

34 See chapter 12, this volume, "Political and Ideological Profiles." However, as shown in this segment, the available data on CACC rank-and-file supporters suggests that its *least* educated supporters were more likely to oppose segregation than otherwise. Unfortunately, no clear explanation can be given for this finding, which goes against national trends in US public opinion of the late 1950s and early 1960s.

35 Adam Fairclough, *Race and Democracy: The Civil Rights Struggle in Louisiana, 1915–1972* (Athens: University of Georgia Press, 2008), 8, 212–15. "Ark-La-Tex School of Anti-Communism," CACCN, November 1961, 2. J. Mark Souther, "Into the Big League: Conventions, Football, and the Color Line in New Orleans," *Journal of Urban History* 29, 694 (2003): 710; "Training to Hit Reds Proposed," *Times-Picayune* (LA), 28 October 1961, 1.

36 Frank Blackford, "Crusade Comes to Tidewater: An Anti-Communist 'Pilot Project,'" *Virginian Pilot*, 31 July 1966, clipping in GRIR, box 364, f. "CACC News Clips – 1966–1967"; Richard Corrigan, "Cold War Crusade Comes to Virginia," *WashP*, 3 September 1966, S7; Wayne Woodlief, "Schwarz May Return: Enthusiasm High, But Cash Low," *Ledger-Star* (VA), 3 September 1966, clipping in GRIR, box 364, f. "CACC News Clips – 1966–1967."

37 A.J. Christopher, *The Atlas of Apartheid* (London: Routledge, 1994), 161.

38 Alex Thomson, *U.S. Foreign Policy towards Apartheid South Africa, 1948–1994* (New York: Palgrave, 2008), 12–26; Darril Hudson, "The World Council of Churches and Racism in Southern Africa," *International Journal* 34, 3 (1979): 477; Miller, *Billy Graham*, 86–7.

39 From CACCN: “Africa,” April–May 1956, 4; “Africa,” October 1957, 4–5; “Africa,” December 1957; E.A.M. to F. Schwarz, 2 October 1958, pub. November 1958, 4–5; “African Challenge – Our Africa,” September 1958, 3; “Our African Work,” June–July 1959, 4.

40 Qtd. in William Strube, “African Challenge – Out Africa,” CACCN, September 1958, 3.

41 *Jy kan die Kommuniste vertrou (... om presies te doen wat hulle sê)!*, trans. Timo Kriel (Baanbraker-Uitgeners: Roodepoort, 1960). From CACCN: “Russia 1917 – Portugal 1974,” 15 May 1974, 1–2; “Soviet Strategy in Southern Africa,” 1 November 1976, 8; “Communist ‘Science’ in South Africa,” 15 February 1986, 2.

CHAPTER SIX

1 Qtd. in “Text of President’s Speech to Nation,” *LAT*, 6 April 1954, 8.

2 “Liberal Anti-Communism,” CACCN, 6 June 1966, 1.

3 Donald Critchlow, *Phyllis Schlafly and Grassroots Conservatism: A Woman’s Crusade* (Princeton, NJ: Princeton University Press, 2006), 72; Richard Gid Powers, *Not without Honor: The History of American Anticommunism* (New York: The Free Press, 1995), 272; A. McDowell to F. Schwarz, 15 November 1962, MLP, box 1, f. 2. As Powers writes, McCarthyism “made liberal anti-communists fearful of grassroots anticommunism.”

4 Kenneth Woodward, “What Qualifications for a Crusader? Fred Schwarz on Communism,” *Catholic Reporter*, 1 February 1963, 16; Brooks Walker, *The Christian Fright Peddlers: The Radical Right and the Churches* (New York: Doubleday, 1964), 116; Schwarz qtd. in John L. Shover, “The Christian Anti-Communism Crusade in San Francisco,” unpub. article, JLSM, 1 portfolio, 2; “The Responsibility of the Average Businessman in the Battle against Communism,” CACCN, June 1962, 1.

5 William Thompson, *Khrushchev: A Political Life* (New York: Palgrave-Macmillan, 1995), 153–9. From CACCN: editorial, July–August 1956, 1; “The Communist Doctrines of Class Morality and Class Guilt,” 27 June 1966, 5–6.

6 Erling Jorstad, *The Politics of Doomsday: Fundamentalists of the Far Right* (Nashville: Abingdon Press, 1970), 62; Bob Considine, “Assails Bankruptcy and Leadership: U.S. Drifting towards Communistic State, Gen. MacArthur Tells Solons,” *Rome News-Tribune* (GA), 25 March 1952, 7.

7 Chesly Manly, *The Twenty-Year Revolution: From Roosevelt to Eisenhower* (Chicago: Henry Regnery Company, 1954), 2.

8 Robert Welch, "The American Opinion Scoreboard," *American Opinion*, July–August 1958, 21–3.

9 Robert Welch, *The Blue Book of the John Birch Society* (Belmont, MA: Western Islands, 1961), 125, 146.

10 Robert Welch, "Foreword," *John Birch Society Bulletin*, December 1959, 2; Welch, *Blue Book of the John Birch Society*, 151; Rick Perlstein, *Before the Storm: Barry Goldwater and the Unmaking of the American Consensus* (New York: Hill and Wang, 2001), 117; Powers, *Not without Honor*, 291; Richard Hofstadter, "The Paranoid Style in American Politics," in *The Paranoid Style in American Politics and Other Essays* (Cambridge: Harvard University Press, 1964), 24–9; Jonathan Schoenwald, *A Time for Choosing: The Rise of Modern Conservatism* (New York: Oxford University Press, 2001), 77. Welch came to incarnate the so-called "paranoid style in American politics," a phrase coined by Hofstadter and still used to this day.

11 Daniel Bell, "The Dispossessed (1962)," in *The Radical Right: The American Right, Expanded and Updated*, ed. Daniel Bell (New York: Doubleday, 1962), 2; Mary Brennan, *Turning Right in the Sixties: The Conservative Capture of the GOP* (Chapel Hill: University of North Carolina Press, 1995), 12

12 Ralph de Toledano, "Choosing Up Sides on Communism," 10 November 1961, RDTP, box 9, printed matter – 1961; Edmund Lambeth, "Anti-Communist Groups Here Show Big Increase in Activity," *Milwaukee Journal*, 4 June 1961, 1; John Corlett, "Communism May Be Top Issue in Elections," *Lewiston Morning Tribune* (ID), 24 September 1961, 4; Norman Birnbaum, "The Coming End of Anti-Communism," *Partisan Review* 29 (1962): 386.

13 Neil McMillen, *The Citizens' Council: Organized Resistance to the Second Reconstruction* (Champaign: University of Illinois Press, 1994), 191–4.

14 Critchlow, *Phyllis Schlafly*, 69; Stanley Allaby, "Local Group Formed to Combat Communism," CACCN, March 1959, 3–4; "Sunday Teachers Pick 'Citizen of the Year,'" *Hartford Courant*, 1 November 1959, 12B. From *Southeast Missourian*: "Delegates Selected to Attend Seminar," 29 March 1961, 10; "Communist Threat Topic of Seminar," 11 December 1961; "Communist Topic," 15 December 1961; "Pleased with Seminar in Cape," 19 December 1961. M. Rogovin, "In re: Four Freedoms Study Groups, Inc.," WSP, file: Internal Revenue Service Study of Ideological Organizations, 31 December 1965, f. "G," 2.

15 Donald Janson and Bernard Eismann, *The Far Right* (New York: McGraw-Hill), 126–7; Dan Kelly, "Birchismo," in *Boob Jubilee: The*

Cultural Politics of the New Economy, ed. Thomas Frank and Dave Mulcahey (New York: W.W. Norton, 2003), 348–9; Alan Westin, "The John Birch Society: 'Radical Right' and 'Extreme Left' in the Political Context of Post World War II (1962)," in *The Radical Right: The American Right, Expanded and Updated*, ed. Daniel Bell (New York: Doubleday, 1962), 239–40. In 1961, the Anti-Defamation League gave a figure of 282 right-wing groups, excluding segregationist and anti-Semitic groups (see Janson and Eismann, *Far Right*).

16 William Hixson, *Search for the American Right Wing: An Analysis of the Social Science Record, 1955–1987* (Princeton, NJ: Princeton University Press, 1992), 56, 60; Jonathan Martin Kolkey, *The New Right, 1960–1968, with an Epilogue, 1969–1980* (Washington, DC: University Press of America, 1983), 113–18.

17 Citizens Committee against Fluoridation, "Say 'NO' to Poison-Fluoride in Your Drinking Water," 1962, 3; Gretchen Reilly, "The Task Is a Political One: The Promotion of Fluoridation," in *Silent Victories: The History and Practices of Public Health in Twentieth-Century America*, ed. John Ward and Christian Waren (New York: Oxford University Press, 2007), 329–30; "From ADL," 8 April 1964, GRIR, box 365, f. "Washington School April 64," 3.

18 Leo Katcher, *Earl Warren: A Political Biography* (New York: McGraw-Hill, 1967), 3; Critchlow, *Phyllis Schlafly*, 62–3; Seymour Martin Lipset, "Three Decades of the Radical Right: Coughlinites, McCarthyites, and Birchers (1962)," in *The Radical Right: The American Right, Expanded and Updated*, ed. Daniel Bell (New York: Doubleday, 1962), 377, 435–46; McMillen, *Citizens' Council*, 201; Schoenwald, *Time for Choosing*, 90; Joseph Lowndes, *From the New Deal to the New Right: Race and the Southern Origins of Modern Conservatism* (New Haven, NJ: Yale University Press, 2008), 45–76. Joseph Lowndes shows well how Southerners became part of the Republican coalition, but he focuses on elite rather than on grassroots discourses.

19 Hixson, *Search for the American Right Wing*, 59–60; Critchlow, *Phyllis Schlafly*, 63, 70.

20 Jorstad, *Politics of Doomsday*, 63; Carmine Sarracino and Kevin Scott, *The Porning of America: The Rise of Porn Culture, What It Means and Where Do We Go from Here* (Boston: Beacon Press, 2008), 54–61; Joel Devine, Joseph Sheley and M. Dwayne Smith, "Macroeconomic and Social-Control Policy Influences on Crime Rate Changes, 1948–1985," *American Sociological Review* 53, 3 (1988): 412; "44,146 Drug Addicts Counted," NYT, 11 September 1958, 5; William Strube, Jr, *The Star over the Kremlin* (Grand Rapids, MI: Baker Books, 1962), 35.

21 George Gallup, "Public Has Long Favored Test Ban," *St Petersburg Times*, 2 August 1963, 17A. Herbert Philbrick described *On the Beach* as Communist propaganda.

22 David Tal, "Missile Gap," in *The Military-Industrial Complex and American Society*, ed. Sterling Michael Pavelec (Santa Barbara, CA: ABC-CLIO, LLC, 2010), 207–8.

23 Philip Potter, "Castro Disowns Communist Tag – Also Denies Seeking U.S. Aid, Hits Sugar Policy," *Baltimore Sun*, 18 April 1959, 1–2; Critchlow, *Phyllis Schlafly*, 95.

24 Fred Kaplan, *1959: The Year Everything Changed* (Hoboken, NJ: John Wiley and Sons, 2009), 8–10.

25 Philip Warden, "Judd Spurns Bid to Dinner with Mikoyan," *ChiTri*, 3 January 1959, 5; David Lawrence, "Mikoyan Proves U.S. Point: You Can't Deal with Reds," *Toledo Blade*, 29 January 1959, 8; "Businessmen and Churchmen Welcome Mikoyan," *CACCN*, March 1959, 1; F. Schwarz to A. Kohlberg, 4 March 1959, AKP, box. 155, f. "Fred C. Schwarz, 1958–1960"; J. Hedberg to W. Judd, 26 January 1959, WHJP, box 222, f. 3, copyright Stanford University.

26 "Visit of Khrushchev: Installment of Surrender," *CACCN*, September 1959, 1–2; Deborah Larson, *Anatomy of Mistrust: U.S.-Soviet Relations during the Cold War* (Ithaca, NY: Cornell University Press, 2000), 94–5; Schoenwald, *Time for Choosing*, 41–2.

27 From *LAT*: George Gallup, "Americans Found to Be for Khrushchev Visit," 10 August 1959, 11; "Visit Hailed and Assailed in Congress," 4 August 1959, 1. "Exchange of Visits," *ChiTri*, 4 August 1959, 18. From *CACCN*: Schwarz, "Visit of Khrushchev: Installment of Surrender," 1; "Khrushchev's Visit Past – Consequences in the Future," November 1959, 1, 4.

28 Arnold Beichman, "From the Bookshelf: What Happened to U.S. Communist Party?," *Christian Science Monitor*, 16 December 1959, 9; Frank Adams, *James A. Dombrowski: An American Heretic, 1897–1983* (Knoxville: University of Tennessee Press, 1992), 246–7; Samuel Walker, *In Defense of American Liberties: A History of the ACLU* (Carbondale: Southern Illinois University Press, 1999), 244–5; Perlstein, *Before the Storm*, 101–2; Richard Fried, *Nightmare in Red: The McCarthy Era in Perspective* (New York: Oxford University Press, 1996), 195; William O'Neill, *Coming Apart: An Informal History of America in the 1960's* (New York: Random House, 1971), 275–7.

29 "Communist Violence," *CACCN*, June 1960, 1–2; "Bridges Praises Unions in Soviet as Democratic," *NYT*, 14 February 1959, 26; George Sokolsky,

"Student Riots Are Weapons in Hands of Communists!," *Florence Times* (AL), 3 June 1960, 4.

30 House Un-American Activities Committee, *Operation Abolition*, film, US House of Representatives, Washington, 1960, 48 min.; "Youth Riots Are Linked to Commies," *Spokesman Review*, 18 July 1960, 5. The idea of a world student strategy was expressed in a report by J. Edgar Hoover (see "Youth Riots Are Linked to Commies").

31 "Film of the Riots," CACCN, July 1960, 6; "Message for Americans," *Nashua Telegraph* (NH), 18 November 1960, 6; "The Investigation: Operation Abolition," *Times*, 17 March 1961, http://www.time.com/time/magazine/article/0,9171,894425-1,00.html; "Film Operation Abolition Under Fire," CACCN, February 1961, 1–2; D. McNeil, notes from CACC Phoenix school, DMP, box 1, f. 1-3. The National Council of Churches encouraged Protestant ministers "not to exhibit the film unless a full and fair presentation" of the circumstances of its production could be made.

32 Murray Illson, "Norman Thomas Hits Birch Group," *NYT*, 20 April 1961, 19; Hicks, *"Sometimes in the Wrong,"* 78; "Anti-Communist Films Stir Nationwide Storm," *LAT*, 26 February 1961, C1.

33 Bell, "Dispossessed (1962)," 1; Craig Schiller, *The (Guilty) Conscience of a Conservative* (New York: Arlington House, 1978), 29.

CHAPTER SEVEN

1 "New Books at Two Libraries," *Ironwood Daily Globe* (MI), 29 October 1958, 3; Lewis Nichols, "In and Out of Books," *NYT*, 23 August 1964, BR8; "Mrs Foster Honored by American Heritage Group," *Nashua Telegraph* (NH), 8 May 959, 3; Ad., "This Week at the Manitowoc Public Library," *Manitowoc Herald-Times* (WI), 12 January 1961, 6-M; Ad., "The Tribune Bookshelf – Best Sellers, Albuquerque," *Albuquerque Tribune*, 8 April 1961, A-4; "Library Offers Commie Book," *Mansfield News-Journal* (OH), 15 October 1961, 6; "Book on Communism Available at Library," *Milford Mail* (IA), 26 October 1961, 10; "New Shipment of Books Augment Library List," *Independent Record* (MT), 24 December 1961, 9; "Club Meetings Highlight Week," *Idaho Sunday Journal*, 28 January 1962, 20.

2 Fred Schwarz, *Beating the Unbeatable Foe: One Man's Victory over Communism, Leviathan, and the Last Enemy* (Washington, DC: Regnery, 1996), 170–1; R. Ettinger, Generic Letter, ACLU, MC001, box 706, f. 9. Teachers received their copies with a letter from Prentice-Hall founder.

3 "Organizations: Crusader Schwarz," *Time* 79, 6 (1962): 19.

4 Fred Schwarz, *You Can Trust the Communists (to be Communists)* (Long Beach: Chantico Publishing Co., 1966), 102–16, 172, 51–66, respectively; "Strange Case of Robert Wesley Wells," *Eugene Register-Guard*, 14 February 1954, 8A. Wells's sentence was commuted in 1954.

5 Schwarz, *You Can Trust the Communists*, 17–25, 58–9; William Edwards, "J. B. Matthews Quits Post as Red Prober – Attacks on Clergy Assailed by Ike," *Chicago Tribune*, 10 July 1953, 1.

6 Schwarz, *You Can Trust the Communists*, 60–1.

7 Fred Schwarz, *Communism, Diagnosis and Treatment: The Story of Brainwashing – How Communism Conquers the Minds of Men* (Los Angeles: World Vision, Inc., 1956). 133; Kenneth Rose, Erwin Levold, and Lee Hilltzik, "Ivan Pavlov on Communist Dogmatism and the Autonomy of Science in the Soviet Union in the Early 1920s," *Integrative Psychological and Behavioral Science* 27, 3 (1992): 267–78; B.F. Skinner, "Pavlov's Influence on Psychology in America," *Journal of the History of Behavioral Sciences* 17, 2 (1981): 242–5; Paul Creelan, "Watson as Mythmaker: The Millenarian Sources of Watsonian Behaviorism," *Journal for the Scientific Study of Religion* 24, 2 (1985): 207–8.

8 Schwarz, *You Can Trust the Communists*, 1.

9 Jack Jones, "Fiery Anti-Communist of 1950's Still Fights the Battle," *LAT*, 26 September 1977, OC1.

10 Ernest Pisko, "How to Raise Your Cold-War I.Q.," review of *You Can Trust* by Fred Schwarz, *Christian Science Monitor*, 16 March 1962, 9; Herman Reissig, "Crusader with a Blunderbuss," review of *You Can Trust* by Fred Schwarz, *United Church Herald*, 3 May 1962, 32; D.L. Lee, "Book Reviews: You Can Trust the Communists," review of *You Can Trust* by Fred Schwarz, *Free China Review* 11 (1961): 49–50; William Chamberlain, "The Bookshelf: The Way of the World Conspiracy," review of *You Can Trust* by Fred Schwarz, *Wall Street Journal*, 12 August 1960, 6; Louis La-Coss qtd. in CACCN, December 1960, 1, 4.

11 Lee Edwards, *The Conservative Revolution: The Movement That Remade America* (New York: Simon and Schuster, 1999), 159; LaHaye qtd. in "Product Description," *Summit Ministries*, http://www.summit.org/store/You-Can-Still-Trust-the-Communists-To-be-Communists-Socialists-Statists-and-Progressives-Too; Stormer qtd. Schwarz, *Beating*, xviii; Richard Viguerie, *The New Right: We're Ready To Lead* (Falls Church, VA: The Viguerie Company, 1981), 47–8.

12 Kenneth Woodward, "What Qualifications for a Crusader? Fred Schwarz on Communism," *Catholic Reporter*, 1 February 1963, 15.

13 From CACCN: "Anti-Communism Schools," July 1960, 6; "Anti-Communism Schools," June 1960, 3; "Stop Press," December 1960, 6.

14 Report, 5/21/62, GRIR, box 363, f. "CACC After-effects"; "Greater St. Louis School of Anti-Communism, April 24–28, 1961 – Attendance Committee," PSC, Communism series, box 3, f. 8; Stanley Mosk, "Broadcast by California Attorney General Stanley Mosk," 02/15/62, KTVU, WFBP, box 22, f. "Schwarz, Fred (1962)"; D. McNeil, notes from CACC Phoenix school, DMP, box. 1, f. 1-3, 2-3.

15 The term was coined by author Kevin Phillips in 1969.

16 Abraham Shragge, "A New Federal City": San Diego During World War II," *Pacific Historical Review* 63, 3 (1994): 333–5; Arthur Verge, "The Impact of the Second World War in Los Angeles," *Pacific Historical Review* 63, 3 (1994): 289–314; "Dallas Asks Why It Happened; Worry over 'Image' Is Voiced," *NYT*, 24 November 1963, 2. J. Mayo to H. Philbrick, 7 September 1960, HPP, box 3, f. 7; Paul Harvey, "Civil Defense Revitalized," *Telegraph-Herald* (IA), 29 September 1960, 20.

17 John Waugh, "Anti-Red Schools 'Arm' U.S. Citizens," *Christian Science Monitor*, 19 November 1960, 15.

18 Irwin Suall, *The American Ultras: The Extreme Right and the Military-Industrial Complex* (New York: New American, 1962), 49.

19 Harvey, "Civil Defense Revitalized," 20; "Ex-Rep James Collins, Texas Republican, Dies," *WashP*, 23 July 1989, B4; Jerome Crossman, Gerald Mann, and Waldo Stewart, "Dallas Trustees Take a Stand," *NYT*, 19 February 1956, X8.

20 Leonard Sloane, "Phoenix: Barry's Brother Minds of the Store," *NYT*, 5 April 1966, 47; "Plan Huge Plant Near Philadelphia," *Prescott Evening Courier* (AR), 21 November 1958, 1; Gene Smith, "Land in Phoenix Is Proving Fertile for Electronics," *NYT*, 8 October 1967, F1.

21 H. Philbrick to Miss E. Hancock, December 1960, HPP, box 49, f. 7; Al Hester, "Dallas' Schools to Teach How to Fight Red Threat: Freedom Forum Offers Material," *Dallas Times Herald*, 4 December 1960, 1. Schwarz also appeared on KERA-TV, an educational station.

22 From *LAT*: "Anti-Communism School Opens Session in L.A.," 8 November 1960, B1; "Ex-FBI Spy Warns of New Moves by Russia," 10 November 1960, B2.

23 Lewis Allbee, "Greater Phoenix School on Anti-Communism," *District Newsletter* 10, 15 (1961): 2; D. McNeil, "Anti-Communism in Phoenix: A Case History," unpub. article, DMP, box 4, f. 4, 18; Elmore Philpott, "Looking for Reds," *Vancouver Sun*, 14 April 1961, 4; "Anti-Red Meets Drawing Big County Crowds," *LAT*, 9 March 1961, D1-2. From the

Register (CA): "See 1,200 Students at Anti-Red School," 7 March 1961, A8; Frank Martinez, "Communist Threat Outlined to 12,000 Students at Rally," 9 March 1961, C1; "'I'm Shocked,' Students Say of Red Menace," 9 March 1961, C1.

24 McNeil, "Anti-Communism in Phoenix," 18–20.

25 Ibid.; Donald McNeil, notes from CACC Phoenix school, DMP, box 1, f. 1-3, 9-10; McNeil, "Anti-Communism in Phoenix," 18–20. A few months later, Schwarz returned to Phoenix and spoke to about twelve hundred people, and the lecture was followed by a fundraising event that allowed the CACC to net a few thousand dollars more.

26 B. Geier to H. Philbrick, 5 January 1961, HPP, box 243, f. 6; Reported by Frank Martinez, "Anti-Communist School Opens Assault on Red Philosophy," *Register* (CA), 7 March 1961, B3; Lisa McGirr, *Suburban Warriors: The Origins of the New American Right* (Princeton, NJ: Princeton University Press, 2001), 54.

27 Edward Soja and Allen Scott, "Introduction to Los Angeles: City and Region," in *The City: Los Angeles and Urban Theory at the End of the Twentieth Century*, ed. Edward Soja and Allen Scott (Berkeley: University of California Press, 1996), 10; Eric Avila, *Popular Culture in the Age of White Flight: Fear and Fantasy in Suburban Los Angeles* (Berkeley: University of California Press, 2004), 46–8; Robert Schuller, *Prayer: My Soul's Adventure with God – A Spiritual Autobiography* (New York: Doubleday, 1995), 143.

28 Martinez, "Anti-Communist School Opens Assault on Red Philosophy," D3.

29 From the *Register* (CA): Ibid.; Martinez, "Communist Threat Outlined to 12,000 Students at Rally," C1; "Kick Reds Out of UN, Anti-Communism School Speaker Says," 8 March 1961, C1; "U.S. Retreat Blasted by University Proxy," 10 March 1961, C3.

30 "School Holds Final Session," *Register* (CA), 10 March 1961, D3; Clancy Franks, "Dr. Schwarz's Crusaders in Orange County, Calif.: Disneyland Meets the 'Red Menace' Heads On," *National Guardian*, 10 April 1961, 3; "Countians Rally Support to Anti-Communism Crusade," *Register* (CA), 12 March 1961, D1; "Anti-Red School Ends," *Long Beach Independent*, 11 March 1961, A4.

31 From *LAT*: "Preacher Sues Birch Group for Slander," 15 April 1961, 3; "Minister Acts to Dismiss Suit," 13 March 1962, 3. Sole exception (*LAT* articles in this note): a Methodist minister from La Habra filed a slander suit against James F. Garry, a Fullerton dentist and Bircher, for allegedly publicly calling him a Communist during the school.

32 McGirr, *Suburban Warriors*, 56–8; Franks, "Dr. Schwarz's Crusaders in Orange County, Calif," 3.

CHAPTER EIGHT

1 H. Philbrick to Mrs S. Richards, 24 January 1961, HPP, box 4, f. 1; CACC leaflet, *School for Anti-Communists, August 23rd–27th.*
2 Simon Casady, "The Hysteria Peddlers Are Back!," *El Cajon Valley News*, 18 August 1960, B6. For the first time, the Crusade was also criticized by Communists, through the California newspaper the *People's World*, whose editorial drew a parallel between the Crusade and early-1920s Nazi movements. Article repub. in *CACCN*, December 1960, 1, 4.
3 Douglas Larsen, "Harness Barks, But Nobody Yet Has Been Bitten," *Pittsburgh Gazette*, 29 August 1947, 16; "Memorandum: Propaganda Activities of Military Personnel Directed at the Public," JWFP, series 4, box 25, f. 4, 1; Fred Cook, *The Warfare State* (New York: Macmillan, 1967), 274–5; James Clayton, "Seminars on the Cold War Spring from a Top Secret Report," *WashP*, 7 August 1961, A2; Randall Woods, *Fulbright: A Biography* (New York: Cambridge University Press, 1995), 284. The program was elaborated by private institutions with a hawkish foreign policy line and close military connections, such as the Chicago-based Institute for American Strategy. The reason Eisenhower signed this directive remains obscure.
4 "People and Events," *ChiTri*, 19 May 1964, B5; F. Schwarz to R. Welch, 19 September 1960, HPP, box 121, f. 6; Fred Schwarz to Arthur G. McDowell, 23 June 1962, MLP, box 1, f. 2; CACC leaflet, *Education for American Security, August 29–September 2, 1960.*
5 F. Vignola to H. Philbrick, 16 August 1960, HPP, box 3, f. 7. From *ChiTri*: Ad., "The United States Naval Air Station"; George Schreiber, "Americanism School to Aid in War on Reds," 14 August 1960, H42.
6 From *ChiTri*: "Ex-Spy of FBI Sees Upsurge of Reds Here," 30 August 1960, A1; "Admiral Raps Ideology Lag of U.S. Youths," 3 September 1960, W7; Cabell Phillips, "Anti-Red Dispute Grips Illinoisans: Intensive Right-Wing Efforts Arouse Controversy," *NYT*, 21 May 1961, 54.
7 From *ChiTri*: "Rips Security School Shown at Glenview: McCarthyism Is Cry of Thompson," 11 September 1960, N2A; "Jury Frees War Hero in Voting Tract Case," 27 May 1961, 3. Phillips, "Anti-Red Dispute Grips Illinoisans," 54.

8 From CACCN: "Was the Naval Air Station Gulled?," *Christian Century*, 14 September 1960, repub. in December 1960, 3; "Liberal Truth," December 1960, 3.

9 Philip Dodd, "Navy Defends Use of Base to Warn of Reds," *ChiTri*, 13 September 1960, 27; H. Philbrick to Mrs S. Richards, 24 January 1961, HPP, box 4, f.1; "Anti-Communism Schools," CACCN, July 1960, 6; Fred Schwarz, *Beating the Unbeatable Foe: One Man's Victory over Communism, Leviathan, and the Last Enemy* (Washington, DC: Regnery, 1996), 257.

10 Robert Welch, *The Blue Book of the John Birch Society* (Belmont, MA: Western Islands, 1961), 152; Gene Blake, "The John Birch Society: What Are Its Purposes?," *LAT*, 5 March 1961, B1.

11 Welch, *Blue Book of the John Birch Society*, 147–9; Gene Blake, "Birch Society's Program Outlined," *LAT*, 7 March 1961, 2; Rick Perlstein, *Before the Storm: Barry Goldwater and the Unmaking of the American Consensus* (New York: Hill and Wang, 2001), 117; Special Agent to J. Edgar Hoover, 20 January 1959, FBIF, F. John Birch Society – HQ 1. "The John Birch Society," Welch wrote, "will operate under completely authoritative control at all levels."

12 H. Philbrick to F. Willette, 28 May 1959, in Donald Critchlow, *Phyllis Schlafly and Grassroots Conservatism: A Woman's Crusade* (Princeton, NJ: Princeton University Press, 2006), 338n38; H. Philbrick to R. Welch, 4 August 1959. From HPP: box 121, f. 6: H. Philbrick to R. Welch, 30 October 1959; R. Welch to H. Philbrick, 25 November 1959; H. Philbrick to R. Welch, 30 November 1959; H. Philbrick to R. Welch, 31 December 1959; R. Welch to H. Philbrick, 6 January 1960; "John Birch Society Backed by Anti-Reds," *Register* (CA), 10 March 1961, C3.

13 Robert Welch, "Foreword," *John Birch Society Bulletin*, December 1959, 3; Blake, "Birch Society's Program Outlined," 23; Robert Welch, *The Politician*, first unpub. edition, 1958, 268.

14 R. Welch to G. K. Smith, 15 August 1960, GKSP, box 55, f. Welch, Robert; B. Goldwater to J. Bell, 17 April 1960, BMGP, MF 48, box 013_REEL021_0003, pdf.,699. When radical right-wing pastor Gerald K. Smith asked for a copy, Welch politely refused.

15 F. Schwarz to R. Welch, 19 September 1960, HPP, box 121, f. 6; Sherm Williams, "Moscow, Schwarz or Who Put Finger on Society? Bircher Welch's Findings Highly Confusing," *Independent* (CA),13 October 1964, B1-2. From AKP: R. Welch to A. Kohlberg, 7 June 1953, box 200, F.

Welch, 1954–1958; A. Kohlberg to R. Welch, 11 January 1960, box 36, F. John Birch Society (in this letter, Kohlberg sent Welch $1,500); R. Welch to F. Schwarz, 6 September 1960, box 121, f. 6, John Birch Society, 1959–1979; Fred Schwarz, *You Can Trust the Communists (to be Communists)* (Long Beach, CA: Chantico Publishing Co., 1966), 181.

16 F. Schwarz to R. Welch, 19 September 1960, HPP, box 121, f. 6.

17 R. Welch to F. Schwarz, 6 September 1960, HPP, box 121, f. 6; "Appendix," *Facts – Published by the Anti-Defamation League of B'Nai B'Rith* (ADL), November–December 1961, 228; Goldwater qtd. in William Buckley Jr, *Flying High: Remembering Barry Goldwater* (Philadelphia, PA: Perseus Books, 2010), 60. Two of Arizona's top JBS organizers were involved in the Phoenix CACC school: banker Frank C. Brophy and attorney Clarence J. Duncan.

18 From *Chicago Daily News*: Jack Mabley, "Bares Secrets of 'Red-Haters': They Think Ike Is a Communist," 25 July 1960, B1; Jack Mabley, "Strange Threat to Democracy: Anti-Red Group Hits Leaders," 26 July 1960, B1.

19 Alex Dorish, "Group Branding Ike as Red Has 10 Chapters in Wisconsin," *Milwaukee Journal*, 31 July 1960, 1; S. Allen to "Russ," 12 April 1962, GRIR, box 3, f. Allen, Steve; "Wisconsin Group Reportedly Views Ike as Red, Traitor," *Chicago Sun-Times*, 1 August 1960, 15.

20 Welch-Schwarz exchange, from HPP, box 121, f. 6: R. Welch to F. Schwarz, 6 September 1960, F. Schwarz to R. Welch, 19 September 1960.

21 Williams, "Moscow, Schwarz or Who Put Finger on Society?," B1, B2.

22 Perlstein, *Before the Storm*, 118. From *LAT*: "Reading before Writing," 29 January 1961, I4; Nick Williams, "A Report to the Public," 5 March 1961, B1; Gene Blake, "The John Birch Society: What Are Its Purposes?," 5 March 1961,B1; "Blue Book Guides Anti-Red Society," 6 March 1961, 2; Blake, "Birch Society's Program Outlined," 2; Gene Blake, "Birch Program in Southland Told," 8 March 1961, 2; Otis Chandler, "Peril to Conservatives," 12 March 1961, G1. David Halberstam, *The Powers That Be* (Chicago: University of Chicago Press, 2000), 295–7.

23 "Sens. Young, Mansfield Assail Birch Society," *LAT*, 9 March 1961, 24; "John Birch Society Is Held 'Patriotic,'" *NYT*, 21 March 1961, 8; Jerry Gillam, "State Senators Watch John Birch Society," *LAT*, 22 March 1961, 2; "Inquiry Is Opposed: Liberties Union Takes Stand on John Birch Society," *NYT*, 28 March 1961, 11.

24 John Morris, "Birch Unit Pushes Drive on Warren," *NYT*, 1 April 1961, 1; Perlstein, *Before the Storm*, 118; David Thorman, "True

Anti-Communism," *Ave Maria*, 8 April 1961, and David Baxter, "The John Birch Society," July 1961, clipping from GRIR, box 3, f. Allen, Steve; "Ohio Senator Raps Welch as 'Little Hitler,'" *LAT*, 4 April 1961, 2; Sydney Gruson, "Birch Unit Ideas Put to U.S. Troops," *NYT*, 14 April 1961, 1.

25 Halberstam, *Powers That Be*, 297; B. Goldwater to J. Bell, 17 April 1961, BMGP, MF 48, box 013_REEL021_0003, pdf., 699.

26 Sam Johnson, "Anti-Red Scores Profs Unwilling to Be Investigated," *Albuquerque Tribune*, 7 April 1961, A1-2; "Fanaticism in Fight against Reds Assailed," *LAT*, 21 June 1961, B2.

27 "Soviet First in Space! Try to Catch Us, Nikita Taunts West," *Milwaukee Sentinel*, 12 April 1961, 1; Perlstein, *Before the Storm*, 119.

28 R. Bevan to L. Speiser, 7 February 1961, ACLU, MC001, 1917– , box 706, f. 5; R. Brown to H. Philbrick, 6 February 1961, HPP, box 45, f. 11; A. Reitman to R. Bevan, 17 February 1961, ACLU, MC001, 1917– , box 706, f. 5.

29 "Anti-Communism Schools," *CACCN*, April–May 1961, 2; Report 5/21/62, GRIR, box 363, f. "CACC After-effects." Figure from Mrs D. Smith to H. Philbrick, 5 May 1961, HPP, box 4, f. 2. Excluding the "Youth Day" event, more than five thousand people attended the St Louis school, roughly the same number as attended the Phoenix and Anaheim schools.

30 St Louis Civil Liberties Committee, *Communism on the Map (Complete text of the tape-film strip) and The Greater St. Louis School of Anti-Communism – April, 1961 (Selected Quotations)*, St Louis, 1962, 27–76; A. Reitman to H. Norman, 5 May 1961, ACLU, MC001, box 706, f. 5.

31 Cabell Phillips, "Physician Leads Anti-Red Drive with 'Poor Man's Birch Society,'" *NYT*, 30 April 1961, 77.

32 Schwarz, *Beating*, 11. From *CACCN*: "Anti-Communism Schools," July–August 1961, 1, 3; C. Daniel to F. Schwarz, 22 August 1961, pub. November 1961, 7; C. Phillips to L. Spivak, 27 August 1962, LSP, box 217, f. "Schwarz, Fred C. – 8/26/62."

33 Schwarz, *Beating*, 7; fundraising letter, 22 June 1961; Merrill Folsom, "'Crusade' on Reds Is Brought East," *NYT*, 10 May 1961, 38; William Tucker, "Troops Chiefs Back Rightist Scouter," *Miami News*, 26 September 1961, C1. The school's "Business" chairman, local realtor Ted W. Slack, was in the local JBS.

34 "Gen. Walker Rebuked for 'Red Label' Charge," *LAT*, 13 June 1961, 1; Cabell Phillips, "Right-Wing Officers Worrying Pentagon," *NYT*, 18 June 1961, 1, 56.

35 J.W. Fulbright to J.F. Kennedy, 28 June 1961, JWFP, series 4, box 25, f. 4. It took two months to Fulbright's staff to gather articles from all over the nation.

36 J.W. Fulbright, "Memorandum Submitted to the Department of Defense on Propaganda Activities of Military Personnel," *Congressional Record*, US Senate, Washington, United States Government Printing Office, 87th Congress, 2 August 1961, 14433. Fulbright told McNamara about the memo in June. Original version: "Memorandum: Propaganda Activities of Military Personnel Directed at the Public," JWFP, series 4, box 25, f. 4.

37 Attachment to "Memorandum: Propaganda Activities of Military Personnel Directed at the Public," 7–9; Report 5/21/62, GRIR, box 363, f. "CACC After-effects."

38 From JWFP, series 4, box 28, f. 3: "ACLU Clippings on 'Project Abolition, 1961,'": J. McKnight to A. Reitman, 24 May 1961; Anonymous to John McKnight, 9 March 1961.

39 Woods, *Fulbright*, 284. From *Congressional Record*, US Senate, Washington, United States Government Printing Office, 87th Congress: Strom Thurmond, "Military Anticommunist Seminars and Statements," 26 July 1961, 13594–618; 29 July 1961, 13998–14008; 31 July 1961, 14169–76.

40 Ralph McGill, "The Hate Mongers," *Miami News*, 19 August 1961, 2A; E.W. Kenworthy, "President Backs Curb on Military," *NYT*, 11 August 1961, 7; "Asks Senate Probe Fulbright Memo," *Chicago Tribune*, 5 August 1961, S5; Ralph de Toledano, 6 August 1961, RDTP, box 9, printed matter – 1961; Allan Ryskind, "Behind the Fulbright Memorandum," *Human Events* 18, 32 (1961): 510. Many anti-Fulbright letters can be found in GHGH, Ms. 76.23, "Militant Anti-Communist" (MAC) series, box 2. In an October 1962 report, the Senate Armed Services Committee criticized the Pentagon's handling of the freedom of political expression among military officials but found no evidence of any "muzzling" of the Department of Defense staff.

41 Philip Horton, "Revivalism on the Far Right," *Reporter*, 20 July 1961, 26–9.

42 Schwarz, *Beating*, 251; H. Philbrick to W. Leimbach, 5 April 1962, HPP, box 274, f. 9.

CHAPTER NINE

1 "No Quiz Of Birch Group, Says Mosk," *Lodi News-Sentinel*, 3 August 1961, 6.

2 E.W. Kenworthy, "President Wins Key Senate Test on Long-Term Aid," *NYT*, 12 August 1961, 1. Fulbright also pushed through a Senate bill that

allowed borrowing from the Treasury to finance foreign aid programs, thus further enraging conservatives.

3 "Junior Chamber Installation to Benefit Anti-Red School," *Van Nuys News* (CA), 20 July 1961, 36A; "Southern California School of Anti-Communism," CACCN, July–August 1961, 4.

4 "Notes on School of Christian Anti-Communist [sic] Crusade, Oakland, California, Jan. 31, 1962 (Shover)," JLSM, 5.

5 Anne Edwards, *Early Reagan* (New York: William Morrow and Company, Inc., 1987), 461–5; Thomas Evans, *The Education of Ronald Reagan: The General Electric Years and the Untold Story of His Conversion to Conservatism* (New York: Columbia University Press, 2006), 111–17; Brad Altman, "Dr. Schwarz's Bank Roll Has Red Lining," *Independent Press-Telegram* (CA), 12 September 1976, B-1; "Communist Eulogy of John Wayne," CACCN, July 1979, 2.

6 Fred Schwarz, *Beating the Unbeatable Foe: One Man's Victory over Communism, Leviathan, and the Last Enemy* (Washington, DC: Regnery, 1996), 214; "Eisenhower Party Returns from Bird Hunting in Mexico," *ChiTri*, 20 March 1961, A4; "Charles S. Jones of Richfield Oil," NYT, 11 December 1970, 50; Frank Martinez, "Anti-Red Crusader Praises Countians: Inside View of Anti-Communist Rally," *Register* (CA), 3 September 1961, A3; W. C. Skousen to R. Skousen, 9 September 1961, "Family News," 9/4/61, WCSP, binder: Hollywood's Answer to Communism, 16 October 1961. Cost of Richfield's sponsorship found in Skousen's notes.

7 Martinez, "Anti-Red Crusader Praises Countians." Locations of rallies included Inglewood, Santa Ana, Garden Grove, Torrance, Santa Monica, Costa Mesa, Whittier, Glendale, Anaheim, Long Beach, and Fullerton.

8 "U.S. Foreign Policy 'Marxist,'" *San Antonio Light*, 11 August 1961, 5; "Kennedy Latin Program Hit by Anti-Red Chief," LAT, 16 August 1961, 36.

9 "Marines to Take Part in Anti-Red Meeting," *Press Telegram* (CA), 29 August 1961, A8.

10 "Dodd Tells 'Stop Reds' Unity Need," LAE, 29 August 1961, 2. From LAT: Louis Fleming, "New U.S. Foreign Policy Urged at Anti-Red School," 29 August 1961, 2, 25; Louis Fleming, "Probe into 'Muzzling' of Military Asked," LAT, 31 August 1961, B1.

11 From WHJP, box 48, f. 4, copyright Stanford University: to Judd by Jenny Lind, Thomas Eagel, George Stewart, Neil Fox, John Fisher, 31 August 1961; Walter Judd to James Colbert, 17 July 1961. Martinez, "Anti-Red Crusader Praises Countians."

12 "$214,496 Net Raised by Anti-Red School," *LAT*, 13 October 1961, B7; "A Report on the Southern California School of Anti-Communism, August 28 – September 1, 1961," GRIR, box 299, f. "Sluis, Joost, 2"; "Dodd Tells 'Stop Reds' Unity Need," 2; Schwarz, *Beating*, 215; R. Moore to W. Judd, 5 September 1961, WHJP, box. 48, f. 4, copyright Stanford University; Schwarz, *Beating*, 221.

13 "A Report on the Southern California School of Anti-Communism, August 28 – September 1, 1961," GRIR, box 299, f. "Sluis, Joost, 4"; "Unconscious Surrender to Kremlin Cited," *LAE*, 30 August 1961, 3; W.C. Skousen to R. Skousen, 9 September 1961, "Family News," 9/4/61, WCSP, binder: Hollywood's Answer to Communism, 16 October 1961; "Health Program Is Attacked," *Lewiston Morning Tribune* (ID), 31 August 1961, 4; "Mental Health Leader Raps Call for Probe," *LAT*, 31 August 1961, B8.

14 "De Seversky Will Replace Teller in Talks," *LAT*, 24 August 1961, B3; "'A-Tests or Face National Suicide,' De Seversky Warns," *LAE*, 1 September 1961, 1; Louis Fleming, "Maj. De Seversky Urges Single Military Service," *LAT*, 1 September 1961, B1; "Judd Says Communism Is Cancer That Perils U.S.," *LAE*, 1 September 1961, 2; GR report on the LA CACC school, GRIR, box 299, f. "Sluis, Joost," 10–11. Louis Fleming, "Anti-Red School Told Victory Plan," *LAT*, 2 September 1961, 3. W.C. Skousen to R. Skousen, 9 September 1961, "Family News," 9/4/61, WCSP, binder: Hollywood's Answer to Communism, 16 October 1961. Considering his notoriety, De Seversky was probably the lecturer whom the CACC paid $750 as compared to the usual rate of $100.

15 "$214,496 Net Raised by Anti-Red School"; Martinez, "Anti-Red Crusader Praises Countians." Earlier in the day, Schwarz affirmed that sales of literature and recordings amounted to $10,000 in the first three days only.

16 From *LAT*: Hedda Hopper, "Entertainment," 2 September 1961, A6; Morrie Ryskind, "How to Put Communists in Red," 6 October 1961, B5. From *LAE*: "Red Expose," 1 September 1961, B2; Vincent Flaherty, "Anti-Red School Impressive," 4 September 1961, 19; "Anti-Communism School on TV," *Register* (CA), 30 August 1961, C14; W. Wagstaff and B. Temple to O. Brandt, 28 September 1961, DSBP, box 36, f. 6; Drew Pearson, "Right Wing Gets Backing from Some Advertisers in California Drama," *Star-News* (NC), 15 February 1962, 4.

17 M. Liebman to F. Schwarz, 4 April 1962, MLieb, box B11, f. "Fred Schwarz."

18 Keith Wheeler, "Who's Who in the Tumult of the Far Right," *Life* 52, 6 (1962): 117; Daniel Bell, "The Dispossessed (1962)," in *The Radical*

Right: The American Right, Expanded and Updated, ed. Daniel Bell (New York: Doubleday, 1962), 4; Carl Greenberg, "Birch Threat Almost Like Reds, Brown Says," LAT, 17 May 1962, A2.

19 J. Sucke to H. Philbrick, 8 December 1959, HPP, box 3, f. 5; CACC leaflet, *Austin Freedom Week, October 15–22, 1960, Austin, Texas.*

20 Scott McNall, *Career of a Radical Rightist: A Study in Failure* (Port Washington: Kennikat Press, 1975), 39–59; L. Skousen to W.C. Skousen, 6 November 1961, WCSP, scrapbook 1961, November–December.

21 "Anti-Communist Seminar Planned for March 11," *Telegraph-Herald* (IA), 27 February 1961, 6; "Nazarere Church Sets Anti-Communist School," *Press-Courier* (CA), 1 April 1961, 8; "Seminar Hears Call to 'Boycott' Russia," *Salt Lake Tribune*, 23 May 1961, 10A; "Raid Retreat, Seize Deserter Hidden by Cult," *ChiTri*, 5 August 1961, S1; James W. Fifield, "Dr. Fifield Says…," LAT, 26 November 1961, E2; E.J. Michaels, "Freedom Forum Tells Way to Beat Reds: Capacity Audience Attends Sessions," *Aurora Beacon-News* (IL), 29 September 1961, 1, 7. "Anti-communist schools of various sorts are breaking out all over. Thanks God for every one of them," Reverend James Fifield wrote in his *Los Angeles Times* Sunday column. At Aurora, Skousen, before a crowd of eight hundred, attacked the ACLU for its criticism of *Operation Abolition.*

22 J. Scott to H. Philbrick, 25 September 1961, HPP, box 4, f. 5. L. Baxter to B. Goldwater, 5 September 1961, BMGP, MF 44, box 0_12_REEL017_0002, pdf. p. 398-9.

23 "Fruitville Sewer Line Approved," *Sarasota Journal*, 22 March 1960, 11. From *Sarasota Herald-Tribune*: "Freedom Forum Breakfast Scheduled Next Tuesday," 21 September 1960, 2; "Gen Trudeau to Kick Off Project Alert," 12 October 1960, 18; Russell Butcher, "Lakeland Group Starts 'Project Alert' Plans," *Lakeland Ledger* (FL), 6 July 1961. For instance, the Project Alert seminar in Green Bay, Wisconsin, in the fall of 1961, began on 5 October with Philbrick's "I Led Three Lives" lecture, followed five days later by Skousen's talk on "Communism and Education." In early December, Bill Strube delivered a lecture titled "Is Co-Existence a Communist Conspiracy?"

24 From *LAT*: "Anti-Red Drive Will Start Today," 25 October 1961, B1; "Dangers of Communism to Be Discussed," 12 November 1961, OC14; Donald Neff, "Kennedy Aides Held Soft on Reds: Project Alert Audience Cheers Demand to Impeach Politicians," 12 December 1961, B1; Donald Neff, "House Quiz Asked in L.A.; Communist Influx Claimed," 15 December 1961, B1; "Thurmond Assails Army 'Muzzling,'" 29 November 1961, 2. Project Alert leaflet, *Act, Inc., Presents: Project Alert, Green Bay,*

Wisconsin. Furthermore, Project Alert had recently sponsored a well-publicized tour by South Carolina's outspoken segregationist Strom Thurmond in a context within which the crusader tried to extend his quietism on the race issue for as long as possible.

25 From *LAT*: Donald Neff, "Kennedy Aides Held Soft on Reds," B1; Donald Neff, "Speaker Regrets Harsh Remarks," 14 December 1961, B1. Bill Becker, "Attack on Warren Boomerangs on Anti-Reds' School on Coast," *NYT*, 17 December 1961, 58. Schwarz, *Beating*, 301–2.

26 Shelby Scates, *Warren G. Magnusson and the Shaping of Twentieth-Century America* (Seattle: University of Washington Press, 1998), 206; Donald Janson, "Vote Push Urged for U.S. Rightists," *NYT*, 31 January 1962, 11; "Right-Wing Campaign in Decline in the U.S.," *Sydney Morning Herald*, 19 April 1963, 2. Boeing lobbyist William Fritz organized anti-communist events in the State of Washington.

27 Michelle Nickerson (interviewer) and Joanne Bennett, CWCP, transcript in F. Bennett, Joanne, 3928, Nickerson, Michelle, 7/22/2002, 2-7; Michelle Nickerson, "Moral Mothers and Goldwater Girls," in *The Conservative Sixties*, ed. David R. Farber and Jeff Roche (New York: Peter Lang, 2003), 60.

28 H. Philbrick to G. Westcott, 7 July 1969, HPP, box 210, f. 8; M. Liebman to F. Schwarz, 4 April 1962, *MLieb*, box B11, f. "Fred Schwarz."

29 Ad., "Local Study Group," CACCN, April 1959, 3; William Strube, *Establishing a Local Study Group: A Method of Effectively Combating Communism* (Houston: CACC, 1960), 3–5.

30 Strube, *Establishing a Local Study Group*, 3–5.

31 Fred Schwarz, "Study Circles," CACCN, June 1960, 3, repub. in Strube, *Establishing a Local Study Group*, 4; "Anti-Communism Schools Continue Its Great Work," CACCN, October 1960, 4.

32 Qtd. in Strube, *Establishing a Local Study Group*, 4; "Anti-Red Group Plans Expansion," *Spokane Daily Chronicle*, 31 May 1961, 1; John Corlett, "Communism May Be Top Issue in Elections," *Lewiston Morning Tribune* (ID), 24 September 1961, 4; M. Rogovin, "In re: Four Freedoms Study Groups, Inc.," 27 October 1965, WSP, Internal Revenue Service Study of Ideological Organizations, 31 December 1965, f. "G," 2. Mrs. T.L. Horn to W. Judd, 11 January 1961, WHJP, box 226, f. 4, copyright Stanford University.

33 Schwarz, "Study Circles," 3–4; D. McNeil, notes from CACC Phoenix school, DMP, box 1, f. 1–3, 2–3. From BMGP: MF 38, Mrs R.J. Leader to B. Goldwater, 7 April 1961, box 011_REEL031_0004, pdf.,164; Mr. and Mrs. Knapp to B. Goldwater, 22 April 1961, box 011_REEL031_0004,

pdf., 128–9; Lisa McGirr, *Suburban Warriors: The Origins of the New American Right* (Princeton, NJ: Princeton University Press, 2001), 62; Fletcher Knebel, "Rightist Revival: Who's on the Far Right?," *Look* 26, 6 (1962): 26; "Facts about: Christian Anti-Communism Crusade," sec. 4, SPEC, 5/1/62, GRIR, box 138, f. "Frawley, Patrick J.," 5; Schwarz, "Anti-Communism Schools Continue its Great Work," 3; Saul Friedman, "Crusade against Commies Grows: Scores Spreading Message to Other Cities and States," *Houston Chronicle*, 5 July 1961, 1–14; Fred Schwarz, "Will the Kremlin Conquer America by 1973?," *Freedom Forum Presentation* (Searcy, AR: National Education Program, 1959), 25; Report on LA CACC school, GRIR, box 299, f. "Sluis, Joost, 13."

34 "Giant Anti-Communist Rally Billed at Bowl," *LAT*, 29 September 1961, C16; Schwarz, *Beating*, 221.

35 Murray Schumach, "Coast Film Rally against Reds Set," *NYT*, 16 October 1961, 33.

36 *Hollywood's Answer to Communism*, leaflet, GRIR, box 363, f. "CACC Correspondence"; W. Wagstaff and B. Temple to O. Brandt, 28 September 1961, DSBP, box 36, f. 6; Bill Becker, "Right-Wing Groups Multiplying Appeals in Southern California," *NYT*, 29 October 1961, 43.

37 From DSBP: box 36, f. 6: W. Wagstaff and B. Temple to O. Brandt, 28 September 1961; KREM Broadcasting Company president (unsigned) to Ben F. Waple, 2 January 1962; L. Schulman to D. Bullitt, O. Brandt, and B. Schulman, 9 October 1961. "The Threat" panel consisted of Arthur S. Flemming, Dr Edward Teller, Richard Rovere, and Gilbert Seldes.

38 Schwarz, *Beating*, 227–9; "Anti-Red Rally Told to Seek 'Total Victory,'" *LAT*, 17 October 1961, B1; James Aronson, "Spectacular Specter," *National Guardian* (NY), 13 November 1961, 12; John Waugh, "Hollywood Glitters as Anti-Red Rally," *Christian Science Monitor*, 19 October 1961, 13; "Biggest Anti-Red Meet Held Here," *Los Angeles Mirror*, 17 October 1961, B1.

39 KTTV, *Hollywood's Answer to Communism*, TV Special 1961-10-16, University of California at Los Angeles, Film and Television Archive, 2 videocassettes of 2 (VHS), 180 mins. (extracts only).

40 "Far-Right Revivalists," *Life* 51, 9 (1961): 39; "Anti-Red Rally Told to Seek 'Total Victory'"; "Life Magazine," *CACCN*, November 1961, 3; Report, 12/10/65, GRIR, box 138, f. "Frawley, Patrick J.," 2–3.

41 W. Cleon Skousen, "Speech from the Hollywood Bowl which was broadcast coast to coast on TV 10-16-61," WCSP, binder: Hollywood's Answer to Communism, 16 October 1961; "Biggest Anti-Red Meet Held Here."

42 Full transcript: "Hollywood Bowl, October 17, 1961, Hon. Walter H. Judd," WHJu, box 79, f. "Hollywood Bowl – 10/16/61."

43 John Waugh, "Hollywood Glitters as Anti-Red Rally," 13; "Anti-Red Rally Told to Seek 'Total Victory,'"; Jack Gould, "TV: Christian Anti-Communism Crusade Here," *NYT*, 3 November 1961, 71; "15,000 Hear Bowl Attack on Reds," *LAE*, 17 October 1961, 1–2; Schwarz, *Beating*, 228.

44 Richard Shepard, "Anti-Red Rallies to Be Televised," *NYT*, 1 November 1961, 79; *Hollywood's Answer to Communism*, leaflet.

45 Gould, "TV: Christian Anti-Communism Crusade Here," 71; Shepard, "Anti-Red Rallies to Be Televised"; *Hollywood's Answer to Communism*, leaflet; Roger Milliken, *The Story of the Presentation of Hollywood's Answer to Communism* (Spartanburg: Deering Milliken, 1962).

46 *Hollywood's Answer to Communism*, leaflet; "Anti-Red TV Show Acclaimed," *Oregon Journal*, 17 October 1961, 3. From DSBP, box 36, f. 6: E. Holmstrom to D. Bullitt, 24 October 1961; Mrs P. Karr to D. Bullitt, 25 October 1961; C. White to D. Bullitt, October 1961; L. Bell to D. Bullitt, 26 October 1961. Schwarz, *Beating*, 228; C.J. Skreen, "Symposium Set on Communism," *Seattle Times*, 17 October 1961, 43.

47 From *LAT*: "Probe of Army's Role in Red Seminar Demanded," 22 September 1961, 16; "Americanism Rallies to Be Held in Valley," 1 October 1961, SG5; "Americanism Rally to Feature W. Cleon Skousen," 17 October 1961, B1; "GOP in Five Districts Sets 'Freedom' Rally," 27 October 1961, 17; "Anti-Red Unit Donates Books," 2 November 1961, D2; "FBI Ex-Agent Urges Law to Cripple Reds," 8 November 1961, A32; "Red Methods Must Be Known, Ex-Spy Says," 9 November 1961, B32; "Red Rule in U.S. in 2 Years Held Possible," 10 November 1961, A23; "Catholics Will Hold Anti-Communism Rally," 12 November 1961, SF6; "Americanism Town Meeting Set in Glendale," 12 November 1961, K6; "2,100 Expected at All-Day Anti-Red Rally," 12 November 1961, CS3; "U.S. Warned of Aid to Reds by Project Alert Speakers," 16 November 1961, A1; "U.S. Still First in Total Power, Meeting Told," 17 November 1961, B2; "Philbrick to Speak," 24 November 1961, B3; "Self-Reliance Lack Criticized at Rally," 26 November 1961, H12; "Thurmond Assails Army 'Muzzling,'" 2. In late October, the aforementioned "Project Alert" began organizing seminars.

48 Becker, "Right-Wing Groups Multiplying Appeals in Southern California." The Crusade sold more than $182,000 worth of books, tapes, and films, but there was a net loss of about $33,400 in this regard because, as the *NYT* reported, "some of the items [were] sold below cost." Charles

Grutzner, "Reports of Dr. Schwarz's Anti-Communist Crusade Show $1,273,492," *NYT*, 24 June 1962, 9.

49 William O'Neill, *Coming Apart: An Informal History of America in the 1960's* (New York: Random House, 1971), 48; Rick Perlstein, *Before the Storm: Barry Goldwater and the Unmaking of the American Consensus* (New York: Hill and Wang, 2001), 149; Jonathan Schoenwald, *A Time for Choosing: The Rise of Modern Conservatism* (New York: Oxford University Press, 2001), 97.

50 Kimmis Kendrick, "Plea of Confidence: Kennedy Assesses U.S. Trek," *Christian Science Monitor*, 20 November 1961, 4.

51 Kevin Boyle, *The UAW and the Heyday of American Liberalism, 1945–1968* (Ithaca, NY: Cornell University Press, 1998), 139–45. Handwritten note taken beside a photocopy of "The Fulbright Memorandum" by H.M. Hauc, WCSP, binder: Hollywood's Answer to Communism, 16 October 1961.

52 Ralph de Toledano, "Choosing Up Sides on Communism," 10 November 1961, RDTP, box 9, printed matter – 1961.

CHAPTER TEN

1 "Crisis in the Belgian Congo," *CACCN*, March 1960, 1, 3; CACC income and expenses (fiscal years 1960 and 1961), GRIR, box 364, f. "CACC General and Financial"; D. McFarland to F. Schwarz, pub. in *CACCN*, April–May 1961, 2; fundraising letter, 11 November 1961; fundraising letter, March 1962.

2 Robin Jeffrey, "Matriliny, Marxism, and the Birth of the Communist Party of Kerala, 1930–1940," *Journal of Asiatic Studies* 38, 1 (1978): 77–98; editorial, *CACCN*, May 1957, 1.

3 "India," *CACCN*, December 1957, http://www.schwarzreport.org; fundraising letter, 15 July 1959. Info on ICM taken from *Commissioner of Income-Tax v. Dr. K. George Thomas*, [1974] 97 ITR 111 (Ker), http://indiankanoon.org/doc/1253492. Thomas got his scholarship through the help of an American branch of the Kerala Brethren. The Brethren was a radical separatist group adhering to a premillennialist theology.

4 Chandrika Singh, *Communist and Socialist Movement in India: A Critical Account* (Delhi: Mittal Publications, 1987), 116; Gene Overstreet and Marshall Windmiller, *Communism in India* (Berkeley and Los Angeles: University of California Press, 1959), 330; Abraham Vazhayil Thomas, *Christians in Secular India, Cranbury* (New Jersey: Associated University Presses, Inc., 1974), 115; George Mathew, *Communal Road to Secular*

India (New Delhi: Concept Publishing Company, 1989), 147–9; "Kerala Communists in Trouble," CACCN, May 1958, 3; fundraising letter, 15 July 1959.

5 From CACCN: "Kerala, India," September 1958, 4; "Kerala, India," November 1958, 2.

6 Singh, *Communist and Socialist Movement in India*, 117; G. Thomas to F. Schwarz, pub. in CACCN, July 1959, 4; G. Thomas to F. Schwarz, 13 August 1959, pub. in fundraising letter, 25 August 1959.

7 Fred Schwarz, *You Can Trust the Communists (to Be Communists)* (Long Beach, CA: Chantico Publishing Co., 1966), 174.

8 G. Thomas to F. Schwarz, 13 August 1959, pub. in fundraising letter, 25 August 1959. From CACCN: K. Wilson to the CACC, pub. April–May 1961, 5; "Miracle in Kerala," September 1959, 3; G. Thomas to B. Strube, pub. in fundraising letter, 2 October 1959; J. Thomas, "Voice of Kerala: A Modern Day Miracle," July 1960, 3; G. Thomas to B. Strube, pub. in fundraising letter, 2 October 1959; Jim Colbert, "India," January 1960, 3; "Kerala, India," November 1959, 3; G. Thomas to B. Strube, pub. in fundraising letter, 2 October 1959; "Anti-Communism Schools Continue Its Great Work," CACCN, October 1960, 4.

9 George Lieten, "Progressive State Governments: An Assessment of First Communist Ministry in Kerala," *Economic and Political Weekly* 14, 1 (1979): 37; S.R. Bakshi, *E. M. S. Namboodiripad: The Marxist Leader* (New Delhi: Anmol Publications Pvt. Ltd., 1994), 327; "From Tragedy to Triumph – Kerala, India," CACCN, March 1960, 1–3; Charles Grutzner, "Reports of Dr. Schwarz's Anti-Communist Crusade Show $1,273,492," NYT, 24 June, 1962, 9; "A Program against Communism," CACCN, April 1962, 2–3; "Study of Ideological Organizations: 1965 (Part I), Appendix F," IRS, 27 October 1965, WSP, file: Internal Revenue Service Study of Ideological Organizations, 31 December 1965, f. "G," 5–8.

10 From CACCN: G. Thomas to F. Schwarz, pub. December 1960, 2; K. Wilson to the CACC, pub. April–May 1961, 5; J. Colbert, "C.A.C.C. around the World," February 1962, 7; "Sentinel" (pseudonym of author), "Christ in Harness: Miracle of Kottayam," *Mainstream* 4, 38, (1966): 18–19. The number in the 1965 Press Registrar's Report of India was 17,821.

11 M. Rogovin to H. Swartz, 27 October 1965, WSP, file: Internal Revenue Service Study of Ideological Organizations, 31 December 1965, f. "G," 5–8; Patrick Heller, *The Labor of Development: Workers and the Transformation of Capitalism in Kerala, India* (Ithaca, NY: Cornell University Press, 1999), 176; *Fred C. Schwarz, M.D. – Announces – The*

Christian Anti-Communism Crusade's Urgent Projects Banquet, 1964, CACC pamphlet, 3; "Kerala, India," *CACCN*, August 1964, 2. Schwarz's plan was the following: "$500 monthly reduction for the first three months followed by a $1,000 reduction for 21 months. There will be a further reduction of $500 a month at 12 monthly intervals, leading to the complete elimination of the subsidy."

12 "Sentinel," "Christ in Harness," 17–19.

13 *Commissioner of Income-Tax, Kerala v. Dr. K. George Thomas*, 1977 108 ITR 1024 (Ker), http://indiankanoon.org/doc/865855/.

14 Ibid.; *Kerala Income Tax Commission: Commissioner of Income-Tax v. Dr. K. George Thomas*, 1974 97 ITR 111 Ker.

15 F. Schwarz to W. Judd, 26 April 1960, WHJP, box 226, f. 4, copyright Stanford University. In a 1960 letter to Judd, he rejoiced in the contribution the CACC made to defeating the Communists through Thomas's project.

16 *Who's Who of Members From 1st to 11th Kerala Legislative Assembly* (Thiruvananthapuram: Secretariat of the Kerala State Legislature, 2006), 71.

17 David Stoll, "Crusaders against Communism, Witnesses for Peace: Religion in the American West and the Cold War," in *The Cold War American West, 1945–1989*, ed. Kevin Fernlund (Albuquerque: University of New Mexico Press, 1989), 133; David Stoll, *The Politics of Evangelical Growth* (Berkeley and Los Angeles: University of California Press, 1990), 68–9.

18 From *CACCN*: "South America," September 1958, 2; "South America," November 1958, 4; "South America," March 1959, 5. Joost Sluis, "Joost Sluis Visits Central America," *CACCN*, July 1961, 2; "Antipathy for U.S. among Latins Cited," *LAT*, 11 November 1960, 30. "I made rounds and saw patients in nearly every country," Sluis wrote.

19 From *Miami News*: Louise Leyden, "Pastor Finds Field in Latin Migrants," 13 November 1954, 4A; "In Spring: Anti-Communist School Planned," 26 November 1960, 5A; Louise Leyden, "Latin Problem: Rev. Hinson Has Look for Himself," 17 February 1962, 5A; Louise Blanchard, "Churchmen Seek Defeat of Demo Hopeful," 5 October 1960, D1; "Anti-Communism Crusade: Ex-Counterspy to Tell Story," 3 June 1961, 5A. William Lissner, "Cuba Refugee Aid is Outlined Here," *NYT*, 25 March 1961, 8. Jack Oswald, "Priests, Nun: Haiti, Wisconsin Visitors Attended," 12 June 1961, C1. CACC leaflet, *Greater Miami School of Anti-Communism*.

20 W.C. Skousen to R. Skousen, 4 September 1961, WCSP, binder: Hollywood's Answer to Communism, 16 October 1961. Extracts from the Mexican version of *You Can Trust* republished in *CACCN*, 9 September 1963, 7; Unknown to F. Ranuzzi, 26 December 1961, FRP, correspondence folder.

21 A. James to F. Schwarz, 5 November 1962, pub. in *Fred C. Schwarz, M.D. – Announces – The Christian Anti-Communism Crusade's Urgent Projects Banquet, 1964*; T. de Queiroz to F. Schwarz, pub. in "Challenge of Brazil," CACCN, February 1963, 6. From CACCN: "Brazil – Land of Destiny for Latin America. Communist of Free?," June 1963, 4; "Brazil," January 1964, 5; caption, April 1964, 3; "Our Biggest Disappointment in 1964," December 1964, 4; Nathaniel Rangel, "Victory in Brazil," July 1964, 1. About twelve thousand copies of *You Can Trust* were distributed in Brazil, mostly to students.

22 Ernst Halperin, "Racism and Communism in British Guiana," *Journal of Inter-American Studies* 7, 1 (1965): 95–6; Eldegard Mahant and Graeme Mount, *Invisible and Inaudible in Washington: American Policies towards Canada* (Vancouver: UBC Press, 1999), 87–8; C. Paul Bradley, "Party Politics in British Guiana," *Western Political Quarterly* 16, 2 (1963): 353–6.

23 Halperin, "Racism and Communism in British Guiana," 97; Cary Fraser, "The 'New Frontier' of Empire in the Caribbean: The Transfer of Power in British Guiana, 1961–1964," *International History Review* 22, 3 (2000): 585.

24 Fundraising letter, 23 May 1961.

25 United Nations, Colonialism Committee, "Chapter X – British Guiana, A. Action Taken by the Special Committee in 1962," *United Nations, Official Records of the General Assembly – Eighteenth Session (Annexes, 17 September-17 December 1963)*, New York, United Nations, 1965, 237; Phil Kerby, "Anti-Red Crusade Seen Expanding across U.S.," *WashP*, 7 November 1961, A4.

26 From NARA: B. Hays to J. Clark, 7 November 1961, RG 59, stack area 150, row 4, compt 13, shelf 4, box 2319; E. Melby to D. Rusk, 3 March 1962, RG 59, stack area 250, row 3, compt 1, shelf 6, box 41; Stephen Rabe, *U.S. Intervention in British Guiana: A Cold War History* (Chapel Hill: University of North Carolina Press, 2005), 72–8; Colin Palmer, *Cheddi Jagan and the Politics of Power: British Guiana's Struggle for Independence* (Chapel Hill: University of North Carolina Press, 2010), 251–2; William Blum, *Killing Hope, US Military and CIA Interventions since World War II* (Noida, India: Gopson Papers Limited, 2004), 108–14.

27 From NARA: RG 59, stack area 250, row 3, compt 1, shelf 6, box 41: E. Melby to D. Rusk, 25 February 1962; D. Rusk to E. Melby, 26 February 1962, compt 1, shelf 6, box 41. US Amb. to Jamaica to Sec. of State, 27 June 1960; Sec. of State to US Amb. to Jamaica, 29 June 1960. Sluis was known by State Department Officials since his 1960 tour.

28 From NARA: RG 59, stack area 250, row 3, compt 1, shelf 6, box 41: "London" to D. Rusk, Mar. 2, 1962; E. Melby to D. Rusk, Mar. 1, 1962; D. Rusk to E. Melby, Mar. 2, 1962.

29 From NARA: RG 59, stack area 250, row 3, compt 1, shelf 6, box 41: E. Melby to D. Rusk, 27 February 1962; E. Melby to D. Rusk, 3 March 1962.

30 From NARA: RG 59, stack area 250, row 3, compt 1, shelf 6, box 41: E. Melby to D. Rusk, 9 March 1962; E. Melby to D. Rusk, 11 March 1962.

31 From NARA: RG 59, stack area 250, row 3, compt 1, shelf 6, box 41: E. Melby to D. Rusk, 17 April 1962; E. Melby to D. Rusk, 18 April 1962; D. Rusk to E. Melby, 25 April 1962; Mr. Guest to D. Rusk, 28 April 1962; Mr Guest to D. Rusk, 28 April 1962; E. Melby to D. Rusk, 22 May 1962; E. Melby to D. Rusk, 24 May 1962; E. Melby to D. Rusk, 31 May 1962; D. Rusk to US Consuls of Georgetown, Paramaribo and the US Emb. of London, 13 June 1962. See also E. Melby to D. Rusk, 23 June 1962, JFKP, National Security Files Counties Reference Copy, box 15, f. "General 6-62 to 12-62." The US officially protested over the deportation order.

32 From *CACCN*: "British Guiana," August 1962, 8; Joost Sluis, "An Alumnus and the Christian Anti-Communism Crusade," independent reprint from the *Harvard Medical Alumni Bulletin*, Spring 1963, 3; "British Guiana," January 1965, 8; "Cheddi Jagan of Guiana – Prohibited Immigrant," 11 December 1967, 7. Joost Sluis to Arthur McDowell, 30 August 1963, MLP, box 1, f. 2.

CHAPTER ELEVEN

1 Carleton Campbell, "Christian Economics," *Lima News* (OH), 4 August 1960, 18.

2 Stanley Allaby, "Local Group Formed to Combat Communism," *CACCN*, March 1959, 3–4.

3 George Thayer, *The Farther Shores of Politics: The American Political Fringe Today, Newly Revised* (New York: Simon and Schuster, 1968), 277; John Andrews III, *The Other Side of the Sixties: Young Americans for Freedom and the Rise of Conservative Politics* (New Brunswick: Rutgers University Press, 1997), 106; Merrill Folsom, "'Crusade' on Reds Is Brought East," *NYT*, 10 May 1961, 38; "Dr. Carleton Campbell, Surgeon, Educator," *Wilton Bulletin*, 5 December 1984, 2; William Lissner, "'Freedom Forum' Begins Talks Here on Tactics of Reds," *NYT*, 7 June

1962, 15; Unknown to L. Merthen, 2 August 1962, GRIR, box 363, f. "CACC Correspondence."

4 C.E. Carver to F. Schwarz, 20 December 1955, pub. in *CACCN*, January 1956, 4. From HPP: M. Ashwill to H. Philbrick, 10 September 1959, box 243, f. 4; C.E. Carver to H. Philbrick, 3 February 1961, box 4, f. 1. C.E. Carver to W.C. Skousen, 11 December 1961, WCSP, binder: Hollywood's Answer to Communism, 16 October 1961.

5 Schwarz, "Schools for Anti-Communists," *CACCN*, March 1959, 3; Scott McNall, *Career of a Radical Rightist: A Study in Failure* (Port Washington: Kennikat Press, 1975), 18–36; Edward Shapsmeier and Frederick Shapsmeier, *Political Parties and Civic Groups* (Westport, CT: Greenwood, 1981), 180; William Lunch, "The Christian Right in the Northwest: Two Decades of Frustration in Oregon and Washington," in *The Christian Right in American Politics: Marching to the Millennium*, ed. John Green, Mark Rozell, and Clyde Wilcox (Georgetown: Georgetown University Press, 2008), 236; Lon Fendall, *Stand Alone or Come Home: As Both Evangelical and a Progressive, Mark Hatfield Separated Himself from the Political Crowd* (Newberg, OR: Barclay Press, 2003), 39.

6 Michelle Nickerson and Patricia Cullinane, CWCP, transcript in f. Cullinane, Patricia, 3933, Nickerson, Michelle, 5/8/2006, 2-7; Robert Novak, "Nixon Forces Cheered by Primary Victory, But a Dilemma Looms," *Wall Street Journal*, 7 June 1962, 1; Bill Becker, "School Post Goes to Conservative," *NYT*, 8 November 1962, 15.

7 From *LAT*: "West Covina Council OKs Smut Drive," 28 November 1965, SG-A1; Bob Jackson, "Obscenity Proposition Raises Stormy Dispute," 6 October 1966, A1. "Assemblyman Names Eight to GOP Committee," 30 March 1969, SG-A5; Jean Merl, "We're the Party: Local Republicans Fill Detroit Scenes," 17 July 1980, CS1; "Mrs. R. P. Feddersen, Jr. (Rusty)," "1-3-79, Agenda," MKP, main folder.

8 Raymond Wolfinger, Barbara Wolfinger, Kenneth Prewitt, and Sheilah Rosenhack, "America's Radical Right: Politics and Ideology," in *The American Right-Wing: Readings in Political Behavior*, ed. Robert Schoenberger (New York: Holt Rinehart and Winston, 1969), 13–17; Raymond Wolfinger, phone interview with author, 5 February 2008.

9 Sheilah Koeppen, "The Radical Right and the Politics of Consensus," in *The American Right-Wing: Readings in Political Behavior*, ed. Robert Schoenberger (New York: Holt Rinehart and Winston, 1969), 49–52. Koeppen eliminated respondents under twenty as well as those who participated in the first study or seemed against Schwarz.

10 The 1964 ANES had a sample of 1,571 respondents, plus a "Black supplement sample" (263). They were asked if they had heard of the CACC. Those who did were then asked to rate it on a thermometer, 0° meaning extreme coolness and 100° extreme warmth. These answers only made sense when compared to those given with regard to other issues or groups.

11 Clyde Wilcox, "The Christian Right in Twentieth-Century America: Continuity and Change," *Review of Politics* 50, 4 (1988): 659–81; Clyde Wilcox, "Popular Backing for the Old Christian Right: Explaining Support for the Christian Anti-Communism Crusade," *Journal of Social History* 21, 1 (1987): 117–32; Clyde Wilcox, "Sources of Support for the Old Right: A Comparison of the John Birch Society and the Christian Anti-Communism Crusade," *Social Science History* 12, 4 (1988): 439–49.

12 Respectively, 47 percent, 23 percent, and 30 percent.

13 "Appendix," *Facts – Published by the Anti-Defamation League of B'Nai B'Rith* (ADL), November–December 1961, 228; Howard Silber, "Sponsors Predict a Huge Success for Schwarz Crusade," *Sunday World-Herald* (NE), 6 May 1962, 6–8; "'Gold for Goldwater' Drive Gains," *Hartford Courant*, 29 July 1963, 3; Fred Schwarz, "The Dallas Freedom Forum," CACCN, December 1960, 1; Michelle Nickerson (interviewer) and Marjorie C. Jensen, CWCP, transcript in F. Jensen, Marjorie C., 3937, Nickerson, Michelle, 7/5/2002, 19.

14 Texas alone had 13.8 percent of all lifetime members.

15 In a year in which all donations to the Crusade amounted to $470,457, 16.3 percent of $100-plus donations came from California (20 percent including institutional donors).

16 Eighty percent of them were suburbanites in Southern California (67 percent in the north).

17 Wolfinger et al., "America's Radical Right," 17; Clyde Wilcox, *God's Warriors: The Christian Right in Twentieth-Century America* (Baltimore: Johns Hopkins University Press, 1992), 9–93; Koeppen, "Radical Right," 53–5. Sixty-seven percent as per Wolfinger, 65 percent according to Koeppen, 51 percent among Bay Area white residents.

18 Koeppen, "Radical Right," 54; Report – LA CACC school, GRIR, box 299, f. "Sluis, Joost, 15"; D. McNeil, notes from CACC Phoenix school, DMP, box 1, f. 1–3; Robert Reilly, "Schwarz Was Here," *America*, 24 March 1962, 821. Reporter Donald McNeil, who attended the CACC School in Phoenix, noted that the bulk of attendees were between thirty and forty-five years old.

19 Wolfinger et al., "America's Radical Right," 38–9, 54.

20 Wilcox, *God's Warriors,* 72–4, 80–1. Among those who attended evangelical churches, "frequency of attendance was a predictor of awareness" of the Crusade.

21 Wolfinger et al., "America's Radical Right," 38–9, 42; Wilcox, *God's Warriors,* 74–6, 84. The ANES study showed that these trends also held among the general public, where both awareness of and support for the CACC was higher among educated and upper-class people

22 William Glaser, "Doctors and Politics," *American Journal of Sociology* 66, 3 (1960): 233–8; Stephen Kunitz, Andrew Sorensen, and Suzanne Cashman, "Changing Health Care Opinions in Regionville: 1946–1973," *Medical Care* 13, 7 (1975): 552–6; John Colomboos, "Physicians' Attitude towards Medicare," *Medical Care* 6, 4 (1968): 320–6; Glaser, "Doctors and Politics," 240–2.

23 James McEvoy, Mark Chesler, and Richard Schmuck, "Content Analysis of a Super Patriot Protest," *Social Problems* 14, 4 (1967): 459; Herman Edelsberg, "Birchites Make Polite Pen Pals," *ADL Bulletin*, April 1962, 7; Seymour Martin Lipset and Earl Raab, *The Politics of Unreason: Right-Wing Extremism in America, 1790–1970* (New York: Harper and Row, 1970), 311–12.

24 Directors and advisory council members from editorial, CACCN, September 1956, 1.

25 G. Westcott to H. Philbrick, 6 February 1967, HPP, box 210, f. 8; Walter Judd, "The Doctor's Place in Public Affairs," *Journal of the Arkansas Medical Society* 61, 7 (1964): 212.

26 Monte Poen, *Harry S. Truman versus the Medical Lobby* (Columbia: University of Missouri Press, 1979), 13; Duane Stroman, *The Medical Establishment and Social Responsibility* (Port Washington: Kennikat Press, 1976), 104–7; Daniel Hirschfield, *The Lost Reform: The Campaign for Compulsory Health Insurance in the United States from 1932 to 1943* (Cambridge: Harvard University Press, 1970), 34–41, 120–30.

27 Judd, "Doctor's Place in Public Affairs," 212–13.

28 Rockey Hendricks, "Medical Practice Embattled: Kaiser Permanente, the American Medical Association, and Henry J. Kaiser on the West Coast, 1945–1955," *Pacific Historical Review* 60, 4 (1991): 453; Lisa McGirr, *Suburban Warriors: The Origins of the New American Right* (Princeton, NJ: Princeton University Press, 2001), 84; G.W. Hawkins to B. Goldwater, 16 August 1961, BMGP, MF 44, box 012_REEL020_0003, pdf. 371-2; W.C. Skousen to H. Skousen, 26 October 1961, WCSP, binder: Hollywood's Answer to Communism, 16 October 1961. In the early 1960s, more than fifty medical professionals founded Doctors for America

in Orange County in support of conservative causes. In Downey, Southeast Los Angeles County, Rotary president and dentist James R. Harvey led a drive that successfully lobbied the local school board to include an American Heritage program in the curriculum, despite opposition from the town's liberals. Skousen spoke before the Californian Medical Association, whose president pushed his book among doctors (see 26 October 1961 letter above).

29 "GOP Forming New Group in Harbor Area," *LAT*, 17 September 1961, OC11; McGirr, *Suburban Warriors*, 91, 116–18; T. Cosgrove to H. Philbrick, 25 January 1961, HPP, box 243, f. 6. Peggy Pearce also recruited Harold and Shirley Muckenthaler, well-respected county citizens, JBS supporters, and members of the Orange County CACC school's finance and youth committees.

30 From *LAT*: Richard Bergholz, "Orange County Doctor Heads GOP Assembly," *LAT*, 17 March 1964, 5; caption, "Elected," 8 April 1964, F10; John O'Dell, "Candidates Abandoned: Democratic Vote Went Elsewhere," 9 November 1980, OC B8; Richard Bergholz, "Delay Installation of UC San Diego Head, CRA Urges," 24 March 1969, A3; "Group Officers of Freedom Foundation to Meet Today," 1 August 1968, G4E.

31 From *LAT*: "1956–1966: Arch-Conservatives and a 'Kooky' Image," 21 March 1976, OC-A5, 9, 10, 12; Jeffrey Perlman, "Orange County Developer Ranks with Top U.S. Donors to Contras," 19 July 1987, OC-A6; David Haldane, "Obituary: W. Brashears; "Developer Left His Mark on Fullerton," 3 November 2000, B13.

32 T.D. Junco, fundraising letter, 2 March 1962. From *LAT*: "Cuban Will Address Grove Club," 8 March 1962, E15; "Republican Fund Dinner Set Tonight," 22 May 1963, B16; "Latin American GOP Group Seeks Members," 12 January 1964, O1; Carl Greenberg, "CRA Chief Says King Paves 'Road to Anarchy,'" 27 March 1965, B6; Carl Greenberg, "CRA Endorses Reagan, Defeats Nixon Backers," 1 April 1968, 3; Richard Bergholz, "State GOP Now Firmly in Hands of Reaganites," 19 February 1979, A3; William Endicott, "Ex-GOP Chief Named to Post," 10 March 1983, B3.

33 Daniel Bell, "The Dispossessed (1962)," in *The Radical Right: The American Right, Expanded and Updated*, ed. Daniel Bell (New York: Doubleday, 1962), 32.

34 The donors' list included thirty-eight small/medium companies that gave a combined amount of $11,856 for an average of $312 each, more than the $221 of individual donors. For instance, Fashion Fabrics from New Mexico; Ward Development Company of Santa Ana; Allen Gwynn Chevrolet, from Glendale; Home Bank from South Long Beach.

35 Lipset and Raab, *Politics of Unreason*, 228–32. See also studies by Burton Levy (political science, University of Massachusetts, 1965) and Barbara Stone (political science, University of Southern California, 1968). In Fred Grupp's study of a group of Birchers, people in business-managerial positions accounted for a third of his sample. More than fourteen out of twenty-four names on the JBS's national council in 1967 had backgrounds similar to that of Robert Welch (i.e., managers of medium-sized companies).

36 Richard Hofstadter, "The Pseudo-Conservative Revolt (1955)," in *The Radical Right: The American Right, Expanded and Updated*, ed. Daniel Bell (New York: Doubleday, 1962), 84; Wilcox, "Popular Backing for the Old Christian Right," 124; Victor Ferkiss, "Political and Intellectual Origins of American Radicalism, Right and Left," *Annals of the American Academy of Political and Social Science* 344, 1 (1962): 9; William Hixson, *Search for the American Right Wing: An Analysis of the Social Science Record, 1955–1987* (Princeton, NJ: Princeton University Press, 1992), 69.

37 Koeppen, "Radical Right," 55–7; Wolfinger et al., "America's Radical Right," 17.

38 Wolfinger et al., "America's Radical Right," 21.

39 Sheilah Koeppen, "Dissensus and Discontent: The Clientele of the Christian Anti-Communism Crusade" (PhD diss., Stanford University, 1967), 60–1.

40 Wilcox, *God's Warriors,* 80; George Gallup, "Most for Integration; Many Deplore Riders," *LAT*, 21 June 1961, 11. Most US citizens outside the South supported integration by 1961, though they were split on civil rights groups themselves.

41 Wolfinger et al., "America's Radical Right," 23–4; Koeppen, "Dissensus and Discontent," 46, 66; Wilcox, *God's Warriors,* 81.

42 Qtd. in "Stanford Survey Depicts Typical Dr. Schwarz Backer," *Oakland Tribune*, 4 September 1963, 2E.

43 Peter Kihss, "Rockefeller Charges Kennedy with 'Opportunism,'" *NYT*, 5 September 1963, 22; Wolfinger et al., "America's Radical Right," 46; "Conservative Traits Found in Anti-Reds," *LAT*, 5 September 1963, 32.

44 "Questions Honesty: Schwarz Attacks Stanford Report," *Daily Review* (CA), 12 September 1963, 6; "Crusader Hits Research Study," *Bridgeport Telegram*, 20 September 1963, 33.

45 *Firing Line* with William F. Buckley Jr, Program 062, "The Decline of Anti-Communism (1967)," Hoover Institution Archives.

46 Clyde Wilcox, "America's Radical Right Revisited: A Comparison of the Activists of Christian Right Organizations from the 1960's and the 1980's," *Sociological Analysis* 48, 1 (1987): 49–56.

CHAPTER TWELVE

1 "Commie Foe Brings His Crusade to City," *Omaha World-Herald*, 17 November 1961, 1; Robert Reilly, "Schwarz Was Here," *America*, 24 March 1962, 820.

2 Fred Schwarz, "Ronald Reagan," *Schwarz Report* 44, 8 (2004): 1; Robert Reilly, "Schwarz Was Here," 821. From *Omaha World-Herald*: "'Rally Crowd Fantastic,'" 17 November 1961, 1, 4; "7,000 Hear Dr. Schwarz Tell of Peril," 17 November 1961, 1.

3 Kenneth Woodward, "What Qualifications for a Crusader? Fred Schwarz on Communism," *Catholic Reporter*, 1 February 1963, 16; E. Berck to W. McCune, 28 May 1962, GRIR, box 363, f. "CACC Correspondence."

4 Fred Schwarz, "Midwest School of Anti-Communism," *CACCN*, June 1962, 3; Reilly, "Schwarz Was Here," 822; "Dr. Schwarz Debate Is Out," *Omaha World-Herald*, 16 April 1962, 18; Morrie Ryskind, "Ryskind Asks: Give Schwarz School Its Chance and Then Form Opinion," repub. in *CACCN*, June 1962, 4. Morrie Ryskind defended Schwarz in his column.

5 "Dr. Schwarz Warns of Kremlin Danger," *St Petersburg Times* (FL), 20 May 1961, 4C. From *St Petersburg Times* (FL): "The Suncoast and Anti-Communism," 3 December 1961, 2E; Bill Williamson, "Unpatriotic Charge Makes Christian 'Sick,'" 3 December 1961, B1; "Demo Women to Observe Anti-Communism School," 17 November 1961, 20B. In 1961, Schwarz was warmly welcomed in west-central Florida.

6 "Thunder on the Right: Fear and Frustration…," *Newsweek* 58, 35 (1961): 28–9.

7 Alan Barth, "Report on the 'Rampageous Right,'" *NYT*, 26 November 1961, SM25, 130, 132; Fred Cook, "Juggernaut: The Warfare State," *Nation* 193, 14 (1961): 334; Fred Cook, from "The Ultras: Aims, Affiliations and Finances of the Radical Right," in *Nation*, 23 June 1962, qtd. in George Seldes, *Never Tire of Protesting* (New York: L. Stuart, 1968), 220.

8 This letter is partly reproduced in Arnold Forster and Benjamin Epstein, *Danger on the Right: The Attitudes, Personnel and Influence of the Radical Right and Extreme Conservatives* (New York: Random House, 1964), 52–3.

9 Leo P. Ribuffo, *The Old Christian Right: The Protestant Far Right from the Great Depression to the Cold War* (Philadelphia: Temple University Press, 1983), 182; John Drabble, "Brown Scare," in *Conspiracy Theories in American History: An Encyclopedia, Vol. 1*, ed. Peter Knight (Santa Barbara, CA: ABC-CLIO, 2003), 137–9.

10 Ribuffo, *Old Christian Right*, 239; D.J. Mulloy, *The World of the John Birch Society: Conspiracy, Conservatism, and the Cold War* (Nashville: Vanderbilt University Press, 2014), 63–4. Interestingly, three of *The New American Right*'s contributors (David Riesman, Peter Viereck, and Daniel Bell) contributed somehow to the Second World War-era Brown Scare.

11 Donald Critchlow, *Phyllis Schlafly and Grassroots Conservatism: A Woman's Crusade* (Princeton, NJ: Princeton University Press, 2006), 103.

12 "Supervisor Challenges Mayor: Anti-Red Week Row," *SFE*, 23 January 1962, 3; Lawrence Davies, "Welch Sees Drive against Military," *NYT*, 13 January 1962, 10; "Schwarz and Mandel in Quiet Debate," *Oakland Tribune*, 27 January 1962, 1, 3; Dana McGaugh, "The Fred Schwarz Story: Crusade for a Million Dollars, *Morning News* (CA), 10 January 1962, 3; Herb Caen, "Anti-Commie Vigilantes Encourage Police State," *Vancouver Sun* (*San Francisco Chronicle* editorial repub.), 15 January 1962, 5; Urban Whitaker, "The Right-Wing Goes to School," *Liberal Democrat* (CA), March 1962, 10–11.

13 From *SFE*: John McDonald, "Crusader Schwarz Speaks Here: Anti-Red Unites in Business Urged," 8 January 1962, 16; John McDonald, "Clergymen Oppose Anti-Red Crusader," 12 January 1962, 1. From *Fresno Bee*: "Mosk, Pike Assail 'Anti Red' School," 25 January 1962, 4-A; "Anti-Red School Supported," 13 January 1962, 6. "Churches to Support Dr. Schwarz," *Oakland Tribune*, 25 January 1962, E5.

14 "Bay 'Anti-Red Week' Tiffs," *SFE*, 19 January 1962, 4; "Mosk, Pike Assail 'Anti Red' School"; "Mosk Raps School for Anti-Reds," *Oakland Tribune*, 25 January 1962, 1; "Christopher Hits Mosk on Anti-Red Issue," *LAT*, 26 January 1962, 6; "Christopher Scores Mosk Red Stand," *Oakland Tribune*, 26 January 1962, E3; "Anti-Red School Backer Quits, Raps Schwarz," *Fresno Bee*, 24 January 1962, 8-A.

15 "Mosk Challenged on Schwarz Stand: School Aide Asks Proof of Charges," *Oakland Tribune*, 30 January 1962, E13; Stanley Mosk, "Broadcast by California Attorney General Stanley Mosk," 02/15/62, KTVU, WFBP, box 22, f. "Schwarz, Fred (1962)"; Fred Schwarz, *Beating the Unbeatable Foe: One Man's Victory over Communism, Leviathan, and the Last Enemy* (Washington, DC: Regnery, 1996), 418–19.

16 John L. Shover, "The Christian Anti-Communism Crusade in San Francisco," unpub. article, JLSM, 1 portfolio, 4; "Dr. Schwarz School in San Mateo," *SFE*, 19 September 1962, 11.

17 "Actress Marsha Hunt Guarded: Terror Bombs, Two Ministers' Homes Blasted, Families Safe," *LAT*, 2 February 1961, 1; Bill Becker, "Homes of Critics of Right Bombed," *NYT*, 3 February 1962, 36. Simmons had publicly opposed *Operation Abolition* at a time when it was shown throughout the Los Angeles suburbs.

18 Drew Pearson, "LA Bombings May Be Only a Beginning," *Free-Lance Star* (VA), 12 February 1962, 6; "Radio Station, Actors' Home Guarded after Bomb Threat," *LAT*, 6 February 1962, A1; "Dr. Schwarz Gives Views on Bombings," *Humboldt Standard* (NE), 5 February 1962, 2.

19 "Radio Debate Cancelled," *Spokane Daily Chronicle*, 8 February 1962, 6; Terry Pettus, "Schwarz Crusade Has a Rough Time at Seattle," *National Guardian* (NY), 5 March 1962, 5; "Clergy Protest: School Is Criticized as Freedom Threat," *Spokane Daily Chronicle*, 12 February 1962, 6; "Anti-Red School: Writer Accused of Aiding Castro," *Honolulu Star-Bulletin*, 27 February 1962, 17; "UPI Background on Wieland Case," *Honolulu Advertiser*, 28 February 1962, A9.

20 Charles Whipple, "Is John Birch Society in Trouble?," *Boston Globe*, 11 February 1962, 1; Critchlow, *Phyllis Schlafly*, 70; Richard Gid Powers, *Not without Honor: The History of American Anticommunism* (New York: The Free Press, 1995), 287–8; William Buckley, "The Question of Robert Welch," *National Review*, 13 February 1962, 82–7; "Nixon Blasts Birch Society," *Free-Lance Star* (VA), 2 March 1962, 8; Harriet Van Horne, "T.V. Review: Voices of Moderation Deserved More Time," *Albuquerque Tribune*, 23 February 1962, A-11; Cynthia Lowry, "TV Program on Rightist Called Bland," *Brainerd Daily Dispatch* (MN), 23 February 1962, 5; Schwarz, *Beating*, 284–92.

21 *Meet the Press*, transcript, recorded 25 February 1962, Guest: Senator Thomas J. Dodd; Thomas Dodd, "Statement," TJDP, box 194, f. "Statement: 'Right Wing Extremism and the Liberal Responsibility,'" 18 February 1962; W. Judd to H. Hof, 3 April 1962, WHJP, box 226, f. 4, copyright Stanford University; H. Philbrick to A.F. Brux, 26 February 1962, HPP, box 4, f. 7.

22 John Abele, "Technicolor Meeting Is Stormy; Projector's Promotion Criticized," *NYT*, 22 May 1962, 49.

23 V. Reuther to R.F. Kennedy, 19 December 1961, JLRP, box 41, f. "Reuther, Walter P. – Personal: 1949, 1954–1965, 1970." John Andrews III, *Power*

to Destroy: The Political Uses of the IRS from Kennedy to Nixon (Chicago: Ivan R. Dee, 2002), 22.

24 *The Radical Right in America Today*, 1961, JLRP, box 41, f. "Reuther, Walter P. – Personal: 1949, 1954–1965, 1970,"

25 Audit Division, National Office, to District Director of the Los Angeles District Office, 25 September 1961; Chief, Exempt Organizations Branch, Tax Rulings Division TR:EO:1-CCG, National Office, to District Director, Los Angeles, California, 2 February 1962, IRS-EOD; Andrews III, *Power to Destroy*, 64.

26 "IRS Memorandum to Regional Commissioners," 27 August 1963, WSP, f. "Internal Revenue Service Study of Ideological Organizations, 31 December 1965, Section E"; Andrews III, *Power to Destroy*, 29–34.

27 "Introduction – Internal Revenue Service Study of Ideological Organizations, December 31, 1965," WSP, f. (same name), 6. Other groups included America's Future, Inc., the Christian Echoes Ministry, the Circuit Riders, the American Economic Foundation, the American Enterprise Institute, the Foundation for Economic Education, and the Freedom Foundation at Valley Forge.

28 M. Rogovin to M. Caplin, 9 February 1963, WSP, f. "Internal Revenue Service Study of Ideological Organizations, December 31, 1965, Appendix D"; CACC income and expenses (fiscal years 1958, 1959, and 1960), GRIR, box 364, f. "CACC General and Financial"; M. Rogovin to H. Swartz, 27 October 1965, WSP, File Internal Revenue Service Study of Ideological Organizations, 31 December 1965, f. "G," 5–8.

29 M. Rogovin to H. Swartz, 27 October 1965, WSP, File Internal Revenue Service Study of Ideological Organizations, 31 December 1965, f. "G," 8.

30 "Australia," *CACCN*, November 1959, 3; Elton Wilson, fundraising letter, 27 October 1962; Forrest Allen, "They Don't Think Much of Schwarz Down Under," *Cleveland Press*, 12 July 1962, B16; Elton Wilson, fundraising letter, 27 October 1962; fundraising letter, 30 September 1963; fundraising letter, 28 September 1965. Wilson was one of Schwarz's friends since 1946. In late 1963, Schwarz wrote his Australian supporters: "To carry on, it has been necessary in the past year for the American Crusade to subsidise the Australian work to the extent of £3,000-0-0. In addition to this a debt of £1,250-0-0 was incurred."

31 Andrews III, *Power to Destroy*, 66; Woodward, "What Qualifications," 17.

32 KREM president (unsigned) to B. Waple, 2 January 1962, DSBP, box 36, f. 6.

33 John Chamberlain, "These Days: Enforcement of 'Fairness' Rule Could Result in Chaos," *Park City Daily News* (KY), 6 November 1963, 4;

Clarence Page, "Fairness Doctrine Works Both Ways," *Blade* (OH), 10 September 1993, 11; "Introduction – Internal Revenue Service Study of Ideological Organizations, December 31, 1965," WSP, f. (same name), 6.

34 Patrick Murphy Malin to Fred Thrower, 3 February 1962, DSBP, box 36, f. 6; "The Reuther Memorandum," *CACCN*, November 1963, 5. For Schwarz, "when we consider ... the death power exercised by the F.C.C. the reluctance of friendly television stations can be understood."

35 *The Radical Right in American Today*, JLRP, box 41, f. "Reuther, Walter P. – Personal: 1949, 1954–1965, 1970," 17; Andrews III, *Power to Destroy*, 22–3.

36 *Dallas Freedom Forum*, leaflet. From FBIF: W.C. Sullivan to A.H. Belmont, 22 September 1960, f. "Dallas Freedom Forum HQ – 1"; f. "Schwarz, Fred HQ – 3": W.C. Sullivan to A.H. Belmont, 13 March 1961; annotated copy of letter from J.E. Hoover to Mrs. B. Mason, 4 August 1961; R.W. Smith to W.C. Sullivan, 13 October 1961.

37 From FBIF: f. "Skousen, W. Cleon – 4": C.D. DeLoach to J. Mohr, 28 July 1960; J.E. Hoover to H. Carlston, 19 April 1961; C.D. DeLoach to M. Tolson, 8 September 1961; J.E. Hoover to D. Moynan, 1 November 1961.

38 From FBIF: C.D. DeLoach to J. Mohr, 26 October 1961, f. "Skousen, W. Cleon – 4"; W.C. Sullivan to A.H. Belmont, 16 January 1962, f. "Skousen, W. Cleon – 1"; W.C. Sullivan to A.H. Belmont, 13 July 1962, f. "Schwarz, Fred HQ – 6."

39 E. Ettinger to W. Judd, 27 October 1961, WHJu, box 70, f. "Judd, Walter H. – Hollywood Bowl, Oct. 16, 1961"; notes by W.C. Skousen, 16 October 1961, WCSP, binder: Hollywood's Answer to Communism, 16 October 1961. The letter from Ettinger confirms that the idea initially came from Frawley.

40 Fundraising letter, May 1962.

41 G. Murphy to M. Liebman, 19 April 1962, MLieb, box B11, f. "Fred Schwarz."

42 From MLieb: box B11, f. "Fred Schwarz": M. Liebman to F. Schwarz, 4 April 1962; M. Liebman to F. Schwarz, 18 April 1962; R. Hunt, "Anti-Communist Says City's Hostility Is Easing," *NYT*, 14 June 1962, 2.

43 M. Liebman to "All Concerned," 26 April 1962; M. Liebman to Schwarz et al., 30 April 1962, MLieb, box B11, f. "Fred Schwarz."

44 "The Case of Fred C. Schwarz," *Facts* (ADL), November–December 1962, 258–9; "The Greater New York School of Anti-Communism," *CACCN*, June 1962, 5–6.

45 Schwarz, *Beating*, 419; Mary Hornaday, "Anti-Red Crusader in N.Y.," *Christian Science Monitor*, 30 June 1962, 5.

46 James Wechsler, "The Have-Nots," *New York Post*, 2 July 1962, 28; Murray Kempton, "The Dinkum Oil," *New York Post*, clipping sent to author, 7. See also numerous columns in Murray Kempton, *America Comes of Middle Age* (New York: Little, Brown and Company, 1963), chap. 7. From MLieb: box B11, f. "Fred Schwarz": M. Liebman to the *New York Post*, 16 May 1962; A. Davis to M. Liebman, 25 May 1962.

47 George Sokolsky, "Washington Is Shaken by McCarthy Noise," *Telegraph-Herald* (IA), 16 April 1950, 12.; George Sokolsky, "Have We Ganged Up?," *Rome News-Tribune* (GA), 21 February 1962, 5; M. Liebman to G. Sokolsky, 2 May 1962, MLieb, box 8, f. "American Jewish League against Communism."

48 G. Sokolsky, "Rightist Movement Not Understood by the Left," *Helena Independent Record* (MT), 13 December 1961, 8; H. Philbrick to G. Sokolsky, 1 March 1962, HPP, box 179, f. 15; George Sokolsky, "The Battle over Right Wing," *Rome News-Tribune* (GA), 25 February 1962, 4; C.D. DeLoach to J. Mohr, 14 March 1962, FBIF, f. "Sokolsky, George E. HQ -1-4"; G. Murphy to M. Liebman, 9 April 1962, MLieb, box B11, f. "Fred Schwarz."

49 C.D. DeLoach to J. Mohr, 14 March 1962, FBIF, f. "Sokolsky, George E. HQ -1-4."

50 "Attack to Discredit Dr. Schwarz & C.A.C.C.," *CACCN*, August 1962, 3–4 ; M. Liebman to W.F. Buckley, 9 May 1962, MLieb, box B11, f. "Fred Schwarz"; A. McDowell to J. Sluis, 3 November 1965, HPP, box 175, f. 6; McDowell to *News and Views*, 22 July 1963, MLP, box 1, f. 2. McDowell also suggested that the Jewish community's hostility revealed its misgivings towards "apostates."

51 M. Liebman to G. Sokolsky, 2 May 1962, MLieb, box 8, f. "American Jewish League against Communism"; Schwarz, *Beating*, 324; F. Schwarz to S.A. Fienberg, 15 April 1963, MLP, box 1, f. 2.

52 "Paying My Debt to History," *CACCN*, 1 July 1996, 2; Schwarz, *Beating*, 321; GR report on the LA CACC school, GRIR, 299, f. "Sluis, Joost," 2; F. Schwarz to J. Garrett, 23 August 1961; G. Hudson to G.K. Smith, 8 January 1962; G.K. Smith to C. Riley, 3 January 1962, GKSP, box 55, f. "Schwarz, Fred – Christian Anti-Communism Crusade."

53 "Case of Fred C. Schwarz," 259; Richard Hunt, "Anti-Communist Says City's Hostility Is Easing," 2; M. Liebman to W.F. Buckley, 9 May 1962, MLieb, box B11, f. "Fred Schwarz."

54 From WFBP: W.F. Buckley to G. Sokolsky, 10 May 1962; G. Sokolsky to W.F. Buckley, 29 May 1962, box 22, f. "Sokolsky, George E. (1962)"; W.F. Buckley to A. Forster, 10 May 1962; A. Forster to W.F. Buckley,

17 May 1962, box 18, f. "Anti-Defamation League (1962)." Buckley text reproduced in Schwarz, *Beating*, 325–30; E. Lyons to A. Forster, 7 June 1962, MLieb, box B11, f. "Fred Schwarz"; Ralph de Toledano, "Choosing Up Sides on Communism," 6 June 1962, RDTP, box 10, printed matter – 1962; Jo-Ann Price, "B'nai B'rith Officer Rips Far Right," *New York Herald Tribune*, 6 June 1962, 11; William Buckley, " 'He Shall Not Be Heard': The Anti-Defamation League," *National Review* 12 (1962): 433–4.

55 Kempton, "Dinkum Oil," 7; "Anti-Communist Crusader Hits 'Insincere' Christians," *NYT*, 24 May 1962, 30; A. McDowell to W. Kintner, 28 March 1963, MLP, box 1, f. 2; Inter-Office Memo, 29 May 1962, *MLieb*, box B11, f. "Fred Schwarz."

56 McCandlish Phillips, "Trade Group's Bid to Anti-Red Sets Off a Membership Dispute," *NYT*, 29 March 1962, 2.

57 "Extreme Right Accused of Anti-Semitism Tinge," *LAT*, 25 June 1962, 28; Morton Puner, "The Language of Fred C. Schwarz," ADL *Bulletin* 19, 6 (1962): 3, 6–7; Buckley, "He Shall Not Be Heard," 434; George Ducan, "Aged Aid Backed by Reform Rabbis," *NYT*, 22 June 1962, 16. The ADL *Bulletin* also portrayed Schwarz as a dangerous demagogue.

58 The only sponsors were Admiral Arleigh Burke, Henry Sargent (American and Foreign Power Company), and Charles Edison, former New Jersey governor.

59 Report by E. Reuther, and J. Schlitt to JLC Field Staff, NTUC, GRIR, box 364, f. "CACC New York School, June 1962."

60 A. McDowell to S. McNail, 11 July 1962, MLP, box 1, f. 2.

61 George Sokolsky, "What Is the Compulsion," *WashP*, 6 July 1962, A15; George Sokolsky, "Questions Raised about Dr. Schwarz," *Evening Independent* (OH), 3 July 1962, 6A; Hornaday, "Anti-Red Crusader in N.Y."

62 "Anti-Red School Due Here Monday," *NYT*, 25 August 1962, 3; "Case of Fred C. Schwarz," 261.

63 *Meet the Press*, transcript, recorded 26 August 1962, guest: Dr Fred Schwarz.

64 Harriet Van Horne, "NBC Presents a Professional Enemy of Reds," *New York World-Telegram and Sun*, 27 August 1962; Len Chaimowitz, "Schwarz's Alarm Just Didn't Ring the Bell," *Newsday*, 27 August 1962; clipping in LSP, box 217, f. "Schwarz, Fred C. – 8/26/62"; W. Wintchell qtd. in Schwarz, *Beating*, 13–14. Letters in all seven folders of LSP, box 217, f. "Schwarz, Fred C. – 8/26/62."

65 "Schwarz Report Cites $75,000 Loss," *NYT*, 1 September 1962, 8; "Anti-Red Crusade in the Red," *Oakland Tribune*, 1 September 1962, 20-B-E.

66 Walter Lippmann, "The Dominant American Majority," *Montreal Gazette*, 9 November 1962, 8.

67 W. Judd to the Christian Century, 2 July 1962, WHJu, box 5, f. 409, Campaign Files – correspondence, misc. papers, 11 October and 2 November 1962; W. Judd to E.B Smith, 1 August 1962, WHJP, box 226, f. 4, copyright Stanford University; Lee Edwards, *Walter H. Judd: Missionary for Freedom: The Life and Times of Walter Judd* (New York: Paragon House, 1990), 270–1; Willmar Thorkelson, "Fraser Urges 'Peace Drive'; Judd Defends Schwarz Ties," *Minneapolis Star*, 5 November 1962, 15A.

68 From GRIR: correspondence between the Jewish Community Relations Committee, the Anti-Defamation League, the American Jewish Congress, and Group Research, box 364, f. "CACC Correspondence"; Report by the Jewish Community Federation of Cleveland in 11 October 1962, box 363, f. "CACC Notes on Individual Meetings."

69 "Schwarz, Bridges, Zing Fiery Words," *Daily Review*, 23 October 1962, 13; Dave Hope, "Bridges-Schwarz Meeting a Brawl," *Oakland Tribune*, 23 October 1962, E13.

70 Irving Leibowitz, "Dr. Schwarz Takes the Stand," *Indianapolis Times*, 2 October 1963, 17; Drew Pearson, "McCormack and JFK on Cordial Terms," *Palm Beach Post-Times*, 9 September 1962, 6; Stephen Young, "They Don't Think Much of Schwarz Down Under," *Congressional Record*, US Senate, Washington, United States Government Printing Office, 87th Congress, 1st session, 7 August 1962, 14732; Julian Krawcheck, "Schwarz School Draws Less Than 50 Listeners," *Cleveland Press*, 1 October 1962, B13; Anonymous to C.D. DeLoach, 5 October 1962, FBIF, f. "Schwarz, Fred HQ – 6."

71 Bill Becker, "Schwarz Says 'Crusade' Will Gross Million in '62," *NYT*, 13 December 1962, 1. From HPP: F. Schwarz to H. Philbrick, 2 November 1962, box 15, f. 18; Strube postcard 1962, box 185, f. 3.

72 W.C. Skousen to R. Skousen, 12 December 1961, WCSP binder: Hollywood's Answer to Communism, 16 October 1961; A. McDowell to F. Schwarz, 15 November 1962, MLP, box 1, f. 2; H. Philbrick to W.C. Skousen, 5 February 1963, HPP, box 178, f. 4; W.C. Skousen to H. Philbrick, 8 February 1963, HPP, box 178, f. 4; W.C. Sullivan to A.H. Belmont, 2 January 1963, FBIF, f. Skousen, W. Cleon – 1; "Christian Anti-Communism General, 8/17/65, WMC," GRIR, box 364, f. "CACC General and Financial."

73 F. Schwarz to H. Philbrick, 10 September 1963, HPP, box 66, f. 1; J. Lynn to W. Judd, 11 September 1963, WHJu, box 69, f. "Judd, Walter H.

– Correspondence, 1963"; "Holy Gum-Smoke," *Criterion* 4 (1963): 4; "Schwarz Raps Catholic Newspaper," *Indianapolis News*, 29 October 1963, 17; "Who Is Dr. Fred C. Schwarz?," *News and Views (Indiana State AFL-CIO)* 5, 14 (1963): 1; James Rourke, "Anti-Red School is $4,000 in the Red," *Indianapolis Times*, 30 October 1963, 7; A. McDowell to M. Lewis, 30 October 1963, MLP, box 1, f. 2.

74 Sokolsky, "Dr. Schwarz's Difficulty," *WashP*, 13 September 1962, A23; "Case of Fred C. Schwarz," 261; From WFBP, box 27, f. "Schvettinger, Robert S. – Schwalbe, A. – Schwarz, Fred C.": F. Schwarz to W.F. Buckley, 20 February 1963; W.F. Buckley to F. Schwarz. S.A. Fineberg to F. Schwarz, 28 April 1963, MLP, box 1, f. 2.

75 Schwarz, *Beating*, 332–4. H. Philbrick to F. Schwarz, HPP, box 66, f. 1.

76 Donald Janson and Bernard Eismann, *The Far Right* (New York: McGraw-Hill, 1963), 55, 67; Richard Dudman, *Men of the Far Right* (New York: Pyramid Books, 1963) 180; Powers, *Not without Honor*, 294; Schwarz, *Beating*, 315.

77 "The Assassin's Accomplice: Marxist Ideology," *CACCN*, January 1964, 1–3.

78 Bill Geerhart, "Anti-Baez: The Ballad of Janet Greene"; "The Freewheelin' Janet Greene: The Conelrad Interview," *Conelrad: All Things Atomic*, http://www.conelrad.com/greene/index.php; "Tuned for Americans: Crusader's Anti-Red Folk Songs Pay Off," *LAT*, 14 October 1964, A8; "New Crusade Dimension: Music," *CACCN*, October 1964, 3–4.

79 Richard Corrigan, "Cold War Crusade Comes to Virginia," *WashP*, 8 March 1966, S7; Jane Clark, "A Girl, a Guitar, and a Message," *St-Louis Globe-Democrat*, 8 April 1966, 12A; Report, 10/15/65, GRIR, box 363, f. "CACC Notes on Individual Meetings"; Eileen Luhr, *Witnessing Suburbia: Conservatives and the Christian Youth Culture* (Berkeley: University of California Press, 2009), 39.

80 Clark, "Girl, A Guitar, and a Message."

81 Mary Brennan, *Turning Right in the Sixties: The Conservative Capture of the GOP* (Chapel Hill: University of North Carolina Press, 1995), 69–81.

82 Gladwin Hill, "Salinger Faces Formidable Foe," *NYT*, 7 June 1964, 78; Kimmis Hendrick, "Murphy on GOP Stage," *Christian Science Monitor*, 12 June 1964, 1; "Salinger and Murphy," *Press-Courier*, 7 October 1964, 12; "Schwarz Hits Salinger, Seeks Equal TV Time," *Fresno Bee*, 19 October 1964, 3A.

83 Darren Dochuk, *From Bible Belt to Sunbelt: Plain-Folk Religion, Grassroots Politics, and the Rise of Evangelical Conservatism* (New York: W.W. Norton and Company, 2011), 229; "Dr. Schwarz Tells of Cheers for

Goldwater," *St Louis Post-Dispatch*, 6 August 1964, 3A; N. Rubin to B. Goldwater, 26 February 1962, BMGP, MF 45, box 012_REEL021_0002, pdf. 532.

84 Peter Coleman, "Crusader Fred Schwarz," *Sydney Bulletin*, 7 April 1962, 18.

85 Shepard, "Anti-Red Rallies to Be Televised," *NYT*, 1 November 1961, 79; Fletcher Knebel, "Rightist Revival: Who's on the Far Right?," *Look* 26, 6 (1962): 26; A.H. Belmont to W.C. Sullivan, 29 January 1962, FBIF, f. "CACC-Fred Schwarz HQ – 7."

86 Leaflet on Schwarz-Whitaker debate, 3 January 1962, San Joaquin County Anti-Communism Group; W. Bartlett to W. Judd, 23 September 1961, WHJP, box 48, f. 4, copyright Stanford University; P. Shelford to H. Philbrick, 24 November 1961, HPP, box 4, f. 4; Urban Whitaker, "Medicine Man from Down Under: Fred Schwarz, Detractor of the Peace," *War/Peace Report* 2, 4 (1962): 8–11. This was the second Schwarz-Whitaker debate.

87 Knebel, "Rightist Revival," 26

88 McGaugh, "Fred Schwarz Story," 3.

89 Woodward, "What Qualifications," 16.

90 Harold Myra and Marshall Shelley, *The Leadership Secrets of Billy Graham* (Grand Rapids, MI: Zondervan, 2005), 82.

91 " 'Blacklist' Charge Kicks Up GOP Storm," *Telegraph-Herald* (IA), 15 October 1965, 3; Gladwin Hill, "Reagan Accused of Bircher Links," *NYT*, 12 August 1966, 15; Rowland Evans and Robert Novak, "Extremist Issue Nil in California," *Boston Globe*, 23 September 1966, 13. In October 1965, Group Research was even accused of reverse blacklisting for its attempts to tie GOP personalities to right-wing groups.

CHAPTER THIRTEEN

1 F. Schwarz to W. Judd, 13 June 1972, WHJP, box 226, f. 4, copyright Stanford University.

2 Jack Anderson criticized Dodd for accepting $1,000 per CACC appearance. Jack Anderson, "Weakness Seen in Nike X System," *WashP*, 12 February 1966, E19.

3 From *Hannibal Courier-Post*: Linda Whelan, "Hannibal Has New Author," 18 November 1977, 1; Gene Hoenes, "Mark Twain III Goes on the Road," 23 May 1980, 1.

4 From *CACCN*: Joost Sluis, "Report on Vietnam," 4 April 1966, 6; "Operation Vietnam," 7 March 1966, 8.

5 Nguyen Van-Tho to James Colbert, 28 January 1968, pub. in CACCN, 6 June 1968; Hoa Minh Truong, *The Dark Journey: Inside the Reeducation Camps of Viet Cong* (Durham, CT: Eloquent Books, 2010), 29; Fred Schwarz, *Beating the Unbeatable Foe: One Man's Victory over Communism, Leviathan, and the Last Enemy* (Washington, DC: Regnery, 1996), 245–6. South Vietnamese author Hoa Minh Truong, who had survived the Vietcong re-education camps and managed to flee to Australia, recalled in his autobiography being given a copy of Schwarz's *Ban co the tin duoc nguoi cong san?* (Do You Believe the Communists?) while attending university in Can Tho in 1969.

6 J. Sluis to H. Philbrick, 27 September 1971, HPP, box 178, f. 6. See, for instance, Joost Sluis, "Dead Men on Furlough," *Christian Cause* 5 (1973): 2. See also correspondence between Sluis and William C. Norris (Control Data Corp.), in which Sluis tried to convince Norris to not do business with communist regimes, WCNP, CB180, box 19, series 9, f. 293.

7 Qtd. in Bill Geerhart, "Anti-Baez: The Ballad of Janet Greene"; "The Freewheelin' Janet Greene: The Conelrad Interview," *Conelrad: All Things Atomic*, http://www.conelrad.com/greene/index.php; G. Westcott to H. Philbrick, 9 April 1972, HPP, box 20, f. 8; H. Philbrick to G. Westcott, 29 May 1974, box 7, f. 6.

8 Wallace Turner, "Coast Millionaire Upset by Publicity and Politics," *NYT*, 14 July 1970, B-47; Charles Powers, "Behavior Modification Treatment Used Successfully on Alcoholics," *Lakeland Ledger* (FL), 21 November 1973, 1C.

9 Schwarz, *Beating*, 190; Deborah Huntington and Ruth Kaplan, "Whose Gold Is behind the Altar: Corporate Ties to Evangelicals," *Contemporary Marxism* 4 (1981–82): 84; Waldemar Nielsen, *Golden Donors: A New Anatomy of the Great Foundations* (New Brunswick: Transaction Publishers, 2009), 174. During congressional hearings about the Tax Reform Act, 1969, which imposed new regulations restricting private foundations from giving money to ideological projects for charity purposes, Bell virulently opposed the idea. After the law had passed, he complied only "minimally with its new rules regarding public disclosure."

10 Brad Altman, "Dr. Schwarz's Bank Roll Has Red Lining," *Independent Press-Telegram* (CA), 12 September 1976, B-1; fundraising letters, 2 October 1967, and 20 November 1967.

11 A. McDowell to J. Sluis, 3 November 1965, HPP, box 175, f. 6; H. Philbrick to F. Schwarz, 9 November 1965, MLP, box 1, f. 2; A. McDowell to J. Sluis, 3 November 1965; handwritten note, 5 November 1965, by McDowell following the later letter, HPP, box 175, f. 6; "The

Name and Nature of the Christian Anti-Communism Crusade," CACCN, 1 October 1997, 1.

12 From CACCN: "Drug Addiction, Demoralization and Communist Conquest," 15 January 1972, 1; "How 'Women's Lib' Promote Rape," 15 August 1975, 1; Brad Altman, "Dr. Schwarz's Bank Roll Has Red Lining," B1.

13 "The Deadly Disease: Communism," CACCN, 1 December 1997, 3; Schwarz, *Beating*, 419; Vladimir Lenin, "Tasks of the Youth Leagues: Bourgeois and Communist Morality," in *Bolshevik Visions: First Phase of the Cultural Revolution in Soviet Russia*, ed. William Rosenberg (Ann Arbor: University of Michigan Press, 1990), 21; Frederick Engels, *The Origin of the Family, Private Property and the State* (Chippendale, NSW: Resistance Books, 2004), 86.

14 See David Hoffman, *Stalinist Values: The Cultural Norma of Soviet Modernity, 1917–1941* (Ithaca, NY: Cornell University Press, 2003), 93–7; Frances Bernstein, *The Dictatorship of Sex: Lifestyle Advice for the Soviet Masses* (DeKalb: Northern Illinois University Press, 2007), 148–50; Schwarz qtd. in St Louis Civil Liberties Committee, *Communism on the Map (Complete Text of the Tape-Film Strip) and the Greater St. Louis School of Anti-Communism – April, 1961 (Selected Quotations)*, St. Louis, 1962, 17; "Cuba, Sex Education, and Homosexuality," CACCN, 1 June 1971, 6. Commenting on the news that the Cuban government would not provide sex education courses and had made it an official state policy to consider homosexuality a pathology, Schwarz claimed that communists desired "to strengthen the character of the community they control and weaken the moral fibre within the areas under capitalist control so that conquest may be easier."

15 Herbert Marcuse, *Eros and Civilization: A Philosophical Inquiry into Freud* (Milton Park, UK: Routledge, 1998), 156. From CACCN: "The Cause of the Campus Revolt," 1 April 1969, 4; "Anti-Red Leader Hits 'Marcusians,'" *San Diego Union*, 3 April 1970, repub. 15 April 1970, 5; "The Campus Revolt – Part III," 1 May 1969, 2.

16 H. Marcuse to M. Chamberlain, 13 March 1970, pub. in CACCN, 1 April 1970, 6; Jack O'Brian, "The Voice of Broadway," *San Antonio Light*, 26 May 1970, A21; "Sauce for Marcuse Is Sauce for…," LAT, 30 March 1970, A8; "Herbert Marcuse Answers," CACCN, 15 April 1970, 1–2.

17 Fundraising letter, 15 April 1970 ; Fred Schwarz, *The Three Faces of Revolution* (Falls Church, VA: Capitol Hills Press, 1972), 75. An interesting part of the book constitutes a dispassionate analysis in which, drawing

on figures on US foreign investment, the crusader tries to debunk the concept of US economic imperialism.

18 "Thank God for the Police," *CACCN*, 24 August 1965, 3; "Schwarz Cheered as He Praises Police, Warns of Red Infiltrations," *Milwaukee Journal*, 13 October 1965, 2–18.

19 "Reds, Race, Riots, and Revolution," *CACCN*, 24 August 1965, 2.

20 "Dr. Schwarz Says Anarchy Is Red Anarchy Is Red Aim," *St Louis Post-Dispatch*, 16 October 1965, clipping in GRIR, box 364, f. "CACC, News Clips – 1966–1967"; "Communism and Race Riots," *CACCN*, 24 August 1967, 4; Report, 10/15/65, GRIR, box 363, f. "CACC Notes on Individual Meetings."

21 "Communism and Race Riots," 1; Report, 10/15/65, GRIR, box 363, f. "CACC Notes on Individual Meetings."

22 "Orders FBI Harlem Probe," *ChiTri*, 22 July 1964, 1; "Red, Watts Link Seen by Schwarz," *Press-Telegram* (CA), 16 September 1965, B1; John Roberts, "Overthrow Whites, 60 Told at Lincoln U.," *Evening Journal* (DE), 20 November 1965, 22; "The Unholy Alliance," *CACCN*, 10 January 1966, 1–2. According to Schwarz, the Chinese were actively promoting "internal disruption leading to anarchy."

23 "Communism and Race Riots," 1–3; fundraising letter, 2 October 1967; F. Schwarz to H. Philbrick, 5 April 1968, HPP, box 66, f. 5; "All Shades," *Oregonian*, 15 October 1965, 14; H. Philbrick to H. Lundy, 26 October 1965, HPP, box 66, f. 2. When the *Oregonian* accused the Crusade of suggesting that "communism is the main force behind the civil rights movement," Philbrick protested by writing a letter to the paper in which he denied this charge.

24 David Lawrence, "Evidence of Planning Is Detected as Race Riots Sweep the Nation," *Day* (CT), 27 July 1967, 14; David Lawrence, "House Group Says Reds Stir Riots," *Sarasota Herald-Tribune*, 22 March 1968, 6; Hazel Erskine, "The Polls: Demonstrations and Race Riots," *Public Opinion Quarterly* 31, 4, 1968: 664–5.

25 Philip Abbott Luce, "The New Left," *CACCN*, 24 July 1967, 4; Jack Roth, "Epton Gets Year in Anarchy Case," *NYT*, 28 January 1966, 31; O'Reilly, "The FBI and the Politics of the Riots, 1964–1968," *Journal of American History* 75, 1 (1988): 108.

26 "The Black 'Ghetto' – A Communist Sanctuary," *CACCN*, 1 September 1969, 1. "Through their association with the Black Panthers, the white communists will be able to operate freely within these areas, store arms within them, and use them as bases from which to launch civil war."

27 "An Analysis of Rebellion at the University of California as Applied Marxism-Leninism," *CACCN*, 18 January 1965, 1–4; LMC to W. McCune, 22 April 1964, GRIR, box 365, f. "CACC Washington School June 64." A Group Research contact reported that Schwarz was "turning [his] interest to college professors and college people."

28 From GRIR: box 365, f. "CACC Washington School June 64": E. Davis to D. Brody, 2 June 1964; Jack S. Landau, "High IQ Student Group Low on 'Red Menace,'" clipping; Nancy Green, Report on 06/16/64 session, and anonymous report.

29 From *CACCN*: "Future Plans," 3 December 1964, 4; "Mixed Emotions," 11 February 1965, 1–4.

30 "The Greater Detroit School of Anti-Communism, June 7–11, Statler-Hilton Hotel," *CACCN*, 17 May 1965, 5. The school of Detroit in June 1965 was in the latter category.

31 Fundraising letter, 5 August 1968; Schwarz, *Beating*, 382. Locations were Detroit (twice), Sacramento, Boston, New York, Chicago, Cincinnati, Indianapolis, San Diego, Washington, San Francisco, and Orange County.

32 Bob Greene, "Red Menace Fading," *Billings Gazette*, 21 February 1974.

33 F. Schwarz to H. Philbrick, 22 March 1972, HPP, box 66, f. 6. Speaking honoraria remained at $200 per lecture, but inflation rates of the late 1960s and 1970s were such that this sum was worth considerably less than it had been in the old days.

34 F. Schwarz to R. Maass, 17 November 1972, GRIR, box 363, f. "CACC Correspondence"; Report on Washington ASS, 1970, GRIR, box 365, f. "CACC Washington Anti-Subversive Seminars, 1969, 1970, 1971, 1972." A film presented during ASS was the NEP production *Republic of Apathy.*

35 J. Colbert to S. Philbrick, 21 April 1969, HPP, box 66, f. 5; "The Exciting Seminar," *CACCN*, 1 August 1972, 2. Scholarships were offered to people from colleges from the area in which the seminar took place. When, at the end of one seminar, attendees were asked to raise their hands to indicate how they had learned about the event, a quarter were from YAF, another quarter from word of mouth, and another quarter from a lecture Philbrick had given at a Catholic university.

36 Report on the Washington, DC, Anti-Subversive Seminar, ADL, GRIR, box 363, f. "CACC Notes on Individual Meetings." From *WashP*: Sanford J. Ungar, "Crusade Hears Opening Attack on Communism," 13 June 1970, B6; Martin Weil, "Anti-Subversive Seminar Opens," 21 June 1969, B3. Only one attendee interviewed by the *Washington Post* reporter came as the result of a newspaper ad. Another journalist (1969) reported a high

number of "love beards, long sideburns and … young men with shoulder-length hair."

37 Ungar, "Crusade Hears Opening Attack on Communism," B6.

38 "The Exciting Seminar," 2; "Dear YAF member," n.d. (1971). The letter inviting YAF in June 1971 stated: "Each scholarship will be worth $60. $20 of this will be for tuition. $40 will be for the individual to cover the cost of rooms and meals."

39 Report on the Washington, DC, Anti-Subversive Seminar, ADL, GRIR, box 363, f. "CACC Notes on Individual Meetings."

40 From GRIR: box 365, f. CACC Washington Anti-Subversive Seminars, 1969, 1970, 1971, 1972: Report on Washington ASS, 1970, Report on Washington ASS, 1971; Baker, "Old Pros of Anti-Communism Lecture on 'Real Enemy,'" *WashP*, 2 July 1972, B9.

41 Schwarz, *Beating*, 467; Dana Rohrabacher, "Honouring Cold War Warriors," *Congressional Record* 159, 44 (2009), House, H3394; Fred Schwarz to Anthony Dolan, 24 March 1983, ARDF, box 76, series IV – Correspondence, f. 2; Fred Schwarz, "Ronald Reagan," *Schwarz Report* 44, 8 (2004): 1.

42 "Philbrick Colleague Collapses," *Lansing State Journal*, 11 November 1964, A8.

43 Eva Smith, "McAfee No Match for Schwarz in 'Big Debate,'" *Visalia Times-Delta*, 2 May 1972, 1B.

44 Committee on the Judiciary, *Subcommittee to Investigate the Administration of the Internal Security Act and Other Internal Security Laws*, US Senate, Washington, United States Government Printing Office, 93rd Congress, 2nd session, pt. 3, 15 July 1974, 155–76.

45 F. Schwarz to W. Judd, 14 August 1978, WHJP, box 226, f. 5, copyright Stanford University; Jack Jones, "Fiery Anti-Communist of 1950's Still Fights the Battle," *LAT*, 26 September 1977, OC1; C. McIntire to F. Schwarz, 20 December 1982; F. Schwarz to C. McIntire, 13 May 1983, CMP, f. "Fred C. Schwarz – Christian Anti-Communism Crusade." The figure of twenty thousand comes from a speech made at the ceremony awarding Schwarz, which was organized by the Council for National Policy. Video copy of the ceremony provided to the author by Political Research Associates. Many thanks to Chip Berlet.

46 F. Schwarz to H. and S. Philbrick, 14 June1977, HPP, box 246, f. 6; "Marvin Olasky, Ph.D.," *CACCN*, 1 July 1977, 3.

47 "Chile – Lenin's Tragic Triumph," *CACCN*, 1 October 1973, 1–4.

48 From *CACCN*: "The New China Policy," 15 November 1971, 1; "Australian Prime Minister Visits Communist China," 15 August 1975, 5.

F. Schwarz to H. and S. Philbrick, 22 September 1970, HPP, box 66, f. 6; W. Judd to F. Schwarz, 28 February 1974, WHJP, box 226, f. 5. He slammed Australian premier Malcolm Fraser for visiting China in 1976.

49 From *CACCN*: "The Paper Tiger," 1 May 1975, 1–3; "The Ford-Carter Foreign Policy Debate," 1 November 1976, 1–2; "The Moral Schizophrenia of Senator Henry M. Jackson," 1 September 1974, 7; "Operation Blindfold," 15 February 1976, 1. Even the most popular political figure among anticommunists during this time, Democratic senator Henry "Scoop" Jackson, was not beyond reproach. Jackson had become famous for his hardline stance on the Vietnam War and his rejection of détente. However, Jackson's relatively soft position on China and his trip to the country in 1974 were akin to a "moral schizophrenia."

50 From *CACCN*: "Morality, Communism and Politics," 1 January 1981, 1–2; "The Primary Objective of the Soviet Union," 15 April 1983, 2.

51 Schwarz, *Beating*, 467. From *CACCN*: "Sadistic Abortion," 15 February 1974, 5; "Morality, Communism and Politics," 1 January 1981, 1–2.

52 From *CACCN*: "Homosexuality, Discrimination, and Communism," 15 July 1977, 1–3; "A Ball for Homosexuals," March 1965, 3. The first salvo he fired in the "culture wars" was actually over this very topic, when, in March 1965, he decried an event that had been held in San Francisco by liberal Protestant clergy to promote dialogue between church bodies and the local gay community.

53 Schwarz, *Beating*, 421–32; "Understanding AIDS?," *CACCN*, 15 July 1988, 1–4.

54 Fundraising letter, 1 July 1982.

55 "The Immediate Need – One Million Dollars," *CACCN*, 15 November 1980, 4; fundraising letter, 15 February 1983. "News Notes from the Organizations," 6–84, GRIR, box 363, f. "CACC General and Financial"; Donation Act, State of Arizona, 31 December 1980, IRS-EOD. In 1980, R.L. Lebrecht, a real estate entrepreneur, donated to the Crusade a twenty-acre (eight-hectare) property in Pima County, Arizona.

56 F. Schwarz to W. Judd, 12 February 1982, WHJP, box 226, f. 5; fundraising letter, 1 June 1983; James Colbert, "African Seminar Safari," *CACCN*, 15 January 1987, 1–4.

57 From *CACCN*: "An Anti-Communist International," 4 September 1967, 3; James Colbert, "An Anti-Communist International," 7 November 1967, 3–6. Scott and Jon Lee Anderson, *Inside the League* (New York: Dodd, Mead and Company, 1986), 54–70. The WACL's first president, Ku Cheng-kang, was one of the Kuomintang's top leaders.

58 "S.E. Asia and the World Anti-Communism League," *CACCN*, 1 February 1969, 2–3; Report prepared for GRI by the National Council of Churches in the Philippines (hereafter NCCP Report), GRIR, box 363, f. "CACC General and Financial." From WHJP, box 226, f. 5: W. Judd to F. Schwarz, 9 June 1972; F. Schwarz to W. Judd, 16 June 1972.

59 From HPP, box 33, f. 4: J. Fisher to H. Philbrick, 11 March 1970; H.A.P. to S.A.E. Rudiger, 17 March 1970.

60 Anderson and Anderson, *Inside the League*, 71–81; 85–6.

61 "MINUTES- Annual Meeting of American Council for World Freedom, Inc. – Mayflower Hotel, Washington, D.C., April 7, 1973," HPP, box 33, f. 5; NCCP Report, GRIR, box 363, f. "CACC General and Financial"; Anderson and Anderson, *Inside the League*, 11. In April 1974, Schwarz apparently attended the league's conference in Washington. A watchdog group report reads: "A rival faction in the WACL clearly noted that Schwarz's role in the 1974 WACL Convention ... was a leading one and counter to their interests." However, Schwarz never publicly discussed his work in the WACL past the 1972 events.

62 Kermit Johnson, *Ethics and Counterrevolution: American Involvement in Internal Wars* (Lanham, MD: University Press of America, 1998), 2–3; Sara Diamond, *Spiritual Warfare: The Politics of the Christian Right* (Boston: South End Press, 1989), 160–1; NCCP Report, GRIR, box 363, f. "CACC General and Financial." Some of these private groups were Catholic (such as the Knights of Malta).

63 F. Schwarz to W. Judd, 12 February 1983, WHJP, box 226, f. 5. In 1982–83, the CACC distributed the pamphlet *Why I Am against Communism* to Taiwanese students.

64 Elton Wilson's report in *CACCN*, 15 October 1975, 1–7; "The Impossible Dream," *CACCN*, 1 February 1976, 1–4; F. Schwarz to W. Judd, 3 November 1975, WHJP, box 226, f. 5. In a letter to Judd, Schwarz explained that no organization providing humanitarian aid had a coherent anticommunist vision.

65 From *CACCN*: John Whitehall, "'Black Is Beautiful,'" 1 September 1989, 4–5; John Whitehall, "Dear Friend and Colleague," 15 December 1985, 2; Michael Leifer, "New People's Army," *Dictionary of the Modern Politics of South-East Asia* (New York: Routledge, 1995), 120.

66 "Communism in the Philippines," *CACCN*, 1 July 1981, 1–5; Diamond, *Spiritual Warfare*, 189.

67 From *CACCN*: "Training Anti-Communist Workers in the Philippines," 15 February 1982, 1–5; John Whitehall, "The White Harvest Fields of

the Philippines," 15 November 1983, 1–5; John Whitehall, "The Danger in the Philippines after Marcos – The Deluge?," 1 May 1985, 3; John Whitehall, "The Past, Present and Future of the Philippines," 1 April 1986, 1–4.

68 NCCP Report, GRIR, box 363, f. "CACC General and Financial."

69 Ibid.

70 Interview with Tom Marty, *Asia-Pacific Backgrounder: A Publication of Third World Reports* 2, 2 (1989): 1–4; P. Brick to W. McCune, 9 November 1987, GRIR, box 363, f. "CACC General and Financial"; Lois A. West, *Militant Labor in the Philippines* (Philadelphia: Temple University Press, 1997), 45; John Whitehall, "Communism in the Philippines," *PCACCN*, April 1987, 6–7; Diamond, *Spiritual Warfare*, 190–1. Whitehall's evidence in support of his argument was largely circumstantial (presence of a KMU leader in an organization controlled by Communists, declarations by KMU leaders, etc.).

71 From *CACCN*: "Opportunity and Danger in the Philippines," 1 October 1986, 2–3; "Sentenced to Death," 15 February 1988, 1–3; Whitehall, "Black Is Beautiful," 5; John Whitehall, "Cory, Karl and the Colonels," private draft by Whitehall, November 1987. In January 1989, Whitehall moved with his family to Canada, where he established a short-lived Canadian CACC.

72 "Deeds and Vision," *CACCN*, 15 November 1982, 1–4.

73 Colbert, "African Seminar Safari," 1–4; James Colbert, "Seminars in Nigeria and Ghana (Feb. 18–Mar. 31)," *CACCN*, 15 January 1987, 3–6.

74 One seminar held in San Jose, Costa Rica, in October 1983 was attended by 250 pastors, "including international evangelists and Catholics," representing thirty denominations. In 1984, in Los Angeles, the CACC held a seminar "for Spanish-speaking pastors" attended by about thirty people. See David Stoll, *Is Latin America Turning Protestant?: The Politics of Evangelical Growth* (Berkeley: University of California Press, 1990), 8–9. From *CACCN*: James Colbert, "Attitudes, Activities, and Opportunities in Central America," 1 December 1983, 1; "Seminar for Spanish-Speaking Pastors," 1 February 1985, 6.

75 From *CACCN*: Colbert, "Attitudes, Activities, and Opportunities in Central America," 3; James Colbert, "Battle for the Minds in El Salvador," 1 April 1984, 6–8; James Colbert, "Teaching Anti-Communism to Campesinos in Costa Rica," 1 December 1985, 1–3.

76 Fundraising letters, 1 April1983 and 1 June 1983. From *CACCN*: Colbert, "Attitudes, Activities, and Opportunities in Central America," 1–3; "Confronting Communism in Central America," 15 March 1985, 2–5;

James Colbert, "The Trail of Truth in Honduras and Belize," 15 May 1983, 4; James Colbert, "Anti-Communism Seminars in Mexico, Paraguay, and Argentina," 1 June 1985, 6; James Colbert, "Seminars and Terrorism in Colombia," 1 March 1989, 2.

77 F. Rogers to H. Philbrick, 27 November 1978, HPP, box 66, f. 8; fundraising letter, 1 July 1979. R. Heimburger to W. Judd, 26August 1980, WHJP, box 226, f. 5. Amateur videotape of the CNP award ceremony, 1987, obtained through Political Research Associates. The 1979 "Silver Jubilee" was sponsored by the National Coordinating Council for Constructive Action, a California-based group led by Frank Rogers, an MD opposed to state healthcare. Afflicted by a burst of shingles, Schwarz did not attend the event organized by the Council against Communist Aggression.

78 Schwarz, *Beating*, xx.

79 Fundraising letter, 6 August 1990; "To Be or Not To Be," *CACCN*, 1 September 1990, 1–4; fundraising letter, 15 February 1988; "The Collapse of the 'Evil Empire,'" *CACCN*, 1 October 1991, 1.

80 "The Life and Death of Rev. James Colbert, 1917–1996," 1 June 1996, letter to CACCN readers.

81 "Reasons for Resigning," *CACCN*, 1 April 1998, 2.

82 Elton Wilson, obituary speech at Fred Schwarz's funeral ceremony, 29 January 2009, private DVD recording provided to author by John and Rosalie Schwarz; Donald Critchlow, John Korasick ,and Matthew Sherman, *Political Conspiracies in America: A Reader* (Bloomington: Indiana University Press, 2008), 130.

83 Laura Jane Gifford, "Girded with a Moral and Spiritual Revival: The Christian Anti-Communism Crusade and Conservative Politics," in *The Right Side of the Sixties: Reexamining Conservatism's Decade of Transformation*, ed. Laura Jane Gifford and Daniel K. Williams (New York: Palgrave Macmillan, 2012), 175.

84 Christmas letter attachment from CACCN, December 1998, 2; Bill Muehlenberg, "Fred Schwarz, RIP," *Christian Today Australia*, http://au.christiantoday.com/article/fred-schwarz-rip/5234.htm.

EPILOGUE

1 Ronald Reagan, qtd. in Jim Hayes, *The Original Reagan Conservative: Ronald Reagan's Conservative Ideas in His Own Words* (Jim Hayes self-pub.: Createspace, 2008), 68; Pat Robertson, "Speech: 1992 Republican Convention," official site of Pat Robertson, http://www.patrobertson.com/Speeches/1992GOPConvention.asp.

2 Lee Edwards, *Educating for Liberty: The First Half-Century of the Intercollegiate Studies Institute* (Washington, DC: Regnery, 2003), 29–30.
3 "Crusader Blasts Apathy in Anti-Red Fight," *Desert News*, 16 December 1961, B1.
4 Schoenwald, *Time for Choosing*, 98.
5 Gifford, "Girded with a Moral and Spiritual Revival," 164; Robert Horwitz, *America's Right: Anti-Establishment Conservatism from Goldwater to the Tea Party* (Cambridge: Polity Press, 2013), 11.
6 S. Campbell to F. Schwarz, 9 June 1978, pub. in CACCN, 4 September 1978, 4; Qtd. in fundraising letter, Nov. 1998.
7 Markku Ruotsila, *Fighting Fundamentalist: Carl McIntire and the Politicization of American Fundamentalism* (Oxford Scholarship Online, 2016), 288–9, DOI: 10.1093/acprof:oso/9780199372997.001.0001; Daniel Bell, "The Dispossessed (1962)," in *The Radical Right: The American Right, Expanded and Updated*, ed. Daniel Bell (New York: Doubleday, 1962); Richard Hofstadter, "The Pseudo-Conservative Revolt: A Postscript," in *The Radical Right: The American Right, Expanded and Updated*, ed. Daniel Bell (New York: Doubleday, 1962), 81–6.
8 Gifford, "Girded with a Moral and Spiritual Revival," 162.
9 David Noebel, fundraising letter, 12 November 1998.

Index

Page numbers in italics refer to figures.